THE DRAMATIC TRADITION
OF THE MIDDLE AGES

THE DRAMATIC TRADITION
OF THE MIDDLE AGES

Edited by

Clifford Davidson

AMS Press, Inc.
New York

Library of Congress Cataloging-in-Publication Data

The Dramatic Tradition of The Middle Ages / edited by
  Clifford Davidson.
    p. cm. ~ (AMS Studies in the Middle Ages ; no. 26)
    Essays previously published in The EDAM newsletter and
    in its successor, The early drama, art, and music review.
    Includes bibliographical references and index.
    ISBN 0-404-64166-0 (alk. paper)
    1. Drama, Medieval—History and criticism. I. Davidson,
    Clifford. II. EDAM newsletter. III. Early drama, art,
    and music review. IV. Series.
PN1751.D76   2005
809.2'02—dc22   2004047608
                                                        CIP

All AMS Books are printed on acid-free paper that meets the guidelines for
performance and durability of the Committee on Production Guidelines
for Book Longevity of the Council on Library Resources.

AMS Press, Inc.
Brooklyn Navy Yard, 63 Flushing Ave – Unit #221
Brooklyn, NY 11205-1005, USA

MANUFACTURED IN THE UNITED STATES OF AMERICA

CONTENTS

Illustrations

Preface

The last generation has been a fruitful one for research in early drama, which previously had been neglected in theater studies and regarded more or less as a stepchild in English and language departments. The groundwork for the necessary interdisciplinary work was laid as far back as the 1960s with serious attention to the relation between drama and liturgy and to the nature of the theatrical event; I am thinking here especially of O. B. Hardison's *Christian Rite and Christian Drama in the Middle Ages* (1965) and V. A. Kolve's *The Play Called Corpus Christi* (1966). And there were other voices, including already the early volumes of Glynne Wickham's *Early English Stages* (1959–63), M. D. Anderson's *Drama and Imagery in English Medieval Churches* (1963), and David Bevington's *From* Mankind *to Marlowe* (1962). Alan H. Nelson's *The Medieval English Stage* (1974) urged returning to records. On account of the issues that he raised, his book would help to inspire the Records of Early English Drama (REED) project. The work of William L. Smoldon, while ultimately not definitive, nevertheless was joined to performance in collaboration with Noah Greenberg and the New York Pro Musica to show that the medieval music drama was splendidly effective—a path also followed by Fletcher Collins, Jr., who was a student of the eminent Karl Young, the author of the still highly respected *The Drama of the Medieval Church* (1933). The early 1970s brought important work by Rosemary Woolf (*The English Mystery Plays*) and Hans-Jürgen Diller (later translated as *The Middle English Mystery Play*). In the mid-1970s several developments occurred, among them the establishment of a triennial colloquium in Europe and in North America the growth of the International Congress on Medieval Studies. These and other venues brought together scholars who shared enthusiasm for early drama and a common scholarly aim.

In 1976 the Early Drama, Art, and Music project was established under my direction at the Medieval Institute at Western Michigan University. Ultimately more than two hundred scholars

from four continents would play some role in this project, the
sponsor of *The Early Drama, Art, and Music Review* (formerly the
EDAM Newsletter) from which the essays in the present volume are
taken. These essays are representative of the range of research from
the liturgical drama to vernacular plays, both religious and secular
mainly from the period before 1600, and include work that focuses
rather precisely on the core mission of the EDAM project. They
hence necessarily exclude notes and articles that deal with art or
music in a relevant but not direct way in relation to drama, and they
also do not comprise essays which are mainly "literary" in scope. It
will seem inevitable to some that in the attempt to be representative
I have, in conjunction with the wishes of AMS Press, been arbitrary,
since there has been so much from which to choose. However, the
index to *The Early Drama, Art, and Music Review* as well as to
other EDAM publications is currently available on the world-wide
web and hence can be consulted by interested persons.

The present volume begins with a section of essays on the
medieval music drama, about which, though I make no pretense of
being a Latinist, I have long been an enthusiast. I have had the opportunity to assist with more than a dozen productions of these
plays and quasi-dramatic ceremonies as produced by the Society for
Old Music, directed by my wife Audrey until her retirement a dozen
years ago, and also more recently with a production of the Beauvais
Daniel, which I suspect will be my last as I too go off into retirement. Such performances today must be based on manuscripts,
which themselves are deserving of a great deal more attention than
they have received heretofore. This is the starting point for
"Women's Liturgical Manuscripts at Klosterneuburg" by Michael
Norton (James Madison University) and Amelia Carr (Allegheny
College). And newly discovered manuscripts of music dramas from
elsewhere are also being called to our attention, as Nils Holger
Petersen (Copenhagen University) demonstrates in his find of a
Visitatio Sepulchri from Swedish archives that can now be added to
the handful known to be extant from Sweden and Denmark. In such
Easter plays and ceremonies, the Easter sepulcher was the central
"stage prop," which might also be incorporated into a kind of
mechanical mime show, as apparently at Bristol, which Mark
Pilkinton (Notre Dame University) has researched in connection

with his REED work. Elsewhere, as Dunbar H. Ogden (University of California, Berkeley) demonstrates, the *Visitatio Sepulchri*, though performed by living people, could in contrast be a hidden rite, very much a *thing done* rather than a show. The dissemination of the *Visitatio* to churches outside monasteries and cathedrals is suggested by its presence in an Eulenspiegel story which spoofs the participation of the clown, a maid, a parish priest, and farmers in a performance. Nicholas J. Rogers (Sidney Sussex College, Cambridge) calls attention to another report of mechanical images, both for Easter and the Nativity, used in a puppet show of sorts at Salisbury. Jennifer Alexander (University of Nottingham) adds a report on an interesting ceremony, performed by women of a parish in Lincolnshire, that in spite of its obscurity seems traceable to the *Depositio*, a quasi-dramatic Good Friday rite with direct links to the Easter morning *Elevatio* and *Visitatio Sepulchri*. Quasi-dramatic Holy Week rites also were performed on Palm Sunday, where in some Continental communities a *Palmesel* or Palm Sunday ass, an image with a carved figure of Jesus, was used; Hans-Jürgen Diller (Ruhr-Universität Bochum) calls attention to an example in Poland, where the *Palmesel* continued to be paraded long after the Council of Trent.

Unique and very different from the usual music dramas is Hildegard of Bingen's *Ordo Virtutum*, which Gunilla Iversen (Stockholm University) speculates had a connection with the abandonment of Hildegard's convent by her favorite nun, Richardis of Stade, as well as her subsequent repentance and death. Hildegard's remarkable play disappeared into obscurity in spite of the attention of the abbot of Sponheim, Trithemius, for whom a copy was made in 1517; however, Audrey Ekdahl Davidson (Western Michigan University) points out that this copy, now in the British Library, was very badly executed and hence, while of real historical interest to scholars, cannot be used for performance.

After absorbing *Medieval Music-Drama News*, which had been edited by Fletcher Collins, *The Early Drama, Art, and Music Review* published many reviews of liturgical drama performances. One of these, written by Rick Johnson (Wind Forest Early Instrument Ensemble), reviewed Sequentia's *Ordo Virtutum* at Ann Arbor which was given as a tribute to Barbara Thornton, who had died one week earlier. Barbara, who had been responsible for this production of the *Ordo* as well as for a previous staging and sound recording of the play in the 1980s, was a larger-than-life figure in early music performance and a truly visionary student of all of Hildegard's work.

The next two essays in some sense treat the topos of the world-upside-down. Michael Milway (Wellesley College) considers the boy bishop, about which much dubious speculation has been concocted, and uses the discovery of a statue in the seventeenth century to counter misconceptions concerning this reversal of roles. John W. Velz (University of Texas at Austin) introduces the term *adoxography* to define the practice of having devils in vernacular drama praise that which is evil and denigrate that which is good, oftentimes to the amusement of the audience.

Interdisciplinary research into iconography is introduced by Yumi Dohi (Landesspracheninstitut, Bochum) and Mikiko Ishii (Kanagawa University), who focus in their comparative studies on the emergence of symbolism in late medieval art and drama, both in their connecting (or not connecting) of Old Testament story and Eucharistic rite and in infusing everyday objects with luminous meaning. History and law are brought to bear by Elza Tiner (Lynchburg College) in her article on law in the York Passion. Mark R. Sullivan (Cross Plains, Wisconsin), in remarks published in one of the initial numbers of the then *EDAM Newsletter*, considers what can be known about the missing York play that dramatized the funeral procession of the Virgin Mary. Mary is also central to the article by Barbara D. Palmer (Mary Washington College), who argues for spectacular show in the English vernacular plays of the Annunciation and Assumption.

Continental drama, with attention to art and iconography, is the subject of commentary by Véronique Plesch (Colby College) on drama and its connections to art in Savoy (she provides a listing of vernacular plays in that neglected and linguistically diverse region), while Alan E. Knight (Pennsylvania State University) ponders a single manuscript of plays from Lille which contains illuminations related to the texts. Jarmila F. Veltrusky (Paris) surveys early drama in Bohemia, and Andrzej Dąbrówka (Institute of Literary Research, Polish Academy of Sciences), in his consideration of the late saint plays of Poland, provides an annotated listing, which, incidentally, includes a play on St. Ambrose by the English Jesuit Edmund Campion that was performed in Calissia in 1592. Susan Verdi Webster (St. Thomas University) turns her attention to the staging of the Descent of Christ from the cross as it was staged in Mexico in the sixteenth century—an instance of Spanish dramatic traditions having been transferred to the New World, and of which iconographic evidence remains in spite of the eventual suppression of the drama by the Inquisition. Francesc Massip (Universitat Rovira i Virgili, Tarragona) takes up a theatrical effect, the cloud used for ascents, in Spain as it has been retained to the present day at Elx (Elche) in its annual Assumption play.

Sandra Pietrini (Università degli Studi di Siena) provides a look at notions of the secular actor of antiquity as he was imagined in the Middle Ages and draws our attention to depictions in the visual arts. These purported views of acting in Roman times differ rather substantially from the medieval Terence illuminations (e.g., Bodley MS. Auct. F.2.13) that have been traced back to actual late antique examples. Finally, Leif Søndergaard and Tom Pettitt (University of Southern Denmark, Odense) offer a translation of and commentary on an anonymous Swedish Shrovetide play fragment which pits Yule against Lent—a classic conflict, in this case in a very rare example of a secular play that we could wish to have been complete, presumably with fighting between the main characters and another character, Mortification, later entering the scene.

The EDAM project and *The Early Drama, Art, and Music Review* owe a great deal to many persons, not least to the scholars who served as members of the advisory board and the numerous others who kindly assisted in so many ways. Space precludes naming them all, but the following may be singled out for special thanks: Richard Rastall, David Bevington, Hans-Jürgen Diller, Lynette Muir, Barbara Palmer, Ann Eljenholm Nichols, Alexandra Johnston, Pamela Sheingorn, Stephen Wright, Véronique Plesch, Peter Happé, the late C. Clifford Flanigan, and, of course, the venerable Fletcher Collins. I am also especially grateful to my wife Audrey, whose knowledge of early music was crucial for the project. Otto Gründler initially accepted my proposal for the EDAM project and until his retirement remained immensely supportive, as was his successor, Paul Szarmach. Thomas Seiler and his successor as managing editor of Medieval Institute Publications, Patricia Hollohan, made *The Early Drama, Art, and Music Review* as well as the EDAM monograph and reference series available under the MIP imprint, while Juleen Eichinger, former production editor of the press, helped to solve many technical problems. Finally, I am grateful to John Hopper, editor-in-chief of AMS Press, for his invitation to publish the present selection of essays.

Clifford Davidson

Women's Liturgical Manuscripts at Klosterneuburg

Amelia Carr and Michael Norton

For most, perhaps all of its medieval existence, the Augustinian convent of Klosterneuburg, on the Danube near Vienna, was a double house.[1] The late twelfth-century life of the first Augustinian prior Hartmann attests to the existence of both men and women in the convent before 1140.[2] Indeed, joint monastic foundations for men and women were common, if not standard, in Austria and Bavaria. The Benedictine abbey at Admont, for example, was founded as double in the late eleventh century, as were most Augustinian foundations during the first half of the twelfth century. But little work has been devoted to the liturgical life of women in these houses, and even the existence of such women seems surprising to many today.

It is useful to review the reasons for this historical eclipse. First, in most cases, there seems to be little difference between the men's and women's manuscripts and, thus, slim motivation for separating the practice. Second, women were subordinate to men within the convent. In Klosterneuburg, the women owned comparatively little property and were not economically self-sufficient. They were supervised by a *Custos dominarum*, responsible for their edification and liturgy. They were also strictly cloistered.[3] Whereas male Augustinians followed an apostolic model of activism, folding public parish duties into their liturgical round, the female Augustinians separated themselves from the world.

Women were outnumbered by men at Klosterneuburg, although not necessarily by choice, since legislation tried to restrict numbers of females in any single house to thirty-two members.[4] During the Reformation, the numbers of men dwindled to seven, and these lived with their wives and children, so that women seem not to have been recruited into the regular life at all. The last canoness, Apollonia Khatzler, died in 1568 at the advanced age of sixty-four. When the convent was later re-catholicized, no role was envisioned for religious females.

What remained of the women's books was consolidated into the splendid library of the main convent. In the catalogues of the collection, some volumes are recognized as belonging to the women, but no one has been motivated to investigate further.[5] Nevertheless, we believe that the women at Klosterneuburg inaugurated and maintained a liturgical existence apart from their male confessors, even while under their direct supervision. In this article we will offer a brief justification for a distinct women's usage at Klosterneuburg. Certain features allow us to assign specific manuscripts to the women, and other inferences can be drawn from those assignments. Finally, we would like to speculate on a narrative of Klosterneuburg's foundation that puts its female heritage into greater prominence.

In fig. 1 are listed the manuscripts provisionally assigned to the Klosterneuburg canonesses. The attribution of these manuscripts to the women is based on a series of interlocking traits that distinguish them from other liturgical manuscripts at Klosterneuburg. These traits include:

1. Inscriptions specifying female use;
2. Decorations featuring female portraits;
3. The use of Laon neumes on four lines with a distinctive four-line clef;
4. A distinct placement for the *Dedicatio Ecclesia*;
5. A distinct pattern of rubrication for the *Visitatio Sepulchri*;
6. A distinct modal and melodic structure for the *Visitatio Sepulchri*; and
7. The use of German inscriptions and rubrics.

ABBREVIATIONS USED IN FIGURE 1

Ins	=	Colophon or Inscription indicating female use
Not	=	Laon Neumes on Four Lines with "Klosterneuburg clef"
Ger	=	German Rubrics
Fac	=	Decorations featuring Women
Rub	=	Distinct Pattern of Rubrics for *Visitatio Sepulchri*
Mus	=	Distinct Modal/Melodic Structure for *Visitatio Sepulchri*
DE	=	Dedication of Church between 22 Sept. & 27 Sept.
Spl	=	Music present only for Men (Angel/Apostles) or only for Women (Marys/Chorus)

Manuscript	Type	Date	Ins	Not	Ger	Fac	Rub	Mus	DE	Spl
Graz, Universitätsbibl., MS. 807	Graduale	12th c.		x						
Klosterneuburg, Stiftsbibl., CCl 588	Graduale	ca. 1300		x	x	x				
Klosterneuburg, Stiftsbibl., CCl 589	Antiphonary	ca. 1330		x	x		x	x		
Klosterneuburg, Stiftsbibl., CCl 592	Breviary	14th c.					x		x	
Klosterneuburg, Stiftsbibl., CCl 969	Breviary	13th-14th c.			x	x	x		x	
Klosterneuburg, Stiftsbibl., CCl 977	Breviary	15th c.			x		x		x	
Klosterneuburg, Stiftsbibl., CCl 996	Seq./Hymnal	14th c.		x	x					
Klosterneuburg, Stiftsbibl., CCl 997	Hymnal	14th c.		x	x					
Klosterneuburg, Stiftsbibl., CCl 999	Hymnal	15th c.		x		x				
Klosterneuburg, Stiftsbibl., CCl 1000	Hymnal	1336	x	x	x					
Klosterneuburg, Stiftsbibl., CCl 1001	Hymnal	14th c.		x						
Klosterneuburg, Stiftsbibl., CCl 1003	Hymnal	14th c.		x	x					
Klosterneuburg, Stiftsbibl., CCl 1004	Hymnal	14th c.		x	x	x				
Klosterneuburg, Stiftsbibl., CCl 1005	Antiphonary	13th-15th c.		x				x		
Klosterneuburg, Stiftsbibl., CCl 1010	Antiphonary	12th c.		x						
Klosterneuburg, Stiftsbibl., CCl 1011	Antiphonary	14th c.		x						
Klosterneuburg, Stiftsbibl., CCl 1012	Antiphonary	12th c.		x	x				x	
Klosterneuburg, Stiftsbibl., CCl 1013	Antiphonary	12th c.		x						
Klosterneuburg, Stiftsbibl., CCl 1015	Antiphonary	14th c.		x						
Klosterneuburg, Stiftsbibl., CCl 1017	Antiphonary	13th-14th c.		x						
Klosterneuburg, Stiftsbibl., CCl 1018	Antiphonary	ca. 1300		x	x		x	x		
Klosterneuburg, Stiftsbibl., CCl 1022b	Rituale	ca. 1330					x			x
Klosterneuburg, Stiftsbibl., CCl 1172	Breviary	1463					x		x	
Klosterneuburg, Stiftsbibl., CCl 1200	Breviary	14th c.					x		x	

Figure 1. Women's Liturgical Manuscripts at Klosterneuburg (Provisional List)

The only unequivocal testimony for female use is found in a fourteenth-century Hymnal, Codex 1000. This manuscript concludes with a Latin colophon indicating its date of completion as 1336 and its scribe as Giesle Ruedwein (*Explicit liber Domine Geisle Ruedweininne. Anno Domini MCCCXXXVI*). The German inscription may have been added later: *Das puech ist unser lieben Fraun gotzhous zu Klosterneuburgk und gehort in das Frauenkloster*. This manuscript is one of a group of manuscripts from Klosterneuburg containing Laon (or Messine) neumes, an important factor considered below.

The inclusion of portraits of nuns, some formal and others more graffiti-like, suggest female use. Codex 969, a thirteenth-century Breviary, includes elaborately-coiffed and bright-cheeked female faces sketched within initials and in the margins, as on fols. 207ʳ, 382ᵛ, and 412ʳ. The oft-cited Gradual Codex 588 opens the first Sunday of Advent with an initial on fol. 4ʳ that depicts a Nun praying to the Virgin and Child. Dragons flank the praying Nun in the initial to the sequence *Oscendit sanctus Gamaliel* in Codex 1004, fol. 109ʳ, evoking the eternal conflict between the serpent and the daughters of Eve. In a fifteenth-century Antiphonary, Codex 999, a female, looking out of the opening initial of the Hymn *Deus Creator Omnium* (fol. 15ᵛ), rejoices that God is the creator of all. A sensuously buxom profile portrait is found later on in the same manuscript (fol. 111ᵛ).

Common to the musical manuscripts presented here is a style of notation that is as distinctive as it is out of place. Derived from a notational style variously called Lotharingian, Messine, or, most recently, Laon (from the city in France hosting its earliest exemplar), the notation in these manuscripts was once thought to represent the notational use of Klosterneuburg as a whole.[6] But this is clearly not the case. Most of the liturgical manuscripts and fragments from Klosterneuburg dating from before the middle of the fourteenth century follow regional norms in employing unheightened German neumes, as in the thirteenth-century Graduale CCl 73. From the mid-fourteenth century and later, Bohemian neumes dominate, as found in Codex 629, a fourteenth-century Rituale.

The manuscripts represented in the ladies' manuscripts, on the other hand, use the typical bird-like neume forms common to their French forebears. All are written on four lines, with the F line in red, the C line in gold (even when C occupies a space), and the

Quis re-vol - vet no - bis ab hos - ti - o la - pi - dem

quem te - ge - re sanc - tum cer - ni - mus se - pul - chrum. -

Quem que - ri - tis o tre - mu - le mu - li - e - res in hoc

tu - mu - lo ge - men - tes.

Ie - sum Na - za - re - num cru - ci - fi - xum que - ri - mus.

Non est hic quem que - ri - tis sed ci - to e - un tes nun - ci - a - te

di - sci - pu - lis e - ius et Pe - tro qui - a sur - re - xit Ie - sus.

Klosterneuburg, Stiftsbibl., CCl 629, fol. 103v-104r (Men's version)

Figure 2a.

Amelia Carr and Michael Norton

Quis re-vol-vet no-bis ab hos-ti-o la-pi-dem

quem te-ge-re sanc-tum cer-ni-mus se-pul-chrum

Quem que-ri-tis o tre-mu-le mu-li-e-res in hoc

tu-mu-lo ge-men-tes.

Ie-sum Na-za-re-num cru-ci-fi-xum que-ri-mus.

Non est hic quem que-ri-tis sed ci-to e-un-tes nun-ci-a-te

di-sci-pu-lis e-ius et Pe-tro qui-a sur-re-xit Ie-sus.

Klosterneuburg, Stiftsbibl., CCl 589, fol. 2r (Women's version)

Figure 2b.

others in either a faint brown or black or simply drypoint. In what must surely be regarded as semiotic overload, clefs are also provided, not just to confirm the locations of C and F, but to show the pitch for all lines. This multiple clef sets these Klosterneuburg manuscripts apart from others using the same, or similar, styles of notation.

This Klosterneuburg style is evident in other manuscripts. These are noted in the table in fig. 1. Most interesting historically are the twelfth-century Antiphonaries Codices, 1010, 1012, and 1013 and the Gradual, Graz, Universitätsbibliothek MS. 807. These manuscripts, Graz 807 in particular, have held the interest of chant scholars for the better part of a century.[7] Numerous studies have been offered with even more numerous efforts to localize these books. Graz 807, for example, has been attributed variously to Klosterneuburg, to Seckau (which owned it), and even to the Augustinian proto-monastery for Bavaria, St. Nicholas in Passau. Scholars agree that these manuscripts were produced in the same scriptorium and, considering the use of the distinctive Klosterneuburg clef, we would argue that the manuscripts were surely produced in or for Klosterneuburg itself. But who used them? Here the placement for the feast for the Dedication of the Church offers a clue and a conundrum.

The men's church at Klosterneuburg was consecrated on 29 September 1136, and the celebration of its dedication is typically placed liturgically between the feasts of Maurice on 22 September and Michael on 29 September. In Codex 1012, the *Dedicatio Ecclesia* falls between the feasts of Maurice, 22 September, and Cosmas and Damian, 27 September. While some have suggested this placement to be in error, the same placement is found in a series of Breviaries from the thirteenth through fifteenth centuries, which are Codices 592, 969, 977, 1172, and 1200. Important to note is that Codex 969 is the Breviary just mentioned containing three female initial portraits.

The date for the consecration for the women's church (or churches) at Klosterneuburg has not survived, and its possible memorial in Codex 1012 and in the Breviaries is thus problematic. The dedication ceremony might have been positioned to correspond to the dedication date for the cathedral at Salzburg (25 September), whence Klosterneuburg was originally settled. It may also have been placed to correspond to the anniversary of the patron of the church's co-founder, Agnes of Swabia (24 September). In any event, the placement of this ceremony alone sets these books apart from other Klosterneuburg manuscripts.

These five breviaries distinguish themselves also with their settings of the *Visitatio Sepulchri*. They have a distinctive pattern of rubrication. The simple rubric *Ad Sepulchrum* is followed by the names of the characters portrayed (rather than the clerical offices portraying them). Thus: *Mulieres, Angelus, Petrus et Johannes*. There are no instructions for movement. The same pattern of rubrication is found in two other Klosterneuburg Antiphonaries, Codices 589 and 1018, both of which employ Laon neumes. While such rubrics may appear commonplace, the pattern is unique to this series among the nearly one thousand exemplars of the *Visitatio Sepulchri*.[8] This format contrasts distinctly with the rubrics of the Klosterneuburg men's version with its lengthier and more explicit rubrics.

The musical settings of the *Visitatio Sepulchri* preserved in Codices 589 and 1018 also vary from the men's sources. Our earliest notated source for the men's *Visitatio Sepulchri* dates from the early fourteenth century, and can be found in a Rituale from c.1330, CCl 629. Following the introductory line, "Maria Magdalena et alia Maria" (fol. 103ᵛ), the seven lines of the form divide neatly into two sections. The opening section, corresponding to the dialogue between the Marys and the angel, is set in E-mode, with the first line transposed to A. The second section, corresponding to the race of the apostles and their announcement to the people, is set in D-mode. The introductory line, "Maria Magdalena," alters the standard setting. Normally set on D, the men's reading at Klosterneuburg moves the melody up one step to E, providing modal balance to the ceremony's opening but creating an effect quite jarring to anyone familiar with the original melody.

The *Visitatio Sepulchri* from Antiphonaries 589 and 1018 also distinguish themselves in their modal structures and in their melodies. In the Antiphonaries, both copied c.1300, the introductory "Maria Magdalena" remains on D, while the next four lines are transposed up a fourth to A. Melodic variations are also evident. Fig. 2 provides a comparison between the lines "Quis revolvet" through "Non est hic" in Manuscripts 629 (for the men) and 589 (for the women). The differences, although subtle, are pervasive.

German rubrics, often a clear signal for female use, are also common among these manuscripts.[9] In the hymnals in particular, German rubrics are frequent, while elsewhere German appears only occasionally. A Graduale from c.1300 (CCl 588), for instance, gives all directions in Latin except for one reference during the Easter procession to take place *vor der heiligen geist* ("before the Holy Ghost altar"). Latin also dominates in Codex 589, an Antiphonary from c.1330. At the head of the Invitatory tones at the end of the manuscript, however, we find the following German couplet that might allude humorously, if not flatteringly, to the sound of women and children singing:

> In die < . . [unreadable].> chind'r / drei chelbel und ein chue sind vier Rinder.
> (Among the < . . . > children, three calves and a cow make four cattle.)

The manuscripts on which we have focused form a cohesive group. Evidence both explicit and implicit suggests that these manuscripts were destined for the women of Klosterneuburg. But who produced them? Could the male scribes at Klosterneuburg have maintained skill with two conflicting notational forms over several centuries? Perhaps more to the point, would they have allowed the kinds of variation in practice that we see with the *Visitatio Sepulchri* to have existed at all? If these manuscripts were commissioned, who commissioned them, and to whom was the commission given? Evidence provided by two of the earliest of our manuscripts suggests that the women of Klosterneuburg may well have produced these books themselves.

The Graduale preserved as manuscript Graz 807 was originally housed in the library of the cathedral at Seckau, founded as a double house for Augustinian canons and canonesses in 1140. Studies of the manuscript's content have revealed its close connection to later manuscripts from Klosterneuburg, to our Codex 588 in particular, and its notation places it clearly among the manuscripts copied for the women at Klosterneuburg. But Graz 807 was not destined for use at Klosterneuburg. Its *Dedicatio Ecclesia* is five months too late. Moreover, Graz 807's close relationship with another twelfth-century Gradual of uncertain provenance suggests an alternate explanation for these manuscripts.

Like Graz 807, Vienna, Nationalbibliothek MS. lat. 13314 is most closely related to sources from Klosterneuburg. Unlike Graz 807, it is set with unheighted German neumes. The Vienna manuscript also shows clear evidence of use at Seckau, in the unique version of the *Depositio Crucis* for Good Friday added in the thirteenth century. Thus, both Graz 807 and Vienna 13314 share an affinity to sources from Klosterneuburg, and both end up at Seckau. Graz 807 suggests a female origin, the Vienna manuscript, a male destination. These manuscripts, we believe, were intended as gifts from the women and men of Klosterneuburg respectively to the women and men at Seckau.

Klosterneuburg Codex 1013 presents problems of a different sort. Copied by the same scribe as Graz 807, it preserves a version of the *Visitatio Sepulchri* that most closely corresponds to that used at the Benedictine abbey of St. Afra in Augsburg. We had originally concluded, based on this recalcitrant setting, that Codex 1013 was destined for use outside of Klosterneuburg. We have come to believe, however, that what we have here in this twelfth-century antiphonary is a distinct women's version of the Easter ceremony in the earliest years of the Klosterneuburg foundation. Our interpretation is based not only on the notational style, which so clearly points to the women at Klosterneuburg, but also to the setting of the ceremony itself. In this manuscript, music is provided only for the Marys and the chorus. If we understand this to be a women's manuscript, then it becomes clear that the music omitted is precisely that which would have been sung by the officiating clergy; the Angel at the Sepulcher is the giver of the Word. Such a pattern is confirmed in Codex 1022b, a Rituale destined for use by the priest in the women's church. In the *Visitatio Sepulchri* from this manuscript, it is the women's music that is omitted, the parts for the Marys and the chorus.

The presentation by the women of a gift manuscript to Seckau and the maintenance of a distinct liturgical practice, all during the earliest decades of the foundation's existence, suggest that the women of Klosterneuburg were in control of their liturgical production and that they were backed by a powerful force. We believe their patron to be none other than Agnes of Swabia. Penelope Johnson has suggested that for many foundations where husbands received the credit, it was the wife who really provided the motivating force.[10] At Klosterneuburg, Agnes has always figured significantly in the foundation legends, but perhaps even those stories only hint at her significance. Let us conclude with a narrative, speculative but fact-based, that restores her to full prominence.

In 1106, Agnes, daughter of Emperor Henry IV, was newly widowed, after nineteen years of marriage to Frederick of Hohenstaufen.[11] Her second marriage to Babenberg Margrave Leopold III cemented the alliance between the Empire and the newly-forming Duchy of Austria. From Swabia, Agnes brought with her the Hohenstaufen tradition of the Hauskloster, a practice of founding monastic establishments as family retreats and burial sites, to serve both as secular strongholds and penitential donations.[12]

Agnes patronized Klosterneuburg immediately, stimulating an imperial donation in 1108 whose record marks the earliest mention of the church.[13] Beginning in 1114, the convent was rebuilt, and thirteenth-century records remember Agnes specifically as *fundatrix*.[14] We presume that Agnes included canonesses in her earliest plans. All ducal donations list both Leopold and Agnes in the transactions. A later medieval legend claims that the monastery was founded at the very spot where Agnes had lost and then found her veil. In any case, the new cloister buildings rose up next to one of the Babenberg residences and fit the Swabian mold of royal burial place with secular chapter, with Agnes and Leopold's young son, the future Otto of Freising, groomed to lead it. Otto frustrated his parents' designs, however, when he entered the Cistercian monastery of Morimond on his return home from studies in Paris in 1132. If Leopold was disappointed in his plans for a dynastic church, Agnes took this development in stride, for the Hohenstaufens always hedged their bets by supporting a wide range of monastic orders. In the next year, Klosterneuburg was given to the reform-minded Augustinians, and the royal couple acknowledged their son's preferences when they founded the Cistercian monastery of Heiligenkreuz nearby.

How far Agnes's patronage extended is not clear, but let us speculate. We propose that Agnes followed custom and retired into the convent at Klosterneuburg following Leopold's death in 1136. The women's church dedicated to Mary Magdalene not only celebrates a woman who was the "apostle to the apostles," but also one who turned from a worldly life to the hermetic one. Agnes would not have been the first nor the last widow to feel kinship here. Magdalene's prominence in the Easter liturgy showed a sensitivity to the presence of the Emperor's daughter at Klosterneuburg, as the prominent altar to St. Agnes in the main church also acknowledged her presence.

According to Jacques Froger, the style of notation used in the women's manuscripts derives ultimately from the Cistercian monastery of Morimond, in France, via Heiligenkreuz.[15] It is easy to imagine the complicity of Agnes and her young son in bringing the more modern, more easily learned, and more easily read style of musical notation to the women of Klosterneuburg. We also suspect Agnes of wielding her influence to introduce the *Visitatio Sepulchri* of her Swabian homeland to the women of her new home.

Agnes died in 1143 at the age of seventy, having spent the last years of her life cementing political ties between her Austrian and Swabian families. Her correspondence with Pope Innocent II procured the documents celebrating Leopold's piety that formed the basis of his canonization in 1485. Her presence lent authority to the life of the women at Klosterneuburg. She generously extended to the women of Seckau the same musical and liturgical benefits. While the women of Seckau seem not to have gained from the gesture, the women of Klosterneuburg were able to maintain their liturgical autonomy for centuries.

Klosterneuburg women and their fundatrix Agnes may be unique, but it is likely that many histories like this one are waiting to be rescued from the archives. A close examination of the evidence allows us at last to hear the Klosterneuburg women singing, in their own voices, in their own mode.

NOTES

Versions of this paper were presented in the conference "Le Drame liturgique: Sens et représentations," Abbaye de Fontevraud, France, Centre Culturel de l'Ouest, and at the International Medieval Congress at Western Michigan University in Kalamazoo, at a session sponsored by the Hill Monastic Manuscript Library in Collegeville, Minnesota. The authors would like to thank HMML for extending its resources to us, particularly the microfilmed copies of the contents of the Austrian monastic libraries.

[1] Floridus Röhrig, *Leopold III. der Heilige, Markgraf von Österreich* (Vienna: Herold, 1985); *Der Heilige Leopold: Landesfürst und Staatssymbol*, Exhibition catalogue, Niederösterreichische Landesausstellung (Stift Klosterneuburg: March 30–November 3, 1985). For a brief discussion of the canoness buildings, see Berthold Černik, *Das Stift Klosterneuburg und seine Pfarren* (Vienna, 1914). Documentary evidence for the canonesses is published by Hart-

mann Zeibig, *Urkundenbuch des Stiftes Klosterneuburg bis zum Ende des 14. Jhr.*, Fontes rerum Austriacum 10 (Vienna, 1857), lxiv–v, hereafter abbreviated as FRA.

[2] In the *Vita Hartmanni* (written c.1200) Hartmann was explicitly credited with keeping the greetings and conversations between men and women to an absolute minimum, only when necessary and then under supervision (cap. VI). Both canons and canonesses were joyful when Hartmann was made Bishop of Brixen in 1140, and then sad as he departed Klosterneuburg (cap. IX). See *Vita Beati Hartmanni*, ed. Anselm Sparber (Neustift bei Brixen, n.d. [1939]), and Anselm Sparber, *Leben und Wirken des seligen Hartmann, Bischofs von Brixen* (Klosterneuburg, 1957). The first document referring to the canonesses dates to 1160.

[3] Elizabeth Makowski, *Canon Law and Cloistered Women: 'Periculoso' and Its Commentators 1298–1545* (Washington, D.C.: Catholic University Press, 1997).

[4] FRA, No. 8 (1 July 1253). A second Chorfrauenstift flourished in Klosterneuburg from at least 1261 through 1432.

[5] All of the manuscripts appear in Hermann Pfeiffer and Berthold Černik, *Catalogus codicum manu scriptorum qui in bibliotheca can. reg. s. Aug. Claustroneoburgi asservantur*, 2 vols. (Vienna, 1931); vols. 3–13, unpubl. MSS. at Klosterneuburg (Ann Arbor, Mich: University Microfilms International, 1922–31). Some manuscripts are discussed by Alois Haidinger, *Katalog der Handschriften des Augustiner Chorherrenstiftes Klosterneuburg*, Teil 1, Cod. 1–100; Teil 2, Cod. 101–200, Österreichische Akademie der Wissenschaften, Philosophisch-historische Klasse, 168, 225 (Vienna: Verlag der Österreichischen Akademie der Wissenschaften, 1983–).

[6] The most recent survey of musical notation at Klosterneuburg is provided by Stephan Engels, "Die Notation der liturgischen Handschriften aus Klosterneuburg," *Musicologica Austriaca* 14–15 (1996): 33–69.

[7] On Graz 807, see Rudolf Flotzinger, "Die Handschrift Graz 807, ihre Notation under der sog. Germanische Choraldialekt," *Musica Antiqua* 8 (1988): 397–411, and the classic treatment by Jacques Froger, *Le manuscript 807 de la Bibliothèque de l'université de Graz*, Paléographie musicale 19 (Bern, 1974). On the Vienna manuscript, see Rudolf Wolfgang Schmidt, "Die Frage nach der Herkunft des Cod. Vindob. Palat. 13314 und die Problematik seines Sequenzrepertoires," *Jahrbuch des Stiftes Klosterneuburg* NF 12 (1983): 43–62. A treatment of both manuscripts is provided by Rudolf Flotzinger "Zu Herkunft und Datierung der Gradualien Graz 807 und Wien 13313," *Studia Musicologica Academiae Scientiarum Hungaricae* 31 (1990): 57–80.

[8] For Easter drama at Klosterneuburg, see Walther Lipphardt, ed., *Lateinische Osterfeiern und Osterspiele*, 9 vols. (Berlin: Walter De Gruyter, 1975–90), and Amelia Carr and Michael Norton, "New Sources for the Visitatio Sepulchri at Klosterneuburg," *Early Drama, Art, and Music Review* 15 (1993): 83–90.

[9] The *Charta Visitationis* of 1419 addressed the literacy of the canonesses among other issues of reform. The reform statutes and the Rule are explicitly to be copied in the vulgar tongue for the nuns, and a brother from the Stift was to be appointed to preach and instruct the women likewise in the vulgar tongue. See Anton Schmidgruber, "Beitrage zur Geschichte Klosterneuburgs in der ersten Hälfte des 15. Jahrhunderts" (Ph.D. diss, Vienna, 1951), 46–56. German sermons preached to the canonesses in 1490 by Chorherr Peter Eckel are also preserved as Codex 845. See also Herbert Grundmann, *Religious movements in the Middle Ages*, trans. Steven Rowan (Notre Dame, Indiana: University of Notre Dame Press, 1995), and David Bell, *What Nuns Read: Books and Libraries in Medieval English Nunneries* (Kalamazoo: Cistercian Publications, 1985), esp. 57–71. At Klosterneuburg, German is by no means exclusive to female usage, but can also be associated with lay brotherhoods, school instruction, parish preaching, communal singing, and chronicle writing.

[10] Penelope Johnson, *Equal in Monastic Profession* (Chicago: University of Chicago Press, 1991), 36.

[11] In addition to sources mentioned in n. 1 above, see Heide Dienst, *Agnes: Herzogin-Markgräfin, Ehefrau und Mutter* (Vienna, 1985), and her shorter essay "Agnes: Herzogin, Markgräfin, Landesmutter," in *Babenberger und Staufer* (Goppingen: Die Gesellschaft für Staufische Geschichte, 1987), 52–69; Klaus Graf, "Der Ring der Herzogin: Überlegungen zur 'Historischen Sage' am Beispiel der Schwäbisch Gmünder Ringsage," in *Babenberger und Staufer*, 84ff; and Ingeborg Petrascheck-Heim, "Der Agnes-Schleier in Klosterneuburg," *Jahrbuch des Stiftes Klosterneuburg* NF 13 (1985): 59–94. Dienst cautions us that the early records of Chorfrauen do not necessarily prove a co-founding of the men's and women's cloisters. The iconography of Agnes as patron of the women's convent dates from the fourteenth century.

[12] Wilhelm Störmer, "Die Hauskloster der Wittelsbacher," *Wittelsbach und Bayern: Die Zeit der frühen Herzöge Von Otto I. zu Ludwig dem Bayern. Beiträge zur Bayerischen Geschichte und Kunst 1180–1350* (Munich: Hirmer Verlag, 1980), 139–50, esp. 142; Stefan Weinfurter, *Salzburger Bistumsreform und Bischofspolitik im 12. Jh. Der Erzbischof Konrad I. von Salzburg (1106–1147) und die Regularkanoniker*, Kölner Historische Abhandlungen 24 (Cologne and Vienna, 1975).

[13] The earliest document relating to the church records was a donation made in 1108 to the altar of Mary by Bishop Hermann of Augsburg (d. 1133) "super altare sancte Marie Niuuburc" (FRA II/4, Nr. 116).

[14] See the thirteenth-century *Chronicon pii marchionis*, fol. 40ʳ: "[1114] Incepta est fundatio in Neuburgensi basilica a marchione Leupoldo et uxore Agnete, fundavit Sanctam Crucem," Vienna, Österreichische National Bibliothek, MS. Cod. Vindob. Palat. 352: fol. 40ʳ, published in Freher-Struve, *Rerum German.*

Scriptores 1 (1717): 443.

[15] Froger, *Le manuscript 807 de la Bibliothèque de l'université de Graz*, 31.

Another *Visitatio Sepulchri* from Scandinavia

Nils Holger Petersen

A previously unknown and unpublished *Visitatio Sepulchri* with musical notation is contained in a fragment of a breviary consisting of a bifolio at Rigsarkivet in Copenhagen.[1] The fragment contains portions of the liturgy for Easter Day on the recto and verso of the first folio and for the first Sunday following Easter on the second folio. The shelf mark is: Fragmentsamlingen (Fragment Collection) E 71. Another fragment, *probably* from the same manuscript and containing part of the liturgy for the feast of St. Nicholas and the octave of St. Andrew, is listed with the above-mentioned fragment as E 72. The service book from which both fragments apparently derive is identified as Breviary no. 9.

The manuscript is written on parchment and measures approximately 30 x 40 cm. The text is written in black ink with rubrics in red and capitals sometimes (but not in the *Visitatio* ceremony) in blue and red. The ceremony or play, which appears on the recto of the first folio of the fragment (fig. 1), is given with full text and music in square-note notation on four lines; the lines are drawn in red ink, the notes in black. At the top of the page is found the conclusion of the verse (to the second respond) *Ecce precedet vos*, followed by the third lectio *Notandum uero*; *Dum transisset* begins at the bottom of this column and continues over into the right-hand column with its verse *Et ualde mane*—all for the Matins of Easter Day. Then, introducing the drama which is set off as a discrete section on the page, appears the rubric *Ordo ad uisitandum sepulchrum. . . .* The play or ceremony ends at the bottom of the column with the *Te Deum*, indicated by its incipit and followed on the verso of the folio by Laudes (fig. 2).

Like E 72, the fragment containing the *Visitatio* survived as a binding for a book. In the case of E 71, the book is not known; E 72, however, was used as a binding for Otto von Sachs, *Coldingische Acten von der Hohen Wàhe*, according to a handwritten notice on

16

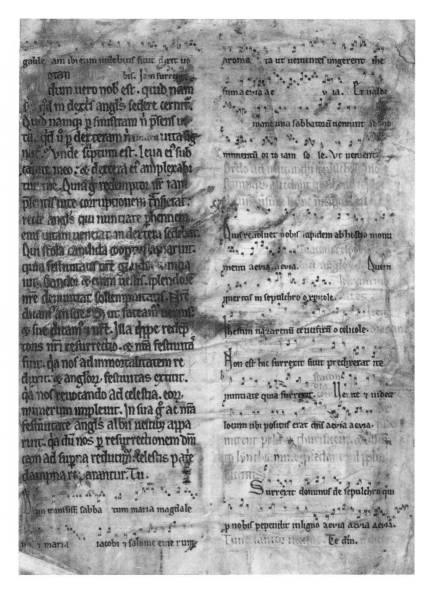

1. Rigsarkivet, Fragmentsamlingen E 71, recto. By permission of Rigsarkivet, Copenhagen.

2. Rigsarkivet, Fragmentsamlingen E 71, verso. By permission of Rigsarkivet, Copenhagen.

the left margin (recto). Nothing is known about the removal of this fragment or the fragment containing the *Visitatio* from its secondary provenance. Very likely *Coldingische Acten* would have been a local archival record from the area of Kolding, a city in the south-eastern part of Jutland which has a large medieval royal castle. Prior to use as binding for archival material, the fragments could have come from anywhere. As in Sweden and Norway, discarded manu-scripts containing pre-Reformation liturgical texts and music were commonly used for binding local and provincial records.

The two fragments have been dated in the thirteenth century by Jørgen Raasted.[2]

Though the primary provenance of the fragment containing the *Visitatio* is not known, there is very good reason to identify it as Scandinavian.[3] Therefore it may be useful within this description also to compare this example, a Type I *Visitatio Sepulchri*, to the Swedish versions of the *Visitatio* which have been edited by Audrey Ekdahl Davidson.[4]

The play or ceremony in E 71 is placed, as noted above, at the end of Matins. After the responsory *Dum transisset*, the "women," played by priests, proceed toward the sepulcher singing *Quis reuoluet*.[5] Deacons take the roles of the angels, and after the *Quem queritis* dialogue and the following antiphon, *Venite et uidete*, the "women" enter the sepulcher and cense it. To be sure, no Easter sepulcher which could actually be entered by those representing the Holy Women seems to have survived in Denmark, but other types, particularly the coffer tomb which holds an effigy of the dead Christ, are extant both in Denmark and elsewhere in Scandinavia.[6] Having picked up and displayed the linens, the "women," proceed-ing back toward the people ("ad populum"), sing *Surrexit dominus de sepulchro*. Then the cantor begins the *Te Deum*.

There are two crucial rubrics: (1) indicating that the "women" should proceed to the sepulcher, and then (2) directing them to enter and cense the sepulcher, to show the linens to the people, and to return to the people ("ad populum"). Similar rubrics are present in nos. 1, 2, 4, and 6 among the Swedish examples; Swedish no. 5, which is a mixture of Type I and Type II forms and containing rubrics which are similar only to the first of the two contained in the Danish *Visitatio*, otherwise differs substantially from the Danish example. This is not to say that there are not other differences which distinguish E 71 from the Swedish examples. Only in

Swedish no. 1 are the "women" definitely known to have been played by priests, though elsewhere to be sure the "clerics" that are specified in the rubrics may have been priests (nos. 2, 4, 6). Another difference involves the *Cito euntes* sung by the "women" at the tomb in the Swedish examples (nos. 1, 2, 4, and 6). Also, all of the Swedish examples give variants of *Non est hic* in the *Quem queritis* exchange which differ from the Danish example in E 71.[7]

Musically the *Visitatio* in E 71 differs from all the Swedish examples which appear accompanied by notation. One will observe that all the melodies in E 71 have the final G except *Surrexit dominus de sepulchro* in which the Mode IV melody begins as in the Swedish examples (but with a different final in nos. 2 and 5, while the ending of this melody in no. 3 is missing).[8] The Swedish examples tend to provide variants even of the finals of the *Quem queritis* melody. The traditional *Venite et uidete* melody in E 71 is close to the versions found in nos. 2 and 3; curiously the melody of *Quis reuoluet* in E 71 is close only to the version in Swedish no. 5.

The *Visitatio* contained in E 71 may also be usefully compared to various other examples of the ceremony or play, especially one from Rheinau which contains incipits only[9] and also the eleventh-century *Consuetudines Sigiberti Abbatis*.[10] The latter includes a *Visitatio* with the same items as those found in E 71. There are some differences, to be sure, in the matter of rubrics, involving, for example, a procession to the sepulcher that includes the entire congregation and also the singing of *Surrexit dominus de sepulchro* by both the *cantores* who sing the role of the Holy Women and the deacons who represent the Angels. However, the rubrics of this ceremony or play are less closely related to the *Visitatio* contained in E 71 than are the Swedish examples.

The *Visitatio Sepulchri* contained in the fragment E 71 in the Danish national archives in Copenhagen may be tentatively seen to be a Danish ceremony or play which is identifiable through its rubrics as part of a Scandinavian tradition. Such an identification is also corroborated by the liturgical evidence of the items and rubrics surrounding the *Visitatio* which seem closely related to the practice of the Linköping and Lund dioceses, in the Middle Ages respectively of Sweden and Denmark.[11] The *Visitatio* in E 71 additionally may provide a link between other Scandinavian examples—found north of Denmark in Sweden—and a continental tradition represented by the *Consuetudines Sigiberti Abbatis*.

A transcription of the *Visitatio Sepulchri* contained in E 71 follows:

Ordo ad uisitandu*m* sepulchru*m* more feminar*um* accedant
quid*dam* ad sepulchrum usum hunc incipientes

Diaconi respond*ent* uice ang*el*or*um*

Iterum mulieres.

Item diaconi.

Statim diaconi.

Ue - ni - te *et* ui - de - te lo - cum u - bi po - si - tus
e - rat do - *mi* - nus al - le - lv - ia al - le - lv - ia.

Deinde intrent pre*sby*teri *et* thurificent. *et* assu*m*pto lynthiamine
pro*c*edant ad po*pulu*m dicentes.

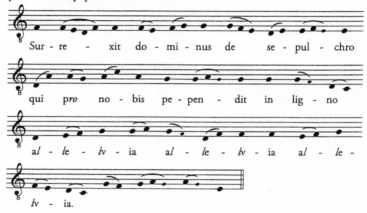

Sur - re - xit do - mi - nus de se - pul - chro
qui *pro* no - bis pe - pen - dit in lig - no
al - le - lv - ia al - le - lv - ia al - le -
lv - ia.

At this point the manuscript fragment continues with the
antiphon of Lauds, *Angelus autem domini.*[12]

NOTES

[1] This fragment was called to my attention by Professor Henrik Glahn, while
the specific reference to the manuscript was provided to me by Professor Jørgen
Raasted. I am also grateful to the staff at Rigsarkivet for helpful assistance and for
permission to publish the facsimile of the *Visitatio* contained in Fragmentsamlingen E 71. It should be noted that the shelfmark has been changed since the initial
publication of the present article.

[2] Rigsarkivet, Folioregister 221; this catalogue was prepared by Jørgen
Raasted in 1975. See also Esben Albrechtson, Specialregistratur (Copenhagen,
1976), folioregister 284.

[3] See also n. 11, below.

[4] *Holy Week and Easter Ceremonies and Dramas from Medieval Sweden*, ed. Audrey Ekdahl Davidson, Early Drama, Art, and Music Monograph Series 13 (Kalamazoo: Medieval Institute Publications, 1990).

[5] On the surrounding musical items of the *Quem queritis*, see Gunilla Björkvall, Gunilla Iversen, and Ritva Jonsson, eds., *Tropes du propre de la messe*, Pt. 2: *Cycle de Pâques*, Corpus Troporum 3 (Stockholm: Almqvist & Wiksell International, 1982), 217–23.

[6] See especially Ulla Haastrup, "Medieval Props in the Liturgical Drama," *Hafnia* 11 (1987): 138–46.

[7] Since the original publication of the present article in 1991, one more Swedish *Visitatio* ceremony has been found; see Nils Holger Petersen, "A Newly Discovered Fragment of a *Visitatio Sepulchri* in Stockholm," *Comparative Drama* 30 (1996): 32–40. Also in Finland, two such fragments have been discovered by Ilka Taitto. See Aasa Ringbom, "Reflections on Liturgical Drama in Medieval Scandinavian Art," in *Roma, Magistri Mundi: Iternaria culturae medievalis*, ed. Jacqueline Hamesse (Louvain-la-Neuve: Fédération Internationale des Instituts d'Études Médiévales, 1998), 737–57. Concerning the German offices mentioned here, see Helmut De Boor, *Die Textgeschichte der lateinischen Osterfeiern* (Tübingen: Max Niemeyer, 1967), 44, for discussion of the short form of the *Non est hic* text in relation to the *Consuetudines Sigiberti* ceremony.

[8] For the traditional Mode VIII melody found in the Winchester Troper, see Susan Rankin, *The Music of the Medieval Liturgical Drama in France and England*, 2 vols. (New York: Garland, 1989), 1:27, and 2:21.

[9] Walther Lipphardt, ed., *Lateinische Osterfeiern und Osterspiele*, 9 vols. (Berlin and New York: Walter De Gruyter, 1975–91), 2:315; see also *Der Rheinauer Liber Ordinarius*, ed. Anton Hänggi (Freiburg: Universitätsverlag, 1957), 137–40. The importance of the Rheinau *Liber Ordinarius* from the beginning of the twelfth century as an early source for Old Norse rubrics has been noted by Lilli Gjerløw; see the Introduction to her edition of the *Ordo Nidrosiensis Ecclesiae* (Oslo: Universitetsforlaget, 1968), 85.

[10] Lipphardt, *Lateinisches Osterfeiern und Osterspiel*, no. 336; see also ibid., 6:338, and Kassius Hallinger, "Die Provenienz der Consuetudo Sigiberti," *Mediaevalia litteraria: Festschrift für Helmut De Boor*, ed. Ursula Hennig and Herbert Kolb (Munich: C. H. Beck, 1971), 155–76. For some other versions of the *Visitatio* that are similar in structure to the example in E 71, see Lipphardt, nos. 179 (Ahrweiler, c.1400), 199 (Bingen-Disibodenberg, early thirteenth century), 274 (Münster Cathedral, thirteenth century), 366–367 and 370 (Worms, fifteenth and sixteenth centuries). Only 199 and 366 include the text of *Non est hic* using the same shortened form as E 71.

[11] The knowledge of medieval liturgy in Denmark is mainly confined to the late Middle Ages, mostly late fifteenth-century, though the situation is somewhat better with regard to the liturgical practices of Sweden and Norway. See especially Sven Helander, *Ordinarius Lincopensis und seine liturgischen Vorbilder* (Lund: C. W. K. Gleerup, 1957). Of interest for further evaluating E 71 is another thirteenth-century fragment of a breviary at Rigsarkivet in Copenhagen—Frag-

24   *Nils Holger Petersen*

mentsamlingen E 73, containing part of the liturgy for Easter Day and identified by Helander (123–24) as Danish. The liturgy of E 71 shows resemblances to the fourteenth-century Ordinary from Linköping, which also seems related to E 73. See additionally two studies by Heinrich Husmann, "Studien zur geschichtlichen Stellung der Liturgie Kopenhagens (unter Zugrundelegung des Missale von 1510)," *Dansk Aarbog for Musikforskning* 2 (1962): 3–58, and "Die Oster- und Pfingstalleluia der Kopenhagener Liturgie und ihre historischen Beziehungen," *Dansk Aarbog for Musikforskning* 4 (1964–65): 3–62. On connections between the earlier medieval liturgy and the later vernacular liturgy especially as related to quasi-dramatic ceremonial forms, see Audrey Ekdahl Davidson, *The Quasi-Dramatic St. John Passions from Scandinavia and Their Medieval Background*, Early Drama, Art, and Music Monograph Series 3 (Kalamazoo: Medieval Institute Publications, 1981).

[12] At least in *Non est hic* b-flat would have been used throughout, although this is only indicated in the fragment from the key (with b-flat), which here has been transcribed into the second line of the item. Based on upon my consulting the manuscript in June 2003, the transcription is a revised version of the one which was published in 1991. I wish to thank Eyolf Oestrem, University of Copenhagen, for valuable help with the transcription and for helpful discussions concerning those places which are difficult to read in the fragment.

The Easter Sepulcher at St. Mary Redcliffe, Bristol, 1470

Mark C. Pilkinton

The Records of Early English Drama (REED) *Handbook for Editors* recommends the exclusion of sepulcher watching from REED volumes, unless such activity directly relates to play production. A 1470 memorandum contained in the parish records of St. Mary Redcliffe, Bristol, discloses the delivery of a new Easter sepulcher to the church, one which by its very nature confirms the inherent theatricality associated with the sepulcher device. The document reads as follows:

> Memorandum that Mayster Canynges hath delyuered the iiijth day of Iule in the yere of our lorde j Mille CCCC lxx to Maister Nicholas Pyttes vicary of Redclif Moyses Couteryn Phelip Bertlemewe & Iohn Browne procuratores of Redclif bi foreseid A New Sepulchre well gilte with fyne golde and a kever þerto

> Item An ymage of god almythy Risyng oute of the same Sepulchre with all the Ordynance that longeth þerto. That is to sey A lath made of Tymbre And the yren worke þere to & cetera.

> Item there to longeth hevyn made of Tymber & steyned clothes

> Item hell made of Tymbue ⌐& Yren worke⌐ with deuellz the nombre of xiij

> Item iiij knyghtes Armed kepynge the Sepulchre with hes wepyns in hare handes that is to sey ij speris ij Axes with ij pavyes

> Item iiij peyre of Angelis whyingez for iiij Angellz made of Tymber & well peynted // Item the ffader the Crowne And visage The Ball with A Crosse vppon well gilte with fine golde

Item the holygoste Comynge oute of heyvn In to the Sepulchre

Item l<o>ngynge to [Angellz] the iiij Angellz iiij Chevelers[1]

This memorandum is fascinating to the theater historian for several reasons. First, the Easter sepulcher and sepulcher watching are obviously associated with the *Elevatio* ceremonies and, less directly, with the *Quem quaeritis* trope and the earliest Christian drama. This particular Easter sepulcher combined heaven, earth, and hell to form a macrocosmic tableau depicting the most important event in the history of Christianity: the victory of Christ over mortal death. The dramatic re-enactment of the victory of Christ over death and the associated human discovery of that victory is one of theater's most exciting reversals. Secondly, the deliberate references to action in the memorandum (God almighty rising from the sepulcher and the Holy Spirit coming out of heaven to meet him) cause one to wonder if in fact this device had some dynamic capability. Did it move and change, and, more importantly, if it did, was it with the help of actors and/or a backstage crew? Thirdly, detailed descriptions of costumes, wigs, and make-up undoubtedly reflect significantly on the overall effect the device must have had on the faithful who viewed it. From the modern perspective, one can almost see a cosmic naturalism in the four wigged angels, the four armed knights, and the thirteen devils.

With evidence coming to light of an Easter sepulcher as complex and grand as the one described in the St. Mary Redcliffe, Bristol, 1470 memorandum and considering the central position the sepulcher plays in the liturgical drama, REED editors should be encouraged to report any similar devices in other English towns and shires. Subject lists of art prepared for the Early Drama, Art, and Music Reference Series, however, have very fortunately included records of Easter sepulchers, both extant and lost.[2]

NOTES

[1] Bristol P/St.MR/Canyngs/1470. I wish to thank the rector of St. Mary Redcliffe who, through Elizabeth Ralph and Mary Williams, Bristol City Archivist, kindly permitted me to examine, transcribe, and photocopy these records, relevant to the *Records of Early English Drama: Bristol* volume when it was in preparation.

A less accurate transcription of this memorandum appears in, of all places, T.

C. Chatterton, *Complete Works*, 3 vols. (London: T. Longman, 1803), 3:305–06, as a "Painter's Bill" copied from a 1736 antiquarian account. This memorandum is clearly *not* a Chatterton forgery, but it is perhaps that fear that caused it to be deleted without mention from Edith E. Williams's splendid book on *The Chantries of William Canynges in St. Mary Redcliffe Bristol* (Bristol: William George's Sons, 1950). Guy Tracey Watts in *Theatrical Bristol* (Bristol: Holloway and Son, 1915) refers to this memorandum as "[t]he earliest allusion to theatrical entertainment in Bristol . . ." (3). Watts uses the 1823 edition of *The Bristol Memorialist* as his source.

The memorandum has also been noted more recently by M. D. Anderson, *Drama and Imagery in Medieval English Churches* (Cambridge: Cambridge University Press, 1963), 27–28, who cites J. Britton, *History and Architecture Relating to Redcliffe Church* (Bristol, 1813), 47.

[2] See especially the listing in Pamela Sheingorn, *The Easter Sepulchre in England*, Early Drama, Art, and Music Reference Series 5 (Kalamazoo: Medieval Institute Publications, 1987), which appeared after the present article was initially published.

The *Visitatio Sepulchri*: Public Enactment and Hidden Rite

Dunbar H. Ogden

More definitely than the compilers of the *Regularis Concordia* of Ethelwold at Winchester in Anglo-Saxon England, the play-wright-composers of the *Fleury Playbook* stepped decisively across the threshold from ritual to drama.[1] The *Playbook* refers to *populus* and to *plebs*. Whether these words designate a monastic community or the presence of a lay congregation one cannot tell except from the context. But it seems that at Fleury (or wherever else the *Playbook* originated)[2] a lay congregation is meant. There in the *Visitatio Sepulchri* the Marys turn *ad populum* with the news of the Resurrection, Mary Magdalene sings the *Congratulamini michi* "to the people" (*ad populum*) after the *Hortulanus* scene—i.e., the episode with Christ as gardener—and the Marys depart from the Sepulcher singing the *Surrexit Dominus* ("The Lord has risen") *ad plebem*; finally, when they lay out the grave-cloth on the high altar, they sing *ad plebem* the words "Cernite, uos socii, sunt corporis ista beati / Linthea . . ." ("Behold, you companions, here is the shroud of the blessed body . . ."). At this moment the congregation becomes directly involved. In fact, it is even given a role as part of the original Jerusalem community that first received the news of the Resurrection from the women; it becomes contemporary with the events that are being depicted.[3]

Yet of all the liturgical dramas, the *Visitatio Sepulchri* could also have a different function. In some primarily monastic churches the exchange between the Marys and the Angel(s) occurred out of sight of the worshipping community, as a private episode. The Marys would then return with the grave-cloth, and the community would celebrate the discovery of the Resurrection with the traditional *Te Deum laudamus*. For instance, where at Magdeburg the dialogue at the Tomb was played out at a stone replica of the Holy Sepulcher (1240) in the nave of the cathedral in the midst of the populace (fig. 1), at Constance it was sung at a stone replica of the

28

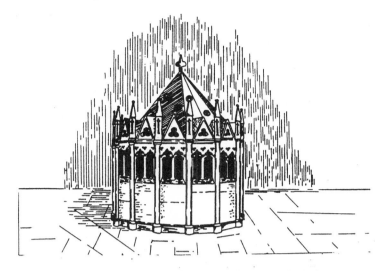

1. The Easter Sepulcher at Magdeburg Cathedral.

Sepulcher (1280) that was quite similar but located in a chapel altogether separate from the cathedral (figs. 2– 3). At Magdeburg it was performed just at the end of Matins; at Constance, just prior to Matins. At Magdeburg one feels the drama; at Constance one feels the ceremony. There, at Constance, the Marys left the church in procession, sang the dialogue with the Angels either while process-ing or at the chapel, and then returned into the church to sing the *Surrexit Dominus* and conclude with the *Te Deum*. Thereupon Matins commenced, eventually to finish with a second singing of the *Te Deum*. The text makes no mention of a grave-cloth. A fif-teenth-century text from Constance also records a pre-Matins ob-servance, an *Elevatio* with a unique antiphon, *Quem queris mulier* ("Whom do you seek, woman?"). There a procession returned to the church with the Host ("cum Corpore Domini") and moved to the choir entrance. The canons with the Host entered the choir, where-upon the Cantor with the chorus (*Cantores*) commenced an anti-phon, presumably the *Surrexit Dominus*, repeating it three times. Finally they sang the *Te Deum*, the procession (*Omnes*) entered the choir area, and then Easter Matins began, the opening proclaimed with an intense voice—"sequitur festive alta voce: 'Domine labia mea'."[4]

To cite another pair of contrasting examples, at Braunschweig, Mary Magdalene actually went searching for Salvator through the crowd of worshippers standing in the nave of the cathedral; whereas prior to 1474 at Sion (Sitten, in Switzerland) the choir members in their stalls and the lay worshippers could only have heard faint music from the Marys and the Angel in the crypt beneath the high altar (a rubric for the Angel specifies "quidam PUER, qui bene sciat cantare"—"a boy who can sing very well").

In these examples, at Constance and Sion a hidden rite was celebrated. At Constance the procession to the tomb actually exited from the cathedral (or formed outside of it) and moved some thirty
.....

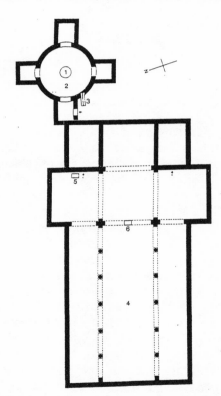

2. Constance. St. Mary's Cathedral and St. Mauritius Rotunda. Based on Erdmann's conjectural groundplan c.1000 with later documented altars. (1) Holy Sepulcher; (2) St. Mauritius Rotunda; (3) grave of Konrad; (4) nave, St. Mary's Cathedral; (5) Altar of the Holy Cross; (6) parish altar.

3. Easter Sepulcher at Constance Cathedral. By permission of Alinari/Art Resource, New York.

or thirty-five meters eastward to enter the ancient (tenth-century)
Chapel of St. Mauritius with its stone replica of the Holy Sepulcher.
The exchange between the angels and the women could have been
neither seen nor heard by the worshippers inside the cathedral.
Similarly, in the Cathedral of Sion the Marys departed from the
raised east choir and descended into the crypt underneath the east
choir to sing their lines with the Angel at the subterranean altar of
St. James and to receive the grave-cloth. Worshippers did not witness the scene at the Sepulcher, and only those near the entrance to
the crypt could possibly have caught even muffled sounds of the
Quem queritis chant down there.

Thus the concealment of the event at Sion bestowed a miraculous nature upon the grave-cloth in the hands of the women as they
emerged from the crypt. That act was akin to the secret miracle of
the Eucharist dramatized at Constance. Where the *Visitatio Sepulchri* served as a public, didactic, and mnemonic instrument as at
Magdeburg and Braunschweig, its lines, music, and its dramatic
characteristics tended to increase, while when the exchange at the
Tomb was hidden away, as at Constance and Sion, the work tended
to remain a brief dramatic ceremony almost indistinguishable in
form from its liturgical contexts.

Regarding *mise-en-scène*, there are two plays that survive from
Sion, and both appear to record very ancient forms. Indeed, in the
strictest sense the second one, an *Officium Stellae*, is really not a
drama. It is not a play acted out but rather a procession with special
props and costumes. Like the early (many Italian) Easter pre-Mass
processions augmenting the Introit with added tropes, both the
Christmas and the Easter observance at Sion augment the *Feierlichkeit* (the celebrative solemnity) of the particular observance. The
populace catches sounds, smells, and glimpses of the *Feierlichkeit*
just as it catches sounds, smells, and glimpses of the sacred
moments of the Mass. On the other hand, for the townspeople in
thirteenth-century Sion the Holy Week festivity at the cathedral was
not on Easter Sunday but on the preceding Palm Sunday when a
great public procession wound its way from the cathedral to various
neighboring churches and eventually back to the cathedral.

Neither the partially secreted *Visitatio Sepulchri* nor the *Officium Stellae* at Sion was intended to teach. It occurs to me that at
times the liturgical drama had a teaching function; at other times it
did not. That is, in some instances its mnemonic function was more

pronounced (i.e., bringing back to mind what was already known), and in other instances its devotional function was more pronounced. Like the tropes added to the Introit of the Easter Mass to make the entering procession more *feierlich*, so some forms of the *Visitatio Sepulchri* and the *Officium Stellae* were included in order to create a more festive event than the liturgy would otherwise allow. Such was the case at Sion. Where the events at the Sepulcher itself are hidden away, as is the situation at the Cathedral of Constance and at other Easter Sepulchers located in removed chapels, the waiting on the part of clergy and congregation creates anticipation toward the re-entry of the Marys into the chancel and the glorious announcement of the Resurrection. That is the augmented *Feierlichkeit*, but not a drama enacted in front of an audience. The mountain isolation of Sion may have resulted in our having texts that although dating to the thirteenth century contain practices and attitudes reflecting a more ancient *Feierlichkeit*. This isolation may also have been the reason for the continued use of these texts in Sion into the seventeenth century.

By contrast, the early liturgical drama in some areas was certainly intended to serve a teaching or mnemonic function within a monastic community. And in a third situation, this drama often served to instruct a general populace. Such was the case at Winchester c.973, teaching apparently both townsfolk and members of the monastic community; and such was the case in churches with texts calling for the singing of a final hymn in the vernacular, often *Christ ist erstanden*.

In other words, it is my hunch that in some monastic communities the overt teaching and mnemonic functions of this drama in its simple form occurred to the monastery's leadership no more or less than the teaching and mnemonic functions of a given hymn or procession, whereas elsewhere, as at Winchester, such purposes became primary elements from the outset, either for the monastic community or for the townspeople, or for both. It is in the latter instances that the drama separated increasingly from the liturgy, became more distinct as a genre, and took on more narrative and characterological features. As to the question of origins, it seems to me that in the tenth century somewhere between the Easter Mass introit tropes of Italy and southern France, and the Easter Matins tropes of German areas—and the Council of Winchester—the idea was born of using this special *Feierlichkeit* in order to bring back to memory and to teach.[5] As time went on, monastic communities whose observances were strictly intramural tended toward the enhancement of their Easter *Feierlichkeit* if they used *Quem queritis* at all, whereas monastic communities and especially cathedral chapters whose observances included extramural congregations, such as townspeople and pilgrims and students, tended toward demonstrating and teaching if they used *Quem queritis*. It was there that the antiphonally exchanged *Quem queritis* lines came to be acted out and expanded—and extended to various sites in the Church—as were the lines of Christmas plays and other music-dramas in the eleventh and twelfth centuries.

NOTES

[1] For the *Regularis Concordia*, see Pamela Sheingorn, *The Easter Sepulchre in England*, Early Drama, Art, and Music Reference Series 5 (Kalamazoo: Medieval Institute Publications, 1987), 20–22, figs. 3–4; for the *Fleury Playbook Visitatio* see Karl Young, *The Drama of the Medieval Church*, 2 vols. (Oxford: Clarendon Press, 1933), 1:393–97, and *The Fleury Playbook: Essays and Studies*, ed. Thomas P. Campbell and Clifford Davidson, Early Drama, Art, and Music Monograph Series 7 (Kalamazoo: Medieval Institute Publications, 1985), figs. 51–56. See also Dunbar H. Ogden, *The Staging of Drama in the Medieval Church* (Newark: University of Delaware Press, 2002).

[2] See the argument for Fleury in Fletcher Collins, "The Home of the Fleury *Playbook*," in *The Fleury Playbook: Essays and Studies*, ed. Campbell and Davidson, 26–34.

[3] On the phenomenological questions which are raised here, see C. Clifford Flanigan, "The Liturgical Context of the *Quem Queritis* Trope," *Comparative Drama* 8 (1974): 45–62.

[4] These texts have been cited from *Lateinische Osterfeiern und Osterspiele*, ed. Walther Lipphardt, 9 vols. (Berlin: Walter de Gruyter, 1975–90), (hereafter *LOO*) as follows:

Braunschweig: *LOO*, no. 780.

Constance: *LOO*, nos. 239, 241. For commentary on Constance see Lipphardt, *LOO*, 7:187. The 1502 rubric reads: "Ad matutinum ante compulsationem fit Processio ad sanctum Sepulchrum cum luminibus, thuribulo et aqua benedicta" (*LOO*, no. 241). This would mean that the *Surrexit Dominus de sepulcro* and the *Te Deum* were sung before Matins. The only other instances that I know where these pieces were performed just preceding Easter Matins occur in texts from Fulda, Rheinau, and St. Gall, also apparently recording very old practice. The positioning of the ceremony or drama was in flux and differed with geographical region. Lipphardt also notes that nowhere else but at Constance does one discover this particular relationship of three antiphons in performance: *Venite et videte*, *Et recordate*, and *Surrexit Dominus*. As mentioned, an earlier text from Constance (fifteenth century, *LOO*, no. 239) also seems to put the procession out to the Sepulcher immediately before Matins, including an antiphon (presumably the *Surrexit Dominus*) and the *Te Deum*, followed thereafter by the opening of Matins in the cathedral with "Domine labia mea" ("Lord, open my lips"). There the initial stage direction reads: "In die sancto Pasce ad Matutinas secundo pulsu angularis DOMINI ibunt ad sacrum Sepulcrum cum candelis et SACERDOS ornatus." The ground plan of Constance Cathedral is from Peter Jezler, "Gab es in Konstanz ein ottonisches Osterspiel?" in *Variorum munera florum: Latinität als prägende Kraft mittelalterlicher Kultur: Festschrift für Hans F. Haefele*, ed. Adolf Reinle, Ludwig Schmugge, and Peter Stotz (Sigmaringen: Jan Thorbecke Verlag, n.d.), 97.

Magdeburg: *LOO*, nos. 608–11.

Sion (Sitten): *LOO*, nos. 746, 746a, b, c. For the early *Officium Stellae* from Sion as well as Easter texts, see Albert Carlen, "Das Ordinarium Sedunense und die Anfänge der geistlichen Spiele im Wallis," *Blätter aus der Walliser Geschichte* 9 (1943): 349–73.

[5] See David A. Bjork, "On the Dissemination of *Quem quaeritis* and the *Visitatio sepulchri* and the Chronology of Their Early Sources," *Comparative Drama* 14 (1980): 46–69, esp. table 1 on 52–53.

Eulenspiegel (Episode 13) as a Theater-Historical Document

Martin W. Walsh

Of the ninety-six episodes that make up the picaresque epic *Ein kurtzweilig lesen von Dyl Ulenspiegel* (1515), one shows the hero participating in theatrical activity.[1] In episodes 11 through 13, Eulenspiegel is, somewhat incongruously, serving as a sacristan with the parish priest of Büddenstedt, a village between Helmstedt and Schoningen in the district of Brunswick, Eulenspiegel's home territory. Episode 13 involves the production of a traditional *Osterspiel* which ultimately ruptures Eulenspiegel's relationship with his employer. The episode is as follows:

> Die 13. Historie sagt, wie Ulenspiegel in der Osternmettin ein Spil macht, daz sich der Pfarrer und sein Kellerin mit den Buren raufften und schlugen.
>
> Nun da es sich nahet den Ostern, da sprach der Pfarer zu Ulenspiegel, dem Messner, es ist ein Gewonheit hie, das die Buren alwegen zu den Ostern in der Nacht ein Osterpil machen, wie unser Her entstet uss dem Grab, und so must er darzu helffen, wann es wär recht also, das die Sigristen das zurichtent unnd regierten. Da sprach Ulenspiegel und gedacht, wie sol das Mergenspil zugon von den Buren und sprach zu dem Pfarrer: "Nun ist doch kein Buer hie, der da glert ist, Ihr müssen mir Euwer Magt dazu leihen, die kan wol schrieben und lesen." Der Pfarer sprach: "Ja, ja, nim nur dazu, wer dir helffen kan; auch ist mein Magt vor mer darbeigewesen." Es waz der Kellerin lieb, und sie wolt der Engel im Grab sein, wann sie kund den Reimen usswendig. Da sucht Ulenspiegel zwen Bauren und nam sie zu ihm und wolten die drei Marien sein. Und Ulenspiegel leert den einen Buren zu latein seinen Reimen. Und der Pfarrer waz unser Hergot, der solt uss dam Grab erston. Da nun Ulenspiegel für das Grab kam mit seinen Buren, als die Marien angelegt warn, da sprach die Kellerin als der Engel im Grab den Reimen zu latein: "Quem queritis. Wen suchen ihr hie?" Da sprach der Buer, die vorderst Merg, als ihn Ulenspiegel gelert het: "Wir suchen ein alte einäugige Pfaffenhur."
>
> Da sie daz hört, daz sie verspottet ward mit ihrem einem Aug, da

ward sie gifftig auff Ulenspiegel und sprang uss dem Grab und meint, sie wolt ihm in daz Antlit fallen mit den Füsten. Und schlug her ungewiss und traff den einen Buren, daz ihm daz ein Aug geschwall. De der ander Buer daz sah, der schlug auch dar und traff die Kellerin an den Kopff, daz ihr die Flügel entpfielen. Da daz der Pfarrer sahe, da liess er daz Van fallen und kam seiner Kellerin zu Hilff und fiel dem einen Buren in daz Har und zohen sich für daz Grab hindan. Da das die anderen Bauren sahen, da luffen sie hinzu und ward ein grosses Gerühel und lag der Pfaff mit der Kellerin under, unnd da lagen die Bauren, die zwo Mergen, auch under, das sie die Buren voneinander musten ziehen.

(When it was getting close to Easter, the priest said to Eulenspiegel his sacristan, "It's custom here that at Easter, during the night, the farmers always hold an Easter play: 'How Our Lord Rises from His Tomb'." Well, he had to help with it, because it was only right for the sacristan to arrange and direct it.

Eulenspiegel thought, "How can the play of the Marys possibly take place with these farmers?" So he told the priest, "Now, there's certainly no farmer here who's educated; so you'll have to lend me your maid for this. She can read and write well."

The priest said, "Yes, yes. Just take whoever can help you with it. Besides, my maid's been in many of these."

His maid was delighted, and she wanted to be the angel in the tomb because she knew the lines by heart. Eulenspiegel then looked for two farmers, and got them, too. Now, he wanted the three of them to be the three Marys, so Eulenspiegel taught one farmer his lines in Latin. Well, the priest was Our Lord God, Who was supposed to rise from the tomb.

Eulenspiegel now approached the tomb with his farmers dressed as the three Marys. At this point, the maid, as the angel in the tomb, spoke her lines in Latin, "*Quem quaeritis?*"— "Whom seek ye here?"

And the farmer who was the first Mary replied as Eulenspiegel had taught him: "We're looking for a priest's old, one-eyed whore."

When she heard this . . . she became furious with Eulenspiegel, sprang out of the tomb, and tried to attack him in the face with her fists. But she struck carelessly, hitting one of the farmers, so one of his eyes swelled up. When the other farmer saw this, he lunged out also, hitting the maid on the head as well, so her wings fell off. When the priest saw this, he let his van fall, came to help his maid, grabbed the hair of one of the farmers, and they pulled one another in front of the tomb. When the other farmers saw this, they ran forward and there was a tremendous uproar. Well, the priest was lying at the bottom with his maid; and the two farmers (the two Marys) were also lying underneath—so the farmers had to pull them apart from one another.[2])

Can we at all employ this comic tale as a theater-historical doc-

ument? How far can we interrogate it, and its accompanying woodcut illustration (fig. 1), with regard to the actual performance of
Easter plays in the hinterland at the turn of the fifteenth-century?
We can begin by rejecting two obvious extremes: (1) that the tale is
an entirely accurate record of an actual historical incident; and (2)
that it is purely a product of the imagination with no bearing whatsoever on early sixteenth-century realities. We need not dwell on
the first extreme. Eulenspiegel, whatever his historical roots might
be, is certainly a creature of the popular imagination, one expression
of that universal archetype, the Trickster. His exploits are satirical
fantasy, and moreover they have wandered into his *vita* from many
different sources, some of them very ancient and very distant. Yet
these exploits are also couched in a grotesque realism and located
quite specifically in actual locales amidst the trades, social types,
and mores easily verifiable as belonging to the milieu of Renais-
sance/Reformation Germany.[3] The background for Tale 13, then,
cannot be total fantasy, for it presumes that the Easter play situation
is, at the very least, a recent memory if not an actual contemporary
practice.

Assuming that certain recognizable social realities underlie it,
what then are the theatrical presumptions and prerequisites in Tale
13? Let us list them:

1. The play is to be performed before dawn on Easter
morning (*Osternmettin*) and has what amounts to a rubric,
"How Our Lord Rose from the Tomb" (*wie unser Her
entstet uss dem Grab*), but is also referred to as the "Marys
Play" (*Mergenspil*). It appears, however, to be conducted
entirely in Latin around the ancient trope: *Quem queritis in
sepulchro*.

2. The parish sexton (*Messner, Sigristen*) acts as producer
and director (*zurichtent unnd regierten*) and moreover
plays one of the Marys. Local peasants (male) are recruited
to play the other Marys in the *Visitatio*. But evidently more
learning or expertise is required for the supernatural roles,
and the sexton naturally turns to the priest's literate household staff, already experienced in such theatrical activities.

1. Woodcut illustrating Episode 13 in *Ein Kurtzweilig lesen von Dyl Ulenspiegel geboren uss den land zu Brunswick* (Strassburg, 1515). Courtesy of Harlan Hatcher Graduate Library, University of Michigan.

The priest himself plays the risen Christ. Both the narrative and the woodcut include the latter's *Van* as a necessary prop. We may therefore conclude that at least the *Noli me tangere* episode with Mary Magdalene (Eulenspiegel's role?) was to conclude a Type III *Visitatio sepulchri* since Christ himself does not appear in the shorter (Types I and II) forms of the play. The audience appears to be simply the peasant population of the district.

3. In addition to the *labarum* of the Risen Christ, the tale mentions a piece of stage architecture, the Tomb, rendered in the woodcut as a plain chapel, little bigger than a child's play-house. It seems to have only one large aperture with a high sill, hardly designed for easy "springing" out. The

Marys are costumed in cloaks and wimples over peasant
male dress, and the tonsured priest appears to be in his
Mass vestments—i.e., in the ancient "costuming" for liturgical drama. The narrative records that the angel's wings
were knocked off, but there are no wings apparent in the
illustration. (The woodcut, it should be pointed out, shows
two sequential acts as simultaneous: the Maid "springing"
from the tomb, and the Priest already in combat with the
Marys. The third Mary, who laughingly retreats from the
neighborhood of the tussle, is presumably Eulenspiegel.)

The situation of Eulenspiegel, Episode 13, appears then to
convey a very plausible small-scale rural performance of an Easter
play. But can we ascertain anything more beyond this general
plausibility? Perhaps, if we compare it with the actual situation of
Osterspiele in the period and if we severely discount those elements
of the tale that are particularly necessary for its comic effect,
namely the housekeeper's playing of the Angel and the peasants'
ignorance of their Latin lines.

With regard to the first procedure, we have an Easter Play from
the tale's purported area in precisely the right time-frame, the
Wolfenbüttler Osterspiel, generally assigned to the city of Brunswick in the early fifteenth-century.[4] It is a typical macaronic (dual-
language) product with its Latin portions containing musical notation and its German portions evidently simply recited, although
toward the end of the piece musical notation is supplied for the
Magdalen's lament in German. The play has over 280 verses in four
episodes: a *Mercator* scene in which the Marys purchase their
ointments; the visit to the sepulcher; the *Hortulanus* scene; and, in
a rather truncated form, a Doubting Thomas scene.

This is obviously *not* the kind of Easter play upon which Tale
13 depends, since its German portions continually clarify what is
being sung in Latin and its scale, moreover, seems much too ambitious. Eulenspiegel's play instead represents the *Osterspiel* in a
much more rudimentary form but nevertheless incorporating the
appearance of Christ to Mary Magdalene—i.e., a Type III *Visitatio*
related to the well-known music-drama included in the *Fleury
Playbook* which contains only some eighty verses of Latin with

musical notation.[5] For Brunswick there are two examples of the Type II *Visitatio*, of 28 and 34 lines respectively, in a twelfth-century Sacramentary and a fourteenth-century Psaltery from the Cathedral of St. Blaise (Kollegiatsstiftkirche St. Blasius). A Lectionary from St. Blaise, assigned to the last half of the fourteenth century, moreover, has an Easter play similar to Fleury's, a Type III *Visitatio* with a *Hortulanus* scene.[6] If we were not dealing with comic fiction, we might be tempted to say that we had definitely located Eulenspiegel's play. This late St. Blaise performance text might be only a generation earlier than the macaronic *Wolfenbüttler Osterspiel* cited above, and it would support the general observation that Latin Easter plays and vernacular elaborations upon the same often existed side by side, in the same district, for considerable periods of time.

With all due caution then, Tale 13 can be used as evidence for the survival and for something of the performance circumstances of very conservative Easter Plays in the Early Modern period. The proto-evangelical satire of the Eulenspiegel author would seem to depend on a more or less accurate rendition of antique practice, with all its subservience to the dead language and rather mechanical reproduction, in order to allow him to craft his subtler satiric effects—how the *Hortulanus* with its *Noli me tangere* speech becomes in fact an exchange of blows "in front of the tomb," and how the false Risen Christ is in fact reburied under a heap of brawling peasants ("the priest . . . at the bottom with his maid").

With regard to the performers and the particulars of performance we can assert less. The situation and the personalities upon which the incident turns are perhaps best left to comic imagination. Wolfgang Lindow, the Reclam editor, finds the housekeeper's playing of the Angel particularly unlikely. We do have records of young actresses in later sacred drama, in the roles of the Virgin and female saints, but not for northern Germany.[7] A mature woman playing an archangel remains rather preposterous in any case, only acceptable within the "emergency" situation required by the joke.

As for the jest itself, the misconstruing of Latin was a staple of jocular literature for centuries, particularly the situation in which an incompetent is coached in Latin responses and proceeds to use them in a completely incorrect context producing either double entendre

or mere absurdity. Yet here again, the prevalence and longevity of
such a motif implies a real social context behind it. There is nothing
inherently implausible about peasants ignorantly learning their lines
by rote for an annual parish play. However, it is impossible to say
whether the contamination of the Easter play upon which the humor
depends is simply the joke-creator's intersection of two separate but
contemporary traditions (vernacular Easter plays in which the laity
participated, and church-bound Latin liturgical drama) or, what is
the more intriguing possibility, the actual contamination of liturgical drama by unschooled lay performers.

   In regard to the set, props, and costumes portrayed in narrative
and woodcut, one would think that they are on a similar level of
general accuracy. The *labarum* seen on the floor in the illustration
appears to be anatomically correct. The tomb there represented
might be a permanent indoor structure or a temporary stage property. The illustration is probably not meant to convey a permanent
stone tomb. Its box-like construction suggests carpentry. German
examples of free-standing stone sepulchers, at Magdeburg, Gern-
rode, Eichstadt, and Constance, are imposing circular structures
echoing the actual Holy Sepulcher in Jerusalem. A closer parallel
to the Eulenspiegel tomb can be found in the fourteenth-century
wooden Easter Sepulcher from St. Michael's Church, Cowthorpe,
Yorkshire, the "Büddenstedt" example, however, being walled in on
its two longer sides. A 1558 churchwarden's account from St.
Helen's, Abingdon, gives some indication of the scale of such, in
this case, temporary wooden structures:[8]

	s.	d.	
Payde for making the sepulture	0	10	0
For peynting the same sepulture	0	3	0
For stones and other charges about it	0	4	6

The Büddenstedt sepulcher's asymmetrical alignment within its
church might suggest that it is also a temporary structure—that is,
a stage-set in the purest terms—but this asymmetry may simply be
due to the exigencies of the woodcut illustration.

   Given the extreme paucity of illustrations of plays *in perfor-*
mance (or thereabouts in our case) for the period prior to 1600, it is
odd that this *Eulenspiegel* illustration has not been given more at-

tention. Together with the details supplied in the narrative it gives such a complete account of a liturgical drama in performance as to preclude any possibility of its being the mere product of fantasy, but to suggest rather strongly that it is directly influenced by contemporary observation. The survival of a Type III *Visitatio* in Brunswick from the late fourteenth century only serves to increase probability here.

One other problem remains to be discussed, the possibility that this Easter play incident has simply wandered in from some earlier era. The linguistic element of the joke, which is communicated completely in German, must, one might be inclined to argue, somewhere have had an all-Latin source. Indeed, it is fairly easy to turn the Marys' traditional response to the *Quem queritis?* into something like the required form: *Jesum nazarenum crucifixum* into *Lascam mereticem sacerdoti* ("the priest's one-eyed whore"). However, no earlier source for Eulenspiegel, Episode 13, is readily apparent. Eduard Kadlec points to a brief allusion to our story in Paulus Olearius' (i.e., Jacob Wimpheling's) parodic treatise *De fide concvbinarvm in svos pfaffos* (?Ulm, c.1501): "*& in nocte pascali, uuen suchen ir hie ir beschelpten frauuen, ein alte hur mit einem auge, & mox responsum est, non est hic.*"[9] But it is quite possible that this simply alludes to an earlier collection of Eulenspiegel material now lost. In any case, even a hypothetical source for the Easter play debacle cannot be pushed back much beyond 1500, and so our general point about the tale reflecting conservative theatrical practice may stand. Indeed it would be hard to imagine such a thoroughly disrespectful handling of sacred drama very much prior to the Reformation.[10]

To conclude, Eulenspiegel, Tale 13, can serve as a secondary theater-historical document. In its general features and perhaps in many of its particulars it presents a plausible picture of the older medieval drama surviving in the hinterland, though soon to be swept away by the tides of Reformation and Counter-Reformation. One should suspect that there are many such theater-historical discoveries waiting to be found in the German jest-book literature of the Early Modern period. In Georg Wickram's *Das Rollwagenbüchlin* (1551), no. 108, for example, we find: *Von einem weyhenactkind und dem Joseph, wie er im ein müsslin kochet inn der kirchen und einanderen in der kirchen schlügen* ("Of a Christmas Child and a Joseph, how he cooked for him a porridge in the church and how in the church they slugged each other").[11] It takes place somewhere in the diocese of Cologne and tells of a rather large choirboy chosen to play the Christ Child on Christmas Eve and duly installed in a cradle by mother Mary. But the rascal so plagued the Joseph-actor with his histrionic wailing that the good old man, who was busy preparing a mess of porridge, jammed a steaming spoonful down the boy-actor's throat, thus precipitating the brawl. Again we seem to have real if antiquated theatrical stuff—the *Kindlwiegen* ceremony, *Breikocher Joseph* in the literal act of cooking—being manipulated for farcical effect. One would respectfully submit, therefore, that the *Schawankbücher*, with all due reservations, be entered into the medieval theatrical record—or at least become an area for further investigation.

NOTES

[1] *Ein kurtzweilig Lesen von Dil Ulenspiegel*, ed. Wolfgang Lindow (Stuttgart: Philipp Reclam, 1966), 39–41.

[2] *A Pleasant Vintage of Till Eulenspiegel*, trans. Paul Oppenheimer (Middletown, Conn.: Wesleyan Univ. Press, 1972), 30–31.

[3] See, for example, the articles by Hans Wiswe and Hans Hagen Hildebrandt in *Eulenspiegel-Interpretationen: Der Schalk im Spiegel der Forschung, 1807–1977*, ed. Werner Wunderlich (Munich: Wilhelm Fink, 1979).

[4] *Der Sündenfall und Marienklage: Zwei nieder deutsche Schauspiele aus Handschriften der Wolfenbüttler Bibliothek*, ed. Otto Schonemann (Hanover: Carl Rumpler, 1855), 149–68.

[5] See Karl Young, *The Drama of the Medieval Church*, 2 vols. (Oxford: Clarendon Press, 1933), 1:393–97.

[6] Walther Lipphardt, ed., *Osterfeiern und Osterspiele*, 9 vols. (Berlin: Walter de Gruyter, 1975–91), 3:534–35; 5:780. The angel's question to the Marys in no. 534 is: *Quem queritis, o tremule mulieres, / in hoc tumulo gementes?* In nos. 535 and 780 the second verse is: *in hoc tumulo plorantes.*

[7] Lindlow, ed., *Ein kurtzweilig Lesen von Dil Ulenspiegel*, 40n. For actresses in Valenciennes, Metz, Saragossa, etc., see *The Staging of Religious Drama in Europe in the Later Middle Ages: Texts and Documents in English Translation*, ed. Peter Meredith and John E. Tailby, Early Drama, Art, and Music Monograph Series 4 (Kalamazoo: Medieval Institute Publications, 1983), 43, 55–56.

[8] Pamela Sheingorn, *The Easter Sepulchre in England*, Early Drama, Art, and Music Reference Series 5 (Kalamazoo: Medieval Institute Publications, 1987), 27, 359. For the St. Helen's record see *Illustrations of the Manners and Expences of Ancient Times in England*, ed. John Nichols (London: John Nichols, 1797), 141–42. Representations similar to our woodcut, with the aperture on the short

side, were used by manuscript illuminators to portray an anchoress's cell, another sort of "tomb."

⁹ Eduard Kadlec, *Untersuchungen zum Volksbuch von Ulenspiegel* (Prague: Koppe-Bellmann, 1916), 98. I have consulted both the *De fide concvbinarvm* edition of 1501 and that of 1505 printed by Johannes Froschauer of Augsburg.

¹⁰The Easter play woodcut was not included in the first French translation of the *Eulenspiegel* (Anvers, 1549), perhaps because of censorship. The tale, moreover, enjoyed an afterlife as a comic *Meistersang* in Protestant Nuremberg at mid-century; see *Dr. Thomas Murners Eulenspiegel*, ed. J. M. Lappenberg (Leipzig: T. O. Weigel, 1854), 232–35. Another curious production was an Eulenspiegel cycle rendered in Latin distychs by Aegidius Periander in 1567, with new woodcuts based on the originals. The Tale 13 illustration shows an even smaller, plainer box for the Tomb with the housekeeper, wings evident in this case, comfortably installed inside and apparently watching the scuffle. Eulenspiegel makes "horns" over the roof of the Tomb. Obviously derivative, this woodcut has little theater-historical value; see Aegedius Periander, *Noctvae specvlvm: Omnes res memora-biles, variasque et admirabiles, Tyli Saxonici machinationes complectens plane nouo more nunc primum ex idiomate Germanico latinate donatum* (Frankfurt am Main, 1567). In the case of this edition I am grateful to the Harvey Firestone Library, Princeton.

¹¹Georg Wickram, *Das Rollwagenbuchlin*, ed. Johannes Bolte (Stuttgart: Philip Reclam, 1968), 178; compare an oafish parish priest's ridiculous sermon on Joseph's porridge in Jacob Frey, *Gartengesellschaft* (1556), tale 117.

Mechanical Images at Salisbury

Nicholas J. Rogers

Many of the lost images of England are only known from single references, usually brief, tantalizing ones in wills. In the case of the mechanical images formerly at Salisbury Cathedral we are more fortunate since we have two descriptions by sympathetic witnesses. In February 1466 Baron Leo von Rozmital, who was seeking support in the courts of Europe for his brother-in-law, the king of Bohemia, arrived in England. Two of his attendants, his squire Schaseck and the Nuremberger Gabriel Tetzel, wrote accounts of the mission which provide vivid impressions of the country, albeit as partial and distorted as those of a modern tourist.[1]

Rozmital's party reached Salisbury just before Palm Sunday. Tetzel's itinerary is somewhat confused (he seems to have muddled reminiscences of Westminster, Reading, and Salisbury), but his description of the images is clear enough:

> We saw also some fine carved figures which were so worked with weights that they moved as if to show how the Three Holy Kings brought gifts to our Lady and her Babe, how our Lord reached out to take the gifts, and how our Lady and Joseph bowed and did obeisance to the Three Kings, and how they took their leave. All this was presented with rare and masterly skill as if they were alive. There was also a similar carving showing our Lord rising from the tomb and the angels ministering to him. This was a splendid and praiseworthy thing to see.[2]

Schaseck's account is essentially the same, but provides a few further details:

> I have nowhere seen more elegant figures. One represents the Mother of God, holding the infant Christ in her arms while the Three Kings offer gifts. The other shows the angels opening the Sepulchre with Christ rising from the dead, holding a banner in his hand. Both scenes are so represented that they do not appear to be fashioned but alive and actually to be moving before our eyes.[3]

46

In his edition of *The Travels of Leo of Rozmital*, Malcolm Letts made the suggestion that there may have been some connection between these figures and the clock installed by Bishop Ralph Erghum (1375–88).[4] The repertoire of gestures ascribed by Schaseck and Tetzel to the Salisbury automata suggests that they were more advanced technologically than the jousting knights or the jacks (the latter only dating from c.1470–80 in their present form) associated with the clock of c.1390 at Wells, also commissioned by Bishop Erghum.[5] However, a date in the late fourteenth century or early fifteenth century is not inherently improbable. The Rood of Boxley, which seems to have been of comparable complexity, if the reports of Protestant commentators are to be trusted, was in existence by 1432.[6]

Although the Bohemians give no clue as to the function of these images, it is to be presumed that they were designed for the dramatic enhancement of the liturgy. Several similar mechanical Resurrection images have been noted, the earliest of 1470 at St. Mary Redcliffe, Bristol.[7] The Salisbury *tableaux* may even have been intended primarily as props in *Quem queritis* and *Stella* plays. Ongoing research into dramatic records at Salisbury and elsewhere may shed further light on this question.

NOTES

[1] Malcolm Letts, ed., *The Travels of Leo of Rozmital*, Hakluyt Society, 2nd ser. 108 (Cambridge, 1957), 43–62.

[2] Ibid., 57.

[3] Ibid., 61.

[4] Ibid., 57, n. 2.

[5] Michael Glenny, "Ingenious and Efficient: The Wells Cathedral Clock," *Country Life* 180 (18 Sept. 1986): 852–54.

[6] Clifford Davidson, "More on Medieval Puppets," *EDAM Newsletter* 10, no. 2 (1988): 33–36; Victoria County History, *Kent*, 3 vols. (London, 1908–32), 2:154.

[7] In addition to Mark C. Pilkinton, "The Easter Sepulchre at St. Mary Redcliffe, Bristol, 1470," reprinted in the present volume, see Pamela Sheingorn, *The Easter Sepulchre in England*, Early Drama, Art, and Music Reference Series 5 (Kalamazoo: Medieval Institute Publications, 1987), 59.

The "Molly Grime" Ritual in Glentham Church, Lincolnshire

Jennifer S. Alexander

In the 1839 Report of the Charity Commissioners, amongst Mr. Charles Humphrey's entries for the Lindsey Division of the county of Lincolnshire, was the description of an arcane practice that had been supported by a charitable endowment in the parish of Glentham. The practice had ceased on the bankruptcy of the last holder of the land in c.1834, but it was evident to Mr Humphrey that the event was well remembered in the parish. The endowment provided an annual sum of 7*s* from an estate in Glentham to pay seven spinsters to wash a tomb in Glentham church, known as Molly Grime, with water drawn from a well on Newel hill in the parish. The custom was performed on Good Friday. The entry is headed "Grime's Rent Charge," but no reference to this name is made in the text.[1]

Early antiquarian descriptions of Glentham, such as that in Allen's *History of Lincolnshire* from 1834, written before the Charity Commissioners Report, make no mention of the "Molly Grime" event, but subsequent histories both repeat and elaborate on the comments in the Report. The *Gentleman's Magazine* for 1865 included a description of the rent charge and identified a damaged female effigy from the fourteenth century in the church as the object of the ceremony.[2] By 1888 an interpretation of the event had been proposed that connected the ritual washing of an effigy with the events of the Easter liturgy, transferring the preparations for the burial of a representation of the dead Christ to a secular, and female, tomb figure. A suggestion was offered for the origin of the name "Molly Grime" in which a local dialect word for "image washing" had been corrupted. The word was 'malgraem' or 'malgraen,' both versions appearing in the printed accounts, but unfortunately no evidence for its use or existence was given beyond the speculation that it was "an ancient local dialect." It has not been possible to trace this word in dialect or other dictionaries. The account appeared in the first volume of the *Lincolnshire Notes and Queries* for

1. The effigy in the "Molly Grime" ritual. Glentham Church, Lincolnshire.

1888, published in 1889, but an almost identically worded piece was reproduced by the same author, Henry Winn, in the *Lincolnshire Chronicle* from an unrecorded earlier date. The text had been sent to him by F. William Allington, but its original source was unknown. The interpretation of the Glentham ritual as a misunderstood version of the events of the Easter ceremonies, carried out after the Reformation, is an interesting one that warrants further investigation.

The medieval ceremonies associated with Holy Week in England can be traced back to the monastic reforms of the tenth century contained in the *Regularis Concordia*.[3] The rubric required that a cross be buried on Good Friday in a site specially prepared for it, for this to be displayed on Easter morning and for a visit by the holy women, represented by men, to take place thereafter on Easter Day. The rituals were incorporated into the Use of Sarum, and additions and variations of the details were introduced. Most importantly for our purposes, a fourteenth-century text, in use at the convent in Barking, makes reference to priests removing the corpus from the cross and washing its wounds in wine and water at the high altar preparatory to its burial. A similar text from this period exists from Hereford Cathedral that again mentions the washing of a representational image, although in this case it took place at the entrance to the sepulcher.[4] It has not been determined when this quasi-dramatic re-enactment moved from the monastic church into the parish churches, but there is considerable documentary evidence that ritual involving an Easter Sepulcher was widespread during the later medieval period in parish churches. Pamela Sheingorn has evaluated this in her studies of the English Easter Sepulchers, citing documents from the fourteenth to the mid-sixteenth centuries that itemize the details and dramatic devices incorporated into the rituals. Apart from the evidence of wills that Sheingorn cites, the surviving stone Easter Sepulchers and records of the timber examples provide evidence of the observance of these rituals in parish churches.

In Lincolnshire itself over three-quarters of the churches listed in the returns of the commissioners into the destruction of images in the 1560s included Easter Sepulchers.[5] The recorded statements of the parishes conform to a standard type, and it is evident that an Easter Sepulcher was expected to form part of the church furnishings. The Lincolnshire sepulchers were clearly made of wood as the description of the secular uses they had been converted to establishes: clothes presses, hen houses, or firewood. Others were reworked for chancel furnishings. Thus the entry for Owmby reads: "Itm one sepulchre broken in peces in A° primo Elizabeth and a co[mmun]ion tabel made thereof."[6] Unfortunately there is no entry for Glentham.

Considerable evidence exists that private individuals wished to associate themselves with the rituals enacted at the Easter Sepulcher either by leaving money to provide candles for sepulcher lights, for example, or by providing items that were to be used in the ritual. A man named Hugh Brown left a silver and gilt cross, containing a relic of the true cross, to the church of St. Leonard, Eastcheap, London with instruction that it was to be used at Easter. His will of 1501 stated that it should "yearly be laid by and with the blessed sacrament in the sepulchere every Goodfriday."[7]

In some cases the cross was replaced by actual images of Christ such as the figure from Lincoln Cathedral that was listed in the fifteenth-century inventory as made of silver weighing 37 ounces that had a hole in its chest "pro sacramento imponendo tempore resurreccionis."[8] There is also an image of the dead Christ, at slightly more than life-size, laid on a bier, carved in stone and fully painted, that was found beneath the floor of the chapel of the Mercers' Hall in London. It has been linked with the will of Thomas, Earl of Ormond, who died in 1515 in which he specified that his burial was to be associated with the site of the Easter Sepulcher.[9] The sculpture is unparalleled in England and perhaps invites comparison with the large-scale corpuses of Continental crucifixes that were intended for removal from their crosses as part of liturgical rites.

There are also many instances where tombs were intended to be associated with the Easter Sepulcher by providing the site for the erection of the sepulcher, evident in the inclusion of resurrection iconography. The will of Thomas de Windsor of Stanwell from 1479 directed that his body should be buried on the north side of the choir of the church "wherupon I will ther be made a playne tombe of marble of a competent hight to th'entent that yt may ber the blissid body of our Lord and the sepultur at the time of Estre, to stond uppon the same. . . ."[10] In some cases flat-topped tomb chests with Resurrection iconography survive, sited on the north side of the chancel, for example at West Alvington in Devon where there is the matrix of a brass showing Christ rising from the tomb on the back panel. A similar tomb panel, with the Resurrection brass in place between kneeling figures, can be seen in Great Coates church near Grimsby.[11] The slab is now let into the floor, but it is reasonable to assume that it originally formed the rear panel to a table tomb placed against the wall.

If the Glentham ritual represents a misunderstood version of medieval liturgical practice, it remains to establish how this rite was initiated in the church and by whom. There were at least three major land owners in Glentham in the medieval period: Barlings Abbey, Lincoln Cathedral, and the family of Tournay. The hospital of St. Edmund at Spital on the Street at the west end of Glentham parish also held two parcels of land in Glentham to support chantries in their chapel during the fourteenth century.[12] The manor of Caenby cum Glentham was given to Barlings Abbey in the thirteenth century, and the manor of Glentham was held by the Dean and Chapter of Lincoln Cathedral, given to them in the fifteenth century as a chantry endowment. Half the advowson of the church had been given to Lincoln Cathedral in c.1190, and further land grants in Glentham had been given for a chantry during the first quarter of the thirteenth century. The land holding was considerable, and the Dean and Chapter built a rectory in Glentham that was described in a document of 1305, when it was in disrepair, as a large house with associated farm buildings although it was not built of stone.[13] None of the charters recorded in the *Registrum Antiquissimum* of the cathedral make any reference to ritual associated with either the church or the church lands. The complex situation of the manors of Caenby and Glentham, with at least four manors in the two parishes during the medieval period and the siting of the boundary between the two parishes, suggests that its division into separate parishes was a later occurance.[14]

Barlings Abbey, founded for Premonstratensian canons in 1154/5, was sited about twenty miles south of Glentham and held lands there and at Caenby from at least the thirteenth century. By 1374 the abbot maintained a house at Caenby and was farming the land there and at Glentham.[15] There is no documented reference to any involvement in the parish of Glentham, either in chantry endowments or in the provision of clergy, and it seems unlikely that the abbey was connected with the "Molly Grime" event.

The Tournays held the manor of Caenby, where their chief residence was, and bought Caenby cum Glentham manor in the sixteenth century but also provided the income for priests at Glentham church from at least the early fifteenth century. In 1404 the vicar of Glentham released back to the widow of John Tournay the lands that had been given on condition that the family provide three priests for Glentham church. This may have been the same chantry that was recorded in the chantry certificates of 1547, although by that time its revenues had been appropriated by John Tournay. It was extant in 1535 when the *Valor Ecclesiasticus* found a chantry priest named Thomas Browne in post; at this time the revenues were estimated at £4 6*s* 8*d*. In 1526 the revenues had been £4 13*s* 4*d*.[16] The Tournay connection with Glentham parish seems to start in the fourteenth century, although their descent from the Thornton family of Caenby extends their local connection back into the thirteenth century.[17] Glentham parish church was used as the Tournay mausoleum; a brass to Elizabeth, second wife of John Tournay, survives from 1452, and the seventeenth-century will of Anthony Tournay specified burial in the "quire belonging theretofore to my ancestors in Glentham church." Further burials continued through the late seventeenth and into the mid-eighteenth century.[18]

Most probably the worn female effigy that was the subject of the washing ritual is to a member of the Tournay family. The figure is broken off at the knees and has been abraded to the extent that the face has been obliterated together with most of the hands and virtually all of the surface carving. It is possible to see that the figure was dressed in a loose gown over a kirtle with tight-fitting sleeves and that the hair was covered with a veil that may have been attached to a wimple. The head is supported on a square-set cushion and damage to the block beneath has removed any trace of angel supporters. The costume detail would suggest a date in the fourteenth century, possibly in the first half.

The tomb effigy was referred to as "Molly Grime" in the Charity Commissioners' Report, which can be interpreted in several ways. One is offered by the colloquial use of the term "Molly Grime" in north Lincolnshire in the late nineteenth century to describe a person who was unwashed.[19] That is simply that the effigy was dirty and required cleaning. If this was the case, then the ritual can be related to the much larger collections of calendar events, some with charitable intentions, of obscure origins. Two factors, however, isolate the "Molly Grime" from the folklore tradition. The most important is that the event took place on Good Friday, and the other is that it involved its participants, seven spinsters, in the strenuous activity of carrying water a distance of over two miles. Parallels for this in folklore are hard to find, and although a number of sculptural images were the focus of activity and water often occurs in connection with calendar events, it has not been possible to locate ritual activity that involves both.

The "Grime" aspect of the name creates links with an earlier period. The name is derived from the Scandinavian personal name Grim, or Grímr, and occurs in the name of the major fishing port in the north of Lincolnshire, "Grimsby." Its use as a personal name, "Grime," is well attested in the later medieval period, although none of the late-medieval wills that mention the name have a connection with Glentham. However, part of the land holding of Barlings Abbey in Glentham included a fieldname, "Grimesgate," listed in an *inspeximus* of 1291, that makes a connection between the name and the parish. The charter records the grant of a piece of land held by William de Herloston from John de Stanford which is described as being "on the north side of Grimesgate."[20]

The same *inspeximus* mentions the "Neuwelhill" in Glentham that is the site of the well from which the water had to be brought for the ritual. It is named for the Newel Well, or "new spring" that lies at its base in a narrow valley, and the hill rises to a height of about a hundred feet to form part of the scarp known as the Lincoln Cliff. The well site is still evident at a deviation in the road and lies about two miles west of Glentham church. The well is a chalybeate spring and is only one of a number of springs and wells recorded in the parish from placename evidence and surviving in the immediate area. Other springs at Glentham are the Blackwell, recorded in 1307, the Grisewell, in 1291, and the Thyrswelles in 1307.[21] It has been noted that the deviation in the road at the Newel Well is aligned with a naturally occurring prominence just to the west of Ermine Street that runs along the top of the scarp and next to the site of a number of further springs.[22] One marked on the Ordnance Survey 1:50 000 map at "Spital Spa" is chalybeate, another further west is fresh water, and there are a series of seven springs at Hemswell.[23] Within this landscape there are sites that suggest the importance of the area in the early period. There are a number of cropmarks, finds evidence from Roman settlement sites in the Caenby/Glentham area, and a major Anglo-Saxon burial from the seventh century at Caenby. It has been suggested that this all forms part of a ritual landscape whose origins stretch back into pre-history, and that the Molly Grime event may even have had its roots in an earlier cleansing ritual.[24] If so, then the Grime element of the name may refer to events in the early, rather than later, medieval period.

The Molly Grime event is reported to have taken place in the parish church at Glentham. The tomb effigy is placed on the floor beneath the stairs at the back of the building, having no tomb chest or other obvious site in the church. It must have been elsewhere when the ritual was enacted since there is little space around it in its current site. The church itself was given a major restoration, which was not documented in detail, in 1855; this may have been in response to the structural problems that are still evident in the angle of the south nave wall. A drawing from 1794 by Claude Nattes shows the building little different than today, although it illustrates the simpler south side rather than the north where changes have been made.[25] On the interior it is clear that the building has been reduced: the chancel east wall and the east wall of the north chancel aisle now cut across the second arch of the chancel arcade, reducing the arch by about two-thirds. There are no piscinas or aumbries to mark altar sites in the east end or in the east end of the nave aisles, although the north aisle east wall has a broad moulded recess as if for a reredos. The nave arcade and south windows suggest a late fourteenth-century date for the church, with a porch of similar date that has a sculpted pietà over the Tournay arms above the entrance. The tower is an eighteenth-century rebuild with a datestone of 1756; recent restoration work on it produced an Anglo-Saxon interlaced grave-cover of late tenth- or early eleventh-century date that had been re-used as a quoin.[26] As noted above, the church was used as the family mausoleum by the Tournay family, with burials in the north chancel aisle and the nave. It is unwise to use the evidence of the current siting of the early brasses and floor slabs since these may have been removed and resited when the east end was reduced, but the seventeenth-century reference to the choir as the previous burial site of the family places it there.[27]

A reasonable assumption is that Glentham celebrated the Easter liturgy at a temporary Easter Sepulcher, in common with a large number of other parishes in north Lincolnshire, with the support of the Tournay family. It is possible a Tournay table tomb was used as the base for the Sepulcher or even that a member of their family may have willed money to prepare a figure of Christ for mock burial in the Sepulcher and that the funds were retained after the Reformation although the figure was not. In the absence of the figure the ritual was transfered to the tomb itself, or more probably to a nearby tomb, that happened to be to a female member of the family, represented in the worn effigy that survives. It is likely that some time had elapsed and that when the ritual was revived the meaning of it had become obscured, with only the element of bringing water from a specified site at some distance and the cleansing of an image remaining. The transformation of activity that would have been the role of clergy to seven spinsters suggests an element of charity entering the procedure. There is an interesting parallel case in the church of Tong in Shropshire where a ritual associated with a religious image was transferred to a secular tomb at the Reformation. A thirteenth-century grant of lands and rights by Roger de la Zouche to Hugh Hugford required that a rentcharge of a chaplet of roses be placed on an image of the Virgin in the church. The custom continued after the Reformation, but the roses were then placed on a female tomb effigy to Lady Elizabeth de Pembruge in the church. The event was noted in the eighteenth century and described in nineteenth-century antiquarian accounts.[28] Doubtless other examples existed of medieval religious practices that had been suppressed at the Reformation only to re-emerge in a changed form after an interval in places where the memory of these events remained. The "Molly Grime" event can be seen as an example of an act of piety, in which people other than the priest could be involved in the mysteries of religion, surviving in a form that divorced it from most of its meaning but retained elements that declare its origins.

NOTES

[1] *Report of the Charity Commissioners* 32, pt. iv (London, 1839): 410.

[2] *GML English Topography* vii (1896), 124–26.

[3] Pamela Sheingorn, *The Easter Sepulchre in England*, Early Drama, Art, and Music Reference Series 5 (Kalamazoo: Medieval Institute Publications, 1987), 26. No reference to rituals of the kind proposed for Glentham have been reported by Stanley J. Kahrl, *Records of Plays and Players in Lincolnshire, 1300–1585*, Malone Society Collections 8 (1974 [for 1969]).

[4] Sheingorn, *Easter Sepulchre in England*, 27, 159.

[5] Edward Peacock, *English Church Furniture, Ornaments and Decorations, at the Period of the Reformation* (London, 1866), with additions by C. W. Foster, "English Church Furniture, A.D. 1566," *Lincolnshire Notes and Queries* 14 (1916–17): 78–88, 109–16, 144–51, 166–73.

[6] Peacock, *English Church Furniture*, 215.

[7] Sheingorn, *The Easter Sepulchre in England*, 227.

[8] Ibid., 209.

[9] Joan Evans and Norman Cook, "A Statue of Christ from the Ruins of Mercers' Hall," *Archaeological Journal* 111 (1954): 168–80.

[10] Sheingorn, *The Easter Sepulchre in England*, 241, quoting the will from Alfred Heales, "The Church of Stanwell, and Its Monuments," *London and Middlesex Archaeological Society* 3 (1865–69): 105–32. It is probable that the tomb of Dean Thomas Balsall, on the north side of the Stratford-upon-Avon parish church, performed the same role; see Clifford Davidson and Jennifer Alexander, *The Early Art of Coventry, Stratford-upon-Avon, Warwick, and Lesser Sites in Warwickshire*, Early Drama, Art, and Music Reference Series 4 (Kalamazoo: Medieval Institute Publications, 1985), 63–68.

[11] See H. F. Owen Evans, "The Resurrection on Brasses," *Transactions of the Monumental Brass Society* 11 (1970): 91–93.

[12] *Calendar of Patent Rolls Preserved in the Public Record Office, 1330–1334*, p. 546, *1384–1387*, p. 343.

[13] Dorothy M. Owen, *Church and Society in Medieval Lincolnshire* (Lincoln: History of Lincolnshire Committee, 1971), 137.

[14] P. L. Everson, C. C. Taylor, and C. J. Dun, *Change and Continuity: Rural Settlement in North-West Lincolnshire* (London: HMSO, 1991), 10.

[15] *Cal. Charter Rolls 1226–1257*, pp. 88–89; *Cal. Patent Rolls 1370–1374*, p. 484.

[16] C. W. Foster and A. H. Thompson, "The Chantry Certificates for Lincolnshire," *Associated Architectural Societies Reports and Papers* (1921): 241.

[17] A. R. Maddison, "The Tournays, of Caenby," *Associated Architectural Societies Reports and Papers* 29 (1907): 1–42.

[18] Ibid., 24.

[19] Ethel Rudkin, *Lincolnshire Folklore* (Gainsborough, 1936), 44–45.

[20] *Cal. Charter Rolls 1257–1300*, p. 399.

[21] I am grateful to Professor K. Cameron for a chance to see the Glentham

entry in his forthcoming *The Place-Names of Lincolnshire VI*, for this area of north Lincolnshire, and to David Parsons of the School of English Studies, Nottingham University, for his help.

[22] P. Everson, "Pre-Viking Settlement in Lindsey," in *Pre-Viking Lindsey*, ed. Alan Vince (Lincoln, 1993), 91–100.

[23] David Marcombe, personal communication.

[24] Everson, "Pre-Viking Settlement in Lindsey," 97.

[25] The Nattes drawing is part of the collection held in the Reference Library, Lincoln.

[26] P. Foster, "Archaeology in Lincolnshire," *Lincolnshire History and Archaeology* 25 (1990): 53–54.

[27] Maddison, "The Tournays, of Caenby," 24.

[28] John Corbet Anderson, *Shropshire: Its Early History and Antiquities* (London, 1864), 42; George Griffiths, *A History of Tong, Shropshire* (London: Horne and Bennion, 1894), 32.

A *Palmesel*
from the Cracow Region

Hans-Jürgen Diller

The fifteenth-century figure of Christ riding an ass (fig. 1) from Szydłowiec (now in the Narodowe Muzeum, Cracow)[1] is a useful reminder that the tradition of the *Palmesel* as described by Karl Young and others[2] is not limited to Germany. In fact, the custom of pulling a wooden Christ on a donkey through the streets and into the churches of Cracow persisted until 1780, when the practice was banned by the Episcopal Curia. Adam Chmiel has an impressive description of the ceremony:

> The figure of Christ on the donkey was put under a canopy, and people threw budding willow twigs, pine twigs, and flowers over it. A church choir and music accompanied the procession, and the participants were town councillors, town authorities, and burghers.

> The commons joined the antiphonal singing, formally prescribed by the church ritual, with their own songs celebrating the occasion. One such song that has come down to us goes back to the first half of the fifteenth century. The Palm Sunday procession was a transformation of a medieval Passion mystery in which the singing of church antiphons went together with the reciting of occasional verses referring to the religious feast. People of the Middle Ages were deeply religious; in church ceremonies and performances they expressed their ideas, perhaps in a naïve way, but with frank straightforwardness and in earnest. Later on, however, these processions lapsed into vulgarity. They became the object of fun and mockery, and especially in the eighteenth century they attracted various abuses and vulgar jokes in the form of schoolboy verses which travestied religious songs:

> Good are layer cakes
> and stuffed sausages.
> Let me, O Christ, taste them,
> let me live and have the Easter Sunday meal.
> I will praise you, Lord, you are good,
> when I have ham for breakfast. . . .

58

1. Palmesel, from the Cracow region (c.1470), formerly used in Palm Sunday processions. Narodowe Muzeum, Cracow.

Such verses testify to the debasement of the Palm Sunday procession. The Episcopal Curia in Cracow issued an edict on August 10th, 1780, which stated: "Pulling the Christ figure on the donkey into the church and arranging for the schoolboys to recite verses on Palm Sunday which almost never have any sense, is hereby forbidden."

Since that time the Christ figure on the donkey was banned from the procession in the diocese of Cracow and probably in other dioceses as well. The wooden figures were put away in church "prop rooms," where they generally fell into decay. Some of them survived, and one such figure was presented to the Cracow National Museum. It hails from Szydłowiec and was given to the museum by Prince Michal Radziwill.[3]

Other customs connected with Palm Sunday in Cracow, and equally banned on 10 August 1780, are remarkably similar to the abuses castigated by Thomas Kirchmayr in his *Regnum Papisticum* (1553).[4] Oskar Kolberg, the founder of Polish folklore studies, reports that people prostrated themselves in front of the figure of Christ on the donkey: "The priest knelt in front of it and beat the figure with a rod made of reed and willow twigs saying: 'I will hit the shepherd and scatter the sheep'."[5] In the *Regnum Papisticum* it is the priest himself who lies down in front of the ass and gets beaten by another priest:

> Mox querno sese coram prosternit asello,
> Sacrificus longa quem uirga percutit alter.[6]

Barnabe Googe's translation, which appeared under the title *The Popish Kingdom, or reigne of Antichrist*, gives the following:

> And straytwayes downe before the Asse, vpon his face he lies,
> Whome there an other Priest doth strike with rodde of largest sise.[7]

Another Cracow custom goes by the name of *puchery* (from Latin *pueri*, presumably going back to the Palm Sunday antiphon *Pueri Hebreorum tollentes ramos*). Young scholars recited facetious "orations" on the poverty of scholarly life, the misery of fasting, etc. For their pains they were rewarded, with alms, eggs, and other foodstuff being the most usual gifts.[8] This, too, looks remarkably like a custom described by Kirchmayr:

> Illico sectantur pueri post prandia certum,
> Dicitur ædituo precium, damnumque cauetur,

Assumuntque asinum, et per uicos atque plateas
Carmina cantantes quædam notissima raptant,
Quis nummo à populo, uel panes dantur, et oua.[9]

They take the Asse, and through the streetes, and crooked lanes they rone,
Whereas they common verses sing, according to the guise,
The people giuing money, breade, and egges of largest cise.[10]

The pertinacity of these customs may be inferred from the fact that after the edict of 1780 many of them emigrated either into neighboring villages or to other parts of the Church year. Christ on the Palm Sunday ass became a Jew leading a group of New Year revellers in fantastic clothes.[11]

The relations between Polish and German Palm Sunday customs are obviously close. It would be interesting to know more about them.[12]

NOTES

[1] This example of Christ on the ass was recorded in an exhibition catalogue, *1000 Years of Art in Poland* (London: Royal Academy of Arts, 1970), fig. 11. The figure is carved of limewood, and is dated c.1470. The figure of Christ is 146 cm. in height, and the total height is 224 cm.

[2] Karl Young, *The Drama of the Medieval Church*, 2 vols. (Oxford: Clarendon Press, 1933), 1:94ff. The German handbooks carry no reference to the existence of the customs outside Germany: *Lexikon der christlichen Ikonographie*, ed. Engelbert Kirschbaum, 8 vols. (Freiburg i. Br.: Herder, 1968–76), vol. 3, *s.v.* "Palmchristus, Palmesel"; *Reallexikon zur deutschen Kunstgeschichte* (Stuttgart: Druckenmüller, 1937–), vol. 4, *s.v.* "Einzug in Jerusalem."

[3] *Szkice krakowskie* [*Cracow Sketches*]. Biblitoteka krakowska nr 100 (Cracow, 1947). This book was ready for the press in 1939, but publication was delayed by the war.

[4] Text of the relevant passages from Thomas Naogeorgus (Kirchmayr), *Regnum Papisticum* (1553), 144f, quoted by Young, *The Drama of the Medieval Church*, 2:526–27; translation of these passages, by Barnabe Googe, *The Popish Kingdom* (London, 1570), fol. 50f, also quoted by Young, 2:532–33.

[5] Oskar Kolberg, *Lud: jego zwyczaje . . .* [*The People: Its Customs . . .*], series 5: Krakowskie, pt. 1 (Cracow, 1871), 273.

[6] Quoted in Young, *The Drama of the Medieval Church*, 2:526; ll. 12–13.

[7] Quoted in ibid., 2:232; ll. 11–12.

[8] Tadeusz Seweryn, *Tradycje i zwyczaje krakowskie* [*Traditions and Customs of Cracow*] (Cracow: Wydawnictwo Artystyczno-Graficzne, 1961), 17–20.

[9] Quoted in Young, *The Drama of the Medieval Church*, 2:526–27; ll. 41–45.

[10] Quoted in ibid., 2:533; ll. 44–46.

[11] Seweryn, *Tradycje i zwyczaje krakowskie*, 17–20. For further information about the survival into the twentieth century of Palm Sunday customs in Poland, published after the present article appeared, see Teresa Bela, "Palm Sunday Ceremonies in Poland: The Past and the Present," *Early Drama, Art, and Music Review* 12 (1990): 25–31.

[12] I need to thank Teresa Bella (Jagellonian University Cracow) for hunting down and translating the Polish sources for me as well as for arranging for the photograph which accompanies this article. The late Hans-Georg Gmelin (Landes-museum Hannover) helped with reference to the German customs.

O Virginitas, in regali thalamo stas; New Light on the *Ordo Virtutum*: Hildegard, Richardis, and the Order of the Virtues

Gunilla Iversen

What is the *raison d'être* and what is the role of the intriguing play on the Virtues, the *Ordo Virtutum*, in the visionary and literary production of Hildegard of Bingen? Even if we can never arrive at a full understanding of all the mysteries behind the existence of the play, the rich textual material which remains certainly invites comparative studies between the different texts.[1] The following will present a few suggestions concerning the relation between Hildegard's musical play and the last Vision of her *Scivias*. In particular I intend to read the two texts in the light of the dramatic events in Hildegard's life during the years 1148 to 1152, years full of great achievements but also marked by a great personal loss.

For, as we know, it was during these years that she managed to establish a convent of her own at Rupertsberg. It was during these years that the Church sanctioned her first writings, the Visions of *Scivias*. But it was also during these years that she bitterly fought to prevent her most beloved pupil and assistant, Richardis of Stade, from leaving her and Rupertsberg—and it was during this period that she received the sad message about the death of Richardis.

We recall the often repeated account, given in the preface of *Scivias* and repeated in her *Vita*, that when Hildegard was a little more than forty years old she decided after great anguish to write down her visions. This work was carried on between the years 1141 and 1151 with the help of the monk Vollmar and Richardis, who had followed her from Disibodenberg when she moved to her own new convent at Rupertsberg with eighteen sisters in 1150.[2] In the beginning of the 1150s she also assembled the collection of her songs, *Symphonia*. And sometime in this decade she also prepared the *Ordo Virtutum*. Thus at least a first version of the Vision, in which

Hildegard describes the Virtues fighting against the Devil in the human soul and which ends in her description of the essence of music, as well as the collection of her songs, the *Symphonia*, and the play *Ordo Virtutum* were all written during a limited period.[3]

Still, we do not have a more precise dating of these texts within this period. From her introduction to the *Scivias* and from her *Vita* we are able to provide a date for the writing of the Visions of *Scivias* as a whole and to discern vague indications concerning the songs, but no direct indication concerning the date of the play. The manuscript sources are slightly later than these dramatic years since the oldest known source of the play and the Vision, the Riesencodex, dates from around 1180–90 and the oldest source of the *Symphonia*, the Dendermonde manuscript, was copied around 1165.[4]

Scholars have suggested different chronologies and relations between the Vision and the play. Thus the editors of *Scivias*—Adelgundis Führkötter and Angela Carlevaris with Marianna Schrader—who follow the indication in Hildegard's preface to her Visions, have assumed that Hildegard had finished the Visions of *Scivias* before the composition of the play.[5] However, Peter Dronke, who has edited the text of the play, has insisted on a reverse order and has claimed that the play existed before the Vision. Dronke, referring to Führkötter and her collaborators in his "Problemata Hildegardiana," says: "The editors assume without discussion that the lyrical works, both songs and play, derive from and are later than 'Scivias'." He continues: "only with a naive and over-dogmatic notion of literary composition could one continue to maintain that lyrics in the Symphonia, and the 'Ordo' itself, are derivatives, not originals." He also says that "In the case of the 'Ordo Virtutum', close attention to the parallel passages can establish that a text of the play was in existence when 'Scivias' III 13 came to be written."[6]

Although Dronke's observations are certainly to be taken very seriously indeed, I would like to modify the conclusion that the play existed before the Vision and to propose a third solution, namely, that there might well have existed a first version of the Vision already in 1147–48, but that this first version (of which we have no manuscript sources) was later followed by a revised one, the one written down together with the play in the Riesencodex, a version which might well postdate the play.

Also concerning the function of the play, different hypotheses have been advanced. Thus Dronke, among others, has suggested that Hildegard had written the play for the ceremony of the official inauguration of the convent at Rupertsberg in 1152.[7] Other scholars have accepted Pamela Sheingorn's view that the play was composed to be performed at the consecration of a new sister in her convent.[8] To these hypotheses I will here propose another, grounded in a close reading of the texts but also on observations based on Hildegard's correspondence. For there seems to be a relation between the dramatic events in Hildegard's life in the years 1151–52 and the composition of the play, a relation which we can trace in her correspondence. The letters thus might help us to a better understanding of the play, its function, and its date in Hildegard's life.

Concerning the existence of a first version of the Vision of the Virtues, I have argued in a previous study that passages in the extant text can be related to the famous letters that Hildegard exchanged with Bernard of Clairvaux in 1147–48 and that her correspondence reflects her dependence on Bernard's opinion at that time in her life in connection with the Council of Trier during that winter. It is in connection with the Council of Trier, which was directed by Bernard's former pupil, Pope Eugenius III, that her visionary texts should be scrutinized.[9] And of course it must have been extremely important to Hildegard at that time to have support from the firm and feared abbot of Clairvaux. In this light we can see how Hildegard, in the words of the Vision, particularly stresses Humility as the first of Virtues in the human soul and Mary as the personification of Humility. In his answer to Hildegard, Bernard repeats the biblical words on humility: "God sets his face against the arrogant but favors the humble" ("Deus superbis restitit, humilibus autem dat gratiam"), a passage which he also comments upon in his Sermons on the Virgin Mother: "Chastity is a laudable virtue, but humility is more necessary" ("Laudabilis virtus virginitas, sed magis humilitas necessaria").[10] Here Hildegard closely follows Bernard's Sermons on the Virgin Mother and his work *De gradibus humilitatis et superbiae* used in the lessons in the convents and churches under the jurisdiction of Mainz at that time. In these works Bernard claims that whereas chastity is important, humility is the most necessary virtue.[11] It is likely that a first version of the Vision on the Virtues might well date to this time—i.e., 1147–48.

In the play *Ordo Virtutum,* the Virtues of Chastity and Obedience are of central importance beside Humility—that is, the three first Virtues in the monastic life (Humilitas, Castitas, Obedientia). In the play sixteen different Virtues have been given speeches of their own, namely Humilitas, Karitas, Timor Dei, Obedientia, Fides, Spes, Castitas, Innocentia, Contemptus Mundi, Amor Celestis, Disciplina, Verecundia, Misericordia, Victoria, Discretio, Patientia. And it is possible, as has often been suggested, that in this way Hildegard arranged individual speeches to be sung by each one of the sisters at Rupertsberg.

But it seems less likely that Hildegard should have created this play for the inauguration and dedication of the new convent at Rupertsberg since there was already a strict and a fairly extensive ritual to be followed for such ecclesiastical ceremonies in the churches in the archdiocese of Mainz.[12] It would certainly have been provocative, even for Hildegard, to dare to depart from the ceremony regulated by the Mainz Pontifical. Another hypothesis is, as noted above, that she arranged the play as a ceremony to be performed at the consecration of a new sister at the convent.[13] But even for this occasion there would have been a strictly formalized ritual in the Pontifical.[14] In the case of the play, therefore, I would like to turn to the rich correspondence and to the dramatic events in Hildegard's life around the middle of the century and to look there for a *raison d'être* and the date of this drama.

It will be recalled that just when the abbey at Rupertsberg had been established and Hildegard and the sisters had moved there, Richardis of Stade, Hildegard's most beloved pupil and assistant, was invited to become the abbess of the rich and influential abbey of Bassum. Richardis herself seems to have been in favor of the move. But for Hildegard it was very inconvenient just as she needed Richardis's help and support during their initially difficult times on the Rupertsberg, and she passionately objected.

In a letter quoted in her *Vita,* Hildegard talks about the role of Richardis as her assistant in the writing of *Scivias,* and about Richardis's decision to leave Rupertsberg:

> Nam cum librum *Scivias* scriberem, quandam nobilem puellam, supradictae marchionissae filiam, in plena charitate habebam, sicut Paulus Timotheum, quae in diligenti amicitia in omnibus se mihi conjunxerat, et in passionibus meis mihi condoluit, donec ipsum librum complevi.
>
> Sed post haec propter elegantiam generis sui, ad dignitatem majoris nominis se inclinavit, ut mater cuiusdam sublimis ecclesiae nominare-

tur: quod tamen non secundum Deum, sed secundum honorem saeculi huius quaesivit.[15]

(When I was writing my book *Scivias*, I deeply cherished a noble-born young girl, daughter of the marchioness I mentioned, just as Paul cherished Timothy. She had bound herself to me in loving friendship in every way, and showed compassion for my illness, till I had finished the book.

But then, because of her family's distinction, she hankered after an appointment of more repute: she wanted to be named abbess of some splendid church. She pursued this not for the sake of God but for worldly honor.)

Evidently, Hildegard could not easily accept that Richardis did not obey her in this matter but rather followed the ambitions of her own powerful and influential family. Hildegard was furious and did not want to lose her beloved assistant. But more than this: in her view, Richardis's pure and innocent soul was in danger. In Hildegard's eyes the invitation to obtain a prestigious position in Bassum was nothing less than the temptation of the old Serpent.

As we know, Hildegard tried by all means to prevent Richardis from leaving Rupertsberg, and we recall that she wrote to all who might possibly help. In 1151–52 she wrote to Richardis' mother, the Marchioness of Stade, to the Archbishop of Mainz, and even to Pope Eugenius III. She wrote to Richardis' brother Hartvig, Bishop of Bremen, to ask him to arrange that she should be sent back to Rupertsberg. In her letter she even alludes to the biblical text on the obedience of Abraham, who was willing to offer his own son to God:

Nunc audi me, cum lacrimis et erumnis prostratam ante pedes tuos, quia anima mea valde tristis est, quoniam horribilis homo consilium et voluntatem meam atque aliarum sororum mearum et amicorum deiecit in carissima filia nostra Richarde, abstrahens eam de claustro nostro per temerariam voluntatem suam. . . .

Ideo obsecro te . . . ut dimittas ad me carissimam filiam meam quia electionem Dei non pretereo nec eam contradico ubicumque fuerit, ita ut Deus det tibi benedictionem quam Isaac dedit Iacob filio suo, et benedicat te in benedictione quam dedit per angelum suum Abrahe in obedientia illius. . . .[16]

(Now, listen to me, as I lay prostrate at your feet with tears and sorrow, because my soul is very sorrowful, since a horrible man has

rejected the plans and wishes which I myself and all the other sisters and
friends have had for my most beloved daughter Richardis. He has taken
her away from our abbey for his own personal desires. . . . Therefore I
implore you . . . that you send back to me my dearest daughter, since I
cannot contradict God's election nor can I oppose God's will, whatever
it is. Send her back, and God will give you the benediction that Isaac
gave to his son Jacob and God will include you in the benediction
which he gave through his angel to Abraham in his obedience...)

When Pope Eugenius III, who had earlier read the Visions of
Scivias, received a similarly insistent letter, he wrote back to Hildegard in 1151; in his reply he told her to support and encourage the
sisters who were left in her care in the convent ("creditas in dispositione tue sorores").[17]
The subsequent development in this story is well known:
Richardis fell seriously ill shortly after her arrival at Bassum, and
Hildegard wrote to her in a letter dated 1151–52 that she herself
always became ill when she had done something that was not right
for her. She complained: "Woe is me, O mother, woe is me, O
daughter—why have you abandoned me like an orphan?" ("Heu me
mater, heu me filia, *quare me dereliquisti* sicut orphanam?")—that
is, in words dramatically quoting the suffering Christ (Matthew
27:46, John 14:18), "Why hast thou forsaken me?"

Heu me mater, heu me filia, *quare me dereliquisti* sicut orphanam?
Amavi nobilitatem morum tuorum et sapientiam et castitatem, et tuam
animam et omnem vitam tuam, ita quod multi dixerunt: Quid facis?
Nunc plangant mecum omnes qui habent dolorem similem dolori meo,
qui habuerunt in amore Dei talem caritatem in corde et in mente sua ad
hominem, sicut et ego habui in te, qui in momento illis raptus est, sicut
et tu mihi abstracta es. Sed procedat te angelus Dei et protegat te Filius
Dei, et custodiat te Mater ipsius. Esto memor misere matris tue Hildegardis, ut non deficiat felicitas tua.[18]

(Woe is me, your mother, woe is me, your daughter: why have you
abandoned me like an orphan? I loved the nobility of your manners,
your wisdom and your chastity, your soul and the whole of your life so
much that some people said to me: What are you doing? Now, let all
who have a sorrow like my sorrow mourn with me, all those who have
ever, in the love of God, had such high love in heart and mind for a
human being as I for you, for a beloved one who has suddenly been
taken away from them, as you have been taken away from me. But may
the angel of God precede you, and the Son of God protect you, and his

Mother guard you. Remember your poor mother Hildegard, that your
happiness may not fail.)

Soon after this, in 1152, Hildegard received the sad news from
Richardis's brother, Bishop Hartvig, that his sister had died. He also
told her that Richardis had regretted that she had ever left Rupertsberg and that she should have returned to Hildegard had death not
intervened. That is, he admitted that Hildegard had been right.[19] We
can imagine that the death of Richardis must have filled Hildegard
with conflicting feelings—on one hand, the pain and grief over the
human loss of her dearest daughter and assistant, on the other, a
joyful release that the victory was won, that in her death the pure
soul of Richardis was saved from the snares of the Devil and Tempter who had tried to seduce Richardis with worldly power.

In a letter that Hildegard now wrote in answer to Richardis'
brother Hartvig, she commented on the death of Richardis as a great
miracle ("O quam magnum miraculum") and a victory:

> O quam magnum miraculum est in salvatione animarum illarum,
> quas Deus inspexit, quod gloria eius in ipsis non obumbratur! Sed Deus
> facit in ipsis velut fortis bellator, qui hoc studet, ne ab illo superetur,
> sed ut victoria ipsius stabilis sit.
>
> Nunc audi, o care. Sic factum est in filia mea Richardi, quam et
> filiam et matrem meam nomino, quia plena caritas in anima mea fuit in
> ipsam, quoniam vivens lux fortissima visione docuit me ipsam amare.
>
> Audi. Deus eam in hoc zelo habuit, quod voluptas seculi illam non
> potuit amplecti ; sed semper contra eam pugnavit, quamvis ipsa velut
> flos in pulchritudine et decore et in symphonia huius seculi appareret.
> Sed cum ipsa adhuc in corpore maneret, audivi de ipsa in vera visione
> dici : "O virginitas, in regali thalamo stas.
>
> Ipsa enim in virginea virga habet societatem in sanctissimo ordine,
> unde filie Sion gaudent. Sed tamen antiquus serpens voluit eam a beato
> honore retrahere per altam generositatem humanitatis. Sed summus
> iudex traxit hanc filiam ad se, abscindens de illa omnem humanam
> gloriam. Unde anima mea magnam fiduciam habet in ea, quamvis
> mundus pulchram formam et prudentiam ipsius, dum in mundo viveret,
> diligeret. Sed Deus illam plus dilexit. Idcirco noluit Deus amicam suam
> dare inimico amatori, id est mundo.
>
> Nunc tu, o care H<artuuige>, sedens in vice Christi, perfice volun-
> tatem anime sororis tue, quam postulat necessitas obedientie. Et ut ipsa
> semper sollicita fuit pro te, ita et tu nunc esto pro anima ipsius, et fac
> bona opera secundum studium ipsius. Unde et ego ibicio de corde meo
> dolorem illum, quem mihi fecisti in hac filia mea. Deus concedat tibi per

suffragia sanctorum rorem gratie sue et beatam remunerationem in futuro seculo.[20]

(O, what a great miracle in the salvation of the souls of those, whom God has looked upon so that his glory should not be overshadowed! But God has acted in these souls like a strong warrior who sees to it that he is not defeated by anyone, so that his victory stands fast.

Now listen, my dear. It has happened so to my daughter Richardis, whom I call both my daughter and my mother, for my soul was full of charity toward her, since the Living Light has taught me in a true vision to love her so. Listen. God had her in such burning love that worldly desire could not embrace her, but always fought against her, although she herself was like a flower in beauty and delight and in harmony with this world. When she was still alive, I heard about her being sad in a true vision: "O Virginitas, you stand in the royal wedding chamber!" For through her virginal lineage, she belongs to the most holy order over which the daughters of Zion rejoice.

But the old Serpent wanted to snatch her away from the blessed honor, because of her noble human birth. But the highest Judge drew this my daughter to him and took away all human glory. My soul, however, has great confidence in her, although the world loved her beauty and prudence while she was still in this world. Therefore, God did not want to give away this beloved friend of his to his enemy—that is, to the world.

Now, O dear H<artvig>, you who sit in the place of Christ, fulfill the wishes of your sister's will which the necessity of obedience bids you to respect. Just as she always cared about you, may you now care about her soul, and make good deeds according to her will. Therefore I throw away from my heart the sorrow and pain which you gave me on behalf of this daughter of mine. May God bring to you the dew of his grace and blessed remuneration in the world to come.)

This letter seems to have significance for our understanding both of the final version of the Vision and of the play. It might help us to understand the songs *O plangens vox* and *O vivens fons*—songs that simultaneously express the greatest sorrow and the most joyful triumph:[21]

> O plangens vox est hec maximi doloris,
> Ach, ach, quedam mirabilis victoria!
> In mirabili desiderio Dei surrexit,
> in qua delectatio carnis se latenter abscondit,
> heu, heu, ubi voluntas crimina nescivit
> et ubi desiderium hominis lasciviam fugit.
> Luge, luge ergo in his, Innocentia,

que in pudore bono integritatem non amisisti,
et que avaritiam gutturis antiqui serpentis ibi non devorasti.

(O this is the voice of deepest sorrow and pain!
Aye! Aye! what a miraculous victory!
In the wonderful desire of God she has risen.
In her, no carnal desire was ever seen.
Alas, alas, in her, the will knew no sin,
and human desires of lust fled away.
Mourn, mourn in this, O Innocence,
in your modest goodness you never lost your pure integrity,
and you did not crave what the old Serpent showed you.)

O vivens fons, quam magna est suavitas tua,
qui faciem istorum in te non amisisti,
sed acute previdisti
quomodo eos de angelico casu abstraheres
qui se estimabant illud habere
quod non licet sic stare.
Unde gaude, filia Syon,
quia Deus tibi multos reddit,
quos serpens de te abscindere voluit,
qui nunc in maiori luce fulgent
quam prius illorum causa fuisset.

(O living Fountain, how great is your sweet compassion!
You never let the straying people out of your sight,
but saw in advance the way that you could save them
from the fate of the fallen angels
who thought they owned what was not theirs to have.
O daughter of Zion, rejoice that God restores to you
many souls of which the ancient Serpent wanted to deprive you:
Now they shine more brightly than ever before.)

In the version of the Vision that appears in the Riesencodex, these songs are placed after the songs to the virgins as the last two of the paired songs of the opening part of the text. Unlike all the preceding songs, they are, however, not part of the collection of songs in *Symphonia*. Was it because these two songs were not part of a first version of the Vision?

In the text of the Vision in the Riesencodex the passage concludes with the speech by the Living Light:

Vivens enim lux de his dicit :

> Tortuosum serpentem scandalizavi in sua suggestione
> que ita plena non fuerat sicut ille putabat.
> Unde iuravi per memetipsum
> quod in his causis feci amplius et amplius
> quam in eis, o serpens, tuum gaudium proderet
> quia in tua suggestione amputavi,
> quod numquam inventum est in tua sevicia,
> o turpissime illusor.[22]

> (*The living Light says about this:*
> I have tripped up the tortuous Serpent in his seduction,
> his work was not as successful as he thought.
> I swore by myself that in these events I did more, far more
> than the delight for you could effect in them, O Serpent.
> For I have destroyed you in your snares,
> ended all joy in your ferocity,
> O wickedest of impostors!)

The entire passage forms a separate unit, and the complex mixture of sorrow and triumph expressed in the songs does not make them easily integrated into the text of the Vision—and makes one wonder if the entire passage might belong to a second redaction of the text.

Also, here the words concerning the temptation and snares of the tortuous Serpent recall the text of Hildegard's letter to Hartvig which was cited above—the letter in which Hildegard remarks of the old Serpent who had tried to seduce Richardis and snatch her away: "But the old Serpent wanted to take her away from beautiful honor" ("Sed tamen antiquus serpens voluit eam a beato honore retrahere").

The text of the Vision continues with the voice of the multitude, singing to encourage the soul to fight against the snares of the Devil. And after this the Virtues appear in person, saying: "We, the Virtues, are in God and remain in God" ("Nos virtutes in Deo sumus et in Deo manemus"). This, in turn, introduces the long dialogue between Anima and the Virtues and the Devil, the dialogue which also constitutes the main part of the play *Ordo Virtutum*.[23]

In the drama, on the other hand, *O plangens vox* and *O vivens fons* make perfect sense as they stand in two different positions (ll. 50–53, 199–208). The songs are well placed in the events of the drama. In the first scene of the play the Virtues sing *O plangens vox* when Anima, in great pain, is pressed by the Devil, just before Humility joins with all the other Virtues to help her. At the end of scene 3, when Anima, strengthened by the encouragement of all the Virtues, has finally come to a state where she bravely opposes the Devil and wants to take her refuge with Humility, the Virtues sing in joy and triumph *O vivens fons*. Quite possibly the text of *O plangens vox* might then refer not only to Anima in general but also specifically to the soul of Richardis. It might belong to a final version of the text of the last Vision and date after Richardis's death. The miraculous victory in the song might be the great miracle ("magnum miraculum") which she remarks upon in her letter.

In the same letter to Hartvig, Hildegard also speaks of Richardis as of a person whom the Living Light in a most powerful vision had taught her to love ("Vivens Lux fortissima visione docuit me ipsam amare"). And she writes that when Richardis was still alive she heard in a true vision that it was said about her: "O Virginity, you are in the royal chamber" ("dum ipsa adhuc in corpore maneret, audivi de ipsa in vera visione dici: 'O virginitas, in regali thalamo stas'").[24] This image of virginity in the chamber of the royal Bridegroom is found both in the text of the Vision in the Riesenkodex and in the play. In the long passage in the Vision, Humility says to the Virtues: "Beloved daughters, I keep you in the King's wedding chamber." She calls them daughters of Israel and daughters of Zion:

> Ideo dilectissimae filiae,
> teneo vos in regali thalamo.
> O filiae Israel, sub arbore suscitavit vos Deus,
> unde in hoc tempore recordamini plantationis suae.
> Gaudete ergo, filiae Sion.[25]

> (O, beloved daughters,
> I keep you in the King's wedding chamber.
> O daughters of Israel, God raised you under his tree,
> so now remember your planting.
> Rejoice, O daughters of Zion!)

In the play however, we find the same passage divided into two parts, forming the introduction and the conclusion of the section where all the individual Virtues sing. Thus, the first part of Humility's speech (74–75) is followed by the long passage of eighty lines (75–155) in which each of the Virtues presents herself to Anima, and in which the choir of the Virtues sing together a response to each of the individual Virtues. After these eighty lines, the second part of Humility's speech (156–58) follows, forming the conclusion of this section. Thus Humility embraces her sister Virtues at first with these words:

> Ideo dilectissimae filiae,
> teneo vos in regali thalamo.

> (O, beloved daughters,
> I keep you in the King's wedding chamber.)

Then, after the speeches of the individual Virtues, Humility sings:

> O filiae Israel, sub arbore suscitavit vos Deus,
> unde in hoc tempore recordamini plantationis suae.
> Gaudete ergo, filiae Sion.

> (O daughters of Israel, God raised you under his tree,
> so now remember your planting.
> Rejoice, O daughters of Zion!)

In the text of the play, Chastity (or Virginity) has an essential place among the Virtues, whereas she is not present in the text of the Vision. Like Humilitas, who in the Vision is represented in her fullest form in the Virgin Mother, Virginitas and all other Virtues are embodied in the person of the Virgin Mary, who is the crystallized gem of all virtues. But the picture seems to be more complex in the realization of the Vision as a play to be performed by the young women in the convent.

Returning to Hildegard's letter to Archbishop Hartvig, cited above, we see that Hildegard speaks about Richardis in the following way: "When she was still alive I heard about her being said in a true vision: 'O Virginitas, you stand in the royal wedding chamber!'" ("audivi de ipsa in vera visione dici: 'O virginitas, in regali thalamo stas'"). These words may be related to the texts of the Vision and the play which then really seem to contain a direct reference to Richardis. Although Hildegard most frequently uses expressions such as "I saw in a real vision," the words "in a most powerful vision" ("in fortissima visione") in her letter might here refer to the Vision of the Virtues in *Scivias*. In fact, this is the only text in which she explicitly talks about Richardis in connection with the words "in regali thalamo."[28] In the play, however, Hildegard uses the expression twice, since she also makes Chastity herself to utter these same words (104–08). The Virtues answer that Chastity (Virginity), the tender flower, is now among the inhabitants of heaven:

> *Castitas:*
> O Virginitas, in regali thalamo stas.
> O quam dulciter ardes in amplexibus regis,
> cum sol te perfulget
> ita quod nobilis flos tuum numquam cadet.
> O virgo nobilis, te numquam inveniet umbra in cadente flore!
> > *Virtutes:*
> Flos campi cadit vento, pluvio spargit eum.
> O Virginitas, tu permanes in symphoniis supernorum civium:
> unde es suavis flos qui numquam aresces.

> (*Chastity:*
> O Virginity, you remain in the royal chamber.
> How sweetly you burn in the King's embraces,
> when the Sun fills you with his light
> so that your noble flower will never fall.
> O noble virgin, the shadow will never touch you and make the flower fall!
> > *Virtues:*
> The flower in the meadow falls in the wind, the rain falls over it.
> But you, O Virginity, remain in the symphony of the heavenly inhabitants:
> you are the tender flower which will never grow dry.)

In her letter to Hartvig, Hildegard finally writes that Richardis in her virginity was now, after her death, a part of "the most holy order in which the daughters of Zion rejoice" ("Ipsa enim in virginea virga habet societatem in sanctissimo ordine, unde filie Sion gaudent"), the holy celestial order of which the earthly order is but a reflection. Also here, in the words of Chastity, who plays a central role in the play but, as we said, not the Vision, there might be another hidden allusion to Richardis.

Of course, we will never fully know the mystery which lies behind the *Ordo Virtutum*. But the correlations between the words of the play and Hildegard's letters from the beginning of the 1150s invite us to conclude that it was not until after Richardis' death in 1152 that Hildegard arranged the Vision into a music drama on the Order of the Virtues, and that it was not until then that she established the final version of the text of the Vision containing also the songs *O plangens vox* and *O vivens fons*. Also it was probably then that, in arranging the Vision into a play, she chose to insert the lines of the individual Virtues into the midst of the speech of Humility which contains words that directly refer to Richardis.

Perhaps such strategies might have been the way that Hildegard handled strong emotions after Richardis' death, to transform the Vision on the Virtues into a drama—a play created and performed to comfort herself and the other sisters, and to express their emotions of pain and sorrow, but also a drama of triumph and joy because of the victory over the old Serpent and Tempter, a celebration of the rescue of Richardis's soul.

At the same time Hildegard appears successfully to have created a morality play for the young women placed under her protection in the convent ("creditas in dispositione tue sorores"), as Pope Eugenius had written to her. In this effort she made it a musical drama in which all the sisters could take part—a play possibly performed not in the abbey church but rather in the chapter house, and not as an official liturgical ceremony. Further, it appears to be a play designed to encourage the sisters in their promise to live a life in humility, obedience, and chastity—to remain in the royal wedding chamber and to resist all temptations of the world. The sisters are themselves to become the daughters of Zion, a true Order of Virtues.

NOTES

[1] A more extensive comparative study in French, "Réaliser une vision. La dernière vision de Scivias et 'le drame liturgique' Ordo Virtutum de Hildegarde de Bingen," by the author has been published in *Revue de Musicologie* 86 (2000): 37–63.

[2] On Hildegard's life and work, see, for example, Peter Dronke, *Women Writers of the Middle Ages* (Cambridge: Cambridge University Press, 1984), 144–201, esp. 145–46, 150–51; Fiona Bowie and Oliver Davies, *Hildegard of Bingen: Mystical Writings* (New York: Crossroad, 1990), 63–70.

[3] *Liber Scivias*, ed. Migne, *PL*, 197: 385–738; *Hildegardis Scivias*, ed. Adelgundis Führkötter and Angela Carlevaris, Corpus Christianorum, Continuatio Mediaevalis, 43A–43B (Turnhout: Brepols, 1978), 614–636. *Symphonia harmonie celestium revelationum,* ed. and trans. Barbara Newman (Ithaca: Cornell University Press, 1988); Pudentiana Barth, Immaculata Ritscher, and Joseph Schmidt-Görg, *Hildegard von Bingen Lieder* (Salzburg: Otto Müller Verlag, 1969). *Ordo Virtutum*, in Peter Dronke, *Poetic Individuality in the Middle Ages* (Oxford: Claren-

don Press, 1970), 150–92, 202-31; *Nine Medieval Latin plays*, ed. Peter Dronke (Cambridge: Cambridge University Press, 1994), 147–84; *Ordo Virtutum* (performance edition, with English translation of the text by Bruce Hozeski and Gunilla Iversen), ed. Audrey Ekdahl Davidson (Kalamazoo: Medieval Institute Publications, 1984; reissued Bryn Mawr: Hildegard Publishing, 2002).

⁴ *Scivias*, in Hessische Landesbibliothek, MS. 1, dated from around 1165, (destroyed in 1945, photocopy from 1927), Bibl. Apostolica Vaticana, Cod. Pal. lat. 311, before 1179; *Scivias, Ordo Virtutum,* and *Symphonia* in Riesencodex, Wiesbaden, Hessische Landesbibliothek, MS. 2, c.1180–90: the Vision of the Virtues, in *Scivias*, fols. 133ᵛ–134ʳ; *Symphonia*, fols. 465ᵛ–478ʳ; and the musical play *Ordo Virtutum*, fols. 478ᵛ–481ᵛ. On the manuscripts, see especially Führkötter and Carlevaris, *Hildegardis Scivias,* 43A:xxxii–lvi. A reduced facsimile of the pages containing the *Ordo Virtutum* in the Riesenkodex appears in Audrey Ekdahl Davidson, ed., *The* Ordo Virtutum *of Hildegard of Bingen: Critical Studies,* Early Drama, Art, and Music Monograph Series 18 (Kalamazoo: Medieval Institute Publications, 1992), pls. 1–7.

⁵ M. Schrader and Adelgundis Führkötter, *Die Echtheit des Schrifttums der heiligen Hildegard von Bingen*, Quellenkritischen Untersuchungen, 10 (Cologne and Graz: Böhlau-Verlag, 1956), 21.

⁶ Peter Dronke, "Problemata Hildegardiana," *Mittellateinisches Jahrbuch* 16 (1981): 100–01, and Dronke, ed., *Nine Medieval Latin Plays*, 152.

⁷ Dronke, *Poetic Individuality*, 151.

⁸ See Pamela Sheingorn, "The Virtues of Hildegard's Ordo Virtutum; or, It *Was* a Woman's World," in *The* Ordo Virtutum *of Hildegard of Bingen: Critical Studies,* ed. Davidson, 52.

⁹ *Hildegardis Bingensis, Epistolarium,* ed. L. van Acker, Corpus Christianorum, Continuatio Mediaevalis, 91–91A (Turnhout: Brepols 1991), 3–6. See Gunilla Iversen, "*Ego Humilitas, regina Virtutum*: Poetic Language and Literary Structure in Hildegard of Bingen's Vision of the Virtues," in *The Ordo Virtutum of Hildegard of Bingen: Critical Studies,* ed. Davidson, 89–91.

¹⁰ *Hildegardis Bingensis, Epistolarium,* 6–7.

¹¹ *Sancti Bernardi Opera Omnia*, vols. 1–8, ed. Jean Leclercq (Rome: Cistercienses, 1957–77), 4:17; see also ibid., 3:4 (Introduction).

¹² The Mainz Pontifical (Romano-Germanic Pontifical), in Cyrille Vogel and R. Elze, *Le Pontifical romano-germanique du X siècle*, 3 vols. (Vatican City: Biblioteca Apostolica Vaticana, 1963–72), vols. 1–2; see also *Medieval Liturgy: An Introduction to the Sources*, trans. and revised William Storey and Niels Rasmussen (Washington: Pastoral Press, 1986), 230–47.

¹³ Sheingorn, "The Virtues of Hildegard's Ordo Virtutum," 43–62.

¹⁴ See, for example, René Metz, *La consécration des vierges dans l'église romaine: Etude d'histoire de la liturgie* (Paris: Presses Universitaires de France, 1954); Vogel and Elze, *Le Pontificale romano-germanique du X siècle*, 1:38–46 ("Consecratio sacrae virginis"); George Klawitter, "Dramatic Elements in Early Monastic Introduction Ceremonies," *Comparative Drama* 15 (1981): 213–30.

¹⁵ *PL,* 197:107.

¹⁶ *Hildegardis Bingensis, Epistolarium,* 27–28.

[17] Ibid., 10–11.

[18] Ibid., 147–48.

[19] Ibid., 29.

[20] Ibid., 30–31.

[21] In the Vision, these texts appear together in Wiesbaden, Hessische Landesbibliothek, MS. 2 (Riesencodex), fol. 133; ed. Führkötter and Carlevaris, *Hildegardis Scivias,* 43A:620–21. In the play, O *plangens vox* is found on fol. 479, O *vivens fons* on fol. 481.

[22] Wiesbaden, Hessische Landesbibliothek, MS. 2 (Riesencodex), fol. 133; *Scivias,* ed. Führkötter and Carlevaris, 43A:621.

[23] The Vision concludes with an argument concerning the function of the music for expressing its meaning. To be understood, she says, the words must reach the heart through the music (*Scivias,* ed. Führkötter and Carlevaris, 43A:630–31). This is what she actually set out to accomplish in adapting the Vision in form of a music drama.

[24] *Hildegardis Bingensis, Epistolarium,* 30–31.

[25] *Scivias,* III.13.325–31; ed. Führkötter and Carlevaris, 43A:625.

[26] Cf. *Scivias,* II.3.486; ed. Führkötter and Carlevaris, 43A:148.

Another Manuscript of the *Ordo Virtutum* of Hildegard of Bingen

Audrey Ekdahl Davidson

The existing manuscripts containing the music of Hildegard of Bingen are Dendermonde Benedictine Abbey MS. 9; Hessische Landesbibliothek, Wiesbaden, MS. 2; and the little-known British Library Add. MS. 15,102. The Dendermonde manuscript contains only the spiritual songs of Hildegard and *not* the *Ordo Virtutum*, while Wiesbaden MS. 2 contains both the songs and the *Ordo Virtutum*. The British Library manuscript includes only the *Ordo Virtutum*.[1] The Wiesbaden manuscript, like the Dendermonde manuscript, is believed to have been written during the decade following 1150, perhaps as early as 1151. On the other hand, the British Library manuscript was copied much later, at the order of Johannes Trithemius (1462–1516), Abbot of Sponheim, from a manuscript apparently borrowed from the library at Rupertsburg, a manuscript which may have been the one that is now located at Wiesbaden.[2]

Trithemius's interest in Hildegard has been noted by Barbara Newman, who finds him to be "[o]ne of the most interesting figures" of his time; according to Newman, Trithemius "rekindled Hildegard's fame and in some ways resembled her."[3] He was a great humanist scholar who, following his election as abbot of Sponheim at the age of twenty-one, began the collection of books which by the time of his departure from the monastery numbered approximately two thousand volumes acquired at the cost of between 1500 and 2000 gulden.[4] Upon his arrival at a monastery, he had found not only an establishment in great disarray but also a library of merely forty volumes, including only ten manuscripts.[5] His additions to the Sponheim library were regarded as a remarkable feat, both in quantity and quality.

An examination of British Library Add. MS. 15,102 reveals that, in the light of the errors made in the musical transcription when it was copied at Sponheim, the only possible judgment is that the single *reliable* existing manuscript of the *Ordo Virtutum* is contained in Wiesbaden MS. 2. Yet it is hard to fault the scribe of the British Library manuscript without knowing the circumstances of its transcription. (1) Was the scribe well-meaning but ignorant, particularly with regard to the earlier conventions of musical notation used in the manuscript which was his source? (2) Was the scribe drunk or incompetent or both? (3) Was the scribe a nun, a monk, or a lay person? The last question brings to mind Alejandro Planchart's observation that the neatest, most accurate manuscripts were those copied by women scribes[6]—an observation that holds for the Dendermonde manuscript and Wiesbaden MS. 2, both copied at Hildegard's abbey in her lifetime. But applied to the British Library manuscript of the *Ordo Virtutum*, Planchart's suggestion argues in this case for a man's work, more likely monastic than lay, and thus corroborates the statement that the manuscript was copied at Sponheim from a borrowed manuscript, either Wiesbaden MS. 2 itself or a copy that has been lost. A note in the manuscript, apparently in Trithemius's own handwriting, provides further corroboration, since it indicates that the copying was done by members of his Order.[7]

The question of the man's care or his carelessness, his competence or incompetence, his ignorance or wisdom, or his sobriety, may be an issue nonetheless. It is not even impossible that the scribe was actively malevolent in attempting to subvert the copy through the errors made in the musical notation. We recall Trithemius' own admission that whenever he thought of his election to the abbacy of Sponheim, he wept. We know that this reforming abbot was not always respected by his monks, who often did not share his ideals and goals for the monastery or its library. To his dismay, his monks eventually forced his resignation from the abbacy of Sponheim in 1506.[8]

British Library Add. MS. 15,102 is a quarto volume, written on paper.[9] The music is notated in *hufnagel* notation from the Rhineland region, already becoming somewhat archaic in the fifteenth century. The *Ordo Virtutum* appears on fols. 207^r–221^r, and is followed by blank pages, in turn followed, on fol. 224^r, by the *Vita S. Hildegardis, cum visionibus et miraculis ejus; in tres libros distincta; opus a Godefrids incoeptum*. Trithemius' note affixed to the volume gives the date of the copying as 1487.

Two examples from the Wiesbaden MS. 2 and British Library Add. MS. 15,102 showing the variations between the two versions

should suffice to indicate the extent of corruption in the later manuscript (Examples 1 and 2). I am providing transcriptions into
modern notation from the Gothic neumes of the Wiesbaden manuscript and the later neumes of the British Library manuscript.[10]

On the basis of the comparison of the musical transcriptions in
the two manuscripts, it is easy to see that the later scribe was unable
to cope with Hildegard's unique musical style or even to reproduce
the characteristic tonalities in his presentation of the music of the
Ordo Virtutum.

Example 1

a. Wiesbaden MS. 2

Patriarche et Prophete:

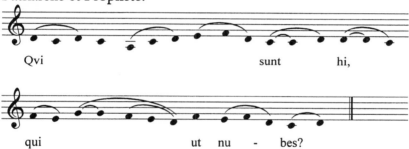

b. BL MS. Add. 15,102

Patriarchis et prophetarum:

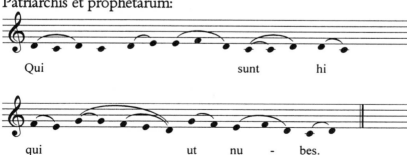

Example 2

a. Wiesbaden MS. 2

[Excerpt from final Procession:]

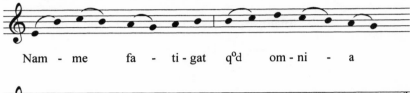

Nam - me   fa - ti - gat q°d om - ni - a

mem - bra   me - a in ir - ri - si - o - nem   ua-dunt.

b. BL MS. Add. 15,102

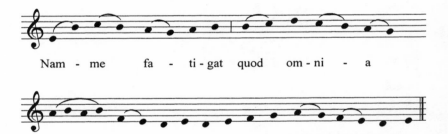

Nam - me   fa - ti - gat quod om - ni - a

mem - bra   me - a, in ir - ri - si - o - nem   va-dunt.

NOTES

[1] Research on Hildegard of Bingen's *Ordo Virtutum* was conducted with the assistance of a Faculty Research Fellowship and Grant in the summer of 1990 which allowed physical examination of the British Library and Wiesbaden manuscripts and determined that the latter is the only one to present the music accurately. Portions of my article, but without the transcription which I include to document my case, were included as an appendix in my "Music and Performance: Hildegard of Bingen's *Ordo Virtutum*," in *The* Ordo Virtutum *of Hildegard of Bingen: Critical Studies*, ed. Audrey Ekdahl Davidson (Kalamazoo: Medieval Institute Publications, 1992), 1–29, and are used here with the permission of the

publisher.

[2] *Catalogue of Additions to the Manuscripts, 1841–1845,* vol.7; this catalogue makes the claim that the manuscript from which British Library Add. MS. 15,102 was copied was "said to have been written by St. Hildegard herself."

[3] Barbara Newman, *Sister of Wisdom: St. Hildegard's Theology of the Feminine* (Berkeley and Los Angeles: University of California Press, 1987), 259–60.

[4] James Westfall Thompson, *The Medieval Library* (1939; reprint New York: Hafner, 1957), 465.

[5] Ibid., 464. As Trithemius lamented, there was for practical purposes upon his arrival at Sponheim "no library because the uncouth monks pursued, not books, but delicious pastimes and pleasures" (quoted by Noel L. Brann, *The Abbot Trithemius [1462–1516]: The Renaissance of Monastic Humanism* [Leiden: E. J. Brill, 1981], 11).

[6] Unpublished paper read at the International Congress on Medieval Studies.

[7] See *Catalogue of Additions to the Manuscripts,* vol. 7.

[8] R. W. Seton-Watson, "The Abbot Trithemius," in *Tudor Studies Presented by the Board of Studies in History in the University of London to Albert Frederick Pollard,* ed. R. W. Seton-Watson (1924; reprint Freeport, New York: Books for Libraries Press, 1969), 78–79; Brann, *The Abbot Trithemius,* 46–53.

[9] Normally Trithemius preferred parchment over paper, which he considered impermanent; see Curt F. Bühler, *The Fifteenth-Century Book* (Philadelphia: University of Pennsylvania Press, 1960), 35.

[10] For comment on the Gothic neumes of Wiesbaden MS. 2, see Ludwig Bronarski, *Die Lieder der hl. Hildegard: Ein Beitrag zur Geschichte der geistlichen Musik des Mittelalters* (Leipzig: Breitkopf und Härtel, 1922), 14. For my transcriptions from Wiesbaden MS. 2 I have used my performing edition of the *Ordo Virtutum* (Kalamazoo: Medieval Institute Publications, 1986; subsequently reissued, Bryn Mawr: Hildegard Publishing, 2002), although I have silently corrected some misreadings that occurred when I had only the microfilm of the manuscript with which to work. For a reduced facsimile of the manuscript, see *The* Ordo Virtutum *of Hildegard of Bingen: Critical Studies,* pls. 1–12.

Sequentia's *Ordo Virtutum* at Ann Arbor: A Performance in Memory of Barbara Thornton

Rick Johnson

As part of the celebration of the nine hundredth anniversary of the birth of Hildegard of Bingen in 1098, the production by the renowned musical ensemble Sequentia of her *Ordo Virtutum* was brought to Ann Arbor, Michigan, under the sponsorship of the University Musical Society.

Sequentia's *Ordo Virtutum* was staged on the evening of 13 November 1998 in the spacious St. Francis of Assisi Catholic Church. Immediately prior to the beginning of the play, the announcement was made that the ensemble's co-founder and musical director for the production, Barbara Thornton, had died just seven days earlier. Appropriately, the performance was given in her memory, and at its conclusion the ensemble performed *O presul vere civitatis* as a further tribute to her.

The drama began with a short instrumental introduction played by three darkly costumed musicians (Rachel Evans, Robert Mealy, and Norbert Rodenkirchen) playing fiddles and a flute. These instrumentalists played sparingly throughout, occasionally offering accompaniment to the singers or providing a subtle but musically important drone.

The *Ordo Virtutum* was presented on two levels, the physical as well as the spiritual. A large raised dais at the front of the church represented the brightly-lit heavenly realm of the eleven Virtues, whose queen is Humility (Maria Jonas). The rest of the sanctuary was in darkness and represented worldly existence. The action took place here within the wide aisles (at audience level) with the characters illuminated by spotlight only.

The human Soul (Anima, played by Pamela Dellal), clothed in a regal white robe, was first noticed at the rear of the center aisle, along which she advanced slowly toward the uplifted Virtues as she

1. Scene from the performance of the *Ordo Virtutum* by Sequentia under the musical direction of Barbara Thornton in July 1998. This presentation was part of Lincoln Center's celebration of the Hildegard of Bingen's birth at the Church of St. John the Apostle on Ninth Avenue in New York City. The staging was based on ideas from Hildegard's other works; thus, as Thornton's program notes explained, Contemptus Mundi stood "within a wheel that revolves without ceasing, within which she remains motionless." Photo courtesy of Lincoln Center.

sang their praises. Suddenly appearing out of the darkness was the menacing Devil (Franz-Josef Heumannskämper, who was also the stage director), whining and screaming (this character is not capable of song), who seduces the Soul to worldly pleasures. At a truly dramatic moment in the play, she dropped her white robe—a sign of her abandonment of her journey toward Heaven. The Virtues immediately lamented the loss of the Soul, and each one stepped forward "to present her case" in a series of chanted "mission statements." This is the portion of the drama—the musical center of the play—in which Hildegard's beautiful arching melodies are used to depict the qualities of perfection in the Christian life. The Devil hissed frequent insults, but he was ignored by the Virtues, who proceeded with their musical presentation of the qualities of the Good. Eventually the Soul reappeared, exhausted from the tribulations of worldly existence. The Virtues, answering her pleas for help, clothed her once again in the white robe of immortality. One last attempt was made by the Devil to win her back, and in a dramatic moment the Virtue Victoria (Marianne Nielsen) descended to overpower and bind him. The weary soul then finally entered Heaven, and the drama concluded with the united singing of *In principio.*

It is always a pleasure to hear (and, in this case, see) recreations of medieval music performed confidently by talented, experienced performers. And the whole endeavor must be supported by adequate scholarship. Sequentia's presentation of the *Ordo Virtutum* succeeded on both counts. Obviously great care was also taken in the choice of the proper venue. St. Francis of Assisi Church offered a handsome interior with enough aisle space for the characters to interact in close contact with the audience. While one missed the reverberant sound of medieval stone walls, this modern sanctuary provided a complementary acoustic for the musicians as well as the benefits of modern lighting. And most importantly, the music of Hildegard of Bingen was sung by the ensemble with the security needed to bring forth all of its emotional appeal. Both the occasional wide note intervals, so unusual for her time, and also the serene chant melodies were performed with great skill. The listener could relax and comfortably enter the world of medieval theology and its musical expression.

The artists of Sequentia, in their fine production, offered the most fitting gift that one could imagine to their founder, Barbara Thornton.

Boy Bishops in Early Modern Europe: Ritual, Myth, and Reality

Michael Milway

At the end of the Thirty Year's War, Bishop John Gregory of Winchester (d. 1647) made a curious discovery in the cathedral of Salisbury. He describes the wonder he felt in a long pamphlet published posthumously in 1649, entitled *Episcopus puerorum in die innocentium* (*The Boy Bishop and the Day of Childermas*).[1] A copperplate print of a small alcove statue adorns the pamphlet's title page and illustrates what the bishop found (fig. 1). His opening paragraph describes the statue and appraises the incredible find:

> In the Cathedral of *Sarum* [i.e., Salisbury] there lieth a Monument in stone, of a little Boie habited all in Episcopal Robes, a Miter upon his head, a Crosier in his hand, and the rest accordingly. The Monument laie long Buried itself under the Seats near the Pulpit, at the removal whereof, it was of late years discovered . . . not without a general imputation of Raritie and Reverence, it seeming almost impossible to everie one, that either a *Bishop* could bee so small in *Person*, or a *Childe* so great in *Clothes*.[2]

The present study begins as did Gregory's investigation with a series of questions about boy bishops: How young were they? What did they do? And how did people perceive them?

> Having consulted with the most likelie men I knew . . . to what Moment of Antiquitie this [statue] could refer, the Answer still was, that They could not tell. . . . The late Learned Bishop Mountague [1641] . . . earnestly appointed mee to make further enquirie after the thing, not doubting but that there would be something in the matter at least of curious, if not substantial observation.[3]

It is hard to believe that a seventeenth-century English bishop was so hard pressed to explain the statue of a boy bishop. Not much earlier, boy bishops were everywhere: in ritual, myth, and reality.

87

1. Title page with illustration of Boy Bishop.

What finally satisfied Gregory's curiosity about the statue and its origin, or so he reports, was his discovery of an ecclesiastical ceremony that featured the appointment of a boy bishop. The ceremony was in fact a popular, pan-European medieval festival that in some regions out-lived Gregory. We have to think, therefore, that his ignorance and surprise stem more from false humility and exaggeration than from genuine bewilderment and scholarly curiosity, perhaps for reasons of rhetorical affect.

The scope of what follows is intentionally broad. I move geographically from England to Austria and chronologically from 1450 to 1650. I touch on the cultural history of drama and the social anthropology of the Church. That breadth allows me to see threads of continuity and stability between the ritual, myth, and reality of early modern boy bishops that are obscured by more focused studies, important in their own right. It also permits me to compare what critics alleged and what masqueraders lampooned, what genuine boy bishops did and what imposter boy-bishops preached.

I

Ritual. The tradition of electing a boy bishop on the Feast of St. Nicholas (6 December) dates to the thirteenth century, and perhaps earlier. By the late Middle Ages rural parishes, cathedral churches, and monastery schools across Europe were celebrating the feast and practicing the ritual.[4] Although customs varied, boy bishops by and large were elected and appointed by their peers, usually the choristers. The boy bishop dressed in episcopal vestments and carried a bishop's staff. He performed all the functions of a real bishop except that he could not administer sacraments. The remaining choristers served him as prebends. He oversaw diocesan visitations, offered blessings, and preached. And he did so for as long as a month, sometimes two, depending on the region. According to an extant medieval office from the cathedral of Salisbury which gives the entire liturgy for the Feast of Holy Innocents, boy bishops were elected on St. Nicholas Day (6 December) and had their first important procession three weeks later on the Feast of St. John (27 December).[5] The following day, on the Feast of Holy Innocents, the boy bishop preached a sermon, and during the month of January, at least in Salisbury, he performed a diocesan visitation collecting alms as he went, sometimes to a considerable sum. In 1440 he col-

lected an amount equal to the yearly earnings of a parish priest.[6] In
some places we find an analogue ritual for girls in nunneries, where
on Innocents' day an "abbess" was elected instead of a "bishop."[7]

Festival behavior of this kind and order was condemned out-
right by the Council of Basle in 1435.[8] But it lived on in many
places until as late as the eighteenth century. Henry VIII forbade the
ritual in 1541 for all of England; Queen Mary later restored it in
1554; then Elizabeth abolished it again when she came to the
throne.[9] In some cases girls were singled out in the prohibitions. Although John Peckham forbade only the office and prayers to be said
per parvulas (by a girl), the bishop of Norwich outlawed any election whatsoever of an abbess on Innocents' Day.[10]

Such measures of control—and these simply scratch the surface
of a long list of suppressions—suggest that the festival of boy
bishops and girl abesses was a farce, a masquerade of sorts that
placed the church in a theater of carnival and put society at risk of
unrest. Indeed, authorities in Regensburg shut down the festival in
1327 after someone was killed.[11] It is hardly surprising, therefore,
that scholars of medieval and Renaissance drama have interpreted
the festival of boy bishops in terms of comic relief and social
catharsis. Arthur Leach remarked that "in the festivities, which cen-
tred round the Boy-Bishop, the mediaeval schoolboy found the
relaxation and reaction which were to compensate him for the re-
straint and repression of the year."[12] Karl Young noted that the feast
was "allied to sheer revelry and hilarity." The boy bishop himself
was "not an *impersonation* of the true presiding bishop, but merely
a ludicrous substitute."[13] Harold Hillebrand wrote that "the pleasure
which the young performers had in their feast is easily compre-
hended when we recollect that out of the whole school year . . . this
was the only holiday the boys had, and it must have come as a
blessed respite. . . . Restraining orders had to be issued to hold in the
enthusiasm of the mob. . . . The whole affair was a glorified
masquerade."[14] These early eminent voices of interpretation have
gone largely unchallenged,[15] and in recent decades have been
strengthened by a vocabulary and method drawn from literary
scholars, cultural historians, and anthropologists. Boy bishops and
the Feast of Holy Innocents are seen as classic examples of the
world turned upside-down: with boys on top.[16]

In spite of its merits, this interpretation needs modification, or
at least amplification. Scholars of drama have yet to study the actual

sermons preached by boy bishops, some of which have been printed and one of which is still famous albeit as the work of Erasmus not as the sermon of a boy bishop. After reading just two sermons by boy bishops, Harold Hillebrand dismissed them as "very moral and very dull."[17] What is equally unsatisfying is the fact that researchers have yet to reconcile their views about the Feast of Holy Innocents as farce with contemporary support of the festival as an admirable expression of piety.

In 1512 when the English humanist John Colet wrote *Statutes* for the foundation of St. Paul's, his new private school for boys, he delineated several examples of required and forbidden behavior, a list that includes injunctions against cockfighting, rabble rousing, and drunkenness, but also embraces admonitions to prayer and punctuality. Among the various statutes, we discover one where Colet charges each pupil to hear the boy bishop preach on the Feast of Holy Innocents and to give him an offering.[18]

As a favor to his friend John Colet, Erasmus of Rotterdam wrote a thirty-minute sermon to be preached by the boy bishop of St. Paul's. Today we know that famous work as Erasmus's *Homily on the Child Jesus*, but he wrote it to be delivered by a schoolboy bishop. And although Erasmus, more than anyone, possessed a gift for subtle satire and biting humor, there is no Erasmian play in this homily. It is serious sermon. Nor would we expect John Colet to require school boys to hold an annual rebellious festival and carnivalesque farce. What we might expect is along the order of what the boy bishop in fact preached (in Erasmus' words):

> It is fitting for us as children to marvel at a child [namely Jesus]. . . . The state of childhood is so pleasing to our leader Christ that he compels even old men to become children again if they wish to be admitted to that society outside which there is no hope of salvation. . . . Christianity is a sort of renewed infancy. . . . Let us remember that the childhood which is acceptable to God lies not in years, but in disposition; not in age, but in behavior. It is then a new kind of childhood which Christ approves: a childhood which is not puerile, but rather a sort of aged childhood consisting not in number of years but in innocence and simplicity of mind.[19]

If Erasmus had wanted to write a farce, he could have waxed far funnier than that.

II

Myth. The early modern literature of discontent about the behavior of bishops is voluminous. Pamphlets and broadsheets,
sophisticated treatises, and *ad hoc* lists of *gravimina* all helped
create and sustain a myth about episcopal vices. Much of the literature draws on a corpus of commonplaces. Bishops were foolish,
lascivious, effeminate, and immature. Critics were quick to use the
word "boy" (*puer*) when describing bishops, and if a harsher terms
were needed, they used "girl" (*puella*).

Of the many prolific and vociferous Church critics of the sixteenth century, I look to Berthold Pürstinger (d. 1543) because he
was a bishop himself. His criticism hails from the rank of those very
clergy impugned for their immoral behavior and extravagant habits.
From 1508 to 1526, he was bishop of Chiemsee, near Salzburg.[20]
Yet even Pürstinger draws on commonplaces to criticize his fellow
clergy: They "work harder at getting laid by prostitutes than at
meeting the needs of the poor."[21] Bishops specifically were "pimps,
sycophants, idiots and low-lifers."[22] He despaired of any chance to
elect a worthy bishop instead of some "young whipper-snapper or
spiritual ignoramus."[23] I use "whipper-snapper" because Pürstinger
employed the word *puer* (boy) in its most caustic, pejorative, and
apocalyptic sense. For he knew that during the Last Days, into
which he himself was born, boys would rule over princes.[24] Compared to his episcopal peers, Pürstinger was relatively old, having
ruled as bishop from age forty-three to age sixty.

The popularity of this anticlerical and apocalyptic myth about
boy bishops inspires us first to wonder how many bishops were in
fact simply young boys, and second to test the literature of discontent for hyperbole. What can we determine from more reliable
sources?

III

Reality. At this point, I move from Pürstinger's Chiemsee to
Freising in Bavaria, an adjacent diocese. I study Freising for three
reasons. First, Freising lies in the heart of Catholic Bavaria, where
Protestant propaganda did not so noticeably affect ecclesiastical
rituals, including those associated with the Feast of Holy Innocents.
Second, political tension between the house of Wittelsbach and the
house of Habsburg, both dynasties adept at placing their sons in

positions of considerable authority, made epsicopal sees in that part
of the Empire especially vulnerable to the designs of young, bene-
fice-hungry, aspiring nobles. Third, Freising is a compelling diocese
to study because one of its teenaged bishops, Ernst von Bayern,
returns this study toward England where it started, far enough into
the seventeenth century to overlap with the life of Bishop John
Gregory and his alcove statue of a boy bishop.

During the two centuries from 1450 to 1650, three of the eleven
"bishops" of Freising were younger than twenty when nominated by
the cathedral chapter and commissioned by the pope, a twenty-five
percent rate of teenaged appointments (table 1).[25] I put the word
"bishop" in quotation marks, because to use that title, bishops had
to be ordained priests. Otherwise—and such cases abounded in
early modern Europe—diocesan heads were called administrators.
Most teenage "bishops" were too young for Holy Orders, so they
oversaw their diocese as "administrators." In some dioceses, the rate
of teenaged episcopal appointments was higher than twenty-five
percent. In many, it was lower. We find the higher rate in dioceses
such as Freising which were ruled by prince-bishops, who wielded
both temporal and spiritual authority. We find the lower rate in
dioceses such as nearby Chiemsee where Berthold Pürstinger
served, where bishops were not *de facto* princes. But money was
money, and benefices were benefices. If a nobleman could not
secure for himself or his son a diocese as prince-bishop, he might
try as bishop alone.

The first teenaged bishop of Freising during the early modern
period was Ruprecht bei Rhein, a man with a rather illustrious, if
not particularly pious, adolescence. At ten, he was appointed prebend in the cathedral chapter. At eleven, he was named co-adjutor
of Freising with right of succession when the incumbent bishop
died, which he did three years later. So Ruprecht became bishop or
rather administrator at age fourteen, then two years later stepped
down in order to get married.

At that point, the chapter nominated Ruprecht's brother, Philipp
bei Rhein, older by one year. Philipp was only four when promised
a position as prebend in the Cologne cathedral which was awarded
finally when he was eleven. Meanwhile, at eight he became prebend
in Mainz, and by twelve had similar benefices in Augsburg, Freising, Eichstätt, and Strassburg. At seventeen he became administrator of Freising when his younger brother Ruprecht left to take
marriage vows. Two years later, Philipp took vows of his own to be

Table 1

The Bishops of Freising c.1450–1650
(and their age when elected "bishop")

1448–52	Johann Grünwalder	(early 50s)
1453–73	Johann Tulbeck	(40s)
1474–95	Sixtus von Tannberg	(late 30s)
1496–98	Ruprecht bei Rhein	(14)
1498–1541	Philipp bei Rhein	(17)
1541–52	Heinrich bei Rhein	(53)
1552–59	Leo Lösch von Hilkershausen	(50)
1560–66	Moritz von Sandizel	(45)
1566–1612	Ernst von Bayern	(11)
1613-1618	Stephan von Seiboldsdorf	(33)
1618-1651	Veit Adam Gepeckh von Arnbach	(34)

come a priest, and thus at nineteen a genuine teenaged bishop, not simply administrator. In fact, he became one of the more reform minded, anti-Lutheran, spiritually guided bishops of his day.

The next teenaged bishop came on the heels of the Council of Trent in spite of its reform mandates. Ernst von Bayern was only eleven when nominated by the chapter and commissioned by the pope as administrator of Freising. He is a classic example of a prince-bishop caught in the middle of conflicting demands between dynastic interests, confessional struggles, and imperial politics. From his birth, he was destined by his father for priestly orders, which he did attain. But his own interests lay rather in mathematics, astrology, hunting, dice, and women. He was administrator of Freising at eleven, then too of Hildesheim at eighteen, of Liège at twenty-six, elector archbishop of Cologne at twenty-eight, and of Münster at thirty. Thus by the end of his third decade, Ernst alone acted as bishop over a large chunk of the Holy Roman Empire. He died in 1612, five years after Bishop John Gregory of Winchester was born. That an English bishop did not know of teenaged bishops —whether in myth, ritual, or reality—is quite unthinkable.

IV

The literature to date on boy bishops, what little there is, does nothing to compare the ritual with the myth, or the myth with the reality. And the work that has been done lurks on the margins theater history, where scholars of drama have done well to view boy bishops as a carnivalesque mockery, but have failed to notice or at least take seriously traces of devout spirituality in the ritual. John Colet and Erasmus of Rotterdam were not admonishing boys to masquerade while turning the world upside down. They were encouraging and equipping them for a "more noble" purpose, beyond the farce of a chorister usurping authority from a legitimate bishop. In the title-page illustration of Bishop Gregory's treatise, the boy bishop is indeed on top, but not above an adult bishop. He is standing on a demon, a she-devil named Lilith according to Gregory,[26] which is the reason why parents in the Middle Ages did not leave their children alone in a crib without lighting a candle. Lilith was a she-devil that killed children, and candlelight would keep her at bay. The statue's iconography is more serious than farcical: boy bishop atop child-killing demon. This is not simply a monument to carnival play.

As we move from ritual to reality, we have even more reason to doubt that boy bishops functioned primarily to satirize church hierarchies or to allow choir boys to vent frustration. If boy bishops could be as old as nineteen—as many of them were in early modern Europe—while real bishops could be as young as eleven—as a few of them were—then in some cases it was impossible for the ritual to turn the world upside down. Bishop Ernst von Bayern was a teen-aged bishop for nine years running, and for three of those years in more than one diocese. Genuine bishops, that is to say, at least in some dioceses, were doubtless younger than boy bishops. The story is more complex and stranger than what Bishop Gregory called, on the title page of his essay, "an ancient custom in the church of Sarum, making an anniversarie bishop among the choristers."

NOTES

[1] The Feast of Holy Innocents, i.e., Childermas, fell on 28 December. John Gregory, *Episcopus puerorum in die innocentium, or a Discoverie of an Antient Custom in the Church of Sarum, Making an Anniversarie Bishop among the*

Choristers (London: William Dugard for Laurence Sadler, 1649), in John Gregory, *Gregorii posthuma, or Certain Learned Tracts . . . Together with a Short Account of the Author's Life and Elegies on his much-Lamented Death* (London: William Dugard for Laurence Sadler, 1650), 93–123 [each treatise except the first has its own title page dated 1649, yet the work is paginated as one continuous volume]. John Gregory was an orientalist and read English, Latin, Greek, Hebrew, Syriac, Chaldee, and Arabic. He cites works in all those languages in this treatise.

² Gregory, *Episcopus puerorum in die innocentium*, 95–96.

³ Ibid., 96.

⁴ Edmund K. Chambers, *The Mediaeval Stage*, 2 vols. (London: Oxford University Press, 1903), 1:336–71.

⁵ For the office, see Chambers, *Mediaeval Stage*, 2:282–89, and Charles Wordsworth, *Ceremonies and Processions of the Cathedral Church of Salisbury* (Cambridge: Cambridge University Press, 1901), 52–59.

⁶ See Chambers, *Mediaeval Stage*, 1:356–57.

⁷ Ibid., 1:361.

⁸ See "De spectaculis in ecclesia non faciendis" (Council of Basel, Session 21, 9 June 1435), in *Decrees of the Ecumenical Councils*, ed. G. Alberigo *et al.*, trans. N. P. Tanner, 2 vols. (Washington, D.C.: Georgetown University Press, 1990), 1:492.13–17.

⁹ "Two Sermons Preached by the Boy Bishop at St. Paul's . . . with an Introduction Giving an Account of the Festival of the Boy Bishop in England by Edward F. Rimbault," ed. John Gough Nichols, *The Camden Society Miscellany*, n.s. 14, vol. 7 (1875): i–xxxvi, 1–34, here at xx–xxi. See also Chambers, *Mediaeval Stage*, 1:367–68.

¹⁰ Chambers, *Mediaeval Stage*, 1:361.

¹¹ Ibid., 1:351.

¹² Arthur Leach, "The Schoolboys' Feast," *The Fortnightly Review* n.s. 59 (1896): 128–41, here at 129.

¹³ Karl Young, *The Drama of the Medieval Church*, 2 vols. (Oxford: Clarendon Press, 1933), 1:110.

¹⁴ Harold N. Hillebrand, *The Child Actors: A Chapter in Elizabethan Stage History* (1926; reprint New York: Russell and Russell, 1964), 24, 28.

¹⁵ One important exception to the trend is found in Richard L. DeMolen, "Pueri Christi Imitatio: The Festival of the Boy Bishop in Tudor England." *Moreana* 45 (1975): 17–28.

¹⁶ See, for example, the article by Martine Grinberg, "L'Episcopus puerorum," in *Infanzie: funzioni di un gruppo liminale dal mondo classico all'Eta moderna*, ed. Ottavia Niccoli, Laboratorio di storia 6 (Florence: Ponte alle Grazie, 1993), 144–58, esp. 146–48.

¹⁷ Hillebrand, *Child Actors*, 26. Rimbault, in his Introduction to his edition of *Two Sermons Preached by Boy Bishops,* mentions that William de Tolleshunte, almoner of St. Paul's, bequeathed in 1329 "all the quires of sermons of the Feasts of the Holy Innocents which the boy-bishops were wont to preach." Unfortunately, these seem to have disappeared (xxxii).

¹⁸ "All these Chyldren shall euery Chyldermasse day come to paulis Church

and here the Chylde Bisshoppis sermon and after be at the hye masse and eche of them offer a jd. to the Childe bisshopp" (John Colet, *Statutes of S. Paul's School*, printed in Joseph H. Lupton, *A Life of John Colet*, 2nd ed. [1909; reprint Hamden, Conn.: Shoe String Press, 1961], 271–84, here at 278).

[19] Erasmus, *Concio de puero Iesu (Homily on the Child Jesus)*, trans. Emily Kearns, in *Collected Works of Erasmus*, vol. 29, ed. Elaine Fantham and Erika Rummel (Toronto: University of Toronto Press, 1989), 56–70, here at 58, 62.

[20] See Johann Sallaberger, "Der Chiemseer Bischof Berthold Pürstinger (1465/66–1543)," *Mitteilungen der Gesellschaft für Salzburger Landeskunde* 130 (1990): 427–84.

[21] "Ecclesiastici plures expenduntur in usus meretricantium quam indigentium pauperum" (Berthold Pürstinger, *Onus ecclesiae* [Landshut, 1524], VIII.4).

[22] "Contra canonum praecepta penes se tenent lenones, adulatores, buffones, vanitatibus vacantes . . ." (ibid., XX.3).

[23] "Ubinam bonus et probatus opere et doctrina in episcopum eligitur, non puer non carnalis spiritualium ignarus?" (ibid., XX.2).

[24] "Sed hodie tumultantur pueri contra senes" (ibid., XXII.7). "Pueri erunt principes eorum et effeminati dominabuntur eorum" [cf. Isaiah 3:4] (ibid., XXIV.2). "Et vae tibi terra cuius rex puer est, et cuius principes mane comedunt" [Eccl. 10:16] (ibid., XXIV.7).

[25] The information that follows was culled from *Das Bistum Freising im Mittelalter*, ed. Josef Mass, 2nd ed. (Munich, 1988); *Das Bistum Freising in der Neuzeit*, ed. Georg Schwaiger (Munich, 1989); and *Die Bischöfe des Heiligen Römischen Reiches 1448 bis 1648,* ed. Erwin Gatz (Berlin, 1996).

[26] Gregory, *Episcopus puerorum*, 97.

Adoxography as a Mode of Discourse for Satan and His Underlings in Medieval Plays

John W. Velz

The devils in medieval plays speak their own language. It is among other things dialectal, earthy,[1] abrupt, scatological,[2] and adoxographic. Of these features, the last is not the least significant. Medieval stage devils regularly indulge in a rhetoric centered in adoxography, that form of irony in which a received value system is turned upside down. *Adoxography* (from Gr. *adoxos,* "ignoble") originally meant writing the ignoble as noble in the manner of the Sophists—to "make the worse appear/ The better reason," as Milton says of his Belial in *Paradise Lost* 2.113–14. As early as the First Sophistic, the converse was also covered by the word *adoxography*—writing the noble as ignoble. Medieval dramatic devils praise the unworthy world of sin and hell and condemn the friends of God as inadequates, sinners, or enemies. It is so outrageous to have the devils fly in the face of all that is holy that scenes in hell are often delightfully ludicrous in medieval plays; audiences laugh heartily because the adoxographs, if done with mock seriousness, are a broad form of irony, related to sarcasm.

Little has been written about the rhetoric of devils.[3] But adoxography itself has been studied from a broadly historical perspective, by Alexander Sackton who forty-five years ago[4] traced "the paradoxical encomium" from the First Sophistic in Socrates' Athens through Roman oratory in the Second Sophistic to the Renaissance Humanists (Erasmus' *Praise of Folly* as a focal text[5]) and from the Humanists to the Tudor and Stuart comic and satiric dramatists, in particular Dekker, Marston, Chapman, Jonson, and Shakespeare. Along this path through the classical tradition, one finds mock serious praise of injustice and tobacco and cuckoldry and prostitution and much more, and (less often) mock disparagement of honor (Falstaff), friendship (Feste), funereal grief (Feste), and virginity (Parolles).[6] An adoxograph is, in this formulation, a set piece of

98

witty choplogic in which the art lies in the tour de force, the clever-
ness with which the inversion is precisely worked out at every point.
As originally conceived, adoxography was display rhetoric, but in
the hands of later artists, Lucian especially, it masked a satiric
purpose.[7] One can work complex variations on the pattern, as when
Shakespeare's Mark Antony "proves" to the doubtful Plebeians in
the Forum scene of *Julius Caesar* that Brutus is a hateful murderer
of a good man while all the time praising this assassin (whom he
loathes) as "an honorable man." (Shakespeare could have found
something very like this in another oration of the historical Marcus
Antonius as recorded by Appian; there his enemies are sarcastically
praised as "boni cives," "solid citizens."[8])

There is no room for devils in Sackton's account of this ironic
rhetorical device; indeed there is little room for anything medieval.
All the same, the Middle Ages appreciated the wit that is inherent
in deliberate disjunction. One thinks of the *Miller's Tale*, a lewd
and disrespectful parody of the *Knight's Tale*, and of Noah's obstreperous wife in the cycle plays, a comic typological echo of
Adam's tragically obstreperous wife—to mention only two familiar
examples. Following the lead of Mikhail Bakhtin in the first two
chapters of *Rabelais and His World*,[9] a number of modern commentators have pointed to the irreverent carnivalesque and/or theatrical spirit of *festivitas* in medieval and renaissance culture.[10]
Among them, Sandra Billington approaches the conception to be advanced here, as she writes of mock kings in medieval culture that
they are not so much subversion as one pole of a quasi-manichaean
dichotomy between order and disorder; the thesis is that order needs
(controlled, licensed) disorder to define what order is—and, to re-
mind all who observe, how fragile and fallible order is.[11] Equally
festive and more ridiculous than threatening are the manuscript illuminations gathered together by John Edwards in which animals,
especially hares, are shown subjugating humans in hunting or siege
situations.[12] As Edwards notes, there is not much likelihood of an
animal rights protest; as in the case of boys as bishops, the delight
lies in the ludicrous reversal of normal roles, not in any politically
correct moral lesson. Despite a sprinkling of errors and one mis-
statement, John D. Cox makes the most important critique to date
of a materialist view of medieval inversion;[13] beginning by applying
the methods of the New Historicists, Cox deftly shows that their
assumption that to invert is to subvert is an oversimplification, at

least in medieval drama.

So inversions, whether of the wise man made a fool or the fool elevated to a place of honor, of the boy made a bishop, of a mock king serving seasonally in place of a true king, however temporarily—these are the heart of the carnivalesque. Bakhtin has only a sentence or two on medieval plays and nothing at all on dramatic devils; indeed he has no interest in adoxography as such. But it is a simple extension of his thought to postulate that the use of adoxographs by devils and other enemies of God originated in the inversions that carnival permitted, even encouraged.[14] It should not, finally, be very much of a surprise to any reader of Bakhtin to find that devils turn the value system of Christianity upside down. And here again we have a link to Feste, who, on the night of the Epiphany at the last gasp of the Christmas season, not only plays the adoxographer as noted above, but in the guise of Sir Topas the curate, making the more or less sane puritan Malvolio out to be mad (and doing it with impunity), echoes the Feast of the Boy Bishop—and sings in context of the Vice and "goodman devil" (end of act 4, scene 2).

The phenomenon that has been defined and placed in a historical context can be illustrated by comments on five or six medieval plays in which devils praise and dispraise, comically.

In the Chester *Harrowing of Hell* (play 17), after the prophets have expressed their hopes for redemption, the devils hold a conference around the throne of Satan during which he instructs them to avenge themselves on Jesus for his "sins"—that is, conspiring to steal Lazarus from their hell fire, healing those whom Satan had made lame and blind, and playing the stubborn fellow as well as acting as if hell were his and as if he could deprive Satan of his power. Jesus, of course, easily triumphs over the power that Satan's cohorts mount against him, and their only consolation in the end, after Jesus has instructed the archangel Michael to lead Adam, the prophets, and the good thief to heaven, is that they are to be allowed to keep a woman who was a dishonest ale-wife in her worldly life. Satan calls her "dere daughter"; another devil calls her "sweete ladye" and offers to marry her; a third devil welcomes the "deare darlinge" to a feast in hell (17.325, 329, 333).[15]

In the York *Harrowing* (and the Towneley play that is based on it), we find Satan voicing the perverse notion that Christ who has done treason to hell in the world is to be the permanent prisoner of the gloating devils. Jesus and the prophets are "boyes,"[16] and the prophets' stirrings of joy at imminent redemption are "þis vggely noyse" (37.101). Christ is "þat dastard" (180) and a "harlot" (i.e., a ne'er do well, 185); he is a mere carpenter's son who lays claim to power that is not his. Then, when Satan is clearly losing the agon with Christ, he portrays Christ as a thief who steals the souls that are citizens of hell—until Satan perceives that Jesus intends "Some measure with malice to melle," leaving the devils some compensation. In wonderful responsive adoxography, Jesus offers Satan a boon in all justice:

> *Jesus.*   3aa, witte þou wele, ellis were it wrang,
> Als cursed Cayme þat slewe Abell,
> And all þat hastis hemselue to hange,
> Als Judas and Archedefell . . .
> (37.305–08)

Making the most wretched of sinners a gift to his old enemy, Jesus shows that God and his friends can play Satan's game and that they can ironically outplay him at it.

The adoxographic pattern in the mentality of devils in Harrowing of Hell plays is a special case of dramatic irony—that irony in which the audience knows more than the speaker does about the full meaning of what is being said. However, here in York, Jesus is a verbal ironist when he purports to avoid doing a great wrong by giving Satan the present of Cain and his ilk. The adoxographic irony in this witty pose cuts more than one way; it would indeed be doing a wrong—an injustice—if Cain and Judas were not to fry in Hell. The psychology of irony is that we the audience are drawn to those who know what we know and are distanced from those who are excluded from our universe of perception. This is, then, shrewd dramaturgy, as we are drawn to Christ who knows as we do that the gift he is praising and giving to Satan is a worthless one. And we are distanced from Satan and his crew, who are adoxographic about Christ without perceiving the ironies they create, though we perceive these ironies perfectly. Adoxography, in such cases, serves ironies that in turn serve dramaturgy and ultimately serve the moral purposes of audience manipulation. If ever the dramatic art of our medieval ancestors was naive, it certainly is not in these adoxographic Harrowing of Hell plays. They are clever, and their purposes run deep.

In the N-Town *Passion Play I*, Lucifer is an implied presenter of the play and an implied controller of its events. He addresses the audience directly and confidentially in an extraordinary 124-line adoxograph which is part social satire[17] and part seriocomic plea for our commitment to his suzerainty that parodies the pleas of medieval street preachers for their hearers' commitment to God. With a straight face, Lucifer offers us as a "reward" for serving him that we "xal sing 'wellaway' evyr in peynes felle" (26.7–8). Praising vanities of dress (specified in loving detail), he reminds us implicitly that Lucifer is the devotee of vain pride. He styles himself a prophet (49–57), thus foreshadowing inversely the much briefer (40 lines) appearance of John the Baptist that immediately follows. In this brilliant tour de force, the author of *Passion Play I* uses adoxography to let the audience know clearly that it is *the Devil* that is the adversary in Christ's agon, about to be portrayed. At the same time the barrier between the world of the audience and the fictive world of the play is breached by the direct appeal, and we are led to see that our sporadic commitment to Satan through lifestyle is the reason for the agon. The dramaturgical and moral device is remarkably sophisticated.[18]

Less well known but as sophisticated is the play of *The Conversion of St. Paul* in the Digby Manuscript from the late fifteenth century.[19] This play follows the account of Saul's journey to Damascus as it appears in the Acts of the Apostles, but it has two unscriptural and very fine subplot scenes that comment on the main action.[20] One is among stablehands who in their pecking order imitate the power structure of the main plot of Saul, the Chief Priests, and God. The other subplot scene is set in hell among the devils, and here the main plot is echoed in another way.

After the news of Saul's conversion is carried to Annas and Caiphas, we get a ninety-line scene of lamentation in hell for the defection of Saul. It begins with Belial, who speaks three rhyme royal stanzas of vainglorious bragging in which he says he is not only second only to Lucifer but also controller of Annas and Caiphas, a god, and so forth. (This false claim to sovereignty is in itself a variant of adoxography; Herod, Satan, Tiberius, Pharaoh, and other enemies of God—in this play ironically enough Saul before his conversion—in many other places in medieval drama abuse through adoxographic loud-mouthed parody the understated *auctoritas* of God.) It is amusing to note that though Belial lays claim to godlike status, he clearly lacks omniscience because he yearns for news from his messenger, Mercury. As a messenger of Jupiter, Mercury is a pagan version of an angel; as the trickster of Roman mythology and as a master of verbal deception in many a myth, Mercury is a fitting guise for one of Satan's minions. At first Belial does not believe the report that Saul has changed sides, defecting to the enemy (God). Mercury wails that the Infernal Law is in decay, that though there are still many adherents to the cause of hell, sinners in Pride and Voluptuousness,

> He þat I most trustyd to,
> And he þat I thowȝte wold haue ben to vs most specyall,
> Ys now of late turnyd, and our cruell foo!
> Our specyall frynd, our chosen Saull,
> Ys becomme seruante to þe hye God eternall! (454–58)

Belial's response is that they have lost "Our darlying most dere, whom we lovyd moste" (466–67). And here we get a stage direction that shows that adoxography can take the form of action as well as of words: "*Here þei shall rore and crye*" (470 *s.d.*). After some reflection, Belial and Mercury plot to kill the defector, and Belial's reaction is as follows:

> Ho, Saul þou shalt repent thy vnstablenes!
> Thou hadyst ben better to haue byn confyrmable
> To our law—for thy deth, dowtles,
> Yt ys conspyryd to reward thy falsnes. (483–86)

Then he consoles himself with the thought that for this one who has "dissayvyd" us, there are twenty loyalists. And he rattles off praise of the Seven Deadly Sins as the scene ends.

In the admirable design of the play, just before this Belial-and-Mercury scene, Annas and Caiphas agree to make Saul "repent hys rebellyous treytory" and his "falsnes":

> We wyll not suffer hym to obtayne, dowtles,
> For meny perellys þat myght betyde
> By hys subtyll meanys on euery syde. (402–04)

They will have the law on him. And just *after* this scene with its adoxograph in praise of the deadly sins, enter the spiritually reborn Saul who launches almost immediately into a diatribe against the seven "mortall synne[s]." In this play, the placement of the scene in hell is carefully contrived to make the most of its adoxography.[21]

Constraints of space prohibit further identification of the pattern in medieval plays, but room must be made for brief accounts of some artistically superior implementations of the tradition in Marlowe and Shakespeare. In *Doctor Faustus* the protagonist is in the posture devils traditionally assume: making God out to be the enemy and torturing his ostensible friends.[22] (In point of fact, the devils in the play never mention God, so Faustus is as it were more infernal than they.) The best adoxograph in the play is an impulsive outburst of anguish from Faustus as damnation nears: "O, spare me, Lucifer!" (5.2.81)—as if Lucifer were concerned with mercy, not at all his medium, which is, of course, harsh justice. The irony is stinging.

Iago, like Faustus associated by his play with the Devil, turns all good things around him toward ignobility.[23] Sexual congress is "making the beast with two backs" (1.1.119–20); the Moor's "free and open nature" is not just a liability on the crooked paths of the world but an attribute that makes him an ass to be led by the nose (1.3.400–03). These adoxographs and others like them are background to the dominant motif of the play: devil-like, Iago portrays Desdemona, an obvious friend of God, associated with St. Mary the Virgin at 2.1.87–88, as a loathsome sinner. It is not the imagery of diabolism that turns Iago into a devil but his appalling insistence on turning the noble into ignobility. In Iago we see Satan's perverse inversion of values, but in this play the result is not the comedy of medieval plays: it is instead the grimmest tragedy.

The comedy of medieval plays is, however, itself more than risible irony. Applying adoxography, this special abuse of rhetoric, to the speeches of devils marks the etymology of Satan's name: "The Adversary" in Hebrew. *Adversary* here does not simply denote *opponent* but also *mirror image*, the turning of something around. As adoxography inverts the rhetorically expected, devils who speak it are inversions of all that God implies. Beneath the laughter that adoxography evokes from audiences, it makes deeper points about natural theology and about the nature of evil. God and Satan are opposite sides of the same coin. Satan may be said to be the converse of God's goodness. Why, then, would he not be precisely within his nature if he should speak in praise of values that are the exact inverse of God's goodness or in dispraise of the virtues that we most admire in God's disciples?

Hell has often been portrayed as an inversion of heaven. In Dante, we wind farther and farther down through the *Inferno* until we reach the very bottom of the cosmos where Lucifer is frozen into ice that symbolizes lovelessness. In the *Purgatorio* we climb up and up the seven-storey mountain until we reach the pinnacle of the *Paradiso* where the ice at the bottom of the *Inferno* is counter-pointed by the light and warmth of God's love. In *The Castle of Perseverance* the battle scenes feature in sequence the Seven Deadly Sins diametrically opposed by the Seven Cardinal Virtues—Castitas in single combat with Luxuria and so on. In later moralities one sees a more subtle opposition in which the vices operate under the names of their innocuous opposites: Lust masquerading as Curiosity; Ignorance as Wit; Pride as Modesty. The diabolical adoxographs that have been identified here are collectively an analogue of such cosmic symmetries as those in Dante or such moral symmetries as those in *The Castle of Perseverance* and later moralities. Miltonists have long recognized the elaborate symmetries of *Paradise Lost* in which the council on the burning lake of hell to debate the future now that heaven has been lost is a parody (in advance) of the council in heaven to determine the future now that a host of heavenly angels has been lost to evil.

It is clear that people in the Middle Ages saw Satan as God's "adversary" and recognized in the symmetry a clear choice for each person to make in life. It might be said that their theology was a bit closer to Manichaean symmetry than ours is. Yet we are Manichaean enough—witness the strongly articulated moral polarities of twentieth-century fantasy literature from C. S. Lewis' science fiction novels to J. R. R. Tolkien's *Lord of the Rings* and on to the Star Wars Trilogy, starring Darth Vader as the adversary of "The Force," Satan as antagonist to God. We can justly say that we are prepared by our own Manichaean secular literature to respond to medieval portrayals of Satan and his cohorts as mirror images of God and his legions of angels. The value—rhetorical, aesthetic, theological, and dramaturgical—of the adoxograph in medieval religious drama is considerable. What it does is to enforce for us (through festive comedy of the kind Bakhtin admires so much in medieval culture) the dreadful cosmic alternatives of Good and Evil. When Evil deliberately inverts the values of Good we laugh at the abuse of the art of rhetoric. But, if we perceive what is intended by these adoxographs we encounter on the stage, we shudder also. Satan sums up the rhetorical abuse and his own nature when he says in book 9 of *Paradise Lost* "Evil be thou my good" (108–10).

NOTES

I am grateful to Margaret Arnold for opening a research door for me by making it possible for an earlier draft of a portion of this paper to be read as part of a session entitled "The Enemies of God Abuse the Arts" at the 1994 International Congress on Medieval Studies at Kalamazoo. Krystyna Kujawinska-Courtney has also been a friendly resource, and I am particularly grateful to Clifford Davidson for a number of informative suggestions. This paper is dedicated to the memory of Alexander Sackton, late Professor Emeritus of the University of Texas, Austin, who first traced the history of adoxography with grace and erudition.

[1] For evidence that the earthly and dialectal dimension of medieval devils' language is still conventional, see the language of Orcs in J. R. R. Tolkien's *The Lord of the Rings.*

[2] For a brief survey of the rationale and history of the use of scatology as a code for diabolism in medieval literature, see the first section of John W. Velz, "Scatology and Moral Meaning in Two English Renaissance Plays," *South Central Review* 1 (1984): 4–21. Cf. Karl P. Wentersdorf, "The Symbolic Significance of *Figurae Scatologicae* in Gothic Manuscripts," in *Word, Picture, and Spectacle,* ed. Clifford Davidson, Early Drama, Art, and Music Monograph Series 5 (Kalamazoo: Medieval Institute Publications, 1984), 1–19. The two essays, written independently and dealing with different materials from discrete perspectives, arrive at very much the same conclusions about the diabolistic implications of scatology in medieval culture.

[3] Barbara D. Palmer's "The inhabitants of Hell: Devils," in *The Iconography of Hell,* ed. Clifford Davidson and Thomas H. Seiler, Early Drama, Art, and Music Monograph Series 17 (Kalamazoo: Medieval Institute Publications, 1992), 20–40, is the best recent study of devils. Palmer is very informative about the varying forms devils have taken in iconographic history, but does not discuss their language in drama.

[4] Alexander Sackton, "The Paradoxical Encomium in Elizabethan Drama," *Texas Studies in English* 28 (1949): 83–104. Sackton found the term *adoxography* in Arthur Stanley Pease, "Things Without Honor," *Classical Philology* 21 (1926): 27–42.

[5] Walter Kaiser, *Praisers of Folly: Erasmus, Rabelais, Shakespeare,* Harvard Studies in Comparative Literature 25 (Cambridge: Harvard University Press, 1963), is the place to start for the centrality of Erasmus' *Encomium Moriae* in the tradition. Kaiser adds an epilogue on Cervantes and many side-glances at Montaigne. One is more likely to find classical than medieval backgounds in this learned and fluent book.

⁶ All of these but funereal grief and honor are mentioned or discussed in Sackton. Kaiser discusses many of them, including honor (in Falstaff's catechism [231–34]).

⁷ Sackton, "The Paradoxical Encomium," 84–85 *et passim.*

⁸ Pat M. Ryan, "Appian's *Civil Wars* Yet Again as Source for Antony's Oration," *Quarterly Journal of Speech* 44 (1958): 72–73.

⁹ Mikhail Bakhtin, *Rabelais and His World*, trans. Helene Iswolsky (Cambridge: M.I.T. Press, 1968), 1–144.

¹⁰ The *locus classicus* is C. L. Barber, *Shakespeare's Festive Comedy* (Princeton: Princeton University Press, 1959). The approach is also anthropological in most of the ten essays in Barbara A. Babcock, *The Reversible World: Symbolic Inversion in Art and Society* (Ithaca: Cornell University Press, 1978); none deals with materials as early as the Middle Ages. The approach is New Historicist in Michael Bristol's influential *Carnival and Theater: Plebeian Culture and the Structure of Authority in Renaissance England* (New York and London: Methuen, 1985); Bristol sees carnivalesque inversions as critiques of authority in an ongoing agon between the governed and their governors. The approach is more directly Marxist in Robert Weimann's *Shakespeare and the Popular Tradition in the Theater* (Baltimore: John Hopkins University Press, 1978); in Weimann's formulation the Vice or other alternative character, speaking subversively from the privileged space of the platea, challenges authority with impunity. Cf. Peter Stallybrass, "The World Turned Upside Down," in *Matter of Difference*, ed. Valerie Wayne (Ithaca: Cornell University Press, 1991), 201–20.

¹¹ Sandra Billington, *Mock Kings in Medieval Society and Renaissance Drama* (Oxford: Clarendon Press, 1991). Also valuable is the erudite article by Jean Klene C.S.C., "Chaucer's Contribution to a Popular Topos: The World Upside Down," *Viator* 11 (1980): 321–34; she relates inversion to various traditions, including *concordia concors*, and *adynatia* (*impossibilities*), the portrayal of what cannot be, sometimes in utopian terms.

¹² John Edwards, "*Monde Renversé* in Medieval Art," *Early Drama, Art, and Music Review* 15 (1992): 5–12. Edwards finds an exemplar as late as the seventeenth century in Brno, Czechoslovakia (11); the motif is actually as contemporary as William Steig's cartoon in a triptych headed "Man and Beast" in which a hunting dog on its hind legs holds a smoking gun in its forepaws, having just shot its master (*New Yorker*, 2 May 1994, 78).

¹³ John D. Cox, *Shakespeare and the Dramaturgy of Power* (Princeton: Princeton University Press 1989), 22–40. Cox, carefully avoiding the transcendent dimension, strikes at Cultural Materialsim and Marxism from their own vantage grounds, power *sub specie temporis.*

¹⁴ Cox has three fine pages (ibid., 32–34) on the moral and social function of devils in medieval plays. His best sentence perhaps is: "Given the fact that [in the N-Town *Passion Play I*] Satan is dressed as a gaudy court gallant and Jesus as a peasant, it is difficult to see how anyone could construe this devil as a radical popular subverter of oppressive orthodox authority [as some have thought him]" (34). In a study published after the present article's initial appearance in print, Cox

comments on the Devil as a ubiquitous scapegoat for moral and metaphysical evil in Medieval society; see John D. Cox, "The Devil and Society in the English Mystery Plays," *Comparative Drama* 28 (1994): 407–38.

[15] Cited from *The Chester Mystery Cycle*, ed. R. M. Lumiansky and David Mills, EETS, s.s. 3, 9 (London: Oxford University Press, 1974–86), vol. 1. Peter Clark has shown that the alehouse and its proprietor (usually a woman) were, by the fifteenth century, becoming an institution of broad and complex significance at the center of town and village life (*The English Alehouse: A Social History 1200–1830* [London and New York: Longman, 1983], esp. 20–38). It is fitting enough that the joke about the one who is singled out to remain in hell should fall upon an ale-wife who has given short measure.

[16] Quotations in this context are from *The York Plays*, ed. Richard Beadle (London: Edward Arnold, 1982); many of them are closely paralleled by phrasing in the Towneley manuscript.

[17] Cox examines this dimension cogently in *Shakespeare and the Dramaturgy of Power*, 32–34.

[18] Cited from *The N-Town Play*, ed. Stephen Spector, EETS, s.s. 11–12 (Oxford: Oxford University Press, 1991), 1:245–95.

[19] Cited from *The Late Medieval Religious Plays of Bodleian MSS Digby 133 and E Museo 160*, EETS, 283 (Oxford: Oxford University Press, 1982), 1–23.

[20] The thematic subplotting among servants and devils in this play is an early example of the technique that Shakespeare made a trademark of his art in dramatic structure.

[21] Another of the few surviving miracle plays in English, *The Play of the Sacrament*, is as ironic for serious purposes as the St. Paul play. Here adoxography is enacted as well as spoken as the antagonists with blasphemous malice re-enact the Passion of Christ—and when miracles result the perpetrators are converted.

[22] Cited from the A-text: Christopher Marlowe, *Doctor Faustus*, ed. David Bevington and Eric Rasmussen (Manchester: Manchester University Press, 1993); See also B-text 5.2.153.

[23] Cited from *The Complete Works of Shakespeare*, ed. David Bevington, 4th ed. (New York: HarperCollins, 1992).

Melchisedech in Late Medieval Religious Drama

Yumi Dohi

In previous scholarship, the figure of Melchisedech that appears in English, French, and German medieval religious plays has not adequately been subjected to comparative study. The starting point in such a study must be to follow the traditions shaping the priest-king in Genesis as a dramatic, semi-dramatic, or liturgical figure—traditions based on exegetical interpretations and their applications. The following investigation explores the hypothesis that the appearance of Melchisedech as high priest in each instance in medieval drama reflects a particular religious, political, or social viewpoint of the period. The well-established analogy between Melchisedech and a Catholic priest offering the Holy Eucharist, acknowledged along with Baptism as the highest sacrament, suggests a special relation to the Christian liturgy, particularly to the Mass and to the liturgy for the feast of Corpus Christi.[1] At the same time, however, it is equally important to pay attention to his status as a secular king if we are to understand how he may have been depicted on the medieval stage.

The meeting of Abraham and Melchisedech, described in Genesis 14:18–20, was not one of the most popular biblical episodes to be brought on stage in late medieval Europe. In England, only the Chester cycle contains the scene of the patriarch and the king of Salem as a section in a three-part Abraham play (play 4). The French counterpart to this scene is found in *Le Mystère du Viel Testament*, and there are also other examples of French plays that treat Melchisedech.[2] Additionally, Melchisedech appears in various dramatizations from German-speaking regions. He appears in the extant Corpus Christi play (*Fronleichnamsspiel*) from Künzelsau,[3] the *Prozessionsspiel* from Zerbst,[4] the *Prozessionsordnung zum Fronleichnam* from Ingolstadt,[5] and the play of *Sündenfall* (*The Fall of Man*) probably written by Arnold von Immessen.[6]

The story of Abraham and Melchisedech itself in the Bible is short: Abraham, having defeated the four kings and delivered his nephew Lot and his family, goes with them and with his soldiers up to the Valley of Shaveh (Vulgate: *Save*; King's Valley). Melchisedech, the king of Salem and the priest of God Most High, blesses Abraham and brings bread and wine. Abraham in return offers him a tenth of all the spoils.

The typological interpretation of this episode identifies it as a foreshadowing of the Last Supper since Melchisedech offers bread and wine. The exegetical tradition in this case is derived from Psalm 109/110:4 and Hebrews 5:4–6, 6:20, and 7:1–28—passages which define him as the type of Christ who is to be born "according to the order of Melchisedech, and not . . . according to the order of Aaron" as "priest forever." The Messiah, who is to come to deliver the Jewish people from their fate of misery, shall be a priest-king like Melchisedech whose name means "the king of justice." He is also "the king of peace" since the king of Salem rules his land for ever. Thus, as the sovereign priest of God, Melchisedech represents the ideal king.

The two iconographical aspects of the Melchisedech and Abraham scene—that is, Abraham's tithing, and Melchisedech's present of bread and wine—are usually not brought together in individual presentations of this episode.[7] In most cases Melchisedech, whose action is associated with the Eucharist, represents only the offering of bread and wine, whereas Abraham's tithe, being associated with the offering of Abel to God, belongs to another typological tradition and is therefore not visualized in the same space where Melchisedech stands.

The earliest representation of the episode appears in the fifth-century mosaics in S. Maria Maggiore in Rome.[8] In this example Melchisedech holds a large basket of bread, and at his feet stands a jug of wine. In appearance like a nobleman rather than a priest, he offers both bread and wine to Abraham, who is depicted as a commander in the Roman army. The story is here identified with the institution of the Eucharist since God, appearing in the sky, gestures toward Melchisedech, who holds the bread and wine with his hand.[9] There seems to have been no depiction here of Abraham's tithe.

Another interpretive tradition in art, appearing as early as the sixth century, connected Melchisedech with the typology of the Sacrifice.[10] A sixth-century mosaic at Sant'Apollinare in Classe, Ravenna, shows the king of Salem together with Abel, Abraham, and Isaac, who prefigure the Sacrifice of the Lamb, the symbol of Jesus' sacrificial death. Such a reference to Melchisedech appears in the *Supra quae* in the *post consecratio* prayer. According to this interpretation, it is not necessary to depict Abraham as the receiver of Melchisedech's offering insofar as the biblical sacrifices must be given exclusively to God.

Ambrose in his *De Sacramentis* has been given credit for systematizing the typological interpretation of Melchisedech's offering, its connection with the bread and wine at the Last Supper, and its meaning as sacrament.[11] Since reference to the offering of bread and wine introduced by Melchisedech in the Bible acquired a Eucharistic sense and became incorporated into the Mass in the sixth century, he has consistently been given the unique role among Old Testament figures of representing the priest celebrating the Sacrifice of the Mass, and hence he has tended to appear without Abraham in religious art. His figure in a relief in a twelfth-century altarpiece at Klosterneuburg, Austria,[12] is recognizably associated with the Sacrifice of the Mass, presenting bread and wine on the altar, although he wears a crown on his head to show his status as king as well as high priest. Here he is not accompanied by Abraham. This iconography was ultimately given authority by Thomas Aquinas, who affirmed Melchisedech's offering as prefiguration of the Sacrament of the Eucharist.[13]

In German-speaking regions, the Corpus Christi plays and processions commonly incorporated the figures of Melchisedech and Abraham. In the *Ingolstädter Prozessionsordnung*, a short reference indicates that Melchisedech and Abraham were in the procession: "Item Melchisedec mit Abraham."[14] The fact that Melchisedech is listed first here may indicate that he rather than Abraham was being presented as the main figure. The sketchy internal evidence about Melchisedech's appearance in this Corpus Christi procession is, however, supplemented by Neil C. Brooks' discovery of the connection between the unchronological order of its biblical figures and an incunambum version of the *Biblia Pauperum*.[15] In this late-medieval picture Bible, two episodes in the Old Testament are combined, according to their typological meaning, with episodes from the New Testament. Melchisedech and Abraham, together with the story of Manna in Exodus, belong to the Last Supper. The same arrangement is found in Dirk Bouts' altar-painting in St. Peter's

1. In the *Speculum*, Melchisedech wears a mitre surrounded by a crown to demonstrate his double status. *Spiegel menschlicher Behaltnis* (Speyer: Peter Drach,
c.1480/81). Bayerische Staatsbibliothek, Rar. 172.

Church in Louvain, Belgium. On the basis of Brooks' investigation
we can assume that the late-medieval dramatization of the King of
Salem in Ingolstadt was based on his figure in the *Biblia Pauperum*.
This picture book and the *Speculum humanae salvationis*, which
also appealed to a broad range of clergy, nobles, and citizens, were
in fact among the most readily available sources of the time for
shaping the biblical personae in in the visual arts.

The visualization of Melchisedech and Abraham in the later
Biblia Pauperum is typically late medieval. Abraham, having van-
quished the four kings in battle, appears in armor like a knight.
Some soldiers are following him with spears in their hands. Melchisedech, usually wearing vestments like those worn by a bishop,
brings Abraham bread and wine. In the background is a medieval
castle or a city wall, probably representing Jerusalem, the city the

King of Salem rules. Neither the Ingolstadt procession nor the *Biblia Pauperum* depicts the tithing of Abraham (see fig. 1).[16]

In Zerbst, processions with figures from the Old and the New Testaments were presented somewhat more dramatically and involved interpretative commentary. The *Grosses Regie-buch* reports texts that were apparently displayed as part of the *tableaux vivants*—e.g., "Anna cum Ihesu: Hir sal Ihesus gebunden gehenn und Annas als eyn bisco[p] uf der eynen seite, uf der andern seite eyn jude, der die hant zum slan ufhebet, und eynen ry[m] in seiner hant: 'Sic respondes pontifici'" ("Annas with Jesus: Here Jesus shall go being bound and Annas as a bishop on one side, on the other side a Jew, who readies his hand to hit [Jesus], and a rhyme in his hand: 'Thus answers the bishop'").[17] The text is remarkably didactic, emphasizing the importance of the Corpus Christi feast and the Sacrament that was exhibited in the procession. It is therefore natural to believe that Melchisedech's appearance in the Zerbst procession and play was directly associated with the ceremony of Corpus Christi and the Holy Sacrament: "Den ehrete Melchisedech mit brot und weyn / Das solt dyszes sacrament bylde seynn" ("Melchisedech honored him with bread and wine, / That shall be this sacrament's image" [37–38]). Just as in the Ingolstadt procession, the Zerbst procession and play depict Melchisedech as a high priest with bread (wafer) and wine (chalice), showing him exclusively on the occasion in which he blesses Abraham and proposing that he as *auctor sacramenti*[18] represents the Eucharistic offering at the Mass. It is, of course, this aspect that is emphasized in the Corpus Christi liturgy; the text of the first antiphon for the second vespers of this feast reads: "Sacerdos aeternum Christus Dominus secundum ordinum Mechisedech, panem et vinum obtulit."

In the Künzelsau Corpus Christi play likewise Melchisedech and Abraham appear unchronologically after the sacrifice of Isaac. The typological tradition used in the Künzelsau play establishes Melchisedech along with Abel, Abraham, and Isaac as a type of the Sacrifice, thus identifying Melchisedech's offering as the highest among the Old Testament sacrifices. The bread and wine symbolizing the sacrifice of God's Son must be valued more than the offering of an animal by Abel or of a child by Abraham. Thus Melchisedech could rightfully take his place after Abel, Abraham, and Isaac in a Corpus Christi procession or play in order to demon-

strate his dominant position established by the typology of the offering.

Since the Künzelsau Corpus Christi play opens with prayer and
veneration of the Holy Sacrament and closes the first part of its
three-part dramatization of the Bible with Melchisedech, this drama
may claim to have its origin in the liturgy. The offering of bread and
wine by Melchisedech representing the Eucharistic offering at the
Mass is appropriately emphasized at the conclusion of the first part,
once again to assist the audience in recognizing the meaning of the
Corpus Christi feast. Abraham is part of the action since Melchisedech calls attention to his entrance—"Da nu her Abraham, der werd
man, / Allen seinen feinden gesigt an" ("There now comes Abraham, the honored man, who / All his enemies has conquered" [665–
66])—and yet he is not given any words to speak when he receives
the bread and wine. Melchisedech, giving the Eucharistic elements
to the blessed patriarch, alone speaks:

> Ich opfer dir bratt vnd wein,
> Du solt ewiglichen gesegent sein.
> Bey dem opfer soltu verstan,
> Das das alt opfer ein end wurdt han.
> Es kumt ein prister, der wurtt ewig sein,
> Dem wurtt man opfern brat vnd wein.
> Das wurt ein newung ordenung
> Vmb aller welt erlosung. (677–84)

> (I offer you bread and wine,
> You shall be blessed forever.
> From the offering you shall understand
> That the old offering has come to its end.
> A priest comes who will be for ever,
> To whom one will offer bread and wine.
> This will be a new law
> For the salvation of the whole world.)

This speech of Salem's king, anticipating Jesus' words to his disciples at the Last Supper, reflects the systematic interpretation of
Melchisedech's role in the Bible. His clear announcement of the
change in meaning of the sacrificial offering from the old law to the
new—an announcement also proclaimed by the Expositor in the
Chester play (4.121–32)—defines him as the prefiguration of Jesus
who will activate the new law through his sacrificial death. The

sacerdotal aspect of both Melchisedech and Jesus is unmistakably emphasized. In contrast to the Chester Melchisedech who is identified as both priest and "kynge," the Künzelsau Melchisedech is never referred to by his secular title: "Melchisedech der erst priester ist,/ Opffert jm zu der selben frist / Zu grossen eren bratt vnd wein" ("Melchisedech, who is the first priest, / Offers him in this moment/ To his great honor bread and wine" [667–69]).

The offering of Melchisedech is seen as an Old Testament type of sacrifice also in the *Sündenfall* of Arnold von Immessen:

> Dat opper abelis, dat duldige lam,
> Dar van abel to dode quam,
>
> . . .
>
> Dat abraham ysaac to sick nam
> Vnde offerde ysaac, syn junge kynt,
> Dar me ock eynen geistliken syn ynne vint. . . .
>   (2124–31)

> (That sacrifice of Abel, that patient lamb,
> Through which Abel was destined to die,
>
> . . .
>
> That Abraham took Isaac to himself
> And offered Isaac, his young child,
> There I find also a religious sense in it. . . .)

In this Low German play, probably staged on the day of or within the octave of Corpus Christi,[19] Melchisedech is placed after Moses, and this position of his appearance can be interpreted from three hermeneutical points of view: (1) he represents the type of sacrifice; (2) he prefigures the New Covenant of the Messiah, Christ, who is to be included in Melchisedech's sacerdotal order but not born after the order of Aaron, the elder brother of Moses who represents the Old Covenant; and (3) Melchisedech himself prefigures Christ, holding bread and wine which here are offered not to Abraham but on the altar: "Her, dut offer dat schal syn (*hic offert.*) / In dussem kelke brot vnde wyn" ("Here, do offer that shall be [here he offers] / In this chalice bread and wine" [2142–43]). The scene foreshadowing the Eucharist in fact ends with the words "sacerdos in eternum" quoted from the first antiphon of second vespers on the day of Corpus Christi, cited above.

The reason for the appearance of Melchisedech in the German plays and processions is thus quite simple once the typological

2. *Kölner Bibel. Biblia* (Cologne: Bartholomäus von Unckel, c.1478). Universitäts-u. Stadtbibliothek Köln, shelfmark GBIV 3322.

---

significance is understood. And yet a remarkable difference appears in representations of this figure when we compare the printed versions of the *Biblia Pauperum* and the *Speculum humanae salvationis*, on one hand, and the pre-Reformation printed picture Bibles from the western and the northern parts of Germany, on the other hand. In the *Kölner Bibel* (c.1478), the earliest printed Bible in Low German with profuse illustrations, Melchisedech does not look like a priest but is shown unmistakably as a secular king (fig. 2). So is he again in the *Lübecker Bibel* (1494), which follows the *Kölner Bibel* in depicting biblical figures (fig. 3). Similarly, in the *Historienbibel* (Berlin, Staatsbibliothek Preussischer Kulturbesitz, MS. germ., fol. 516) he wears only a royal crown without religious headdress. We thus may assume that the type of Melchisedech as a secular king became dominant in the Low German region in the second half of the fifteenth century and that this depiction then spread, along with the popularity of the picture bibles themselves, further into the northwestern parts of Europe. Later, Melchisedech as a monarch would have been much more welcome to Martin Luther and other reformers than as a priest since the emphasis on him as Salem's king would not suggest a relationship between him and a Roman Catholic bishop at the Mass.

From the standpoint of its iconography the Chester Melchisedech and Abraham scene is exceptional: it contains the complete institution of both the Eucharistic offering of bread and wine and the tithe. The French counterpart to this dramatization, *Le Mystère du Viel Testament*, also consists of the two events as they are presented in the Old Testament, and, as far as I have been able to determine, these are the only examples of this sort among the late medieval English, French, and German dramatizations of this story.

The Chester scene of Abraham and Melchisedech is divided into two parts, one dramatic and another explanatory. The dramatic part contains Abraham's voluntary tithe-making and Melchisedech's offering without any further exegetical anticipation. The explanatory part consists exclusively of the Expositor's speech which interprets the occasion from a theological viewpoint, particularly emphasizing the typological relation between the Old and the New Testaments.

Abraham, who plays the main role in the Chester dramatization, decides voluntarily, therefore ideally as a Christian, to offer a tenth of his plunder to God since he believes it was God who gave him the victory over the four kings. The voluntary character of Abraham's offering is likely to have been derived from the *Stanzaic Life of Christ*, the probable main source for the Chester dramatization of this scene.[20] In both texts Abraham's decision to to give a tenth of his spoils (see *Chester* 4.25–32 and *Stanzaic Life*, 2385–88) occurs before Melchisedech brings him bread and wine. It is thus apparent that Abraham is represented as not knowing in advance of the manner of Melchisedech's welcome.

Melchisedech, being informed by his armiger of Abraham's coming "this ilke night" (*Chester* 4.53), orders the armiger to prepare bread and wine:

> Ah, blessed bee God that is but one.
> Agaynste Abraham will I gonne
> worshipfullye and that anonne,
> myne office to fulfill,
> and presente him with bread and wyne,
> for grace of God is him within. (57–62)

Melchisedech, characterized as a high priest, explains his obligation to "fulfill" his "office." Interestingly, this passage rests entirely on

the basic description in Genesis. No passage in the dramatic text of
the Chester Melchisedech and Abraham scene suggests the typological relationship of this event and the Last Supper.[21]

Thus the exegetical interpretation of the event is left to the
Expositor who subsequently appears before the audience and
speaks:

> In the owld lawe, without leasinge,
> when these too good men were livinge,
> of beastes were there offeringe
> and eke there sacramente.
> But synce Christe dyed one roode-tree,
> in bred and wyne his death remenber wee;
> and at his laste supper our mandee
> was his commandemente.
> (*Chester* 4.121–28)

Here the Expositor's explanation places the Chester Melchisedech
in an interpretive framework similar to the tradition drawn upon by
the Künzelsau play. It is in fact worth noting that there are some
obvious similarities between the speeches of the Chester Expositor
and the Künzelsau *Rector Processionis*. Both define a general idea
of how Melchisedech should be understood for an audience that
possesses only a rudimentary understanding of typology.

The speech of the Chester Expositor contains some theologi-
cally significant remarks: (1) the old style of sacrifice was replaced
by the bread and wine at the Last Supper through Jesus, who died
on the cross to save all mankind; Melchisedech prefigured this
replacement of the sacrifice when he presented bread and wine to
Abraham; (2) Jesus Christ said to his disciples at that time that they
should repeat the Last Supper and/or the washing of feet; (3) all
Christians must therefore repeat "our mandee" to remember the
death of Jesus.[22] In the Künzelsau play, by comparison, the second
and the third of these points, mostly derived from John 13:12–20,
are not clearly mentioned, though of course they may be implied.
However, the first point is very similarly emphasized by the Künzelsau *Rector Processionis* with the only difference being the question
of whether the dogma of transubstantiation is affirmed. In the
Künzelsau play this dogma is unmistakably invoked (670–77),
whereas in the late texts of the Chester play— copies produced after
the Reformation—not even a suggestion of the dogma can be found,

3. *Biblia, mit Glossen nach den Postillen des Nicolaus de Lyra, niederdeutsch* (Lübeck, 1494). Herzog August Bibliothek, Wolfenbüttel, shelfmark Bibel S. 2° 105.

although in the Expositor's speech the figure of Melchisedek "ministers the sacrament," by which bread and wine, the symbols of Christ's offering of himself, are presented with the words of the institution at his Last Supper as an affirmation of subsequent liturgical practice in a manner consistent with the Thirty-Nine Articles of the Church of England:

> Melchysedecke, a pryest to his paye
> to minister that sacramente
> that Christe ordayned the foresayde daye
> in bread and wyne to honour him aye.
> (*Chester* 4.139–42)

In *Le Mystère du Viel Testament*, a gigantic Old Testament play of nearly 50,000 lines, the meeting of Abraham and Melchisedech is dramatized most creatively in comparison with its German and English counterparts. Its narrative content is in part similar to the Chester play, and in fact Rosemary Woolf has advanced the hypothesis that the *Viel Testament* may have been a principal source for the playwright writing or revising the Chester Old Testament plays.[23] The following similarities have been noted between the Chester and *Viel Testament* scenes of Abraham and Melchisedech: (1) Lot plays the third important role; (2) both plays include both Melchisedech's present of bread and wine and Abraham's tithe-making.

There are, however, some differences between these dramatizations which might tend to prove that in this case the Chester play owed little or nothing at all to the *Viel Testament* in the course of its development. In the Chester play, Lot, who offers Melchisedech a royal cup as his tithe, is not Abraham's nephew but his brother—proof that some parts of the Chester dramatization of this scene were taken directly from the Vulgate.[24] Also in the *Viel Testament* Lot does not offer anything to the High Priest but simply mentions his wish to reside again in the city of Sodom, which he had been given by God.

It is worth mentioning that Melchisedech in the *Viel Testament* prepares bread and wine exclusively to fill the appetite and thirst of Abraham and his troop:

> Preparer je vois pain et vin,
> Affin de leur en presenter,

> S'il leur plaist icy arrester,
> Affin qu'ilz soient confortez
> Des grans travaulx qu'ilz ont portez,
> Car jamais on ne fait bataille
> Que le corps d'homme ne travaille
> Et endure beaucoup de peine;
> Par quoy, refection humaine
> De pain et de vin delectable
> Si est droit que je leur en donne.
>   (8191–8202)

> (I am going to prepare bread and wine,
> In order to present them,
> If they should wish to stop here,
> In order that they should be comforted
> From the hard work they have undertaken,
> Because one never fights
> Except without the human body suffering
> And enduring much pain;
> Therefore, human refreshment
> Of bread and delightful wine
> It is fitting that I offer them.)

This scene seems thus to have a basis in realistic representation, for his offering of bread and wine to Abraham and his troop seems grounded in the soldiers' natural needs after their hard work in the battlefield. No dogmatic reasoning is present.

While in the Chester play Abraham's tithe was first motivated only by his own thanksgiving to God, the *Viel Testament*, on the contrary, does not include this voluntary aspect of Abraham's offering. Abraham in the *Viel Testament* mentions his tithe to Melchisedech initially after having received the bread and wine from him and sharing them with his company:

> Abel presenta les presices
> Par sacrifice legitime;
> Je vueil presenter le decime,
> Comme je croy qu'il soit requis,
> De tous les biens que j'ay conquis.
> Melchisedech, prestre de Dieu,
> Les disme des biens de ce lieu
> Je vous donne en oblacion.
>   (8243–50)

(Abel presented the proper thing
As a legitimate [lawful] sacrifice;
I would give the tithe,
Just as I think necessary,
Of all the goods that I have conquered.
Melchisedech, priest of God,
The tithe of the goods from this place
I give you as offering.)

Here, interestingly, it is Abraham's tithe and not Melchisedech's bread and wine that is regarded as the offering ("oblacion"), categorized as the second legitimate sacrifice after Abel's. The passage shows no clear differentiation between the offering and the tithe, and consequently Abraham in this play is not the pioneer of tithing that he is in the Chester play, for instead he is a follower of the tradition of making sacrifice that Abel first established. This is a fundamental difference in interpretation.

Melchisedech in the *Viel Testament* is presented consistently as a high priest—"Souverain prestre" (8218), "le grant prestre," (8228), "prestre de Dieu" (8248)—but without being specifically identified as associated with either the priest in the Mass or Jesus at the Last Supper. In actual production he probably was represented as a Jewish high priest as typically depicted in the visual arts when showing figures from the Old Testament; and quite possibly his costume would have reflected the lack of interest in typology. In any case, the Abraham-Melchisedech scene in the *Viel Testament* does not share the same tradition as its German counterparts, which in contrast stress the symbolic figure of the Sacrament of the Eucharist and hence also the relationship to the Catholic priests or bishops who are privileged to perform the sacramental act which is the Eucharist.[25]

By way of conclusion, we can observe that within the German-speaking regions, particularly in its southern parts, the connection between the dramatization of the Melchisedech-Abraham episode and the liturgy must be seen as very close. Melchisedech, wearing the vestments of a priest or bishop and holding bread (wafer) and wine (a chalice) in his hands, presumably appeared like the figure seen in the *Biblia Pauperum*, or he might have worn the mitre-crown headdress of the *Speculum humanae salvationis*. He appeared outside of the chronological order recorded in the Bible since the German dramatizations of this scene were less concerned with the normal sequence of history and instead focused on matters liturgical and theological—especially on typology. The strong association of the episode with the feast of Corpus Christi is reflected in the form of presentation to the extent that Abraham's institution of tithe-making is omitted. Exclusively in the northern and the north-western parts of the German-speaking area, another tradition also developed that would shape Melchisedech as a secular king and contemporary, as we have seen.

It seems provable that originally the Chester Melchisedech, de-spite his title as a priest-king, followed the same tradition as the German dramatizations of this figure. His iconography, which is found exclusively in the description by the Expositor after the dramatic presentation, clarifies the typological relation between him and Jesus Christ at the Last Supper; further, he is also regarded as a priest ordained to minister the Sacrament—an interpretation which links him with typical liturgical acts and which appears most strikingly in the stage directions in MS. Harley 2124: "Mel-chis[edech] extendens manus ad coelum"; "Tunc Melchisedech equitabit versus Abraham et offerrit calecem cum vino et panem super patenam."[26] While a direct connection has not been identified to relate the choice of this episode to the Feast of Corpus Christi within the Chester plays, nevertheless the typological reference in the Expositor's speech still suggests the possibility that this feast might have been a reason to present Melchisedech in the repertoire of the cycle before the Chester cycle was transferred to Whitsun week. In any case, Melchisedech was a regular figure in the pro-cession of Corpus Christi, as Lydgate notes in his poem celebrating the feast:

> Remembreþe eeke in youre Inwarde entente
>   Melchysedec, þat offred bred and wyne,
> In fygure oonly of þe sacrament,
>   Steyned in Bosra, on Calvarye made red,
>   On Sherthorsday to-fore er he was ded,
> For memoryal mooste souereyne and goode,
>   Gaf hees appostels, takeþe here off goode heed,
> His blessid body and his precyous bloode.[27]

The appearance of Melchisedech in the extant Chester play could possibly provide at least a hint concerning the problem of the origin of the cycle since this figure does point toward a connection with

Corpus Christi, a feast that was introduced into England in approx-imately 1318.[28]

The French Melchisedech in the *Viel Testament* must, as noted above, have been informed by a tradition different from that which stood behind both its German and English counterparts. For the author of the Abraham play in the *Viel Testament* it was more im-portant to retain the narrative coherence within the whole Abraham story as "a story" rather than to meddle with the dogma. The atti-tude that was taken in the adaptation of the biblical story was that of a dramatist who was interested in a realistic depiction of past events, especially when he allowed Melchisedech to speak of his motivation for presenting bread and wine to Abraham and his troop. This approach is very different from that taken by the Chester play-wright, as noted above.

Undoubtedly the Corpus Christi processions and/or plays were most brilliant religious functions in many late medieval cities throughout Europe. This is an observation that also holds true for Italian and Spanish cities. We can observe, for example, Gentile Bellini's painting (now in the Galleria dell'Academia, Venice) of what is probably a typical example of a Corpus Christi procession at the Place San Marco in Venice (1496). Shown in this painting are many prominent civic leaders joining in the procession along with the clergy and laity who are escorting the golden reliquary in which the relic of the True Cross, the most precious relic belonging to the Cathedral of San Marco and evidence for the sacrificial death of Christ, is enshrined. Further research concerning the possible ap-pearance of Melchisedech in Italian or Spanish processions is clearly in order.

But German processions also seem to have been lavishly splendid. In Zerbst, the *Fronleichnamsprozession* in 1506 was also magnificently presented in the presence of political and religious dignitaries such as the Cardinal of Gurk and the Archbishop of Magdeburg, who was at the same time the Duke of Saxony, the Landgrave of Doringen, and the Margrave of Meissen.[29] This pro-cession was presented on the last day of the octave of Corpus Christi with figures from the Old and New Testaments.[30] Since the city of Zerbst did not have any special relics to match the Host, the Holy Body of Christ itself was the focal point of the procession.[31] In front of the dignitaries, the "Melchisedech and Abraham" scene was possibly brought out in which these figures were depicted as a

Catholic high priest and a knight just as in the *Biblia Pauperum* or even in the *Speculum humanae salvationis*—that is, wearing the mitre with crown. As a living picture of social stratification and of the power relationships between the religious and the secular orders, reflecting the present archbishop who also holds high secular titles, the procession must have represented the ecclesiastical and secular realities that formed the basic structure of the society of the day.

NOTES

[1] For Melchisedech as a priest at Mass, see Lynette R. Muir, "The Mass on the Medieval Stage," *Comparative Drama* 23 (1989–90): 320.

[2] *Le Mystère du Viel Testament*, ed. James de Rothschild (Paris: SATF, 1878). Muir identifies another mention of Melchisedech from French-speaking areas: in the prologue to the first Lille Abraham play (it is reported "that Melchisedek will offer bread and wine 'en priant pour lui' . . . but [the playwright] does not stage the meeting") (Muir, "The Mass on the Medieval Stage," 320). For the Chester cycle, see *The Chester Mystery Cycle*, ed. R. M. Lumiansky and David Mills, EETS, s.s. 3, 9 (London: Oxford University Press, 1974–86).

[3] *Das Künzelsauer Fronleichnamsspiel*, ed. Peter K. Liebenow (Berlin: Walter de Gruyter, 1965).

[4] *Das Zerbster Prozessionsspiel 1507*, ed. Willem Reupke (Berlin and Leipzig: Walter de Gruyter, 1930). See also Bernd Neumann, *Geistliches Schauspiel in Zeugnis der Zeit*, 2 vols. (Munich: Artemis Verlag, 1987), 1:781– 809.

[5] Neil C. Brooks, "An Ingolstadt Corpus Christi Procession and the *Biblia Pauperum*," *Journal of English and Germanic Philology* 35 (1936): 1–16; Neumann, *Geistliches Schauspiel*, 1:408–11.

[6] Arnold Immessen, *Der Sündenfall*, ed. Friedrich Krage (Heidelberg: Carl Winter, 1913).

[7] Louis Réau, *Iconographie de l'art Chrétien*, 3 vols. (Paris: Presses Universitaires de France, 1955–59), 3:128–29.

[8] G. Seib, "Melchisedech," in *Lexikon der Christlichen Ikonographie*, ed. Engelbert Kirschbaum *et al.*, 8 vols. (Frieburg i. Breisgau: Herder, 1968–76), 3:241–42.

[9] Ibid., 3:241–42.

[10] Ibid., 3:242.

[11] See Miri Rubin, *Corpus Christi: The Eucharist in Late Medieval Culture* (Cambridge: Cambridge University Press, 1991), 129–31.

[12] Altarpiece (completed in 1181), by Nikolaus von Verdun, in the Stift Klosterneuburg.

[13] Thomas Aquinas, *Summa Theologia*, Q. LXXIII, Art. 6.

[14] Neumann, *Geistliches Schauspiel*, 1:409.

[15] Brooks, "An Ingolstadt Corpus Christi Procession," 8.

[16] In the printed versions of the *Biblia Pauperum*, his figure does not have a crown, whereas he has the mitre with a crown in the *Speculum humanae salvationis* from Speyer (see fig. 1, above). Manuscript versions of the *Biblia Pauperum*, however, show both mitre and crown, as in the case of the example from Peter Cloister, Erfurt (1350–60), now in the Staatsbibliothek at Weimar, Cod. max.4.

[17] Neumann, *Geistliches Schauspiel*, 1:785. Another, and perhaps better, example is as follows: "Die bruwer knechte: S. Petrus mit eynem langen mantel, eyn diadem; in eyner hant eynen rym: 'Nescio quid dicis?' In der lincken hant eynem rym: 'Non novi hominem.' Zu ichlilcher seite eyne maget mit rymen. Die eyn: 'Et tu cum Ihesu Naszareno eras,' die ander: 'Et hic era[t] cum Ihesu Naszareno'" ("The brewery servants: St. Peter with a long coat, a diadem; in one hand a rhyme: 'I do not know what you mean.' In his left hand a rhyme: 'I do not know the man.' On each side a young woman with rhymes. One of them: 'And you were with Jesus of Nazareth,' the other: 'And this man was with Jesus of Nazareth'" [ibid.]).

[18] Ambrose, *De Sacramentis* IV C.3.10; *PL*, 16:457.

[19] Immessen, *Der Sündenfall*, 71.

[20] See Frances Foster, ed., *A Stanzaic Life of Christ*, EETS, o.s. 166 (London, 1926), xlii. Peter Travis, however, does not mention the Abraham play in his list of probable sources in his *Dramatic Design in the Chester Cycle* (Chicago: University of Chicago Press, 1982), 50–51.

[21] See my article "Ein gewisser protestantischer Einfluss? Eine vergleichende Untersuchung der Handschriften Huntington 2 und Harley 2124 des 'Chester Cycle'," in *Mittelalterliches Schauspiel: Festschrift für Hansjürgen Linke zum 65. Geburtstag*, ed. U. Mehler and A. Touber (Amsterdam: Editions Rodopi, 1994), 161–82.

[22] Concerning the word 'mandee,' see ibid., 174.

[23] Rosemary Woolf, *The English Mystery Plays* (London: Routledge and Kegan Paul, 1972), 306.

[24] See *The Chester Mystery Cycle*, ed. Lumiansky and Mills, 2:46.

[25] The tradition of costuming the Jewish high priests in a way similar to Catholic bishops finds expression in a stage direction in the N-town collection: "*Here xal Annas shewyn hymself in his stage beseyn aftyr a busshop of þe hoold lawe in a skarlet gowne, and ouyr þat a blew tabbard furryed with whyte, and a mytere on his hed after þe hoold lawe*" (*The N-Town Play*, ed. Stephen Spector, EETS, s.s. 11–12 [Oxford: Oxford University Press, 1992], 1:252). In the *St. Galler Passionsspiel* (*Das Mittelrheinische Passionsspiel der St. Galler Handschrift 919*, ed. Rudolf Schütyeichel [Tübingen: Niemeyer, 1978]), Caiphas is called "Herre bischof" (567).

[26] The text edited by Lumiansky and Mills from Huntington MS. 2 provides instead the following English stage directions: "Here Mechysedech, lookinge up to heaven, doth thanke God for Abrahams victorye, and doth prepare himselfe to goe present Abraham"; "Mechysedech, comminge unto Abraham, doth offer to him a cuppe of wynne and bred" (4.56 *s.d.*, 72 *s.d.*).

[27] John Lydgate, *The Minor Poems*, ed. Henry Noble MacCracken, EETS, e.s.

107 (London, 1911), 36.

[28] Rubin, *Corpus Christi*, 199.

[29] Neumann, *Geistliches Schauspiel*, 1:782.

[30] Ibid.

[31] Ibid., 1:785. It is mentioned here that the figures (of the twelve apostles) had to remain standing for a long time "vor dem sacrament" until Jesus was arrested. The description does not specify where the Sacrament was exhibited during the procession—i.e., whether in the procession, or on/before the altar built on the street.

A Spoon and the Christ Child

Mikiko Ishii

The symbolic meaning of the gifts in the Shepherds plays in the Towneley collection have received much attention and have been frequently and intensively studied. However, the significance of the homely and rustic gifts in the other Shepherds plays still remain to be explored fully. In particular, the gift of a spoon has never been examined.

The roots of the symbolic naturalism presently under discussion here have been traced back to a statement by St. Thomas Aquinas; Erwin Panofsky, writing of the disguised symbolism of the Master of Flémalle (fl. 1406–44), quotes Aquinas' terminology: "spiritualia sub metaphoris corporalium."[1] Physical appearances were thus indeed frequently interpreted in the arts as "corporal metaphors of things spiritual." Disguised symbolism, though inherent in medieval iconographic practice previously, emerged as a concomitant of the perspective interpretations of space in the Italian trecento and reached its highest development in the great Flemish painters. Ingvar Bergström has noted that this period not unnaturally coincides "more or less with the happy, rich period in the history of symbolic sacred art between the Council at Constance (1414–18) and that at Trent (1545–63)."[2]

One of the most remarkable paintings from this period when hidden meaning was attached to everyday objects is the *Holy Family* (fig. 1), attributed to Joos van Cleve (c.1490–1540), at the Metropolitan Museum of Art, New York. Almost all the attributes associated with Jesus and the Virgin Mary are on display. On a narrow ledge in the foreground are placed a covered glass vessel of wine, half of a walnut, a knife, and a pewter dish containing fruit. On the shelf behind the family, there are a glass vessel and a wooden box. These are all objects laden with symbolic meaning. Wine, like bread, is a Eucharistic symbol, while a knife is a symbol of circumcision and sacrifice, potentially emblematic of Christ. On the pewter dish are: a pomegranate, typifying the Resurrection; Eucharistic grapes; an apple, regarded as a sign of original sin to be

1. *Holy Family, with Jesus at His Mother's Breast.* Attributed to Joos van Cleve. The Metropolitan Museum of Art, New York. Bequest of Michael Friedsam, 1931. The Friedsam Collection. (32.100.57)

overcome by Christ's act of sacrifice; cherries, symbolic of the Incarnation; and a pear, a symbol of redemption. The apple that the Child holds may be a sign of his bearing the weight of man's sins, while the glass vessel and wooden box on the shelf are very likely designed as maternal symbols.[3] Even the whisk hanging under the shelf may be intended as a symbol of the perfection of the Mother, who is commonly described as characterized by her "cleanness" on account of her virginity and her immaculate conception.

It is thus interesting to find that the homely gifts offered by the English shepherds in the English drama have parallels in Northern European paintings, particularly in Flemish paintings of the fifteenth and sixteenth centuries. In the *Prima Pastorum* in the Towneley manuscript,[4] one shepherd offers a spruce coffer, another a ball, and a third a gourd bottle, while in the *Secunda Pastorum* the offerings are a bird, a ball, and a bob of cherries. The symbolic values of the gifts in the latter play in relation to Continental tradition have already been thoroughly examined by Lawrence J. Ross[5] and E. B. Cantelupe and Richard Griffith.[6] The bird, the ball, and the cherry are among the most common attributes of the Christ Child and represent his divinity, his kingship, and his incarnation and sacrifice on the cross. The three gifts in the *Prima Pastorum* seem to present similar symbolism. The little spruce coffer offered by the First Shepherd may represent "the evergreen nature of man's spirit which aspires toward heaven," while the Third Shepherd's gourd may be a sign for the work of the Incarnation, as John P. Cutts has suggested.[7] Also, a bottle, which contains water, may (like the box) be a symbol of the maternal body. In a number of paintings of the Virgin and Child resting during the Flight to Egypt in the fifteenth and sixteenth centuries, a gourd bottle is placed at the feet of the Virgin or is carried by Joseph on the end of a stick. Filled with wine or water, it will provide the Holy Family with refreshment on the journey. Several versions of this theme were painted by Joachim Patinir (1485–1524); in one example at the National Museum, Stockholm, the Child is holding a ball (a symbol of his kingship) in his right hand, a bird (a sign of his divinity) in his left, while at the feet of the Virgin lies a gourd bottle.[8]

In the Shrewsbury fragments, perhaps from a neighborhood in Cheshire or north Staffordshire, a horn spoon is presented to the Christ Child by a shepherd (III Pastor).[9] In the corresponding play in the York cycle, one shepherd offers a brooch with a tin bell, another two cob-nuts (hazelnuts) on a ribbon, and the third a horn spoon.[10] In the Chester Shepherds' plays, Primus Pastor offers a bell, Secundus Pastor a set comprising a flask and spoon, and Tertius Pastor a cap, while the master's boys offer a bottle, a hood, a pipe, and a nuthook.[11] The Shepherds' gifts in the Coventry Shearmen and Taylors' play are a pipe, a hat, and mittens.[12] All these articles are characteristic of rural life and have equivalents in medieval pastoral literature.[13] While they are necessary accouterments of the pastoral vocation, they also are likely to convey symbolic significance. For example, the nuthook and pipe (a musical instrument) may be connected with the role of the Child as the Savior of the soul and the embodiment of the principle of harmony in the cosmos.

The bell, useful for shepherds to keep track of their sheep, has long had symbolic value, even being interpreted as a symbol of fertility[14] or as an attribute of the fool. As Sandra Billington demonstrates in her book *A Social History of the Fool*, at the basis of Christian belief about the fool lies St. Paul's teaching, which insists that the Christian is a fool in the eyes of the world.[15] The greatest fool of all, of course, is Christ himself. The bell was also felt to be a useful defense against the devil, who in fact was believed to be fearful of bells.[16] The symbolism of the nut, though usually depicted as a half of a split walnut, was held to refer to Christ: the outer green case is the flesh of Christ, the shell the wood of his cross, and the kernal his divine nature.[17] The spruce coffer, on the other hand, is not only a feminine symbol, suggestive of the mother of the Redeemer, but also an ordinary wooden box such as those carried by shepherds for keeping needles or tar, the latter used as a healing agent to treat lacerations or cuts in the skin of sheep (e.g., at shearing time).

Special attention should, however, be given to the gifts of Secundus Pastor in the Chester Shepherds play who presents the Child with a set comprising a flask and a spoon:

> Hayle, the emperour of hell
> and of heaven alsoe;
> the feynd shalt thow fell,
> that ever hath binne fals.
>
> Hayle, the maker of the stare
> that stoode us beforne;

hayle, the blessedesfull baronne
that ever was borne.
Loe, sonne, I bringe thee a flackett.
Therby hanges a spoone
for to eat thy pottage with at noone,
as I myselfe full oftetymes have donne.
With hart I praye thee to take yt.[18]

It is clear from this speech that Secundus Pastor regards his gift, humble as it may seem to be, as very appropriate for the Child, "emperour of hell," "maker of the stare." As for the flask, here called a "flackett" (an alternate word is 'flaggen' or 'flaggette'), this term denoted a sort of small flask. A metal bottle with a screw cap such as was carried by pilgrims is also a possibility, however. Interestingly, a clear glass flask, partially filled with liquid (wine, presumably), is often depicted in the Annunciation or Madonna and Child. Carol J. Purtle comments on the significance of the glass vessel in Flemish paintings:

> This transparent vessel filled with light has traditionally been interpreted as a reference to the virgin birth of Christ. As the light passed through this glass, illuminating before passing beyond, so "the word of God, the splendor of the Father, entered the virgin chamber and then came forth from the closed womb." Taken in terms of the general meaning, then, the glass vessel becomes . . . [a] symbol of the womb of the Virgin. . . . Christ is light, and the womb of the Virgin receives that light and allows it to pass on to the space beyond.[19]

Significantly, the pairing of the spoon and the flask makes its appearance in the *Virgin and Child with Four Saints* by Rogier van der Weyden (1400–64) in the Städelsches Kunstinstitut, Frankfurt.[20] One of the two doctors at the right of the Virgin nursing the Child is holding a flask in his right hand, while the other doctor holds a spoon. As the Chester shepherd says in presenting the spoon to the Child, it is a useful utensil for eating soup, but it is unlikely that the writer of the Chester play is not conscious also of the symbolic meaning in his pairing of "flackett" and spoon.

The spoon thus is given as a gift to the Christ Child in three English pageants. It is not surprising that the spoons given in the York play and the Shrewsbury fragment are made of horn because this material would be most easily available to actual shepherds. The spoon of the York Shepherd can hold forty peas, and hence it

2. Gerard David, *Madonna à la Soupe au Lait*. Koninklijk Instituut voor het Kunstpatrimonium, Brussels.

may have been used not only for eating soup but also as a measure of volume. Peas often formed a significant portion of the diet of the poor in the Middle Ages.[21]

The Christ Child is actually depicted holding a spoon in the *Madonna à la Soupe au Lait* (fig. 2) by Gerard David (1460–1523), a painter whose work was associated with the city of Bruges. This

3. Gerard David, *Virgin and Child Resting during the Flight to Egypt.* Prado Museum, Madrid.

painting, very much admired in its day, shows the Virgin seated at a table and about to feed milk soup to her Child with another spoon made of wood, while the Child himself is grasping his spoon and fixing his attention on it. Actually the *Madonna à la Soupe au Lait* exists in six versions,[22] and further there is another painting on the same subject by David but with cherries substituted for the implement originally held by the Child.[23] A sprig from a cherry tree with seven cherries was painted over the wooden spoon which the artist had originally placed in the infant's hand. Lawrence Ross comments on this alteration: "it is perhaps understandable that a student of the painting has balked at the idea that the fruit has any more symbolic significance than than spoon."[24] Nevertheless, all the other versions of the same subject by David retain the spoon, and he has also used the same motif of the wooden spoon held by the Child in the *Virgin and Child Resting during the Flight to Egypt* in the Prado (fig. 3). Thus it is not possible to favor the assumption that replacing the spoon with cherries "resulted from the demand for a detail of established symbolic propriety."[25]

However, in versions of the *Virgin and Child Resting during the Flight to Egypt* by David in the Metropolitan Museum, New York, and in the Prado the Child does not hold anything, though a twig with small apples is laid beside the Mother nursing the Child.[26] In yet another version of David's painting, in the National Gallery of Art, Washington, D.C. (fig. 4), the Child is holding a bunch of grapes. The grapes and apples clearly have symbolic meaning, and the objects held by the Child always in other instances signal the central meaning of the painting. Hence it is very plausible that, like such objects as grapes, apples, and cherries,[27] the spoon held by the Christ Child also should have symbolic meaning, specifically in his role as conqueror of the infernal powers as the "emperour of hell."

Interestingly, the paintings by David in which a spoon is depicted usually represent the Virgin nursing the Child. That the pairing of the milk (Mother) and spoon (Child) is unlikely to have been an accident is proved by its frequent appearance also in the paintings of David's contemporaries and followers. For instance, in the *Virgin and Child* by Quintin Matsys (1465–1530) a bowl of milk with a wooden spoon in it is placed before the Mother and Child.[29] In the *Adoration of the Shepherds* by Maarten van Heemskerck (1498–1574) at the Wallraf-Richartz Museum in Cologne, a bowl of milk is placed on the table where the Child is lying.[30] In the

4. Gerard David, *Virgin and Child Resting during Flight to Egypt.* Andrew W. Mellon Collection, National Gallery of Art, Washington, D.C.

Adoration of the Shepherds by Jacob Jordans (1494–1578) at the Metropolitan Museum of Art, New York, St. Joseph is holding a candle in his right hand and a bowl of milk with a wooden spoon in his left while the Virgin is nursing the Child.[31] We may wonder if the interest in the milk ingested by the Child was connected with popular devotion, for at Bruges there was a cult of the relic of

Mary's milk which was believed to have nourishing and healing power.[32] In England, relics of the Virgin's milk were venerated at Walsingham, Coventry, Waltham Abbey, and elsewhere.[33] But the use of the spoon in the paintings, and in the plays, is certainly connected with the paradox of the Christ Christ (being fed) as the nourisher of mankind.

Superficially, then, the homely gifts of the shepherds in the English plays are most appropriate to the rustic shepherds and to the poverty of the Holy Family.[34] But in spite of their apparent simplicity they are extremely significant attributes of the Christ Child in an age not yet affected by ideas that contradicted the notion of physical things being "corporal metaphors of things spiritual." Other layers of symbolism are of course available from the study of archetypes and folklore,[35] but it is not possible to deal with such matters in the present paper.[36]

NOTES

[1] *Summa Theologia* I, qu. I, art. 9c, as quoted by Erwin Panofsky, *Early Netherlandish Painting*, 2 vols. (Cambridge: Harvard Univ. Press, 1953), 1:142.

[2] Ingvar Bergström, "Disguised Symbolism in 'Madonna' Pictures and Still Life, II," *Burlington Magazine* 97 (1955): 348.

[3] Ibid., 347.

[4] References to the Towneley plays are to *The Six Pageants in the Towneley Cycle*, ed. Mikiko Ishii *et al.* (Tokyo: Society for Medieval English Drama, 1987).

[5] Lawrence J. Ross, "Symbol and Structure in the *Secunda Pastorum*," *Comparative Drama* 1 (1967): 122–49.

[6] See E. B. Cantelupe and Richard Griffith, "The Gifts of the Shepherds in the Wakefield 'Secunda Pastorum': An Iconographical Interpretation," *Mediaeval Studies* 28 (1966): 328–35.

[7] John P. Cutts, "The Shepherds' Gifts in *The Second Shepherds' Play* and Bosch's *Adoration of the Magi*," *Comparative Drama* 4 (1970): 122.

[8] Görel Cavalli-Björkman, *Dutch and Flemish Paintings, 1: c.1400–c.1600* (Stockholm: National Museum, 1986), no. 51.

[9] *Non-Cycle Plays and Fragments*, ed. Norman Davis, EETS, s.s. 1 (London: Oxford University Press, 1970), 2.

[10] *The York Plays*, ed. Richard Beadle (London: Edward Arnold, 1982), 132.

[11] *The Chester Mystery Cycle*, ed. David Mills and R. M. Lumiansky, EETS, s.s. 3, 9 (London: Oxford University Press 1974–86), 1:150–53.

[12] *Two Coventry Corpus Christi Plays*, ed. Hardin Craig, 2nd ed., EETS, e.s. 87 (London: Oxford University Press, 1957), 11–12.

[13] Helen Cooper, *Pastoral: Medieval into Renaissance* (Ipswich: D. S.

Brewer, 1977), 50–71.

[14] Ad de Vries, *Dictionary of Symbols and Imagery*, 2nd ed. (London and Amsterdam: North-Holland, 1976), 44.

[15] Sandra Billington, *A Social History of the Fool* (Brighton: Harvester Press, 1984), 16–20.

[16] William Durandus, *The Symbolism of Churches and Church Ornaments, being a Translation of the First Book of the Rationale Divinorum Officiorum*, trans. John Mason Neale and Benjamin Webb (London: Gibbings, 1893), 71.

[17] Gertrude Grace Sill, *A Handbook of Symbols in Christian Art* (London: Cassell, 1976), 55.

[18] *Chester Mystery Cycle*, 150 (ll. 563–75).

[19] Carol J. Purtle, *The Marian Paintings of Jan van Eyck* (Princeton: Princeton University Press, 1982), 33.

[20] Martin Davies, *Rogier van der Weyden* (London: Phaidon, 1972), fig. 73.

[21] See Fernand Baudel, *The Structures of Everyday Life*, rev. Siân Reynolds (Berkeley and Los Angeles: University of California Press, 1992), 112–14.

[22] These paintings are located at Brussels, Bruges, Genoa, Strasbourg, Prague, and New York; see J. van Miegroet, *Gerard David* (Antwerp: Mercatorfonds, 1989), 302–03.

[23] R. Langton Douglas, "*La Vierge à la Soupe au Lait* by Gerard David," *Burlington Magazine* 88 (1946): 290; see also Leo van Puyvelde, *The Flemish Primitives*, trans. D. I. Wilton (London: Collins, 1948), pl. 99.

[24] Ross, "Symbol and Structure," 131.

[25] Ibid., 147n. I would like to express my gratitude to Finola Hurley for drawing my attention to the Child holding a spoon in David's *Virgin and Child Resting during the Flight to Egypt*.

[26] The version in the Prado is reproduced in Van Miegroet, *Gerard David*, pl. 234.

[27] See E. de Jongh, "Grape Symbolism in Paintings of the 16th and 17th Centuries," *Simiolus* 7 (1974): 166–91.

[28] For a symbolic spoon in Italian art, see Sandro Botticelli's *St. Augustine and the Child with a Spoon* (San Barnaba Altarpiece, Uffizi, Florence). This painting "illustrates the legend of the child who was attempting to empty the sea into a hole in the sand with a spoon. When the saint dryly remarked on the futility of this exercise, the child answered that it was no more hopeless than Augustine's attempt to achieve a rational understanding of the Trinity" (Martin Kemp, "The Taking and Use of Evidence; with a Botticellian Case Study," *Art Journal* 44 [1984]: 211, fig. 6).

It is more significant to the iconography of the spoon under consideration in this paper that this implement was used as one of the items of the English coronation regalia. The anointing spoon from the twelfth century is extant; see John Cannon and Ralph Griffiths, *The Oxford Illustrated History of the British Monarchy* (Oxford: Oxford University Press, 1988), 116. Interestingly, in ancient China the constellation of the Great Dipper, which was interpreted to look like a spoon, was a symbol of the Emperor. In an unpublished lecture on the "Consecration of the Japanese Emperor" (Japan Christian Center, Tokyo, April 1989), a Japanese folklorist, Yuko Yoshino, noted that the oldest compass in China is in the shape of a spoon and that the Emperor, like the Great Dipper, is the guide of the people in darkness. The Emperor, the son of the supreme God, offers food to his Father, represented by the Pole Star just as the Great Dipper seems to do. There is a comparison with an essential part of the ritual of the Consecration of the Japanese Emperor, a religious communion of sharing food.

[29] Van Puyvelde, *The Flemish Primitives*, pl. 118. For another example, see *The Virgin and Child* (c.1520) attributed to Simon Bening, a Flemish painter contemporary with David, at the Metropolitan Museum of Art. In this painting the Child, who is nursing, holds a spoon.

[30] Ilja M. Veldman, *Maarten van Heemskerck and Dutch Humanism in the Sixteenth Century*, trans. Michael Hoyle (Amsterdam: Meulenhoff, 1977), pl. 17.

[31] Walter A. Liedtke, *Flemish Paintings in the Metropolitan Museum of Art* (New York: Metropolitan Museum of Art, 1984), color pl. IX, pl. 52.

[32] Van Miegroet, *Gerard David*, 242.

[33] For the Coventry St. Mary's Cathedral relic list, see Clifford Davidson and Jennifer Alexander, *The Early Art of Coventry, Stratford-upon-Avon, Warwick, and Lesser Sites in Warwickshire*, Early Drama, Art, and Music Reference Series 4 (Kalamazoo: Medieval Institute Publications, 1984), 171; for Waltham Abbey, see Nicholas Rogers, "The Waltham Abbey Relic-List," in *England in the Eleventh Century: Proceedings of the 1990 Harlaxton Symposium*, ed. Carola Hicks (Stamford: Paul Watkins, 1992), p. 179. For Walsingham and other sites, see Edmund Waterton, *Pietas Mariana Britannica: A History of English Devotion to the Blessed Virgin Marye* (London: St. Joseph's Catholic Library, 1879), 195–205.

[34] The meaning of the spoon in folklore would, of course, be a separate study which would note "love spoons" given to girls as a token of affection by boys and christening spoons presented to children at their christening.

[35] A word should probably be added concerning the gift of headgear to the Child in the Chester and Coventry plays. These gifts represented useful garments, but again would seem to have symbolic value. Helen Cooper points out that the hat became one of the marks of the Good Shepherd in medieval pastoral literature (*Pastoral*, 53). A hood might also imply a certain level of folkloric understanding of the situation—a hint that the Child is regarded by the shepherds as a guardian spirit of the type identified by Hilda Ellis Davidson; see her "Myth and Symbols in Religion and Folklore," *Folklore*: 100 (1989): 105–42, and "Hooded Men in Celtic and Germanic Tradition," *Cosmos* 5 (1989): 105—24.

[36] I wish to thank Hilda Davidson and Richard Axton for their many helpful ideas during the preparation of the present essay.

English Law
in the York Trial Plays

Elza Tiner

While the Passion sequence of the York mystery plays is broadly based on the New Testament, the pageants depicting the trials of Christ employ English legal procedures not in Scripture or in any of the other sources for the plays.[1] The six trial scenes (*The Conspiracy* [play 26]; *Christ before Annas and Caiaphas* [29]; *Christ before Pilate 1* [30]; *Christ before Herod* [31]; *The Remorse of Judas* [32]; and *Christ before Pilate 2* [33]) are connected by the progress of a case of heresy and treason through ecclesiastical and secular courts.[2] In the trials, Christ becomes one of the local citizens, convicted and crucified through the English judicial system, by which he redeems them all. Thus the abuses of the law by Christ's accusers become a kind of inverted mirror, instructing members of the audience to respect their own legal system and to use it justly.

The York trial plays are, of course, part of a larger cycle of approximately fifty biblical plays depicting the history of the world from Creation to Doomsday which were performed annually in York on the feast of Corpus Christi from possibly as early as 1376 until the latter half of the sixteenth century. Subjected to numerous revisions and annotations, the manuscript of the plays is dated c.1475,[3] a date which is important when considering the legal ramifications of the trial scenes in the plays.

Legal references in the York plays suggest an author or authors with knowledge of the English courts. R. H. Nicholson, who has examined the procedures by which Christ is tried as a sorcerer, comments on the sophisticated use of law in the trials to convey the religious message, the contrast between earthly and divine justice.[4] In her analysis of the York trial plays, Pamela King suggests that the point of the legal proceedings in these plays is not only to depict events from Scripture, but also to warn the audience against obeying evil authority. She believes that for the contemporary York audience in particular, the plays could have resonated historically with the trial of Archbishop Scrope, who was convicted of treason and put to death for leading a rebellion against Henry IV in 1405.[5]

Trial scenes and legal references are not unique to the York plays. Jody Enders, exploring the parallels between legal rhetoric and medieval French drama, argues broadly for the influences of courtroom oratory on the dramatic dialogue in medieval plays.[6] Lynn Squires has demonstrated that the author of the N-Town plays had considerable knowledge of English law and incorporated such background into the court scenes to make them plausible and effective for a contemporary audience.[7] Likewise, the ecclesiastical and secular courts in the York plays create a powerful dramatic context for the events of Scripture.

Fifteenth-century York was a center of ecclesiastical courts which could have served as models for the process in *Christ before Annas and Caiaphas*. Located there were the courts of the arch-diocese and diocese, which until 1541 encompassed Yorkshire, Nottinghamshire, Cumbria, and North Lancashire.[8] A possible source for the setting of the trial plays was the Court of Audience or Chancery, a provincial court with jurisdiction over heresy and other major ecclesiastical offenses. In this court, the Vicar General, acting on the authority delegated to him by the Archbishop of York, could remove ecclesiastical dignitaries if their crimes required such an extreme measure.

The archbishops of York were directly involved in developing the procedure for putting heretics to death. In 1384 they requested the king to institute a formal procedure. At this time, the penalty which the secular arm could inflict on heretics was limited to imprisonment. Confiscation of property was added in 1388. Then, in 1401, the statute *de heretico comburendo* was introduced: "When sentence of condemnation was made against a person who had refused to abjure or who had relapsed after abjuration, the sheriff or other local officer was to be present, if the bishop required it, to receive the heretic for public burning."[9]

In the ecclesiastical court depicted in *Christ before Annas and Caiaphas*, the defendant, Jesus, is examined by two bishops, of whom Caiaphas is clearly the leader while Annas functions like a legal advisor. A plaintiff in an ecclesiastical court retained an advocate whose job it was to advise him and the judge on matters of fact and law.[10] While Caiaphas is chiefly concerned with the end result, having Jesus put to death, Annas is anxious to mount charges that will produce the desired result—or as he says in *The Conspiracy* (26.110), "prophite" their "pele," a technical term for an accusation of crime. Annas tries to relate the case to a violation of civil law that Pilate will accept.

When Caiaphas commands that Jesus be put to death in *Christ before Annas and Caiaphas* (29.334–35), Annas reminds the bishop that he would violate canon law: "Nay sir, þan blemysshe yee prelatis estate,/ 3e awe to deme no man to dede for to dynge" (336–37). Annas advises Caiaphas that he must send the defendant to the secular courts, specifically to Pilate, the "domysman nere and nexte to þe king" (341) who has power over life and limb.

In the remaining trials, the majority of the plaintiffs' charges are a reiteration of ecclesiastical crimes, including false preaching, apostasy, effecting conversions, thereby causing many to fall into error, defamation, witchcraft, and sorcery, all grounds for excommunication.[11] In Scripture, Jesus is charged with false preaching, subversion, and treason, but the other ecclesiastical charges appear in medieval significations of excommunication, writs in which the aid of the secular arm in punishing the excommunicate was sought.[12]

The death penalty, public burning, was reserved for relapsed heretics.[13] For example, in March 1430/31, Humphrey, Duke of Gloucester, had been present at the burning of a priest convicted of heresy. Later accused of treason himself, he was arrested in January 1446/47 and died shortly after. In 1441, his second wife, Eleanor Cobham, was accused of witchcraft and sorcery and finally imprisoned for treason. Echoing major peerage trials like these, the York playwright creates vivid associations between the trials of Christ and contemporary law courts. The plaintiffs try to charge Jesus as if he were a heretic who refuses to recant or as a traitor claiming the throne of England.

In the secular courts (plays 26, 30–33), failing to convince the judges that Jesus should be put to death for ecclesiastical crimes, Caiaphas and Annas persuade the secular judge Pilate and the king, Herod, that Jesus is guilty of treason. In England, if a cleric were convicted of treason against the king, he had no "benefit of clergy" protection. Like everyone else, if found guilty, he was drawn and hanged by award of the secular justices—a medieval analogue for the final conviction and crucifixion of the preacher Jesus in the plays.[14]

In a major administrative center such as York, a playwright also had access to models for the secular trial scenes. Throughout the later Middle Ages, York was the administrative headquarters for the north of England and hence was a center of law courts. Richard II transferred the courts to York as a means of disciplining the citizens of London who opposed royal policy and thus would have to plead at a distance.[15] In the latter half of the fifteenth century, Richard, Duke of Gloucester (Richard III), made York the headquarters of the King's Council in the North.[16] The cast of characters and the language in the *Conspiracy, Christ before Pilate 1, Christ before Herod,* and *Christ before Pilate 2* are suggestive of procedures in trials such as those before the King's Council in which the chancellors were clerics, assisted by bishops and doctors of the civil law.[17]

At the opening of *The Conspiracy,* Pilate identifies himself as "regent of rewle" for the region, under the "ryallest roye of rente and renowne" (26.1–2). Pilate claims judicial authority over not only the laity but also "busshoppis" (3). He is higher in authority than the nobility of the realm; as he says, "The dubbyng of my dingnité may noȝt be done downe, / Nowdir with duke nor duge-peres" (7–8), and his word is law: "My desire muste dayly be done / With þame þat are grettest of game" (9–10). In lines 19–21, Pilate makes it clear that he has power over life and limb, as would a royal justice: "He schall full bittirly banne þat bide schall my blame / . . . For sone his liffe shall he lose or left be for lame." On one level this is Pilate boasting, but on another level it identifies the legal attributes of the speaker to the audience. Fifteenth-century ana-logues to "regent of rewle" might be the Regent of England or Protector of the Realm—posts which the Duke of Gloucester held during the minority of Henry VI[18]—or the Lord Chancellor. Unlike the conspiracy in the Gospels and other narratives of the Passion, where Pilate's presence is not mentioned, Annas and Caiaphas seek his approval for their plans, like the Lord Chancellor to whom peti-tions were addressed at the start of a case.

As in a major criminal case brought before English ecclesias-tical and secular judges in the late Middle Ages, each of the trial plays employs summary trial by verbal examination. Without legal counsel, the defendant is questioned by the judge and the plaintiffs, and must answer the charges on his own. His answers, and also reports by prominent citizens, are judged as evidence of his guilt or innocence.

In *Christ before Annas and Caiaphas*, four knights, who are not in Scripture, give their testimony (29.250–51, 254–55, 258–61, 263–64, 266–71, 279–83); these accusations are reiterations of the charges made in *The Conspiracy*. That these knights are cast as witnesses is also clear by Jesus' rebuke in line 329: "A wronge wittenesse I wotte nowe are ʒe." When Caiaphas questions him as to whether or not he is God's son (290–92), and Jesus answers, "Sir, þou says it þiselffe" (293), it is taken as an affirmation of guilt. On a higher level, it signals Caiaphas' unwitting admission of Jesus' higher power, analogous to the reverence of Jesus in *Christ before Pilate 2*, where Annas and Caiaphas complain at the bowing of the banners when the defendant enters the courtroom and Miles III explains, "And þis werke þat we haue wrought it was not oure will" (33.183).

Unlike the presentation of the case in the ecclesiastical court, no witnesses giving evidence are present in *Christ before Pilate 1*. The procedure is either analogous to a highly abbreviated segment of that used in a common-law criminal trial (where the indictment is read to the defendant, who must then accept or reject the charges) or else to proceedings before the King's Council. Council handled matters outside the jurisdiction of the ordinary courts. Sometimes it would be addressed in cases of heresy, sorcery, and witchcraft, and also had jurisdiction in all matters affecting the king's person and all rights pertaining to the crown.[19] In criminal cases tried in Council or Chancery, the defendant was not allowed the aid of counsel. There were no juries and rarely witnesses. If the facts could not be obtained readily, the Council could apply the inquisitorial examination, which was borrowed from the ecclesiastical courts, where it was used for heresy trials.[20]

In *Christ before Herod*, Christ is also brought before a foreign King and Council: Herod, the two dukes, and Herod's three sons. Jesus is led in by two knights representing the plaintiff. With the exception of Christ, Herod, and his one son, none of these characters are in Scripture.[21] Herod acquits Jesus, who he is still convinced is a fool, witless and dumb: "Wherfore schulde we flaye hym or fleme hym / We fynde noʒt in rollis of recorde; / And sen þat he is dome, for to deme hym, / Ware þis a goode lawe for a lorde?" (31.

400–03). The "rollis of recorde" is a common-law technical phrase referring to the written documents of a court. These contain previous judgments as well as evidence touching the case at hand. No precedent for incriminating Jesus appears in Herod's court record. Therefore the plaintiffs bring the case back to Pilate and again charge Jesus with treason.

Pilate functions like the head of a commission of oyer and terminer which has been set up to investigate charges of treason in *The Remorse of Judas* and *Christ before Pilate 2*. For individual cases of treason, the commission might resemble the King's Council or a part of it. In fifteenth-century England, the commission of oyer and terminer was used to hear and determine accusations of treason. This was a special commission, often including local justices of the peace and always magnates and men of high standing in the royal service. The chairman of the session might be an important local official, but at least one member of it had to be a justice of either the King's Bench or Common Pleas. These commissioners had wide powers and could inflict any penalty they wished on those whom they found guilty. Rarely was a defendant acquitted if charged with treason.[22] The overall trial procedure was that used in Council. As soon as the defendant was brought into court, the indictment was read to him or her. By the fifteenth century the proceedings were conducted in English. The prisoner was not given a copy of the indictment beforehand, nor was he allowed to retain counsel, as in the preceding trials. All he could do in court was to answer with a plea of guilty or not guilty to the charges.[23] This kind of procedure is used in the last trial, in *Christ before Pilate 2*.[24] After the charges have been made, Pilate asks Jesus, "Say man, / Consayues þou noȝt what comberous clause / Þat þis clargye accusyng þe knawse? / Speke, and excuse þe if þou can" (33.296–99). As the true judge of the whole process, Jesus replies that his accusers will have to account for their charges later (306–07).

As Jesus' answer implies, the whole trial sequence is full of legal errors committed by the prosecution. These legal "sins" serve to undermine the bishops' case and reinforce Christ's innocence as he redeems mankind. First of all, throughout the trial sequence, the plaintiff and his advocate are guilty of malicious prosecution, as Pilate repeatedly points out. His comments start in *The Conspiracy*: "Beware þat we wax noȝt to wrothe" (26.40); "ȝoure rankoure is raykand full rawe" (93); "Forsothe, ȝe ar ouer-cruell to knawe" (95).

These lines identify both his judicial authority and his suspicion of the conspirators. In medieval England, malicious prosecution was a violation of both canon and secular law.[25]

Caiaphas demonstrates his own guilt in *Christ before Annas and Caiaphas* when he accuses Jesus of defamation of God the Father (29.296–99). Annas recommends the punishment: "He sclaunderes þe Godhed and greues vs all, / Wherfore he is wele worthy to be dede—" (302–03). In medieval English secular courts, given the slanderous charges of these plaintiffs, the defendant could return to court and sue for defamation. In the Church courts, if as a result of trial it was determined that the ill-fame was unfounded, then "those who spread the calumny have themselves committed a crime" and would be subject to excommunication.[26]

Secondly, the way Jesus is summoned to trial is also illegal, as the defendant himself points out (*Christ before Annas and Caiaphas*, 317–19). In medieval English law, bringing a defendant into court by force was illegal unless he had been caught in the act of committing a crime.[27]

Finally, Caiaphas also violates canon law in his active request for the death sentence in the secular courts. For example, in play 30 (*Christ before Pilate 1*) Caiaphas begins, not as he should, with a charge, but with the sentence he desires: "To deth for to deme hym with dewly device" (30.409). Canon law states that no member of the clergy may actively participate in a case affecting life and limb.[28]

Throughout the trial sequence, such legal errors create a paradox. While violating secular and ecclesiastical laws, the two bishops and their followers are completing a necessary stage of salvation history. On a higher level, Jesus is condemned to death to redeem the sins of mankind—sins which are in fact symbolized by the clerics' violations of law in the plays. Through these trials, the citizens of York are thus warned against dishonest proceedings in their own legal system.

NOTES

[1] This article is based on research presented in my doctoral dissertation, "*Inventio, Dispositio*, and *Elocutio* in the York Trial Plays" (University of Toronto, 1987), esp. chap. 2 ("Law as a Source for the Trial Plays," 44–78). For a collation of Scripture and Middle English Passion narratives as sources for the plays, see ibid., 212–32. I am grateful to Alexandra F. Johnston for her guidance in the

original research, to Helen Ostovich for her editorial suggestions, and to the Lynchburg College Faculty Research and Development Fund for its support. The article as it appears here is a revised version of my text published in 1996 in *The Early Drama, Art, and Music Review.*

[2] These plays have been attributed to a skilled dramatist sometimes referred to as the "York Realist"; see Clifford Davidson, "The Realism of the York Realist and the York Passion," *Speculum* 50 (1975): 270. All references to the York plays follow the lineation and numbering in *York Plays*, ed. Richard Beadle (London: Edward Arnold, 1982).

[3] *The York Play: A Facsimile of British Library MS Additional 35290 together with a Facsimile of the* Ordo Paginarum *Section of the A/Y Memorandum Book*, introd. Richard Beadle and Peter Meredith, Leeds Texts and Monographs, Medieval Drama Facsimiles 7 (Leeds: University of Leeds School of English, 1983), xlv.

[4] R. H. Nicholson, "The Trial of Christ the Sorcerer in the York Cycle," *Journal of Medieval and Renaissance Studies* 16 (1986): 125–26. While Nicholson is accurate in explaining the legal procedures by which Christ is tried as a sorcerer in the York plays, he fails to take into account that sorcery is but one of a series of ecclesiastical charges in the plays.

[5] Pamela M. King, "Contemporary Cultural Models for the Trial Plays in the York Cycle," in *Drama and Community: People and Plays in Medieval Europe*, ed. Alan Hindley (Turnhout: Brepols, 1999), 200–16.

[6] Jody Enders, *Rhetoric and the Origins of Medieval Drama* (Ithaca: Cornell University Press, 1992).

[7] Lynn Squires, "Legal and Political Aspects of Late Medieval English Drama," unpubl. Ph.D. diss. (University of Washington, 1977), and "Law and Disorder in *Ludus Coventriae*," *Comparative Drama* 12 (1978): 200–13.

[8] These ecclesiastical courts included four episcopal courts, lesser courts, and twice-yearly synods of the diocesan clergy. See D. M. Palliser, *Tudor York*, Oxford Historical Monographs (Oxford: Oxford University Press, 1979), 4–5.

[9] F. Donald Logan, *Excommunication and the Secular Arm in Medieval England: A Study in Legal Procedure from the Thirteenth to the Sixteenth Century*, Studies and Texts 15 (Toronto: Pontifical Institute of Mediaeval Studies, 1968), 69.

[10] On the duties and training of advocates, see Carson I. A. Ritchie, *The Ecclesiastical Courts of York* (Arbroath: Herald Press, 1956), 61–64.

[11] Examples of the ecclesiastical charges, repeated throughout the trials, are as follows: Breaking the ecclesiastical laws: 26.96, 29.271, 30.471, 31.273; preaching falsely: 26.86–90, 32.67, 70–71, 33.96–101; apostasy: 36.77; effecting conversions: 36.77, 113, 30.444; defamation: 29.297; witchcraft and sorcery: 29.58, 30.293, 33.288–89.

On ecclesiastical crimes see Paul Fournier, *Les officialités au Moyen Âge: Étude sur l'organisation, la compétence et la procédure des tribunaux ecclésiastiques ordinaires en France, de 1180 à 1328* (Paris, 1880), 90–94. Witchcraft and sorcery are included under crimes against the faith (91).

[12] Logan, *Excommunication and the Secular Arm*, 23–24, 50–53, which lists

examples of fourteenth- and fifteenth-century cases including these charges.

¹³ Norman P. Tanner, ed., *Heresy Trials in the Diocese of Norwich, 1428–31, Edited for the Royal Historical Society from Westminster Diocesan Archives MS. B.2*, Camden 4th Series 20 (London: Royal Historical Society, 1977), 10. For an example, see the Latin account of the 1428 trial of Lollard Margery Baxter (ibid., 43). She is warned by the Bishop of Norwich that she will be subject to the death penalty if she reverts to her old ways and beliefs.

¹⁴ *Statutes of the Realm*, 25 Edward III (1351–52), Stat. 6, c. 4, 325, where protection is granted to clergy for all crimes except treason. See also J. G. Bellamy, *The Law of Treason in England in the Later Middle Ages*, Cambridge Studies in English Legal History (Cambridge: Cambridge University Press, 1970), 138.

¹⁵ John H. Harvey, "Richard II and York," in *The Reign of Richard II: Essays in Honour of May McKisack*, ed. F. R. H. du Boulay and Caroline M. Barron (London: University of London, Athlone Press, 1971), 202–03.

¹⁶ Palliser, *Tudor York*, 4.

¹⁷ James F. Baldwin, *The King's Council in England During the Middle Ages* (Oxford: Clarendon Press, 1913), p. 280.

¹⁸ See G[eorge] E. C[okayne], *The Complete Peerage of England, Scotland, Ireland, Great Britain, and the United Kingdom Extant, Extinct, or Dormant*, 13 vols. (1910–59; microprint reprint Gloucester: Alan Sutton, 1982), 5:732. On the Lord Chancellor as a judicial and administrative authority next to the king, see Baldwin, *The King's Council*, 236–61.

¹⁹ During the reign of Richard II, the King's Council functioned as a sort of *ad hoc* tribunal, varying in its combination of bishops, lords, justices, serjeants-at-law, and clerks. See ibid., 244–45, and also the examples of cases given by Baldwin, 275–76.

²⁰ Ibid., 296. See also King, "Contemporary Cultural Models," 205–08, particularly on the accusations of riot, one of Annas and Caiaphas' attempted justifications for the arrest of Jesus.

²¹ Soldiers, flanking Christ, are present in the depiction of the trial before Herod in painted glass of 1420–30 in a window in the south choir aisle of York Minster; see Clifford Davidson and David E. O'Connor, *York Art*, Early Drama, Art, and Music Reference Series 1 (Kalamazoo: Medieval Institute Publications, 1978), 73. Scenes depicting Christ on trial before the high priests, Herod, and Pilate do not seem to have been popular in the visual arts in the region.

²² See Bellamy, *The Law of Treason*, 147–49.

²³ According to Bellamy, "The judges were not passive hearers of evidence but as in all criminal cases active protagonists for the crown. They seem to have tried to cajole the accused into admitting his guilt or to have browbeaten him for the same reason" (ibid., 166).

²⁴ For an alternative reading of this procedure as one used in a felony trial, where the knights serve as a jury, see King, "Contemporary Cultural Models," 209–12.

²⁵ On malicious prosecution in canon law, see Gratian, *Decretum*, C. 3, q. 5, c. 3–4, in *Corpus Iuris Canonici*, ed. Aemilius L. Richter and Aemilius Friedberg, 2nd ed., 2 vols. (Leipzig, 1879–81), 1:514–15; Gregory IX, *Decretales*, Lib. 5, Tit.

l, c. 7, in *Corpus Iuris Canonici*, 2:734; and Justinian, *Digest*, 48, 2.4, 2.7, sect. 3, and 2.9, in *The Digest of Justinian*, ed. Theodor Mommsen and Paul Krueger, trans. Alan Watson, 4 vols. (Philadelphia: University of Philadelphia Press, 1985), 4:797–98. On malicious prosecution in the secular courts, see William Holdsworth, *A History of English Law*, rev. A. L. Goodhart, H. G. Hanbury, and S. B. Chrimes, 7th ed., 17 vols. (London: Methuen, 1956–72), 1:57.

[26] Theodore F. T. Plucknett, *A Concise History of the Common Law*, 5th ed. (London: Butterworth, 1956), 484.

[27] Sir Frederick Pollock and Frederic W. Maitland, *The History of English Law Before the Time of Edward I*, rev. S. F. C. Milsom, 2nd. ed., 2 vols. (Cambridge: Cambridge University Press, 1968), 2:582–83.

[28] According to the authoritative fifteenth-century collection of English synodal constitutions, William Lyndwood's *Provinciale*, which was completed in 1433 and accepted by the Convocation of York in 1462:

> Praesenti Decreto Statuimus, ne Clerici Beneficiati, aut in Sacris Ordinibus Constituti villarum Procuratores admittantur . . . nec Jurisdictiones exerceant Saeculares praesertim illas quibus Judicium sanguinis est annexum.
>
> His quoque duximus adjungendum, ne scilicet Judicium sanguinis in locis Sacris tractetur, in Ecclesia videlicet vel coemeterio. Auctoritate quoque Concilii districtius Inhibemus, ne quis Clericus Beneficiatus, vel in Sacris Ordinibus constitutus literas pro poena sanguinis infligenda scribere vel dictare praesumat, vel ubi Judicium sanguinis tractatur vel exercetur, intersit. (*Provinciale [seu Constitutiones Angliae]* [Oxford, 1679], 269–70 [III.29])

See Arthur Ogle, *The Canon Law in Mediaeval England: An Examination of William Lyndwood's "Provinciale," in Reply to the Late Professor F. W. Maitland* (1912; reprint New York: Burt Franklin, 1971), 33–34.

The Missing York
Funeral of the Virgin

Mark R. Sullivan

The Funeral of the Virgin play, known from the civic records as *Fergus*, is not extant. Nevertheless, from references to the play from the York dramatic records and from its portrayal in art and literature, much about this missing play can be deduced. But the legend itself does not really explain why the play had such an apparently stormy history in York.

The earliest reference to the play is in Roger Burton's *Ordo Paginarum* of 1415 which specifies four apostles carrying the bier of Mary "et fergus pendens sup*er* feretrum."[1] Fergus is accompanied by other Jews, probably two in number, and another hand in the manuscript also indicated the presence of an angel.[2] The pageant is attributed to the "Lynweuers," but this attribution is written over an erasure and points to practice later in the century (i.e., in 1476, when this guild took up the "pageant and play Called ffergus," and in 1485, when "the padgeant called ffergus late broght furth by the lynweves" was "laid ap*art*").[3] In Burton's shorter list the play of *Fergus* is described simply as "Portac*io* corp*or*is marie."[4]

The most interesting document relating to the York *Fergus* is a petition of the Goldsmiths dated 1431 in which they state that the Masons were unhappy about their play in the Corpus Christi cycle "vbi ffergus fflagellatus erat" because the play's content was not found in the Scriptures and because, coming near the end of the cycle, the play could not be performed in daylight. More importantly, the play caused more laughter and shouting than devotion ("magis risu*m* & clamore*m* causabat q*u*am deuotione*m*"), even provoking quarrels to the point of fighting. As a result of this petition, the Masons were given the Herod play which had previously been one of the Goldsmiths' plays and were "freed and quit of the pageant of Fergus."[5] Perhaps this reaction to this play before it was given up by the Masons is suggested by Friar William Melton's criticism in 1426, when he noted undesirable audience response at the plays—"carousing, drunkenness, shouting, singing, and other insolences."[6]

The York play's subject matter may be traced back to legends associated with the Assumption of the Virgin in the *Transitus Beatae Mariae*, which was given an English translation as early as the *Blickling Homilies* and which was provided with wide currency through the *Golden Legend*.[7] All the English versions seem to follow the Tischendorf B Text except for minor details.[8] In the funeral procession, John carries a palm at Peter's insistence; the other apostles sing. The singing arouses the townspeople, and when they learn the nature of the procession they become violently angry. An angel strikes the Jews blind, but one of their princes reaches up toward the bier and tries to overturn it. His arms wither, and he asks Peter for help. Peter advises him that only God can assist him and that he must accept Mary as mother of Christ. The Jew agrees and is partially healed, with complete healing following more complete acceptance of Jesus as Son of God. Then, taking the palm from John, he offers it to each of the other Jews, who are healed if they will believe. The procession then proceeds to the sepulcher to bury the body of Mary. In the Middle English drama, this story receives dramatization only in one of the N-Town plays which also includes the Death of the Virgin and Assumption.[9]

The Prince in the N-Town play is described in the stage directions as madly (*"insanus"*) leaping at the bier of Mary and as then hanging there by his hands (*"et pendet per manus"*). The wording is similar to that in Burton's list as quoted above. The Prince in the N-Town play would appear to have hung *over* the bier, however; the actor must have held steady with his hands and proclaimed:

> Allas, my body is ful of peyne!
> I am fastened sore to this bere!
> Myn handys are ser bothe tweyne.
>   (41.423–25)

The Jew standing over the bier with his hands stuck is shown in a woodcut in the York Hours printed on the continent in 1517 (fig. 1). But more relevant to the lost York play might well be the portrayal of the funeral procession of the Virgin in mid-fourteenth-century glass in the choir clerestory of York Minster; here the impious person actually *hangs by his hands from the bier*, which he has

1. Funeral procession of the Virgin, with the Jew (called "Fergus" in the now-missing York play) attempting to overturn her bier. *Hore beatissime Marie* (Rouen, 1517), fol. xxiv.

attempted to overturn, whereupon his hands "remain stuck and severed while he has fallen to the ground."[10]

The identification of the impious Jew in the York play is unique but also suggests another factor that may have stirred the emotions of the audience. "Fergus" is a Scots name—a fact with far-reaching ramifications when considering the biases of a medieval audience from the North of England. While the expulsion of the Jews had taken place long before in 1290, the creators of the York play of *The Funeral of the Virgin* nevertheless could turn to a people, the Scots, who were thoroughly disliked as aliens and as organizers of border raids into England. Of course, the more alien and evil Fergus could be shown, the more miraculous would be his conversion to faith.

As a final point concerning this play in the York cycle, I believe that we can establish at least one line from the lost text. Music is necessary to the plot and symbolism of the play. In the N-Town play, the angelic choir sings "*in celo*," echoing the singing of the "Alleluia" of Peter and the apostles so that "[t]he erthe and the eyer" are filled with "melodye" (41.368ff). The Jewish reaction to this music provides the initial motive for them to consider attacking the funeral procession. But the music begins with Peter's singing of a line from Psalm 113: "Exiit Israel de Egipto, domus Jacob de populo barbaro" (41.369). This line, followed by the apostles singing the second verse—"Facta est Judea sanctificacio eius, Israel potestas eius" (41.370)—includes the incipit of the psalm that appears not only in the N-Town version of the story but also in Melito, the *Golden Legend*, and the *Blickling Homilies*.[11] The first lines of the psalm reflect Mary's own exodus from this world, and are the only lines that we can reasonably feel certain to have been likewise included in the York *Fergus* play.

NOTES

Some of the documentation in the following endnotes, including reference to editions and scholarship available only after this article was initially published, has been supplied by the editor.

[1] Alexandra Johnston and Margaret Rogerson, *Records of Early English Drama: York*, 2 vols. (Toronto: University of Toronto Press, 1979), 1:23; see also Richard Beadle, ed., *York Plays* (London: Edward Arnold, 1982), 391, 360.

[2] See Richard Beadle and Peter Meredith, introd., *The York Play: A Facsimile of British Library MS Additional 35290, Together with a Facsimile of the Ordo*

Paginarum Section of the A/Y Memorandum Book (Leeds: University of Leeds School of English, 1983), lvii.

[3] Johnston and Rogerson, *REED: York*, 1:110, 136.

[4] Ibid., 26.

[5] Ibid., 1:47–48, 2:732.

[6] Translation mine; for the Latin text, see ibid., 1:43.

[7] See Anna Mill, "The York Plays of the Dying, Assumption, and Coronation of Our Lady," *PMLA* 65 (1950): 867.

[8] M. R. James, trans., *The Apocryphal New Testament* (Oxford: Clarendon Press, 1924), 209.

[9] *The N-Town Play*, ed. Stephen Spector, EETS, s.s. 11–12 (Oxford: Oxford University Press, 1991), play 41; quotations are from this edition.

[10] Clifford Davidson and David O'Connor, *York Art* (Kalamazoo: Medieval Institute Publications, 1978), 103. Ann Eljenholm Nichols, "The Hierosphthitic Topos, or the Fate of Fergus: Notes on the N-Town Assumption," *Comparative Drama* 25 (1991): 29–41, supplies a more detailed analysis of the iconography, though not directed to the specific problems involved in the York play.

[11] Psalm 113 as used here derives from the Sarum Burial liturgy. See JoAnna Dutka, *Music in the English Mystery Plays* (Kalamazoo: Medieval Institute Publications, 1980), 27, and Richard Rastall, *The Heaven Singing*, Music in Early English Religious Drama 2 (Cambridge: D. S. Brewer, 1996), 290.

Staging the Virgin's Body: Spectacular Effects of Annunciation and Assumption

Barbara D. Palmer

Nothing is more ordinary or physiologically normal than the two bookends of common human experience, birth and death. All who are human entered this world through the portals of sexual intercourse, conception, birth; and all shall exit this world through the humble gates of death, decay, burial. Unlike ordinary mortal bodies, however, the body of the Virgin Mary is not subject to these human laws either in legend or in the portraiture of early art and drama. By definition her physical experiences are extraordinary and to represent them visually invites extraordinary spectacle. In particular, to represent the conceiving of the Virgin's son and the assumption of her body calls for spectacular effects. Through what means those effects are achieved remains a trifle elusive, particularly in relation to early English drama, which is notoriously soft-spoken on the apparatus of staging, acting, and other performance-based explication. The observations which follow thus are positioned on the somewhat slippery critical slope of the human experience, pictorial representation, dramatic presentation, and their hypothetical relation to each other.[1]

Nevertheless, there is an appreciable amount of "hard data" which can be applied to explicate how Jesus' conception and his mother's Assumption either were or else could have been effected on stage. From the N-Town Annunciation text's challenging stage direction of the *"thre bemys,"* about which Peter Meredith marks "no representation that pictures the scene quite in the way described here,"[2] to the confirmation of Annunciation and Assumption performance light, fire, fireworks, and thunder from extant Valencian and Florentine accounts, staging the Virgin's spiritually redemptive body seems to call for dramatic and spectacular techniques similar to those required for the effective stage representation of spiritual

1. The Annunciation. Painted glass, Church of St. Mary, Elland, West Yorkshire.
From Barbara D. Palmer, *The Early Art of the West Riding of Yorkshire*, with the
permission of Medieval Institute Publications.

damnation.

Although the stagecraft of damnation and virtue suggests remarkably similar techniques, far more heed has been paid to the
spectacular effects attached to devils, Antichrists, tempters, the

doomed, and the damned. That diabolic myopia is explicable on any number of grounds, not the least of which was the challenge of staging early drama in the 1970s and 1980s. Many scholars now writing or reading articles like the present devoted something of their younger lives learning how to blow things up—with terrific effect on audience but nothing dismembered of actor.[3] The ending of *Doctor Faustus* served jointly as inspiration and warning. Numerous conference sessions and post-performance symposia were devoted to discussions of evil—the stagecraft of damnation, complete with fire and thunder and flame; the appearance of evil, in all of its costumed guises of fur and feathers and misplaced bits of anatomy.

That less heed has been paid to the potential for spectacular staging of spiritual virtue is perhaps a human tendency to find evil more fascinating than good, devils more interesting than angels.[4] Student curiosity over the years about Belyal's "pyrotechnic accoutrements" in *The Castle of Perseverance* (Philip Butterworth's tactful phrase for "gunnepowdyr brennynge In pypys")[5] far surpasses any inquiries about the Goode Aungyl. Perhaps, too, is an uneasiness about mixing "miracle" with "magic," a willingness to allow stage tricks for representing sinners but reluctance to color saints with similar smoke and mirrors. Two resources for fashioning this stagecraft of virtue in fact were identified early on and of late have come under scrutiny for what they suggest about potential performance conditions. First, the corpus of saints' lives and legends as rich materials for dramatic performance was identified as transferable by such scholars as Darryll Grantley, who addressed some of the early accounts of miracles and the pragmatic challenges such accounts suggest. Second, civic pageantry was brought into the realm of dramatic possibility by Gordon Kipling's and others' recognition that staging a queen and staging a virgin saint ask for similar spectacular effects.[6]

Although one might suppose that the present age, this jaded, weary post-Reformation world, would find it difficult to imagine the popular appeal of the Virgin, of recent years a respectable amount of scholarly attention has been devoted to her historic ubiquity, iconography, attire, facial portraiture, relics, diction, and characterization.[7] Perhaps more surprising than academic attention has been a popular revival reflected in such mainstream films as *Elizabeth* and *Shakespeare in Love*, both of which somewhat fashion the queen as Protestant saint or deity.[8] Most startling, however, was Mary's gracing the cover of *Newsweek* magazine on 25 August 1997 as the featured "Lifestyle" subject. Inspired by petitions that His Holiness, John Paul II proclaim a new dogma of the Roman Catholic faith to designate the Virgin Mary "Co-Redemptrix, Mediatrix of All Graces and Advocate for the People of God," the article notes that between 1993 and 1997 the pope received 4,340,429 signatures from 157 countries.[9]

As one probably cannot overestimate the popularity of the Virgin Mary, one probably ought not underestimate the sophistication of devices used to play her miraculous life, in particular the events of Annunciation and Assumption. Both have the potential to be spectacular moments of early theater performance, but both have suffered from the naive presumption that action primarily is limited to words and gestures rather than to staging effects. One reason for that presumption, besides insufficient knowledge of early theater stage technology, is that the few surviving English texts are in general quite deficient in stage directions, and surviving production records are sparse on the ground. Nevertheless, a useful analytical tool is simply to read the English texts quite literally, to assume that if a surviving play text describes certain events as happening in front of the audience's eyes then they must have done so, and, theater being what it is, they must have done so effectively. Any assessment of "staging the Virgin's body" needs first to acknowledge what effects are described in the text rather than being constrained by ignorance of how those effects could be produced.

Unencumbered by theoretical or non-physical considerations, one thus notes that in the York Drapers' *Death of the Virgin* pageant, Jesus gives a palm to Gabriel in Heaven, and Gabriel delivers the palm to Mary on earth.[10] Peter, James, and Andrew appear suddenly and miraculously at her deathbed with none of them (nor the text) clear on the means of their appearance, although Peter reports that a cloud covered him in Judea. Jesus appears suddenly to tell her that the fiend in full foul figure must be at her end but angels shall be about her. He seems to stay in "heaven" ("And þerfore my modir come myldely to me" [159]), and she acknowledges him from below as she dies:

Mi sely saule I þe sende
To heuene þat is highest on heghte,
To þe, sone myne þat moste is of myght,
Ressayue it here into þyne hende. (171–74)

He instructs angels to fetch her body, and four angels in addition to Gabriel, apparently on the same heavenly level as Jesus, exit singing "[c]*um vno diabolo. Et cantant antiphona, scilicet 'Aue regina celorum'*."

In the York Weavers' *Assumption* (titled *Appearance of Our Lady to Thomas* by Lucy Toulmin Smith in her 1885 edition of the York plays), twelve angels, each with one line, call Mary to rise and "Come vppe to þe kyng to be crouned" (117). Thomas, as stage observer and commentator, marks gleams gliding, angels' company, mirth, melody, and Mary's progress to dwell in bliss. At an intermediate position, she tells Thomas to report to the apostles that "þou sawe me assendinge" and gives him her "fresshe of hewe" girdle as proof, a girdle explicitly made so precious because "hir wombe wolde scho wrappe with it" (162, 168, 277). She continues toward the peerless empire where Christ sits with a crown. In the

2. Assumption of the Virgin. Fourteenth-century roof boss (destroyed), York Minster Nave; drawing by John Browne, *History of the Metropolitan Church of St. Peter, York* (1847).

following pageant, the Hostelers' *Coronation of the Virgin*, Jesus tells six "bright and schene" angels to go to Mary and bring her body to him "here so high in blis," a partial ascent accompanied by *"Cantando"* (1, 16; 81 *s.d.*). He descends part way to welcome her ("Come forth with me my modir bright,/ Into my blisse we schall assende" [101–02]) and leads her up as he tells the Five Joys of Mary: the Annunciation; his birth, Resurrection, and Ascension; and her own Assumption and Coronation.

Although no markedly "spectacular effects" are noted in the lines, the acting between Mary and Jesus, with each joy a physical stage of their ascent, can be miraculously moving as he ultimately places the crown on her head, instructs the angels to sing in her honor, and blesses all who have been watching. Conversely, "spectacular effects" could indeed complement the lines, as is detailed below in Continental accounts. The York textual attention to ascents, descents, appearances, disappearances, physical place, and movement marked with music seems to suggest no little experience in the visual dimension of drama.

Neither the Towneley nor the Chester Annunciation pageant seems to demand much by way of spectacle and are briefly noted here. The Towneley Annunciation God explains that Mary will conceive "Wythouten wem, os son thrugh glas" (37), with the moment of Gabriel's word and her hearing the moment of conception. The Towneley editors note that the metaphor of "light shining through glass is a familiar figure in medieval drama for the conception of Christ" but do not suggest that the metaphor is staged, except in the rather inane suggestion that "[p]ossibly the stage of the Towneley play was designed as a room in a middle-class home. . . ."[11] Although the Towneley manuscript does not include an Assumption text, nor much Marian material at all, some sort of ascending device with heavenly clouds seems to be suggested by the Ascension text (Play 29). Jesus says, "In erthe will I no longere be;/ Opyn the clowdes, for now I com/ In ioy and blys to dwell with the" (287–89). The following stage direction reads *Et sic ascendit cantantibus angelis 'Ascendo ad patrem meum'*"; he certainly seems to go up rather mysteriously, the angels point out how he is sitting in heaven as a marvel, and Mary confirms that "[a] clowde has borne my chylde to blys" (336).[12]

It will come as no surprise that of surviving early English drama only the N-Town pageants, both "Mary Play" and "cycle," draw fairly pointed textual attention to the Virgin's physical body.[13] *The Trial of Mary and Joseph* detractors invite the audience to leer at her in sexual marketplace terms: "fresch and fayr," "a mursel," "of schap so comely," "[o]f hire tayle . . . lyght," "fresche wench," "bolde bysmare" (91–92, 95–96, 98, 298). With greater sanction but no less voyeurism is the Nativity itself. Although the Chester *Nativity* has a sceptical Salome testing Mary's cleanliness with the withered hands consequence, the N-Town has a faithful Zelomy testing at Mary's invitation. In a clever deflection of audience attention, Zelomy focuses on the baby's cleanness, without birth filth, calling Salome to note Mary's full breasts and spotless baby ("Beholde þe brestys of þis clene mayd/ Ful of fayr mylke how þat þei be,/ And hyre chylde clene" [235–36]); the sceptical Salome doubts virginity, Mary tells her to test, and her hand withers, to be restored by touching the baby's garments. This N-Town pageant seems to have had not only the withered hand property but also a spectacularly full breast, not an unseemly property in light of the numerous reliquary vials of Mary's milk and frequent lactation images. The N-Town text alone, by the way, points to her breasts, a body image reinforced by the N-Town Doctors' sarcastic charge that the twelve-year-old Christ still nurses at his mother's breast. And the N-Town Annunciation pageant, with its infamous *"thre bemys"* stage direction, hardly neglects the Virgin's body, but that pageant is reserved for later comment below.

Of the surviving English texts, most potentially complex in spectacle is the N-Town *Assumption of the Virgin*, which begins with the Jews' threats to burn her body and ends with her glorious physical ascent. The text suggests numerous actions, and the equally numerous stage directions suggest that those actions were meant to be played, not just reported. In response to Mary's prayer and Christ's instructions, an angel descends playing a cithara, tells her that she will die in three days and ascend to where her son is, and gives her the palm branch which God bids should be born before her bier. She asks that the apostles be present and that she not have to see the fiend. The angel ascends, and two holy maidens, the servants of God, appear to attend her until she will "passe to that hye toure" (182). She wishes that her brethren the apostles were here "[t]o bere my body, that bare Jesu, oure Savyoure" (187). John the Evangelist suddenly appears in front of Mary's door and says that he has been brought to these hills by a white cloud. He knocks on the door at the

entrance of Mary's house, and she gives him the palm branch to
bear before her bier. All of the apostles miraculously congregate in
front of her door. Feeling her flesh fail, she will rest "in this bed"
(298), to which she is moved and modestly arranged ("*Hic erit
decenter ornatus in lecto*") as the apostles keep watch with their
lamps and lights.

Mary then calls to Jesus, who hears the "voys of my moder"
(312) and descends. She tells him in another marvelous acting line:
"A, wolcom, gracyous Lord Jesu, sone and God of mercy!/ An
aungyl wold a ssuffysed me, hye Kyng, at this nede" (314–15). He
responds that nothing short of his proper person and the heavenly
choir would suffice to read her dirge. In due course her soul exits
from her body into God's bosom; the two virgins "wasche this
gloryous body" (349), Peter bears the palm before "this gloryous
body" (357), and Paul helps to carry "[t]his blessid body" (366).
And so follow the play's numerous other actions, through the
apostles' carrying Mary's bier to the sepulcher, the unbelievers'
attempt on the bier, the conversion of the Jews, the descent of Jesus
and return of Mary's soul into her body, and, finally, the triumphant
ascent of Jesus and Mary into heaven with organs playing.

As noted above, the N-Town *Assumption*'s stage directions are
plentiful. While some directions are quite clear, such as "here the
angels sing sweetly in heaven" ("*Hic angeli dulciter cantabunt in
celo*" [371]), others are nearly opaque, such as "here Mary's soul
exits from the body into God's bosom" ("*Hic exiet anima Marie de
corpore in sinu[m] Dei*" [330 *s.d.*]) or "here suddenly all of the
apostles congregate miraculously in front of the door" ("*Hic subito
omnes apostoli congregentur ante port[a]m mira[n]tes*" [234 *s.d.*]).
One knows what needs to happen, what the text specifies that the
audience should see, but to explicate how the spectacle might have
been accomplished incurs an enormous debt to Peter Meredith and
John Tailby's *Staging of Religious Drama in Europe in the Later
Middle Ages* as well as to other remarkable EDAM publications
over the years. From the Continental accounts, however, the spectacular effects which were employed to stage the Virgin's Annunciation and Assumption are sufficiently documented to suggest that
one should not undervalue the technical means available to portray
stage virtue.

Whether those effects were employed on both sides of the
Channel is presently a moot discussion, but the Continental records

nevertheless underscore the extraordinary spectacle which potentially could be devoted to portrayal of stage virtue. In the most basic terms, all of the Virgin Annunciation and Assumption texts require different levels or heights on which to stage the events; means of descent and ascent for the actors; and miraculous effect, however that effect is accomplished. To meet those requirements, the Continental accounts can speak to three basic categories of stage effects: first, heavens and heavenly properties; second, clouds; and, third, representations of soul, spirit, or the Holy Spirit.[14]

Extraordinary ingenuity and no mean expense were devoted to the heavens and "heavenly" properties. In 1453 at Barcelona, the Corpus Christi Creation float calls for a finely-carved gilded or silvered throne, a revolving globe, and either a wheel or a circular platform on which angels stand. Additionally, the vaulted heaven of the Nativity float holds "stars and clouds, in the center of which God the Father shall be visible at least from the waist up. From him shall descend rays of light or fire . . . which shall pass between the said structures and reach down to where the infant Jesus is lying . . . quite naked, . . . glowing with light." Kings come up through the door of the float and climb steps to Jesus; hidden stairs and doors are common features.[15]

The 1509 Romans accounts specify a wooden heaven and hell with entrances, exits, and trapdoors. Carpenters are contracted to devise towers, turrets, castles, towns of wood, stakes, and canopies as necessary, with portals and openings for the effects and steps. Alençon's 1520 Paradise scaffold commanded three levels, three floors, curved canopies, and a height at least as tall as the town's outer rampart. The Bourges Parade's 1536 float for Paradise was eight feet wide and twelve long:

> All the way round it was a circle of open thrones painted like passing clouds and within and without small angels, such as cherubim, seraphim, powers, and dominions in the round (*élevés en bosse*) with folded hands and moving continually. In the middle was a seat made like a rainbow on which sat the Godhead (*la Divinité*), Father, Son, and Holy Spirit, and behind two golden suns in the midst of a throne which turned ceaselessly in opposite directions. At the four corners were the four Virtues—Justice, Peace, Truth, and Mercy—richly dressed, and at the sides of the said Godhead were two other small angels singing hymns and canticles to the accompaniment of the players on flutes, harps, lutes, rebecs, and viols, who were walking along all round the Paradise.[16]

A second basic category of spectacular effects in Virgin plays (and, of course, in Ascension and Pentecost plays as well) is clouds. Their construction is too complex a subject for the present writing, and it also is well outside the technological ken of this writer: those who want to know more must consult the exposition of Francesc Massip, Pamela King, and others.[17] Massip's generic definition of a "spherical machine representing a cloud, normally opening during its descent to show in its interior its celestial nature" is adequate here, although one must needs note that Spanish and English clouds may have varied greatly in materials and appearance. Regardless, clouds seem to have been a relatively ordinary property requirement, however remarkable their effect on the audience. The Bourges effects list of 1536 takes quite for granted that "there must be thunder in Paradise and a white cloud to come and snatch up St. John preaching in Ephesus and transport him to outside the door of the Virgin Mary's house. There must be another cloud to snatch up the apostles in various countries and let them be brought to the front of the said house."[18]

In 1498 Rome all sorts of cloud-masked pulleys were constructed for the Virgin's assumption, but their "*exact functioning the records do not make clear.*"[19] Perplexed editorial understatement aside, what *is* clear is the Rome shopping list, which requires iron strips, big iron bars, some sort of wooden frame with crossbars, a big iron rod, an iron cross-bar with hinges, a hinged iron girdle to hold the Virgin actor's body, and "clouds" to cover the iron apparatus of "flying," a fifteenth-century Italian prototype for those generations of children who later believed that Peter Pan could fly.

That the English, even outside London, were not unfamiliar with cloud construction for dramatic effect is suggested by a surviving 1520 Ripon Minster fabric roll, which contains a detailed account of building clouds for a movable image of the Holy Ghost. Because the detail of the account is rare, it probably is worth recording in full for those who would wish to study it:

Et de 78*s*. receptis de denariis collectis per garciones villae Ripon hoc anno et datis tam ad novam cellaturam parcell' del Rooff in navi ecclesiae praedictae quam pro nova factura cujusdam nebulae pro lee Holy Goost, ut patet indentura inter dictos garciones et istum computantem confecta super hunc compotum ostensa. Summa, 78*s*. . . . De quibus allocatus ei 18*s*. 3½*d*. pro tot denariis per ipsum solutis pro nova

factura cujusdam nebulae in navi ecclesiae praedictae, ut in opere car-
pentr' pro Spiritu Sancto in eadem ascendendo et discendendo in die
Ascensionis Domini et Pentecostes; empcione stuffurae pro le paynting,
cum vadimonia Thomae Payntour pro pictura praedicti operis hoc
anno. . . .[20]

If the "stuffurae" of cloud construction rather confounds modern understanding, the means by which the third category of stage
spectacle suggested by the Virgin's Annunciation and Assumption
—visual representations of soul, spirit, or the Holy Ghost—could
be effected well may boggle the literary mind. Although dolls or
small images moving on a wire (*filium*) sometimes were used for
souls' ascending or descending,[21] other effects were far more
elaborate. For the Whitsuntide tongues of fire, a fifteenth-century
Paris Resurrection text specifies that "[h]ere shall descend a fiery
brand (*brandon de feu*) from Paradise that shall be round like a
circle and shall be all soaked in burning spirit (*eaue vive*), and in the
middle of this blazing circle should be a pigeon of white metal (*fer
blanc*) surrounded by fire which does not burn it. And all round the
circle should be tongues of fire (*langues ardentes*) which should fall
on Our Lady, on the women, on the apostles and disciples."[22]

A 1453 Barcelona record commissions a mechanical dove "to
issue from the mouth of God the Father in the float of the Annunciation and descend with its wings extended . . . until it reaches
Mary. And it is to emit certain rays of light or fire which are to do
no damage when it is before Mary. And afterwards it shall return to
God, 'flapping' its wings."[23] A live dove clearly is less reliable. Preliminary directions for a Lucerne 1583 Crucifixion note "that a live
dove is to be hidden in the cross, to fly out at the death of Christ,"
arrangements which were canceled in 1597 with a marginal "*nüt*"
("no").[24]

These records, among many others, suggest five generalizations
which cannot be ignored when "staging the Virgin's body," either
in classroom study or in performance. First, early theater production clearly was capable of fakery, if not quite of Titanic proportion
at least of convincing illusion. Besides the hollow cross for the Holy
Spirit, other inventory items include a pre-painted Veronica, one
platter with two breasts for St. Agatha, one platter with two eyes for
St. Lucy, and a two-sided rock with one side whole, the other split.
Those who teach or produce English medieval religious drama need
entertain no squeamishness or political correctness about "faking"

the Virgin Mary.

Second, any number of silent actors or stage hands can be used to bring about spectacular effects, a possibility often overlooked when teaching a bare-bones play text. In 1597 Lucerne, for example, the Operator of the Star, Holy Ghost, and Eclipse Maker (with the Crucifixion play's two-sided Sun and Moon) is a paid staff member positioned "in the topmost room of the *Haus zur Sonne*," from which strings are run to the pillar of the fountain. Cautioned to have his equipment at the ready and to test it for reliability, the Operator's duties include lowering the Holy Ghost (with a live dove) over Mary at the Annunciation and over Jesus at the baptism, as well as lowering and raising the Star for the Magi's progress.[25]

Third, the role of music in these Annunciation and Assumption pageants can be extensive; again, the bare text seldom guides a reader to full appreciation of musical possibilities and effects. Music seems to have been specially written for the York Assumption of Mary and Appearance to Thomas, but that instance probably is just one among many for which no record survives.[26] Fourth, sound effects clearly may contribute to the Virgin pageants, including a soft peal of thunder for the coming of the Holy Spirit, loud thunder, and explosions of various volume, as noted below. Finally, and as always in effective theater, the primary and essential dimension in these Virgin plays is the acting, the emotional power of the embodied text. Spectacle enhances acting; it does not replace it.

When all of these dimensions are combined, however, the result can be spectacular indeed, as in the 1536 Bourges effects list for the Assumption incidents, which sound remarkably close to those in the N-Town text. These Book Five effects start with the "false magic" of the Jews, calling for a bronze serpent which moves along the ground, a singing dog, a laughing idol, withered hands, detached and rejoined hands, blinding fire flung by angels, and fire in the form of lightning. These devices are contrasted with the "miracle" of the Virgin's body, including the sudden great light at her tomb, the reunion of her soul with her body, "her face bright as the sun," and the cloud which conceals the apostles' departure.[27]

Even more detailed, and very attentive to the acting, is the early fifteenth-century Valencia Assumption play,[28] which calls for a scaffold, a chamber enclosed with curtains which can be pulled back to see Mary inside, a door with a knocker, a seat on which she sits, and a bed. Thunder is made for an angel's descent, for the approach of the three princes, and yet more for the opening of heaven (*obras lo cel*) while apostles, princes, and others help Mary to her bed. Christ descends and takes the soul from her body (*trahent la anima del cors*), while loud thunder accompanies the handmaidens' placing her body under the stage and carrying *la ymage* "up." The second day of the play begins as St. Michael brings down the image; under the stage thunder and smoke are made as the living actor (*la viva*) suddenly emerges on a monument tomb, looking amazed as if she had never been in this world before —i.e., the actor must make it quite clear that she has died and is now new.

A procession forms through which Mary walks in a very emotional farewell. At the end of the procession she kneels before Christ and makes to take off her chaplet, which angels reverently remove and give to the handmaidens in a wonderful stage moment, since the audience knows that she will exchange it for a crown. "And after Christ has [asked the archangels to bring her to him], the angels are to lead Mary humbly and raise her up with Christ. Then the angels, apostles, and everybody else are to crowd round Christ and Mary, and thunder and smoke are to be made, and Christ and Mary are to exit. And at once the lifting machinery (*la ara celi*) is to rise."[29] When it begins rising, the apostles and angels sing praises to Mary. It seems fairly clear that the apostles sing as the machinery ascends; a second song is by the angels in the dome as the machinery with Christ and Mary arrives in heaven; and the angels' "another song" is to allow the full spectacle of Christ and Mary in majesty to be displayed at some length. After the heaven has been closed and the apostles have led the *Te deum laudamus*, they head to the chapter house, disrobe, and "have their lunch if they have food with them."[30]

One final representative of spectacular effects, the 1439 Florence Annunciation and Ascension, is too extraordinary to omit here. From this eyewitness account of Abramo, a Russian bishop in Florence for the Ecumenical Council, "heaven" is a scaffold at the entrance to SS. Annunziata Church, very high up and 10½ feet square with God's throne rising above the platform; 175 feet away, in the middle of the church, is a stone platform on columns 21 feet high and 17½ feet deep. Stretching from the stone platform to the heaven scaffold are five thin but strong ropes; two of them are fastened on the left side near the Virgin's bed and seat with the other three fastened precisely to the center of the platform.[31]

Following extensive activity of the seven heavens, the heavenly powers, the inextinguishable angelic light, many children artfully arranged, angel musicians, and a half hour dispute among the four prophets, the Annunciation proper begins:

> [T]he curtains of the upper scaffold open and from there comes a volley of shots imitating Heaven's thunder, and the Prophets with their scrolls are not seen again. Up on the scaffold is God the Father surrounded by more than five hundred burning lamps which revolve continually, going up and down. Children dressed in white, representing the angels, surround him, one striking the cymbals, others playing flutes or citterns in a scene of joyful and inexpressible beauty. After some time, the angel sent by God descends on the two ropes already mentioned to announce the conception of the Son. The angel is a beautiful, curly-headed youth, dressed in a robe as white as snow, adorned with gold, exactly as celestial angels are to be seen in paintings. While he descends he sings in a low voice, holding a branch . . . in his hand. The descent is effected in this way: behind him there are two small wheels secured, invisible from below because of the distance, into which the two ropes fit, while some people who cannot be seen stand up above and by means of the third very thin rope lower and lift up the angel.[32]

Even more stunning are the moment of the Incarnation and Gabriel's ascent:

> [A] fire comes from God and with a noise of uninterrupted thunder passes down the three ropes towards the middle of the scaffold, where the Prophets were, rising up again in flames and rebounding down once more, so that the whole church was filled with sparks. The angel sang jubilantly as he ascended, and moved his hands about and beat his wings as if he were really flying. The fire poured forth and spread with increasing intensity and noise from the high scaffold, lighting the lamps in the church but without burning the clothes of the spectators or causing any harm. When the angel arrives back at his point of departure the flames subside and the curtains close again.[33]

In the face of this wondrous Italian spectacle, one almost feels embarrassed to return to the enigma of the N-Town Annunciation stage direction, that *"Here þe Holy Gost discendit with thre bemys to Our Lady, the Sone of þe Godhed nest with thre bemys to þe Holy Gost, the Fadyr godly with thre bemys to þe Sone, and so entre all thre to here bosom, and Mary seyth. . . ."*[34] Meg Twycross, in an ex-

haustively researched article on light, illumination, multiple verbal
meanings, and various ways of illustrating light as it is connected to
the Virgin, also puzzles over the N-Town stage direction and notes
that "[we] still do not really know how this was done. Were the
bemys, as in the recent Toronto production, painted wood? in which
case this shows an extreme reification of the concept of light. . . ."
Finding the wooden beams "posed, static, and expository," Twycross judges Florence's flaming ropes "breathtakingly dynamic."[35]
Although she was not able to attend either the 1988 or the 1439
Annunciation performance, her *in absentia* assessments highlight a
central dimension to this subject of staging the Virgin's body.

The Toronto wooden beams were constructed for reliability,
portability, and a deliberate subordination of spectacle to the power
of acting.[36] With no means (or ability) to devise Incarnation special
effects, the actors had to focus on the remarkably dynamic N-Town
text, which became less and less "posed, static, and expository" the
more it was explored in rehearsal. Without flaming ropes, the Mary
actor had to show the audience through her physical body the
moment of Incarnation: "A, now I fele in my body be/ Parfyte God
and parfyte man . . ." (293–94). Moreover, the actors quickly discovered that the relationship between Mary and Gabriel was
anything other than "posed, static, and expository." The N-Town
Virgin is not easy of persuasion, Gabriel's explanations are not
especially compelling, and the stage tension between them is readily
available in such a text as "*Here þe aungel makyth a lytyl restynge
and Mary beholdyth hym, and þe aungel seyth*":

> Mary, come of and haste the,
> And take hede in thyn entent
> Whow þe Holy Gost, blyssysd he be,
> Abydyth þin answere and þin assent.
> Thorwe wyse wereke of dyvinyté,
> The secunde persone, verament,
> Is mad man by fraternyté
> Withinne þiself in place present.
>
> Ferthermore, take hede þis space
> Whow all þe blyssyd spyrytys of vertu
> Þat are in hefne byffore Goddys face,
> And all þe gode levers and trew
> That are here in þis erthely place. . . .
>   (261–73)

The passage, among many others in the Virgin plays, calls for fine acting, which most certainly would not be diminished by fine spectacle as well. One clearly envies Archbishop Abramo's 1439 privilege to observe both achievements in one performance, but one also is grateful that his eyewitness account so feelingly acknowledges the totality of what moved him. "Staging the Virgin's body" long has been a multi-dimensioned challenge, a challenge which simultaneously must communicate the female body, the human experience, the ordinary and normal, along with the miraculous, the extraordinary, the spectacular. These present remarks suggest that one need not underestimate either the textual or technological resources to hand, then as now.

NOTES

[1] An earlier version of this paper was delivered in the Medieval and Renaissance Drama Society-sponsored session on "Before Hollywood: Pyrotechnics and Spectacular Effects in Medieval and Renaissance Drama" at the 1998 International Congress on Medieval Studies; that version was illustrated by the slides which cannot of course be supplied here. For examples of the Annunciation and Assumption from locations associated with the kind of biblical drama discussed in the present article, however, see Barbara D. Palmer, *The Early Art of the West Riding of Yorkshire*, Early Drama, Art, and Music Reference Series 6 (Kalmazoo: Medieval Institute Publications, 1990), 71–75, 145–47, figs. 39–40; Clifford Davidson and David E. O'Connor, *York Art*, Early Drama, Art, and Music Reference Series 1 (Kalamazoo: Medieval Institute Publications, 1978), 39–43, 103–07, figs. 9, 31; Clifford Davidson and Jennifer Alexander, *The Early Art of Warwickshire*, Early Drama, Art, and Music Reference Series 4 (Kalamazoo: Medieval Institute Publications, 1985), 21, 35, 88, 112–14, 136, frontispiece, fig. 5; Sally-Beth MacLean, *Chester Art*, Early Drama, Art, and Music Reference Series 3 (Kalamazoo: Medieval Institute Publications, 1982), 26–28, 46–47, figs. 7–9, 24; and Ann Eljenholm Nichols, *The Early Art of Norfolk*, Early Drama, Art, and Music Reference Series 7 (Kalamazoo: Medieval Institute Publications, 2002), 52–57, 102–04. For a general discussion of the Annunciation, see Gertrud Schiller, *Christian Iconography*, trans. Janet Seligman, 2 vols. (Greenwich, Conn.: New York Graphic Society, 1971–72), 1:33–52.

[2] Peter Meredith, ed., *The Mary Play* (London: Longman, 1987), 75, 116.

[3] Philip Butterworth, "Gunnepowdyr, Fyre and Thondyr," *Medieval English Theatre* 7 (1985): 68–76; "The Light of Heaven: Flame as Special Effect," in *The Iconography of Heaven*, ed. Clifford Davidson, Early Drama, Art, and Music Monograph Series 21 (Kalamazoo: Medieval Institute Publications, 1994), 128–45; "Hellfire: Flame as Special Effect," in *The Iconography of Hell*, ed. Clifford Davidson and Thomas H. Seiler, Early Drama, Art, and Music Monograph Series

17 (Kalamazoo: Medieval Institute Publications, 1992), 67–101. Butterworth rightly has become something of the scholarly authority on "blowing things up."

⁴ Both theatrical virtue and evil, however, receive attention in a special issue of *Comparative Drama* edited by Grace Tiffany on "Drama and the English Reformation." See R. Chris Hassel, Jr., "Painted Women: Annunciation Motifs in *Hamlet*," *Comparative Drama* 32 (1998): 47–84; and John D. Cox, "Stage Devils in English Reformation Plays," *Comparative Drama* 32 (1998): 85–116, and *The Devil and the Sacred in English Drama 1350–1642* (Cambridge: Cambridge University Press, 2000).

⁵ Philip Butterworth, *Theatre of Fire: Special Effects in Early English and Scottish Theatre* (London: Society for Theatre Research, 1998), 25.

⁶ Darryll Grantley, "Producing Miracles," in *Aspects of Early English Drama*, ed. Paula Neuss (Cambridge: D. S. Brewer, 1983), 78–91; and Gordon Kipling, "The London Pageants for Margaret of Anjou: A Medieval Script Restored," *Medieval English Theatre* 4 (1982): 5–27.

⁷ Two of the many thoughtful works on the Virgin Mary which inspired this present study are Marina Warner, *Alone of All Her Sex: The Myth and Cult of the Virgin Mary* (London: Weidenfeld and Nicolson, 1976); and Gail McMurray Gibson, *The Theater of Devotion* (Chicago: University of Chicago Press, 1989).

⁸ In an unpublished paper, "The Face of the Virgin: Mary in English Words and Windows," delivered at the 1997 International Congress on Medieval Studies, the present writer noted that the facial portraitures of Elizabeth I and pre-Reformation female saints, as pictured in English painted glass, were surprisingly congruent.

⁹ Kenneth L. Woodward, "Hail, Mary," *Newsweek*, 25 August 1997, 48–56.

¹⁰ Richard Beadle, ed., *The York Plays* (London: Edward Arnold, 1982): Pageant 44, Drapers, *The Death of the Virgin*, 386–91; Pageant 45, Weavers, *Assumption of the Virgin*, 392–99; Pageant 46, Hostelers, *Coronation of the Virgin*, 400–04; I also have consulted Lucy Toulmin Smith, ed., *York Plays* (Oxford: Clarendon Press, 1885), and in one instance I have followed her (correct) reading of a line. I have given line numbers in parentheses for quotations from Beadle's edition in my text.

¹¹ Martin Stevens and A. C. Cawley, eds., *The Towneley Plays*, EETS, s.s. 13–14 (Oxford: Oxford University Press, 1994), 2:476, who broadly note that "[t]he Incarnation was represented variously in late medieval art and drama." Quotations from the Towneley plays in my text are from this edition; line numbers are given in parentheses.

¹² The notes in *The Towneley Plays*, 2:627, suggest the editors' lack of familiarity with such ascension devices as they puzzle that "this stage business was no doubt the most difficult in the play and perhaps in the whole cycle. As the central scene in the play, it had to be made credible, and the play itself must have been one of the most spectacular in the cycle."

¹³ Stephen Spector, ed., *The N-Town Play*, EETS, s.s. 11–12 (Oxford: Oxford University Press, 1991): *Trial of Mary and Joseph*, 139–52; *The Nativity*, 152–63; *The Assumption of Mary*, 387–409. Except where otherwise noted, quotations from these plays in my text are from this edition; line numbers are given in parentheses.

172 *Barbara D. Palmer*

¹⁴ Peter Meredith and John E. Tailby, eds., *The Staging of Religious Drama in Europe in the Later Middle Ages: Texts and Documents in English Translation*, Early Drama, Art, and Music Monograph Series 4 (Kalamazoo: Medieval Institute Publications, 1983).

¹⁵ Ibid., 71–72.

¹⁶ Ibid., 92.

¹⁷ See Francesc Massip, "The Cloud: A Medieval Aerial Device, Its Origins, and Its Use in Spain Today," in the present volume; Pamela M. King and Asunción Salvador-Rabaza, "*La Festa d'Elx*: The Festival of the Assumption of the Virgin, Elche (Alicante)," *Medieval English Theatre* 8 (1986): 28–50; Pamela M. King, "Elche Again—The *Venida* and *Semana Santa*," *Medieval English Theatre* 12 (1990): 4–20; and Clifford Davidson, *Technology, Guilds, and Early English Drama*, Early Drama, Art, and Music Monograph Series 23 (Kalamazoo: Medieval Institute Publications, 1996), 81–100.

¹⁸ Meredith and Tailby, *The Staging*, 95.

¹⁹ Ibid., 96.

²⁰ James Fowler, *Memorials of the Church of SS. Peter and Wilfrid, Ripon*, 4 vols., Surtees Society, 74, 78, 81, 115 (Durham, 1881–1908), 3:180, 182, as quoted in Palmer, *The Early Art of the West Riding of Yorkshire*, 143–44.

²¹ Meredith and Tailby, *The Staging*, 113.

²² Ibid., 107.

²³ Ibid., 119.

²⁴ Ibid.

²⁵ Ibid., 148.

²⁶ See Richard Rastall, *The Heaven Singing*, Music in Early English Religious Drama 1 (Cambridge: D.S. Brewer, 1996), for an essential study with an enormous bibliography. Published since the present article was initially published is the same author's *Minstrels Playing*, Music in Early English Religious Drama 2 (Cambridge: D. S. Brewer, 2001).

²⁷ Meredith and Tailby, *The Staging*, 101–02.

²⁸ Ibid., 230–31.

²⁹ Ibid., 238.

³⁰ Ibid., 239.

³¹ Ibid., 243. For the visual context of these Florentine plays, see Nerida Newbigin, "Art and Drama in Fifteenth-Century Florence," *Early Drama, Art, and Music Review* 19 (1996): 1–22.

³² Ibid., 244.

³³ Ibid., 245.

³⁴ Meredith, *The Mary Play*, 75 (l. 1356 *s.d.*).

³⁵ Meg Twycross, "'As the Sun with His Beams when He Is Most Bright'," *Medieval English Theatre* 12, no.1 (1990): 48.

³⁶ A cast from Chatham College, Pittsburgh, Pennsylvania, performed the N-Town *Parliament of Heaven and Annunciation to the Virgin* pageant in May 1988 at Victoria College, University of Toronto. The present writer directed the production.

Ludus Sabaudiae:
Observations on Late Medieval Theater in the Duchy of Savoy

Véronique Plesch

By now multiculturalism is a required virtue. Not long ago an issue of the *New York Times Magazine* celebrated the diversity of the city.[1] The traditional metaphor of the melting pot, in which the different nationalities and origins are melted and recombined into a unified mass, has mutated into that of a mosaic, in which the individual components retain their diverse identity. For those interested in fifteenth-century culture, the Duchy of Savoy offers a fascinating case of a multicultural state *avant la lettre*.

By 1414 the Holy Roman emperor had given the title of Duke to Count Amadeus VIII of Savoy, a result of the steady increase in the possessions and the consequent importance of the County. The fifteenth century was indeed a period of climax for the Duchy, when it fully deserves its nickname of "porter of the Alps." This is a time when the House of Savoy ruled over the Western Alps and beyond, from the lake of Neuchâtel in present-day Switzerland to the Mediterranean, and from the Saône to the Po rivers. It takes a mental effort to consider fifteenth-century Savoy, which is today split between Italy, France, and Switzerland, as a political entity. And yet this is the state Olivier de la Marche called "the richest, the safest and the most plentiful of its neighbors."[2] As might be expected, these prosperous circumstances gave rise to interesting artistic productions. In the visual arts the 1979 landmark exhibition on Giacomo Jaquerio,[3] a painter active on both sides of the Alps, has certainly constituted an impetus for the consideration of a characteristic Savoyard artistic expression. It may seem surprising that I would cite an event that took place only two decades ago as the starting point for this type of reflection. Yet the lag in recognition may indeed be seen as caused by the very pluricultural nature of

173

Jaquerio's art in particular and of Savoyard culture in general. As a court artist for Amadeus VIII, Jaquerio was exposed to a network of connections that linked the House of Savoy to the ducal courts of Berry, Burgundy, and Milan. Amadeus was the son of Bonne de Berry (herself granddaughter of the king of France John the Good), and in 1403 he married the daughter of Philip the Bold, Duke of Burgundy. These dynastic links generated many artistic exchanges: the presence of artists from Lombardy, Tuscany, Germany, Flanders, Fribourg in Switzerland, Lyon, Grenoble, Geneva, Venice is documented at the court of Savoy in the fourteenth and fifteenth centuries.[4]

In the field of visual arts as in that of literature, we find a lack of studies dealing with the Savoyard state as a unity, with contemporary scholarship tending to focus on the production of sub-areas ("Savoie propre"—that is, present day French departments of Savoie and Haute-Savoie—Piedmont, Val d'Aosta, etc.). These categories tend to follow modern political subdivisions, and this is even more marked in the literary field, with a marked division between Italy and France, between Italian and French languages.

As it turns out, the linguistic situation in Savoy was far from simple. As Claudio Marazzini expressed it, the Duchy was "plurinazionale e plurilingue" ("multinational and multilinguistic"),[5] for it lies at the junction of several linguistic zones: French (Francoprovençal, to be precise), Italian, and Provençal; and to these one must add the use of French at the Court and in official documents. In other words, in considering the ensemble of Savoyard literary creations one must be willing to accept a wide range of languages and to go beyond linguistic borders. And again, our conception of modern states, unified by a common language, certainly undermines such understanding. A case in point is Piedmont, with Piedmontese dialect in the north, Provençal in the southern valleys, and Francoprovençal in western areas such as the Val d'Aosta.[6]

In this essay, I shall attempt to develop a sketch of the theatrical production in the Duchy of Savoy. Without any claims to comprehensiveness, I would like to indicate some important works and studies dealing with religious drama and reflect on some of the issues paused by this material. But first, one might ask, how pertinent is such a topic? How important was drama in an area so overwhelmingly absent from surveys and histories of late-medieval theater? To answer this question I include as an appendix a list of the performances documented in the regions under Savoyard domination in the fifteenth and sixteenth centuries. I have chosen to conclude that list with the end of the sixteenth century, although in many places the theatrical production continued, sometimes well into the nineteenth century.[7]

This information has been collected in only a very few published sources and studies. The second volume of Petit de Julleville's *Les Mystères*[8] remains an important resource, for it lists some three hundred performances between 1290 and 1603 and analyzes extant texts, and among these are several from Savoy.[9] Another important early study for the French side is François Mugnier's *Le théâtre en Savoie*.[10] More recently, some of the material discussed by Mugnier may be found in a study which Jacques Chocheyras published in 1971. As its title indicates, *Le théâtre religieux en Savoie au XVIe siècle* is solely concerned with the flourishing of religious theater in Savoy in the sixteenth century. In his introduction Chocheyras specifically states that he has not focused on the independent Duchy of Savoy, an area that was not under French rule.[11] However, an appendix devoted by him to religious theater at the court of Savoy in the fifteenth century[12] does fit into the limits of our inquiry. When necessary this short notice updates data from Mugnier and Petit de Julleville. Another useful appendix in Chocheyras's book concerns "Le théâtre religieux au pays de Vaud aux XVe et XVIe siècles" (79–80), which relies on information from an article by Paul Aebischer published in 1937.[13] Additional information on the appreciation of theater at the court of Savoy is available from Sheila Edmunds' studies on the ducal library.[14] Through careful combing of inventories, Edmunds was able to reconstruct a comprehensive picture of its book collection, which contained several texts of plays. For example, in the inventory of the Castle at Moncalieri, executed on 2 March 1479 after the death of Duchess Yolanda, the following are listed: a "passion nostre seigneur en parsonnaiges," a "destruction of jherusalem a parsonaiges pour jouer," "le jeu saincte marie par personaiges," "ung livre en papier a xxiij parsonaiges," "listoire saint allexis en parsonaiges."[15] That these volumes were considered precious is made clear by their

reappearance in later inventories.[16] An important event for the study
of Savoyard theater was the reappearance of a series of manuscripts
that had been collected by Florimont Truchet (1842–1916), a local
scholar. Discovered by Truchet's heirs in 1985, the manuscripts
were microfilmed (unfortunately rather badly) by the Archives
Départementales de la Savoie in Chambéry and were studied by
Graham Runnalls in his recent *Les mystères dans les provinces
françaises*. The Truchet collection comprises manuscripts of five
plays (*Le mystère de l'Antéchrist et du Jugement de Dieu*, *La
Dioclétiane*, *Le mystère de saint Sébastien*, a *mystère de la Passion
de Jésus en deux journées*, and a fragment of another *mystère de la
Passion*), some complete, others fragmentary. It also contains
a fascinating text documenting the organization of a Passion in
Saint-Jean-de-Maurienne in 1573.

On the Piedmontese side, the article published by Ferdinando
Neri in 1928 remains fundamental.[17] Neri starts with liturgical
drama, with the fourteenth century *Breviarium ecclesiae S. Mariae
Yporiensis* in the capitular library in Ivrea which contains offices
for Christmas (on the Nativity) and Easter (on the Resurrection).
Other documents in that library make reference to expenses for a
"ludo" performed yearly at Whitsuntide, with the first mention in
1376, followed by some eighteen others stretching until 1489. Neri
proceeds to list some thirty performances documented in Piedmont
and then spends the rest of the article in a discussion of the *Passione di Revello*, a very important play to which I shall return later.
The data from Neri's article may be supplemented by Anna
Cornagliotti's introduction to her edition of the *Passione di
Revello*.[18] Few manuscripts or printed editions have survived, of
which a very small portion is available in modern editions. This is
probably why the above mentioned *Passione di Revello*, which was
edited and published as early as 1888,[19] has attracted such attention.
Prior to further discussion of this play, however, a brief overview
of the extant texts and of editions is in order.

In the concluding part of his book on theater in the sixteenth
century, Chocheyras provides a series of analyses of hitherto unpublished plays and includes accompanying quotations. We find *La
Patience Job*, performed in Lanslevillard in 1542 (109–24), a *Histoire de saint Laurent*, performed in Lanslevillard in 1553 (54–58,

129–40), a *Passion* performed in Bessans once, perhaps in 1553, and again in 1583 (160–69),[20] and the *Mistère de la passion, mort et résurrection de N.S.J.C.*, performed in St-Jean-de-Maurienne in 1573 (5–12, 171–76). The surviving pages from a *Vie et Histoire de Madame Sainte Barbe* now in the Archives de Savoie in Chambéry are edited *in extenso*. This fragment contains the role of St. Barbara, and was probably originally from the Maurienne region.[21] Another fragment published in its entirety comes from the *Mystère de l'Antéchrist et du Jugement*, performed in Modane in 1580. The manuscript was once held in the parish archives of Modane which burned during the bombing of 1943. The fragment published by Chocheyras is in the Archives Départementales de Savoie, but other fragments from this play are in the Bibliothèque Nationale de France as well as in the Truchet collection.[22] Among the texts studied and quoted by Chocheyras, two have received extensive editions. The *Histoire de Saint Martin*, performed in Saint-Martin-la-Porte in 1565, was edited in 1881 by Florimond Truchet,[23] and the first day of the *Histoire de Monseigneur Saint Sébastien*, performed in Lanslevillard in 1567, was edited in 1872 by François Rabut.[24] Another play published early on is the *Mystère de Saint-Bernard de Menthon*, which was edited in 1888 by Lecoy de la Marche.[25] The play recounts the life of Bernard, a young noble from Menthon (a town overlooking the lake of Annecy), founder of the Hospice du Mont-Joux (the monastery at the Grand-Saint-Bernard). What survives today of the play are 4,340 lines, which were performed over two days.[26]

The *Mystère de Saint-Bernard de Menthon* has generated considerable discussion, starting with Paul Aebischer's 1925 article in which he claimed that this mid-fifteenth-century play originated in the Val d'Aosta.[27] Aebischer is indeed quite sure that the author was from the Val d'Aosta or at least was born "somewhere at the foot of the Mont-Blanc" (114; translation mine). He also contends that he was a clergyman, and was very likely to have been attached to the Hospice of the Grand-Saint-Bernard, as suggested by the use by the *Meneur de Jeu* of phrases such as "celle mayson" ("this house" [4,283]) when referring to the Grand-Saint-Bernard. Aebischer additionally suggests that the mystery might have been written with the purpose of lobbying in favor of the return of St.

Bernard's relics from the abbey of St. Lawrence in Novara to the Hospice. He concludes: "The *Mystère de Saint Bernard de Menthon* therefore bears witness of French literary culture in the Val d'Aosta or at least in the neighboring regions" (115; translation mine). Some of these conclusions were challenged by Chocheyras in a paper delivered in 1983.[28]

Considering the play in the context of the dramatic creation of its time, Chocheyras argues that "far from being an exception, this mystery is perfectly integrated within the dramatic production of neighboring francophone regions, with a Francoprovençal or Provençal substratum" (185; translation mine). He contends that the performance(s) did not take place by the monastery but rather in the town of Aosta, specifically at the Maison de Saint-Jacquême, where canons from the hospice lived. This then would also account for the use of the demonstrative in "celle mayson." Although Chocheyras retains the idea that the play was aimed at recovering the saint's relics, he also considers that here as elsewhere an outbreak of plague may have been responsible for initiating the tradition, and he notes that an epidemic struck the region in 1471. Previously Philippe Godet had suggested that the play could have originated in French-speaking Switzerland.[29] Godet noted that "many details, many customs touched on in this truly touching and pathetic work, link it in a direct way to our land"—for example, one of the characters swears "Par Nostre Dame de Lausonne" ("By our Lady of Lausanne" [2,112]), and an inn-keeper boasts of the wine he serves the pilgrims: "Il est bien frès;/ C'est du vim roge de Valez" ("it's well chilled, this is red wine from the Valais" [817–18]). If I have quoted these diverging opinions at length it is because there is certainly a common thread to all of them, and that is that the possible origins claimed by these scholars were part of the Duchy. In other words, we can affirm that this is truly a Savoyard work.

As noted above, the *Passione di Revello* was first published over a century ago in Promis's 1888 edition, which has been superseded by the 1976 edition of Anna Cornagliotti.[30] A *petizione* at the beginning of the only extant manuscript (Florence, Biblioteca Laurenziana, MS. Ashburnam 1190) is addressed to the officials of Revello, a town some forty kilometers southwest of Turin. At the time Revello was part of the Marquisate of Saluzzo, and indeed a second *petizione* follows, this time addressed to the Marquis of Saluzzo and his court.[31] The manuscript gives an explicit date of 15 July 1490 (R III, after 2,385), and Cornagliotti assumes that, given the date in the text announcing a performance spread over three days between 23 and 25 April, it could have taken place in 1492 when Easter fell on 22 April. Cornagliotti also considers that the performance might have been planned as part of the festivities in honor of the arrival of Marguerite de Foix, who, at the beginning of that month, had been betrothed to the Marquis of Saluzzo, Ludovico II. The wedding took place later, in the following November. Cornagliotti also stresses that the lack of accounts documenting a performance casts doubts on whether the play was ever in fact staged.

Revello is the most famous of the plays produced in the area, and it is the only one which is discussed in English-speaking scholarship. When considered within the field of Italian theater, its uniqueness is always emphasized.[32] The general consensus is that *Revello*'s singularity lies in its adherence to French prototypes.[33] Its length (close to a total of 13,000 lines) and division into three *giornate* are indeed comparable to the great cyclical plays of Arnoul Gréban and Jean Michel. Cornagliotti acknowledges the play's debt to French theater with regard to its structure, but she sees connections with Italian theater for its sources.[34] Nevertheless, the principal texts which she cites—sermons, the *Meditationes Vitae Christi*, the *Golden Legend*, apocrypha, etc.—also constitute essential textual sources for French theater. Indeed, Madeleine Le Merrer has revealed links between *Revello* and the *Passion Rouergate*.[35] To understand better the use of the Tuscan rather than the Piedmontese dialect in the *Passione di Revello*, one can benefit from Gaston Tuaillon's remarks about the *Mystère de Saint-Bernard de Menthon*; here we have a play in French which was performed for members of an audience who, in their daily lives, spoke dialect—in this case *valdôtain*: "From the fifteenth century to the end of the nineteenth, in Val d'Aosta as in Maurienne, dialect and French maintained relations of harmonious coexistence based on the principle that the dialect was the language for everyday and that French was the language for Sunday, the language for solemn occasions."[36] Priests preached in French, and logically, since mystery plays represented "des actes solennels de la vie religieuse et culturelle" ("solemn acts of the religious and cultural life" [Tuaillon, 182]), they were written and performed in French as well. Tuaillon also stresses that dialect and the French language were then closer to each other than they are today. But even if the French text was understandable for the *patoisants* (dialect-speakers), it both impressed ("le texte impressionnait" [183]) and expressed the sacredness of its message.

As Graham Runnalls has argued, for the audience of a mystery play the visual element was paramount: what one saw was more important than what one heard—or, we might add, what one understood![37] On the other hand, French or Italian, sacred and solemn languages, would stand in relationship to the dialect the same way Latin would stand to French in plays performed in French-speaking areas.[38] Tuaillon also reminds us that French was "the language the House of Savoy had been promoting for several centuries in its administration, the language of culture which was of the same family as the dialect from Savoy or from the Val d'Aosta, the language that the mountain *patoisants* could learn without too much effort, thanks to the linguistic kinship with their native dialect" (184; translation mine). These observations may be applied to the relationship between Piedmontese and Tuscan in the Marquisate of Saluzzo. The choice of Tuscan in the Marquisate might also reflect the tensions the small state experienced with the house of Savoy. Alessandro D'Ancona stressed that if the official language of the Duchy was French, the Marquis of Saluzzo promoted Tuscan.[39] Once again, things are far from being that clear-cut, for only a few generations before the *Passione* the Marquis of Saluzzo, Tommaso III (1396–1416), had chosen French to write his allegorical poem *Le Chevalier Errant*.[40]

Likewise, in areas under Savoyard domination we do find plays in Italian. Such is the case of the *Judicio de la fine del Mondo*, a play on the Last Judgment published in Mondovì by the printer Vincenzo Berruerio on 12 April 1510. Luigi Berra was the first to discover the text, which only exists in a unique copy now in the Vatican Library[41] and which Gian Luigi Beccaria edited in 1978.[42] Berra and Beccaria agree that the author of this short piece (1,312 lines) was most likely from Mondovì and that he wrote in a language not unlike that of the *Passione di Revello* and of the *Laudi* from Carmagnola and Bra.[43] His origin is nevertheless revealed by the presence of many expressions and words which seem specifically to belong to the area around Mondovì, the Monregalese.[44] In Berra's discussion of points of encounter between the play and the paintings in St. Sebastian's chapel in nearby Bastia Mondovì,[45] he argues that one of Bastia's frescoes, completed in 1472 and representing the Heavenly Jerusalem and Hell, provided a direct source of inspiration for the play. This is not the place to discuss this assertion, although I would like to seize the opportunity to stress that, along with its rich theatrical production, Savoy also witnessed a remarkable flowering of pictorial decorations, in particular cyclical depictions of Christ's Passion and of saints' lives, and that these two forms of expression do share many common features.[46]

Similarly, we can note the coexistence of pictorial cycles and records of performances in the same localities. This is the case of Lanslevillard, a mountain village in Maurienne. There, as mentioned above, a play on the life of St. Sebastian was performed in 1567, while the chapel dedicated to that saint contains an extensive cycle on his life (the paintings date from about 1490–1500). In the nearby village of Bessans, the Chapel of St. Anthony contains an extensive Passion cycle, while the parish archives contain fragments of a Passion play. These fragments belong in fact to two manuscripts. According to Chocheyras, the first and earliest dates from the first half of the sixteenth century and was more likely the director's copy. The second, in a hand datable to the second half of the century, states that this play had been performed in Bessans twice in the past and that it will be staged again, in the current year of 1583. This second and more recent fragment bears witness to the intervention of censorship, with curses either replaced by more proper terms or simply canceled. It also divided the *journées* into numbered chapters in a rather arbitrary grouping of scenes. Chocheyras established that the Bessans *Passion* follows Jean Michel's *Passion* rather closely. A noteworthy addition, which Chocheyras cited *in extenso*, occurs during Judas' Pact. The text painstakingly highlights the counting of the silver coins, each of them, from one to thirty. Interestingly enough, the chapel's depiction of the Pact of Judas also alludes to the process of the counting of the coins. On the table the thirty deniers are neatly arranged in

1. The Pact of Judas, c.1500. Bessans, St. Anthony's Chapel.

six groups of five (fig. 1).

Albeit fragmentary, the Bessans *Passion* still bears witness to a series of fundamental issues with regard to the late-medieval and early modern theater: it speaks of the process of adapting texts—in this case it confirms the fame of Jean Michel's *Passion*. But the marks left by the censors reveal the changes brought about by the Council of Trent. The division of the later manuscript into chapters hints at a new purpose—that is, not for the stage only, but also as devotional reading. As a matter of fact, in the later manuscript the stage directions have been translated from Latin to French, and thus we are informed about the level of culture of the potential user/ reader. The points of contact with local pictorial culture show how these two forms of expression interacted better in the hope of successfully conveying their message to the faithful. Indeed, such plays and such pictorial cycles are quite comparable in their communal sponsorship, and if more often than not they expressed campanilistic pride, they were nevertheless always aimed at a spiritual goal. A frequent impetus for financing the building of chapels and their pictorial decoration and likewise for supporting dramatic productions was to invoke divine help in times of calamities, particularly during epidemics of the plague.[47] Another frequent incentive was to combat the Waldensian heresy, then widespread in the Alpine parts of the Duchy and in neighboring areas. Chocheyras has shown how, in the beginning of the sixteenth century, religious theater in Provençal was used by the monastic orders as a means for anti-Waldensian propaganda.[48] The recourse to plays in Provençal makes perfect sense if one remembers that it was the language spoken in the so-called "Vallées Vaudoises"—that is, the Piedmontese valleys some fifty kilometers south-east of Turin, with Torre Pellice as its center. A fascinating example of such drama is the manuscript in the National Library in Turin published in 1984 by Alessandro Vitale-Brovarone.[49] This fragmentary text (the manuscript was damaged by fire in 1904) contains notes for the staging of a Passion play. Vitale-Brovarone has remarked that it displays linguistic features belonging to the northern Pays d'Oc and more specifically to Alpine regions. Chocheyras was to be more specific in affirming that the manuscript originated in Provençal-speaking Piedmontese valleys.[50] The presence of the manuscript in what originally was the ducal library, as well as the many connections between the text and Savoyard passion iconography, serve to support this hypothesis.[51]

The list which follows in the Appendix to this paper cannot, as noted above, claim to be comprehensive. It nevertheless bears witness to the vitality of theatrical life in the Duchy of Savoy, and in the future no doubt additions will be made as more records of performances are discovered and texts are edited. I have begun this article by remarking how the Duchy of Savoy, in the fifteenth and sixteenth centuries, was a plurilingual and pluricultural state. What is also clear from this list is the variety of Savoyard religious performances; indeed they span the entire spectrum of society. Besides plays performed at the ducal court and performances held in important urban centers, we also find plays being staged in rural settings, often remote mountain villages.

Appendix: Performances in the Duchy of Savoy from 1400 to 1600

For purposes of simplification, references are generally limited to one reference per performance, usually the most recent and, in terms of sources, the most comprehensive.

1376–	Ivrea, *ludo* performed annually at Whitsuntide (Cornagliotti,[52] xiv).
Early 15th c.	Chieri, *Lamentatio Domini* (Cornagliotti, xiv).
	Turin, *Lamentazione sulla 'Passione'* (Cornagliotti, xiv).
1402	Bourg en Bresse, *feste appelee des desperas*, payment on 22 January by the treasurer of Savoy to the actors. Cordero di Pamparato (342)[53] suggests this could have been a performance of Hell.
1406	Lausanne, performance for Mary of Burgundy, countess of Savoy (Aebischer,[54] 114).
1410	Thonon, court of Savoy, *Passion*, payment on 12 January to "Maistre Pierre lescrivain" (Cornagliotti, xv).
1426	Cuneo, main square, *ludo de stella que apparuit tribus regibus* (Cornagliotti, xv).
1427	Thonon, court of Savoy, *Histoire de saint Christophe* (Chocheyras,[55] 73, 75).
	Lausanne, *Disputacionis Corporis et Anime*, 30 March (Aebsicher, 114).
1429	Thonon, court of Savoy, *La Passion de saint Georges*, April (Chocheyras, 73).
1432	Grandson, *Passion* (Aebischer, 118).
1438	Lausanne, Place de la Palud, performance (Aebischer, 114).
1440	Lausanne, morality to welcome Amadeus VIII of Savoy, who had just been elected Pope (Aebischer, 114).
c.1446–50	Chambéry, *Histoires de saint Sébastien et sainte Anastasie*, to celebrate the arrival of Duke Louis and his wife Anne de

	Lusignan (Chocheyras, 73–74).
1453	Lausanne, *Passion* (Aebischer, 114).
1454	Pinerolo, *Passion*, Corpus Christi, (Cornagliotti, xv).
1456	Pinerolo, cloister of the monastery of St. Francis, *ludus seu iocus sancte Margarite* (Neri,[56] 85).
1459	Orbe, *fiction* (possibly a *Passion)*, Corpus Christi (Aebischer, 116: probably annual performances for the feast of the Corpus Christi).
1460	Moncalieri, *sancta luda*, after 27 April, date of the request of the Duke of Savoy to build scaffolds (Neri, 86; Cornagliotti, xv).
	Chambéry, *l'Histoire du bienheureux Laurent*, Whitsuntide (the performance was canceled because of a death in the ducal family and the duke of Bourbon's war in the Bresse; Chocheyras, 74).
	Lausanne, *Miracle de Sainte Suzanne*, 10 August (Aebischer, 114).
1461	Lausanne, *Creatio Ade*, 3 May (Aebischer, 114; Chocheyras, 79, suggests it may be a *Creation* from the *Vieux Testament*).
	Lausanne, *Ystoriam Status Mundi*, 3 July, for Bishop Georges de Saluces (Aebischer, 114).
1463	Turin, *Vita e passione di Santo Stefano* (Neri, 86).
1464	Barge, church of San Giovanni Battista, *Passion*, 4 May (Cornagliotti, xv–xvi).
	Orbe, *Ystoire*, perhaps of St. Germain, 28 May (Aebischer, 116).
	Orbe, *Passion*, Corpus Christi, 31 May (again in 1467 and 1497; Aebischer, 116).
1465	Chambéry, castle, *Descolacion de Mons. Saint Jean Baptiste* (Cornagliotti, xvi).
1466	Chambéry, *Passion*, Good Friday (Cordero di Pamparato, 344).
	Villeneuve, *Miracle de St. Paul* (Aebischer, 116; Chocheyras, 79, suggests it may be *Conversion de Saint Paul*).
1467	Orbe, *Passion*, Corpus Christi, 31 May (already in 1464 and again in 1497; Aebischer, 117).
	Pinerolo, *Nativity* and *Passion*, 28 May (Cornagliotti, xvi).
1468	Turin, *Passione di S. Vittore* (and again in 1506; Neri, 86).
	Turin, *Martirio di S. Vincenzo* (Galante Garrone,[57] 85).
1470	Chambéry, *Mistère de sainte Suzanne*, 1–2 July before Amadeus IX and his wife Yolande de France (Chocheyras, 74).
1473	Orbe, *Moralité de Saint Jean l'Ermite*, 10 October

(Aebischer, 117; Chocheyras, 79, suggests it probably is about St. John the Baptist).

pre-1475   Borgo d'Ale, inventory mentions texts for a *Passion* and *Infancy* (Cornagliotti, xvi).

1476   Orbe, "estueres," Corpus Christi, 13 June (Aebischer, 117).

1477   Cuneo, Church of Saint Francis, *Passion*, Holy Week (Cornagliotti, xvi).

1479   Revello, performance for feast of St. Mary Magdalene, 15 July (Cornagliotti, "Dimensioni culturali," 14–15).

1480   Orbe, *Moralité de Adam et de Evez*, 7 May (Aebischer, 117; Chocheyras, 79, suggests it may be a *Creation* from the *Vieux Testament*).

          Moudon, *Passion*, 21–22 March and 9 April (Aebischer, 115).

1481   Yverdon, *Passion*, Good Friday (Aebischer, 118).

          Yverdon, *Resurrection*, Easter Monday (Aebischer, 118).

1482   Savigliano, *Martyrdom of St. Catherine* (and again in 1484 and 1485; Neri, 86).

          Geneva, *Robert le diable*, before Charles of Savoy (d'Ancona,[58] 286).

1484   Savigliano, *Martyrdom of St. Catherine* (already in 1482, and again in 1485; Neri, 86).

1485   Savigliano, *Martyrdom of St. Catherine* (already in 1482 and 1485; Neri, 86).

          Geneva, *Myroir de Justice*, before Charles of Savoy (d'Ancona, 286).

1486   Savigliano, *St. Peter* (Neri, 86).

1488   Lausanne, cathedral's cemetery, mystery play (Aebischer, 115).

1489   Orbe, morality on the Sunday after St. George, 26 April (Aebischer, 117).

1490   Lausanne, Palud neighborhood, *historias*, 5 September (Aebischer, 115).

1491   Barge, *Passion*, 22 March (already in 1461, and again in 1492, 1495) (Cornagliotti, xvi).

          Turin, castle, *Purificazione di Maria*, September (Cornagliotti, xvi).

          Turin, square, *Resurrection*, September (Cornagliotti, xviii).

1492   Barge, *Passion* (already in 1461 and 1491, and again in 1492, 1495; Cornagliotti, xviii).

1494   Turin, *tableaux vivants* for the passage of Charles VIII (Orsi,[59] 23).

<table>
<tr><td></td><td>Chieri, *tableaux vivants* for the passage of Charles VIII (Orsi, 23).</td></tr>
<tr><td>1495</td><td>Barge, *Passion* (already in 1461, 1491, 1492; Cornagliotti, xviii).</td></tr>
<tr><td>1496</td><td>Orbe, *Miracle de Notre-Dame* (Aebischer, 117).[60]</td></tr>
<tr><td>1497</td><td>Orbe, *Mistere de Dieu* (*Passion* and *Resurrection*) (Aebischer, 117).</td></tr>
<tr><td>1502</td><td>Borgo San Dalmazzo, *San Dalmazzo* (Neri, 87).
Pinerolo, *Passione*, Easter (Cornagliotti, xviii).</td></tr>
<tr><td>1506</td><td>Turin, *Passione di S. Vittore* (already in 1468) (Neri, 86–87).
Seyssel, *St. Blaise* (Petit de Julleville, *Les mystères*, 2:88–89).
Orbe, Corpus Christi (Aebischer, 117).</td></tr>
<tr><td>1507</td><td>Saluzzo, performance to celebrate the return of the marquis, 2 March (Cornagliotti, xviii–xix).
Pinerolo, *Representatio Mundi*, 2 June (Cornagliotti, xviii).
Moudon, *Mystère de St. Etienne*, 5 September (Aebischer, 115; Chocheyras, 79).
Grandson, *Nativité* (Aebischer, 118).
Lausanne, cemetery, *Ludo moralizato*, 13 August (Aebischer, 115).</td></tr>
<tr><td>1508</td><td>Saluzzo, performance (Neri, 87).
Orbe, *Nativité*, 6 August (Aebischer, 118).
Grandson, *Jeu des Rois* (Aebischer, 118).</td></tr>
<tr><td>1510</td><td>Turin, procession for the feast of Corpus Christi, *Nativity* and *Ascension* (Cornagliotti, xix).</td></tr>
<tr><td>1511</td><td>Borgo San Dalmazzo, *San Giovanni Battista* (Cornagliotti, xix).</td></tr>
<tr><td>1514</td><td>Verzuolo, *Ludus in ecclesia* (Neri, 87).</td></tr>
<tr><td>1515</td><td>Pinerolo, *Resurrection* and *Annunciation*, 7 April (Cornagliotti, xviii).</td></tr>
<tr><td>1516</td><td>Chambery, "in plathea castri," *Passion*, Good Friday (Cornagliotti, xviii, n. 2).
Vevey, morality, June (Aebischer, 119).
Saluzzo, performance for the entry of the bishop (Neri, 87).</td></tr>
<tr><td>1517</td><td>Payerne, *Miracle de St. Nicolas* (Aebischer, 116; Chocheyras, 79).</td></tr>
<tr><td>1518</td><td>Villeneuve, *Passion*, in the parish church (Aebischer, 115–16).</td></tr>
<tr><td>1521</td><td>Yverdon, *Ludus sancti Jobi*, 18 August (Aebischer, 119; Chocheyras, 33, 79).</td></tr>
<tr><td>1522</td><td>Grandson, *Passion* (Aebischer, 118).</td></tr>
<tr><td>1523</td><td>Lutry, *Ystoria imperatorum* (Aebischer, 119–20; Chocheyras, 79).</td></tr>
</table>

Lutry, *Ystoria Sancte Susanne* (Aebischer, 119–20; Chocheyras, 74, 79).

Lutry, *Ystoria Pueri prodigi* (Aebischer, 119–20; Chocheyras, 79).

Geneva, *Ste. Hélène*, 4 August, for Beatrice of Portugal, wife of the Duke of Savoy (Godet,[61] 32–33).

1526   Moudon, *Mystère de Lazare* (Aebischer, 115; Chocheyras, 80).

Orbe, *jeu* performed by members of the clergy, Whitsuntide (Aebischer, 118).

Vevey, *Historia morale*, 19 May, eve of Whitsuntide (Aebischer, 120).

1529   Orbe, morality, 30 May (Aebischer, 118).

1530   Lutry, *Ystoery* (Aebischer, 119).

Aubonne, performance on the Feast of the Assumption (Aebischer, 118).

1531   Moudon, *Passion*, 2 and 10 April (Aebischer, 115).

Moudon, morality *Loz poure commung*, 27 August (Aebischer, 115).

Aubonne, Miracle plays for the Annunciation (Aebischer, 118).

1532   Vevey, *Passion,* Good Friday (Aebischer, 120).

Grandson, *Passion* (Aebischer, 118).

1533   Chivasso, *Rappresentazione di Tobia* (Neri, 87).

Aubonne, miracle play for Annunciation and Easter (Aebischer, 118).

1534   Borgo San Dalmazzo, *Apostles* (prepared but not performed) (Cornagliotti, xix–xx).

Yverdon, *Ludus Magdalene* (Aebischer, 119; Chocheyras, 80).

1536   Lausanne, performance (last before the proclamation of Reformation in Lausanne, in October of that year) (Godet, 31).

1541   Borgo San Dalmazzo, in the Church, *Resurrection* (Cornagliotti, xx)

1542   Modane, *Passion* and *Resurrection* (Chocheyras, xv, 3–5).

Lanslevillard, *Patience of Job* (Chocheyras, 29–34; analysis and quotations, 108–24).

1546   Salbertrand, *Mystère de saint Jean Baptiste*, 24–27 June (Chocheyras, xix).

Beaune, *Ystoire de Monseigneur sainct Sebastien* (Chocheyras, xv, xxi, 47).

1551   Rumilly, *Sacrifice d'Abraham* (Chocheyras, xv, 35– 36).

1553	Bessans, *Passion* (two performances) (Chocheyras, xv, 12–15; analysis and quotations, 159–69).
	Lanslevillard, *Histoire de saint Laurent* (Chocheyras, xv, 54–58; analysis and quotations, 129–40).
1562	St-Jean-de-Maurienne, Collège, *Sacrifice d'Abraham* (Chocheyras, xv, 35–36).
1564–65	Albiez-le-Vieux, *Passion* (Bulard,[62] 262).
1565	Beaune, *Ystoire de Monseigneur sainct Sebastien* (Chocheyras, xv, xxi, 47–48).
	Albiez-le-Vieux, *Ystoire de Monseigneur sainct Sebastien* (Chocheyras, xv, xxi, 48).
	St-Martin-la-Porte, *Histoire de la vie du glorieux sainct Martin, evesque de Tours* (Chocheyras, xv, xxii, 59–64).
1567	Lanslevillard, *St. Sebastien* (Runnalls, 25–28).[63]
1572	Modane, *Mystère de l'Antéchrist et du Jugement.*
1573	St-Jean-de-Maurienne, *Passion* (Chocheyras, xvi; analyzed, 5–12; analysis and quotations, 171–76; Runnalls, 127–28); there had been earlier performances of the *Passion* in St-Jean-de-Maurienne.
1574	Modane, *Mystère de l'Antéchrist et du Jugement.*
1580	Modane, *Mystère de l'Antéchrist et du Jugement* (Chocheyras, 20–27; analysis, quotations, and unpublished fragment, 181–224; Runnalls, 17–23).
1583	Bessans, *Passion* (Chocheyras, 12–15; analysis and quotations, 159–69).
c.1585	Fontcouverte, *Passion* (Chocheyras, xvi, 15).
c.1597	Aime, *Passion* (Chocheyras, xxi, 15).
1598	Jarrier, *Vie et Passion de saint Pierre* (Bulard, 262).

NOTES

I wish to express my gratitude to André Palluel-Guillard (as always with things Savoyard), to Graham Runnalls, to Lucinda Scanlon of the Interlibrary Loan office at Colby College for her indefatigable help in tracking books and articles, and to my assistant, Yuliya Komska. Since the initial publication of this essay, a major contribution to the study of early religious theater in Savoy has been made by Graham Runnalls' *Les mystères dans les provinces française (en Savoie et en Poitou, à Amiens et à Reims)* (Paris: Champion, 2003). I have included references to this work wherever relevant.

[1] *The New York Times Magazine*, 19 October 1997; special issue entitled "New York's Parallel Lives: A City of Subcultures, Side by Side."

[2] *Mémoires d'Olivier de la Marche, maître d'hôtel et capitaine des gardes de*

Charles le Téméraire, ed. Henri Beaune and Jules d'Arbaumont (Paris, 1883), as quoted in Bernard Demotz, "Amédée VIII et le personnel de l'Etat savoyard," in *Amédée VIII–Félix V premier duc de Savoie et pape (1383–1451)*. *Colloque International Ripaille-Lausanne, 23–26 octobre 1990*, ed. Bernard Andenmatten and Agostino Paravicini Bagliani (Lausanne: Bibliothèque historique vaudoise, 1992), 123. Unless otherwise noted all translations are mine.

[3] *Giacomo Jaquerio e il gotico internazionale*, ed. Enrico Castelnuovo and Giovanni Romano (Turin: Città di Torino *et al.*, 1979). This was preceded by a monograph by Andreina Griseri, *Jaquerio e il realismo gotico in Piemonte* (Turin: Fratelli Pozzo, 1965).

[4] For an introduction to Savoyard art, with an updated bibliography, see Sheila Edmunds and Robert Oresko, "Savoy," *The Dictionary of Art*, ed. Jane Turner, 34 vols. (New York: Grove's Dictonaries, 1996), 28:1–20.

[5] Claudio Marazzini, *Il Piemonte e la Valle d'Aosta* (Turin: UTET Libreria, 1991), 1.

[6] Ibid., 3.

[7] See, for example, the performances held in the Canavese region of Piedmont during the nineteenth century: Costantino Nigra and Delfino Orsi, *Il Natale in Canavese* (Turin: Roux, 1894), *La Passione in Canavese* (Turin: Roux Frassati, 1895), *Il Giudizio Universale in Canavese* (Turin: Roux Frassati, 1896).

[8] L. Petit de Julleville, *Les Mystères*, 2 vols. (1880; reprint Geneva: Slatkine, 1968).

[9] Ibid.: 1460, Chambéry, *St. Laurent* (28ff); 1470, Chambéry, *Ste Suzanne* (32); 1506, Seyssel, *St. Blaise* (88); 1546, Salbertrand, *St. Jean* (143); 1567, Lanslevillard, *St. Sebastien*, (164; analyzed, 557ff); 1573, St-Jean-de-Maurienne, *Passion* (166; earlier—but undated—performance of the *Passion* in St-Jean-de-Maurienne, 168); 1580, Modane, *Passion* and *Jugement Dernier* (169; analyzed, 460ff). One also finds, among the texts that are analyzed, *St Bernard de Menthon* (488–91).

[10] François Mugnier, *Le théâtre en Savoie* (Paris: Champion, 1887).

[11] Jacques Chocheyras, *Le théâtre religieux en Savoie au XVIᵉ siècle* (Geneva: Droz, 1971), xiv.

[12] Ibid., 73–74 ("Le théâtre religieux à la cour de Savoie au XVᵉ siècle").

[13] Paul Aebischer, "Le théâtre dans le Pays de Vaud à la fin du Moyen Age," *Recueil de travaux publiés à l'occasion du quatrième centenaire de la fondation de l'Uuniversité, Juin 1937*, Université de Lausanne, Faculté des Lettres, Publications, 3 (Lausanne: F. Rouge, 1937), 113–26; reprinted in *Neuf Etudes sur le théâtre médiéval*, Université de Lausanne, Publications de la Faculté des Lettres, xix (Geneva: Droz, 1972), 155–74.

[14] Sheila Edmunds, "The Medieval Library of Savoy," *Scriptorium* 24 (1970): 318–27; 25 (1971), 253–84; 26 (1972), 269–93.

[15] Ibid. (1971), 277–80 (entry no. 148, items no. 33, 35, 56, 65, 79).

[16] See for example the inventory of the Castle of Chambéry, on 25 October 1498, Edmunds, 26:269 (entry no. 162, item no. 6) and 26:273 (no. 138).

[17] Ferdinando Neri, "Per la storia del Dramma sacro in Piemonte," *Annali dell'Istituto superiore di magistero del Piemonte* 2 (1928): 83–95.

[18] *La Passione di Revello: sacra rappresentazione quattrocentesca di ignoto*

piemontese, ed. Anna Cornagliotti (Turin: Centro Studi Piemontesi, 1976), xiii–xxii. See also Ludovico Zorzi, "Notizia sul teatro piemontese dei primi secoli," *Communità,* May 1965, 75–86.

[19] Vincenzo Promis, *La Passione di Gesù Cristo, Rappresentazione sacra in Piemonte nel secolo XV* (Turin: Bocca, 1888).

[20] For the date of this first performance see Chanoine Adolphe Gros, *Histoire de la Maurienne,* 6 vols. (Chambéry: Imprimeries Réunies, 1946–60), 2:184, who does not indicate a source for this information. See also Marcel Bulard, "Un manuscrit du mystère de la Passion découvert en Savoie," in *Mélanges de la Société d'Etudes classiques* (Toulouse: Edouard Privat, 1946), 245–63.

[21] Chocheyras, *Le théâtre religieux en Savoie,* 41–46 and, for the text, 93–108.

[22] Ibid., 20–27; analysis, quotations, and unpublished fragment, 181–224; Runnalls, *Les mystères dans les provinces françaises,* 17–23, 30–31. Runnalls considers that "keeping in mind both the Fonds Truchet's four manuscripts and those in Paris and in the Archives Départementales de la Savoie, we possess traces of at least two and maybe even three versions of the text" (ibid., 19).

[23] "Histoire de saint Martin," ed. Florimont Truchet, *Travaux de la Société d'histoire et d'archéologie de la Maurienne,* 1st ser., 5 (1881): 193–367. See Chocheyras, *Le théâtre religieux en Savoie,* 59–64; analysis and quotations, 141–53. See also André Duplat, "Comparaison des quatre Mystères de saint Martin récités ou représentés aux XVᵉ et XVIᵉ siècles, en français ou en provençal," in *Atti del IV Colloquio della Société Internationale pour l'Etude du Théâtre Médiéval,* ed. M. Chiabò, F. Doglio, M. Maymone (Viterbo: Centro Studi sul Teatro Medioevale e Rinascimentale, [1984]), 235–49, and Nadine Henrard, *Le Théâtre religieux médiéval en langue d'oc,* Bibliothèque de la Faculté de Philosophie et Lettres de l'Université de Liège, 273 (Geneva: Droz, 1998), 371.

[24] *Histoire de Monseigneur saint Sebastien (1ere journée),* ed. François Rabut (Chambéry: Albert Bottero, 1872; extract from *Mémoires et Documents publiés par la Société Savoisienne d'Histoire et d'Archéologie,* 13); Chocheyras, *Le théâtre religieux en Savoie,* 49–50; quotations, 155–57. See also Runnalls, *Les mystères dans les provinces françaises,* 25–28, for other versions of this play, in particular that found in the Truchet collection.

[25] *Le Mystère de Saint-Bernard de Menthon,* ed. Lecoy de la Marche, Société des Anciens Textes Français (Paris: Didot, 1888). Previously, the play had been briefly analyzed by Petit de Julleville, *Les Mystères,* 2:488–91.

[26] In the manuscript edited by Lecoy de la Marche the beginning and end are missing. The beginning can be read in a later manuscript; see Paul Aebischer, "Une oeuvre littéraire valdôtaine? Le 'Mystère de Saint-Bernard de Menthon',"*Neuf études,* 95–116, esp. 97, n. 5. This article is reprinted from *Augusta Praetoria* 7 (1925): 49–61.

[27] See n. 26, above.

[28] Jacques Chocheyras, "La place du mystère de Saint-Bernard de Menthon dans le théâtre de son époque," in *Histoire linguistique de la Vallée d'Aoste du Moyen Age au XVIIIᵉ siècle. Actes du séminaire de Saint-Pierre (mai 1983)* (Aosta: Région Autonome de la Vallée d'Aoste/Assessorat à l'instruction publique, 1985), 185–89.

²⁹ Philippe Godet, *Histoire littéraire de la Suisse française* (Paris: Fischbacher, 1895), 31–32. Christopher Lucken has taught a course on the play at the University of Geneva while working on a study of the representation of mountains in the hagiographic texts devoted to St. Bernard de Menthon. We eagerly await his contribution to this discussion.

³⁰ See n. 18, above. Citations to this edition in my text follow the abbreviation R. See also Anna Cornagliotti, "Dimensioni culturali della *Passione di Revello*, sacra rappresentazione del XV secolo," *Bollettino della società per gli studi storici, archeologici ed artistici della provincia di Cuneo* 77 (1977): 13–17.

³¹ The inclusion of this play in a survey of theater in the Duchy of Savoy could be challenged because the Marquisate was not part of the states under domination of the Savoy. The relations between the Duchy and the Marquisate were, as a matter of fact, far from being harmonious; starting in 1486 there was a war between the two states; by 1488 the Marquisate was occupied by the Savoyard armies; in 1490 Lodovico of Saluzzo, assisted by the French and the Milanese, regained the state (Alessandro d'Ancona, "Misteri e Sacre rappresentazioni in Francia e in Italia," *Saggi di letteratura popolare* [Livorno: Raffaello Giusti, 1913], 280).

³² For Douglas Radcliff-Umstead, *Revello* "stands apart from the usual Italian sacred dramas" (*A Companion to the Medieval Theatre*, ed. Ronald W. Vince [New York: Greenwood Press, 1989], 187). Similarly, Joseph Spencer Kennard, *The Italian Theatre: From its Beginning to the Close of the Seventeenth Century* (New York: William Edwin Rudge, 1932), 29, declared it "unique in Italian literature."

³³ See, for example, ibid.: "This great Piedmontese cyclical drama is, in construction, versification, and proportions, influenced by the French mysteries" (29); Radcliff-Umstead: "shows the influence of French mystery plays" (*A Companion to the Medieval Theatre*, 187); Lynette Muir: "on the French model" (*The Biblical Drama of Medieval Europe* [Cambridge: Cambridge University Press, 1995], 35); d'Ancona: "example until now unique in Italy of a cyclical drama, following the norms of the art beyond the Alps" ("Misteri e Sacre rappresentazioni," 312; translation mine).

³⁴ Cornagliotti, *La Passione di Revello*, xxxv: "some motifs, for example the procession of the sibyls and prophets, affirm an unchallengeable knowledge of certain forms of Italian theater" (translation mine).

³⁵ In a personal communication to Jacques Chocheyras, mentioned by this latter in "Les relations ouest-est dans le théâtre religieux du XVᵉ siècle au sud de la Loire," in *Actes du XVIIIᵉ Congrès de Linguistique et de Philologie Romanes. Université de Trèves, 1987* (Tübingen: Niemeyer, 1988), 377–84. In both Revello and the Passion Rouergate, and contrary to the tradition, Gamaliel is not depicted as an enemy of Christ. On the apocrypha and southern French theater, see Madeleine Le Merrer, "D'une source narrative occitane de la Passion provençale et des Mystères rouergats: L'Evangile de Gamaliel," in *La vie théâtrale dans les Provinces du Midi, Actes du IIᵉ colloque de Grasse, 1976*, ed. Yves Giraud (Tubingen: Gunter Narr, and Paris: Jean-Michel Place, 1980), 45–50.

³⁶ Gaston Tuaillon, "Le théâtre religieux en Maurienne au 16ᵉ siècle et la situation linguistique dans les Alpes," *Histoire linguistique de la Vallée d'Aoste du Moyen Age au XVIIIᵉ siècle. Actes du séminaire de Saint-Pierre (mai 1983)*

(Aosta: Région Autonome de la Vallée d'Aoste/Assessorat à l'instruction publique, 1985), 178–84 (translation mine).

[37] Graham Runnalls, "Were they Listening or Watching? Text and Spectacle at the 1510 Châteaudun *Passion Play*," *Medieval English Theater* 16 (1994), 25–36.

[38] See Alan E. Knight, "Bilingualism in Medieval French Drama," in *Jean Misrahi Memorial Volume: Studies in Medieval Literature*, ed. Hans R. Runte *et al.* (Columbia: S.C.: French Literature Publications, 1977), 247–64.

[39] See d'Ancona, "Misteri e Sacre rappresentazioni," 288.

[40] Begun in 1394. See Marvin J. Ward, "A Critical Edition of Thomas III, Marquis of Saluzzo's 'Le Livre du Chevalier Errant'," Ph.D. diss. (University of North Carolina–Chapel Hill, 1984).

[41] Luigi Berra, "Una ignota rappresentazione sacra di Mondovì 'Lo Iudicio de la fine del mondo'," in *Miscellanea Giovanni Mercati*, 6 (Vatican City: Biblioteca Apostolica Vaticana, 1946), 432–41.

[42] Gian Luigi Beccaria, *Il "Judicio de la fine del mondo." Sacra rappresentazione piemontese del primo cinquecento* (Turin: G. Giappichelli, 1978).

[43] *Le laudi del Piemonte*, ed. Ferdinando Gabotto and Delfino Orsi (Bologna: Romagnoli dall'Acqua, 1891).

[44] Berra, "Una ignota rappresentazione sacra," 436.

[45] Ibid., 440–41.

[46] See my "Walls and Scaffolds: Pictorial and Dramatic Passion Cycles in the Duchy of Savoy," *Comparative Drama* 32 (1998): 252–90.

[47] Ibid., 279, 290.

[48] Jacques Chocheyras, "Le théâtre religieux provençal et la propagande antivaudoise: Personnages en quête d'auteurs," *Réforme, humanisme, renaissance* 44 (1997): 49–54.

[49] Alessandro Vitale-Brovarone, *Il quaderno di segreti d'un regista provenzale del Medioevo. Note per la messa in scena d'una Passione*, ed. Alessandro Vitale-Brovarone (Alessandria: Edizioni dell'Orso, 1984). See also Alessandro Vitale-Brovarone, "Devant et derrière le rideau: Mise en scène et *secretez* dans le cahier d'un régisseur provençal du moyen âge," *Atti del IV Colloquio*, ed. Chiabò *et al.*, 453–63.

[50] Jacques Chocheyras, "Le théâtre religieux provençal" and "Les relations ouest-est," 377–84. On this manuscript, see also Henrard, *Le Théâtre religieux médiéval en langue d'oc*, 163–65.

[51] Véronique Plesch, "Notes for the Staging of a Late-Medieval Passion Play," in *Material Culture and Medieval Drama*, ed. Clifford Davidson, Early Drama, Art, and Music Monograph Series 25 (Kalamazoo: Medieval Institute Publications, 1999), 75–102.

[52] In the appendix, "Cornagliotti" refers to her 1976 edition of the *Passione di Revello*.

[53] Stanislao Cordero di Pamparato, "Di alcune rappresentazioni sacre negli antichi stati sabaudi," *Bollettino Storico-bibliografico Subalpino* 5, no. 5 (1900), 340–47.

[54] Here and subsequently "Aebischer" refers to his "Le théâtre dans le Pays de Vaud à la fin du Moyen Age," in *Recueil de travaux*, 113–26.

[55] Here and subsequently "Chocheyras" refers to his *Le théâtre religieux en Savoie.*

[56] Here and subsequently "Neri" refers to his "Per la storia del Dramma sacro in Piemonte."

[57] Virginia Galante Garrone, *L'apparato scenico del dramma sacro in Italia* (Turin: Rosenberg and Sellier, 1935).

[58] Here and subsequently "D'Ancona" refers to his "Misteri e Sacre rappresentazioni."

[59] Here and subsequently "Orsi" refers to Delfino Orsi, *Il Teatro in Dialetto Piemontese: studio critico* (Milan: G. Civelli, 1890).

[60] This reference appears in accounts, but clearly performances were held at Orbe for the Corpus Christi on a yearly basis.

[61] Here and subsequently "Godet" refers to Godet, *Histoire littéraire de la Suisse française.*

[62] Here and subsequently "Bulard" refers to Bulard, "Un manuscrit du mystère de la Passion découvert en Savoie."

[63] Here and subsequently "Runnalls" refers to his *Les mystères dans les provinces françaises.*

Manuscript Painting and Play Production: Evidence from the Processional Plays of Lille

Alan E. Knight

In the Herzog August Bibliothek in Wolfenbüttel, Germany, there is a remarkable manuscript collection of seventy-two fifteenth-century French plays (Cod. Guelf. 9 Blankenburg). Though the manuscript had been listed since 1966 in the library's published catalogue,[1] only in the 1980s did it come to the attention of scholars working in medieval French theater studies. Sixty-five of the plays are dramatizations of biblical events, while the remainder are based on Roman history and Christian legend. They were written for the *Procession de Lille*, an annual religious and civic observance for which that city was renowned for over five hundred years. Plays were associated with the procession during the fifteenth and most of the sixteenth centuries. Like the cycle plays at York in England, they were mounted on *charettes* or pageant wagons. They were staged by companies of neighborhood youths, who vied for prizes in a contest that was for many years under the aegis of the Bishop of Fools, a canon of the collegiate church who organized civic entertainments.[2] The Lille plays are unique in that no other examples of this type of processional drama have survived from France.[3]

The manuscript is not dated, but based on physical and stylistic evidence it can be attributed to the last quarter of the fifteenth century, possibly between 1485 and 1490.[4] The text of each play is preceded by a painting that depicts one or two scenes from the action of the drama. In addition, the first page has a painted border in which, among the decorative leaves and branches, we find six occurrences of a highly stylized initial *h*, possibly the initial of the person for whom the manuscript was made. Originally, the owner's coat of arms was painted at the bottom of the page, but at an apparently early date someone crudely tore out the shield and took with it nine lines of text on each side of the folio. All that remains of the shield is a tantalizing fragment of its lower left corner, not enough to identify the owner.

All of the paintings in the manuscript, which is of paper, are ink and watercolor drawings. They exhibit a variety of styles, indicating that a number of different painters were involved in the work. The best of the paintings from a technical point of view is the first, which illustrates the play of Adam and Eve (fig. 1). The Garden of Eden is shown surrounded by a wall with a Flemish gate. Inside we see the creation of Eve on the left and the temptation scene in the center background. Outside the gate on the right an angel expels the fallen pair from the earthly paradise. This kind of continuous narration is found in a number of the paintings, though most of them are divided into two distinct scenes. The first painter, who was probably the master of the shop, was proficient enough to fill in fine details in the background and to draw faces that express emotion. The first three paintings of the manuscript are probably by the same master. The remaining seventy are more cartoon-like in style. Some are competently drawn; others seem to be the work of apprentices. The coloring is done in a variety of styles as well, ranging from light pinks and yellows in some illustrations to deep blues and greens in others. In some of the New Testament illustrations Jesus is depicted with a cruciform nimbus; in others he is portrayed without nimbus. Jesus and the apostles usually wear long, formless robes, while the other characters in the paintings wear identifiable fifteenth-century garments. The armor and weapons in the battle scenes are also contemporary with the painters.

There are many fascinating elements in these paintings that will engage art historians in the future. The question that interests us here, however, is the relationship between the paintings and the plays. Though much of what can be said at this stage is hypothetical, we can begin with an observable fact. In none of the seventy-three paintings in the manuscript is there a depiction of a stage. The painters have not portrayed plays being performed at the procession in Lille, as Fouquet portrayed the staging of the *Mystère de Sainte Apolline* in the Hours of Etienne Chevalier. Instead they have depicted historical scenes from the Bible, just as the playwrights represented historical actions from the same source. Thus the paintings and the plays have parallel functions for readers and spectators. Their relationship to each other, however, still remains problematical.

The pursuit of this elusive relationship brings several corollary

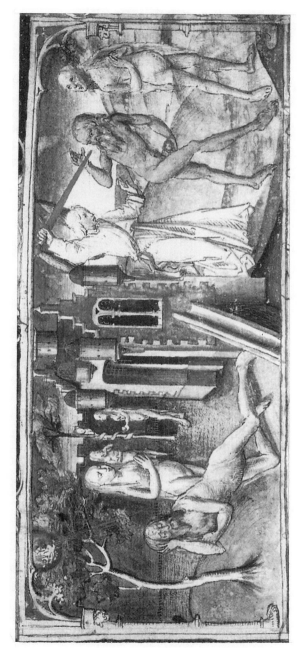

1. Adam and Eve in the Garden of Eden and their expulsion from the Garden. Herzog August Bibliothek Wolfenbüttel, Cod. Guelf. 9 Blankenburg, fol. 1ᵛ.

questions to mind. How, for example, were the scenes selected and how were they laid out? Is it possible that the painters saw the plays and then made their drawings on the basis of what they had seen? This seems rather unlikely. Obviously the plays came before the paintings, but how much before? The styles of clothing and armor in the illustrations, along with the watermarks in the paper, suggest that the manuscript was made in the late fifteenth century. The plays, on the other hand, were most likely written and played over a period of years, since the neighborhood groups who staged them were far fewer than the total number of plays in the manuscript. Two of the plays have, in fact, been dated to 1467 and 1474.[5] Since new plays were required each year, the painters would have to recall details of a performance they had seen some ten or twenty years earlier in order to base their illustration on what they had seen. This seems unlikely in the extreme. Still, they may have seen similar productions, since the procession was always adorned with dramatic representations in the late fifteenth century.

It is possible, of course, that the painters or someone in charge read the plays and then selected incidents from the action to be illustrated. It is also possible that the scenes depicted were based on a reading of the biblical text without reference to the plays. A third possibility is that the subjects of the paintings were derived from another series of illustrations such as one finds in the *Bible moralisée*. In any case, one notes a high degree of conformity between text and illustration. Moreover, the plays themselves conform very closely to their biblical sources. One notes also that when the painters treat well-known scenes, the composition of the picture tends to reflect the iconographic conventions found in other paintings of the same scenes. One example of such conventional iconography is the illustration for the Adam and Eve play already decribed. Another is the illustration for the play of Abraham and Isaac, where we see father and son, accompanied by servants and a pack animal, on their way to Mount Moriah. In the distance we see the climactic moment of the sacrifice, when the angel stays Abraham's sword. The illustration for the play about Jacob's ladder is no less conventional. In the foreground Jacob dreams of the angels ascending and descending, while in the background he constructs the pillar to commemorate the event.

Of the sixty-five biblical plays in the manuscript, forty-three are drawn from the Old Testament. Many of these are dramatizations of

2. Judith places the head of Holofernes in a bag held by her servant. Herzog August Bibliothek Wolfenbüttel, Cod. Guelf. 9 Blankenburg, fol. 134ᵛ.

events that were largely unfamiliar to the spectators, a fact that is evidenced by the need for long prologues to explain the circumstances of the action. Such unfamiliarity would suggest that the painters, working with less conventional iconography, had a freer hand in designing the illustrations. In most of these cases, however, the paintings follow the biblical and dramatic texts very closely. The rape of Tamar, David's daughter, was most likely not the subject of frequent illustration; yet the two scenes depicted in the manuscript follow the text quite closely. The left scene shows Amnon forcing Tamar into his bed, while the right scene shows Absalom's revenge on Amnon. The story of Naboth's vineyard is also illustrated in close accord with the play and the biblical text. On the right Naboth is seen kneeling before King Ahab; on the right he is being stoned by two of his townsmen as a result of Jezebel's machinations. Probably even less familiar to spectators and painters alike were the stories taken from Roman history. The play about Atilius Regulus is based on an incident narrated by Valerius Maximus and repeated by Augustine. The painter has followed the play quite closely in the two scenes he chose to illustrate. On the left we see Regulus, a prisoner of the Carthaginians, kneeling before King Xanthippus. Historically the latter was a Greek captain of mercenaries, but was transformed into a king in the play. On the right Regulus is put to death for his steadfast loyalty to Rome by being forced to starve in a barrel lined with nails.

Not all of the paintings, however, match the action of the plays they illustrate. One such painting illustrates the play that treats the death of King Ahab. In both the play and the biblical narrative Ahab disguises himself and rides in a chariot in the battle against the Syrians. He is struck by a random arrow and dies of the wound. The illustration of this scene, however, shows the king wearing his royal regalia rather than a disguise. The illustrator may not have been familiar with the story, or he may simply have wanted to make the dramatic situation more immediately comprehensible to the viewer. Far more difficult to explain is the illustration for the play of Joab and Abner. The painting shows two battle scenes in which all participants are wearing plate armor. On the left one soldier is killing another, while a third lies on the ground already dead. On the right we see a number of troops engaged in combat. Apparently, the illustrator had read neither the play nor the biblical narrative, in which the principal action is the killing of Abner by Joab. According to both texts, when Abner returned to Hebron, Joab took him aside at the gate where he pretended to speak with him quietly and there killed him (2 Samuel 3:27). In neither text is there a battle.

Though some of the paintings betray a lack of close relationship with the plays, others suggest techniques of staging that cannot be derived from the texts alone. In the play about Dinah, for example, the sons of Jacob take revenge on the city of Sheckem for the rape of their sister. The Israelites, pretending to accept the Sheckemites, require that all the males of the city be circumcised. On the third day, when the men are sore, Dinah's brothers attack and kill the Sheckemites. The painting shows one of them killing King Hamor in bed. Neither the play nor the Bible indicates that the men were in bed because of their soreness, yet this is certainly a highly visible and dramatic way of conveying the situation to the audience. In the play in which Joseph interprets Pharaoh's dreams, the ruler rewards Joseph by giving him power over all Egypt second only to his own. According to Genesis 41:42, the Pharaoh gives Joseph his ring, clothes him in fine linen, and places a gold chain around his neck. In the play the Pharaoh mentions only a garment. The painter, however, following the biblical text, has depicted the moment when the chain is placed around Joseph's neck. It is not unreasonable to suppose that the players too might have followed the Bible in their staging of the scene. Finally, the illustration for the play of Judith provides us with a detail that is not in the play, but which may well have been presented on the stage. The dramatic text tells us only that Judith left her maid outside the chamber when she beheaded Holofernes and that she took his head back to the besieged city of Bethulia. Here again the painter has followed the biblical text, which states that Judith gave the head to her maid, who put it in her food-bag (fig. 2). Clearly, if the players were at all realistic in their staging of the scene, they would have had Judith conceal the head in order to get past the guards and back to the city.

Though such connections may at this point be hypothetical and speculative, one hopes that the paintings in this unique collection of processional plays from Lille will ultimately contribute to our understanding of the relationship between illustration and staging in the late medieval theater.

NOTES

[1] *Kataloge der Herzog August Bibliothek Wolfenbüttel* (Frankfort: Vittorio Klosterman, 1966), 11:20–26.

[2] See Alan E. Knight, "The Bishop of Fools and His Feasts in Lille," in *Festive Drama*, ed. Meg Twycross (Cambridge: D. S. Brewer, 1996), 157–66.

[3] A critical edition of the plays is currently in progress, with two of the projected five volumes having already appeared. See Alan E. Knight, ed., *Les Mystères de la Procession de Lille*, vol. 1: *Le Pentateuque*; vol. 2: *De Josué à David* (Geneva: Droz, 2001–03).

[4] See Pamela Sheingorn, "Illustrations in the Manuscript of the Lille Plays," *Research Opportunities in Renaissance Drama* 30 (1988): 173–76.

[5] Knight, ed., *Les Mystères de la Procession de Lille*, 1:88–89.

Medieval Drama in Bohemia

Jarmila F. Veltrusky

My purpose in the present article is to offer a brief account of what is known about the medieval drama of Bohemia—a corpus which has hitherto been largely ignored outside its country of origin. The neglect of early Bohemian drama is due in part to the Czech language, which is understood by few specialists in medieval drama. The religious character of the extant material has evidently been a problem for Czech scholars, who have published little on the subject in recent decades. Difficulties of a different sort arise from the fact that most of the texts, aside from the Latin liturgical drama, are fragmentary and corrupt.

Moreover, the plays provide very few stage directions, and we are lacking independent accounts of dramatic performances or even references to them in records, though there is a prohibition that was promulgated by Archbishop Jan Očko of Vlašim in 1366 and repeated by the Synod of 1371 which concerns the inclusion of *ludos theatrales* in Corpus Christi processions. While these records are an early indication that plays of some kind were associated with the Corpus Christi procession, we do not know the type of plays that were presented nor are we able to ascertain how they are related to the procession. The absence of information about staging is a grave loss because the existing texts demonstrate that the plays were meant to be *seen*; hence when read as texts only by readers they must be a lesser experience than attending the fully staged dramas. This is true also on another level, since the plays contain a large number of sung passages, sometimes unprovided with musical notation or else reduced to incipits that cannot now be identified. The use of music clearly drew upon well-established and often quite elaborate practices of performing the text and creating a dynamic relationship with the audience.

It is thus unfortunate that matters of production—both visual elements and the use of music—can only be deduced very imperfectly from the available evidence. Nevertheless, in spite of the frustrating deficiency of the available information, the early drama of Bohemia deserves attention both for the light that it throws on the wider tradition to which it belongs and for the sake of its own particular contribution to this tradition.

The history of early drama in Bohemia begins in the late twelfth century, the date of the two oldest Bohemian versions of the *Visitatio Sepulchri*, and terminates in the sixteenth century with the final liturgical dramas as well as bilingual (Latin-Czech) and vernacular plays of the medieval type. At the beginning of this period Bohemia was a relatively backward country, dependent upon its German neighbors for virtually all its limited contacts with the civilizations of Western Europe. It did not even have an independent ecclesiastical organization since the Bishop of Prague owed obedience to the Metropolitan See of Mainz. But change came to this region rapidly, in part through large-scale immigration from German-speaking lands; and there was encouragement by ambitious rulers eager to improve their country economically and culturally. By the middle of the fourteenth century, King Charles IV of Bohemia, who was also Holy Roman Emperor, had begun to realize his plan to make Prague not only an independent archiepiscopal see but also the site of the first university in Central Europe and the political, intellectual, and artistic capital of the Empire. Determined to endow his hereditary kingdom with as much power, prestige, and magnificence as possible, he brought to Prague many leading artists and craftsmen of the day. Throngs of clerics, scholars, artists, poets, and courtiers were drawn from across the whole of Europe, and the country witnessed an extraordinary upsurge of intellectual and artistic life. Together with the other arts, drama flourished.

Because of the fact that the extant plays are sacred rather than secular in subject matter, it is important to remember that the religious life in Bohemia was characterized over a long period by ferment. On the one hand, the enormous wealth of the Church led to corruption and abuse; on the other, there was a steadily growing movement for reform, powerfully expressed by a succession of preachers who addressed the laity in their own tongues— German (e.g., Waldhauser) as well as Czech (e.g., Milíč, Matěj of Janov)— and enjoyed immense popularity. The reform movement culminated in the figure of John Hus, who won a wide popular following but was ultimately condemned by the Council of Constance and burned at the stake in 1415. The Hussite wars that followed were of a national and social as well as religious nature. While the Hussite movement was admirable in many respects and is often regarded as the high point of Czech history, its effect on the drama was wholly negative. The movement was opposed in principle to theatrical performance, and the upheaval caused by the war was so great that even defenders of the theater would have had difficulty in continuing to stage plays. In contrast to neighboring countries, therefore, the life of Bohemia's drama was abruptly cut short except in some German-speaking areas near the frontiers such as Cheb (German: Eger), the home of the famous *Egerer Fronleichnamspiel*. The few late dramatic texts that employ Czech are clearly reworkings of earlier models and show certain signs of adaptation to the changed atmosphere of their age. While at times they illustrate serious attempts to revive the dramatic tradition after the worst of the upheaval was over, in other cases they merely seem to have been written down as monuments of an already dead tradition. Toward the end of the sixteenth century a new form of drama appears that is Renaissance in form and content, and, aside from the three Easter plays by Šimon Lomnický (1522–after 1622) of which only fragments survive, they bear absolutely no traces of the medieval tradition.

Another unfortunate consequence of the Hussite wars and their aftermath was the destruction of many manuscripts, among which we may assume were included many texts of plays as well as documents which might have thrown light on their original performance. What remains must be only a tiny proportion of the original corpus of texts, but the extant texts nevertheless prove that Bohemia had a flourishing and varied dramatic culture.

The extant examples of the *Visitatio Sepulchri* originating in Bohemia[1] fall into two groups. One group is closely akin to other Central European ceremonies which dramatize the Visit to the Sepulcher, and the other, originating from the Convent of St. George in Prague, is distinguished by several unusual features. This type of *Visitatio Sepulchri*, as distinct from the more specifically dramatic form known as the *Ludus Paschalis*, is unique in including the episode of the Apothecary or vendor of spices to the Marys, and it contains a singular version of the *Hortulanus* episode in which the risen Christ appears to Mary Magdalene. Further, it also offers one of the earliest examples of the roles of the Marys being performed by nuns.

There are bilingual Easter plays, all of them usually identified under the generic title *The Plays of the Three Marys*; the earliest of these are untitled and are identified simply as *The First Play of the Three Marys*, *The Second Play of the Three Marys*, and *The Museum Fragment of a Play of the Three Marys*,[2] while two further examples, both found in the same manuscript (Czechoslovak State Library, MS. XVII E 1O) of 1516–26, are entitled *Ordo trium personarum in die resurectionis domini sepulcrum visitancium* and *Ludus pasce*.[3] These bilingual plays are based on a type of the *Visitatio Sepulchri* tradition associated with what Wilhelm Meyer called the *Zehnsilberspiel*,[4] not otherwise found in Bohemia. The Latin text provides a framework which is augmented by the addition of passages spoken and sung in Czech. Though the precise relationship between the Latin and the Czech components varies from play to play—occasionally a segment of dialogue or even an entire episode employs a single language throughout—as a rule not only each episode but also every unit of dialogue or "speech" is bilingual. Typically in each instance in which a participant intervenes in the dialogue, he sings a traditional Latin item and then adds a vernacular rendering, spoken or sung.[5] Sometimes, as in the later plays, there are two vernacular renderings, first a sung and then a spoken.

The vernacular passages made the Easter drama more accessible to a wider audience, and undoubtedly this was one reason for their introduction. The Church was engaged in a widespread effort to evangelize the common people at the time when this type of drama emerged, and thus it may be seen as consistent with the encouragement of the vernacular in other situations such as preaching and even certain liturgical acts. Instead of being able to attend only to the visual and musical aspects of the performance, those unlearned in Latin could now understand more of the general content of the plays. However, the vernacular speeches were intended not simply to duplicate the Latin chants but rather to complement them. The plays were in fact designed to appeal to educated audiences capable of understanding both languages and of appreciating how the vernacular paraphrase both reflects and modifies the Latin text. Two characteristics which appear in these *Plays of the Three Marys* serve to show that they were not primarily aimed at the same general audience as the dramas written fully in the vernacular: (1) some of the traditional passages receive no Czech rendering, while additions to the traditional framework include both Latin and Czech passages; and (2) these dramas as a whole are highly stylized.

The *Plays of the Three Marys* are akin to some of the Latin-German *Osterspiele*. Like the *Osterspiele*, they sometimes include a burlesque episode featuring the Apothecary who supplies the Marys with their spices or unguents. Although the only completely extant Latin-Czech play to contain such an episode is the late *Ludus pasce*, two fragmentary versions of the episode alone—the texts known as *Masti čkář Musejní* or *Museum Apothecary*, and *Masti čkář Drkolenský* or *Schlägl Apothecary*[6]—survive in manuscripts older than the earliest complete *Play of the Three Marys*.

The third category of plays consists of dramas which are mainly vernacular, though they usually contain a number of sung Latin items as well. The only complete text of this kind is the late *Ludus de resurrectione domini*[7] which is found in the manuscript which also contains the *Ordo trium personarum* and *Ludus pasce*. Another example in this category that appears to be almost complete is a work known as *The Play of Gay Magdalene* (*Hra veselé Magdaleny*), which presents Mary Magdalene as the typical sinner who finally repents.[8] All the others are mere fragments of what appear at least in some cases to have been quite elaborate productions. There is a small piece of a Resurrection play;[9] the beginning of an Ascension play;[10] the conclusion of a Passion play, followed by two burlesque sermons which may have been intended for presentation following it;[11] the first part of a Palm Sunday play and a very short beginning from another on the same subject;[12] and two fragments which are thought to belong to a Corpus Christi play, though the second of these may in fact be the conclusion of an independent Christmas drama.[13] The latter is remarkable for containing a speech by the infant Jesus, while the penultimate example in the above list records the ending of what may have been a unique dramatization of the story of Elijah as well as the beginning of an episode from the story of Moses. Finally, there are two examples of a dramatized *Planctus Mariae* which were sung entirely or almost entirely in Czech;[14] and two examples of a quasi-dramatic Christmas ceremony in which a group of "persone" standing around a manger, a choir, and a group of "pueri" sing a number of both Latin and Czech pieces *alternatim* in honor of the Nativity.[15]

The Latin-Czech and Czech plays belong to a family of texts which spans the linguistic divide between Czech and German. Their nearest kin among the German plays are the Trier, Innsbruck, Vienna, and Erlau *Osterspiele*[16] and the *Fronleichnamspiel* from

Eger—to which may be added the Melk *Salbenkrämerspiel* (related
to the two Apothecary or *Mastičkář* fragments) and the Erlau *Ludus
Mariae Magdalenae in gaudio* (related to the *Play of Gay
Magdalene* or *Hra veselé Magdaleny*). The precise nature of the
relationship between the German and Czech plays is, however,
difficult to establish. Internally they are linked by broad family
resemblance rather than by direct dependence or close parallelism
between entire plays. The initial impetus for this drama no doubt
came to Bohemia from its German-speaking neighbors, but there is
no reason to assume that influence necessarily continued to operate
in only one direction. Czech expressions appear in some of the German texts, and it has been argued that at least one passage in the
Apothecary episode in both German and Czech plays is actually of
Czech origin.[17] In any event, none of the extant plays appears to be
an original version or the possible ancestor of the others in either
Czech or German; instead the evidence points to a common tradition
upon which both the Czech and German plays drew. The older
models are now evidently lost. The questions of priority and dependence, which seemed of great importance to certain nationalistic
scholars in the past, now appear to spring from a misconception
about how such plays were composed and above all about the ways
in which medieval dramatists used already existing plays as models
to be freely copied, reshaped, and adapted to each new audience and
setting. Insufficient documents survive to enable us to observe the
process in any detail with respect to the texts in question. In particular we have no examples of the German-language plays which
must have been performed in the Bohemian towns with a sizable
German-speaking population.[18]

The Latin, bilingual, and Czech plays actually represent three
different genres of drama, each of which uses different means to
produce different effects. Each implies a different kind of reception
on the part of the audience. As is well known, the liturgical *Visitatio
Sepulchri* was integrated into the liturgy of the Church. In
Bohemian practice it was performed in conjunction with Easter
Matins by persons who visibly remained clerics or nuns and who
used the same or similar chants, garments, and objects as those
otherwise involved in the office. Moreover, it dramatizes the subject
matter of the lessons which report the revelation of the Resurrection, and it presents the story in a spirit of communal praise and
thanksgiving similar to the liturgy which surrounds it. The events of

the first Easter are represented in a distinctly ceremonial fashion which remains sufficiently transparent for the members of the audience-congregation to remain aware that they are participating in an act of communal worship. The purpose of the representation is to bring these events before the spectators' eyes with the vividness that characterizes even highly stylized drama in order to make them participate more actively and fervently in the celebration. The liturgical drama is a drama of communal worship.

The bilingual *Plays of the Three Marys*, again representing the events of the first Easter morning, were also performed during Matins at least in some and perhaps in all cases.[19] Their close relationship with the liturgical drama is clearly apparent since they incorporate all the Latin items that make up a complete *Visitatio Sepulchri*. However, the addition of the passages spoken or sung in Czech serves to modify them, for thus they are given a fundamental duality which in turn underlies their entire structure. The ritual world of the items sung in Latin confronts the personal world of the vernacular; the latter also involves representation in a highly stylized fashion, though by contrast it appears more immediate, more emotional, and more discursive, especially in its emphasis on humanity's sinfulness and the cost at which Christ redeemed it. While the Latin passages still invite spectators to respond as participants in a communal celebration to the ritual announcement of the Resurrection, the Czech speeches place them rather in the position of individual Christians invited to identify in spirit with the original recipients of the revelation. At the same time the juxtaposition of two or even three versions of every utterance (Latin chant, followed by a Czech speech or chant, or both) promotes reflection and invites meditation about the full meaning—both from a ritual and a personal point of view—of the event represented. Here the emphasis shifts between communal worship and personal devotion.

Some of these plays take the characteristic dichotomy a step further and introduce elements which are strikingly at odds with the generally pious atmosphere—even extending to blasphemous parody. Such elements heighten the characteristic dichotomy by inserting into the event not only a more humanly personal devotion but also flagrantly ribald laughter of the sort traditionally associated with festive celebration in general and with the *risus paschalis* tradition in particular. At the same time, some of the most outrageous scenes, perceived as merely comic by perhaps the major portion of the audience, offered the better educated spectators, the clerics and students accustomed to analyzing the theological message of Easter, the additional pleasure of detecting (under the comic surface) playfully concealed allusions to various aspects of this message, which forms the basic theme of the Easter drama as a whole, whether Latin, vernacular, or bilingual. The dialogue of the burlesque *Apothecary (Mastičkář)* suggests that it was performed by students. Whether the serious parts of the bilingual plays were also performed by students or by more senior clerics is not known, and indeed the practice may have varied from one location or occasion to the next.

The Czech language plays are designed to instruct and entertain in varying proportions. Some of the fragments seem entirely didactic, but elsewhere there are comic scenes or again passages of profane singing perhaps accompanied by dancing. Whether serious or light-hearted, all the scenes in these plays place the spectators in the position of a true audience, watching the represention of events from the outside, as it were, rather than participating ritually (as in the liturgical drama) or devotionally (as in the bilingual plays). This is not, of course, to imply that there is a hard-and-fast division between the world of the play and the world of the audience. Whereas the liturgical and bilingual plays represent the best-known part of the Gospel story and shape it into a repetitive and hence foreseeable pattern of quest-and-revelation—a pattern that encourages the spectator to celebrate the mystery directly or as a focus of meditation—and hence remove any suspense about what will happen next, the vernacular plays tend to arouse curiosity (if not suspense) about what is said and what is shown to happen on the stage.

There is some evidence to suggest that these plays may have been associated with student productions. Nevertheless, the more straightforwardly didactic, plain, and serious texts seem to me to be less likely candidates for staging in schools. There is here no external documentation to tell us whether they were the independent work of religious organizations responsible for the edification of the laity, or whether lay bodies such as guilds or civic authorities shared in their presentation.

A certain amount of interpenetration exists between the three kinds of drama surveyed above. In the bilingual *First Play of the Three Marys*, one episode, the questioning of Mary, remains entirely in the form of the Latin chant in the *Visitatio Sepulchri*. The two fragmentary versions of the Apothecary episode seem to present typical examples of vernacular drama, though the earlier (and by far the longer) of the two plays includes a Latin-Czech passage that dramatizes the laments of the Marys as well as the beginning of their meeting with the Apothecary—a bilingual passage that proves the original placement of the fragment in a bilingual play. The three plays found together in MS. XVII E 1 also exemplify a mixture of these two kinds of drama. The *Ordo trium personarum*, for the most part a typically bilingual example of the *Play of the Three Marys*, gives the Hortulanus an unusual burlesque speech of a sort associated with vernacular dialogue; it also portrays the Doubting Thomas episode through purely vernacular dialogue until the moment of Christ's appearance, whereupon it returns to the dominant bilingual form. The *Ludus pasce* provides the passages, mostly in Czech, to be added to a bilingual play like the *Ordo trium personarum*.[20] The *Ludus de resurrectione domini* is an essentially vernacular play but contains two Latin-Czech scenes akin to those in the bilingual plays.

Very likely the mixture of forms in these three plays is related to their late date. Perhaps it was felt that bilingual drama was out of date and hence unlikely to elicit the desired response from a contemporary audience. Thus a deliberate effort may have resulted in order to adapt the play to the vernacular mode. At the same time, however, it may have been decided that passages alternating Latin singing with Czech speech would provide a suitable means of introducing ceremonial solemnity at certain points in the action of a vernacular play.

NOTES

[1] *Lateinische Osterfeiern und Osterspiele*, ed. Walther Lipphardt, 9 vols. (Berlin: Walter de Gruyter, 1975–91), 2:528–30 (no. 387); 4:1165–1219 (nos. 661–69, 671–81); 5:1540–46 (no. 789), 1579–1604 (nos. 798–806); 6:167–86, 204. There are also examples of the *Depositio* for Good Friday and the Easter *Elevatio*, ceremonies which are not discussed here.

[2] For these plays, see Jan Máchal, *Staročeské skladby dramatické původu liturgického* (Prague: Rozpravy České Akademie, 1908), 98–125.

[3] Both plays are edited by Máchal; see ibid., 149–86.

[4] Wilhelm Meyer, *Fragmenta Burana* (Berlin: Weidmann, 1901), 106–20.

[5] The male pronoun 'he' is used advisedly since in Bohemia these plays were almost certainly all male productions.

[6] Máchal, *Staročeské skladby dramatické původu liturgického*, 63–80, 86–93.

See also Jarmila F. Veltruský, *A Sacred Farce from Medieval Bohemia: Mastičkář* (Ann Arbor: Horace H. Rackham School of Graduate Studies, University of Michigan, 1985).

⁷ Máchal, *Staročeské skladby dramatické původu liturgického*, 186–215.

⁸ Ibid., 82–86.

⁹ Ibid., 93–94.

¹⁰ Ibid., 94–97.

¹¹ Ibid., 127–34.

¹² Ibid., 134–40, 145–46.

¹³ Ibid., 141–45.

¹⁴ For the first of these, which has a Latin opening, see Josef Truhlář, "O staročeských dramatech velikonočních," *Časopis Českého Musea* 37 (1871): 191–97; for the other, entirely in Czech, see Zdeněk Nejedlý, *Dějiny husitského zpěvu*, 6 vols. (Prague: Československá Akademie Věd, 1954), 1:401–05.

¹⁵ Josef Truhlář, "Pabĕrky z rukopisů Klementinských XVII: Latinsko-česká slavnost vánoční z doby okolo r. 1400," *Vĕstník České Akademie* 7 (1898), 660–62; A. Brückner, "Ein böhmisches officium ad cunabulum in Nativitate Domini," *Archiv für slavische Philologie* 16, no. 2 (1894): 606–07.

¹⁶ For the origin of the so-called *Innsbrucker Osterspiel* in Thuringia and of the so-called *Wiener Osterspiel* in Upper Silesia, see Heinz Kindermann, *Theatergeschichte Europas* (Salzburg: Otto Müller Verlag, 1957), 249.

¹⁷ Walter Schamschula, "The Place of the Old Czech Mastičkář-Fragments within the Central European Easter Plays," *American Contributions to the 8th International Congress of Slavists, Zagreb and Ljubljana, September 3–9, 1978*, 2: *Literature*, ed. Victor Terras (Columbus, Ohio: Slavica, 1978), 678–90.

¹⁸ The *Egerer Fronleichnamspiel* is a special case since Eger (Cheb), located on the frontier, was wholly German-speaking.

¹⁹ There is no evidence to show where and when the earlier *Plays of the Three Marys* (to which the two Apothecary fragments no doubt belonged) were performed; but the Erlau *Osterspiel*, which has an even longer and bawdier Apothecary episode, was performed in the customary position of the *Visitatio Sepulchri* immediately prior to the *Te Deum* at the end of Matins. The Erlau play attests that such ribaldry was no bar to performance in a liturgical setting.

²⁰ It seems that the scribe who copied the two plays, one after the other, saw the *Ludus pasce* as an optional expansion of the *Ordo*, but in fact the relationship between the two texts is more complex: the *Ordo* contains, in the Doubting Thomas episode, a passage which is based on the Emmaus episode of the *Ludus pasce*. Thus the two texts in their present form were not destined to be performed together; see Stanislav Souček, "Ke Komedii vánoční o narození Syna božího, pocházející z Vlachova Březí," *Strahovská Knihovna* 12–13 (1977–78): 122–58.

SELECT BIBLIOGRAPHY

Baumann, Winfried. *Die Literatur des Mittelalters in Böhmen.* Munich and Vienna: R. Oldenbourg Verlag, 1978. [Drama: 123–47.]

Bogatyrev, Petr. "Zur Frage des gemeinsamen Kunstgriffe im alttschechischen und im volkstümlichen Theater," *Slavische Rundschau* 10, no. 6 (1938) [Festschrift for Franz Spina]: 154–61; trans. Jaroslav Kolár: "Kotázce společných postupů v staročeském a lidovém divadle." In Petr Bogatyrev, *Souvislosti tvorby*, ed. Jaroslav Kolár. Prague: Odeon, 1971. 132–38.

Brückner, A. "Ein böhmisches officium ad cunabulum in Nativitate Domini," *Archiv für slavische Philologie* 16, no. 2 (1894): 606–07.

Černý, Václav. *Staročeský Mastičkář* [*The Old Czech Mastičkář*], Rozpravy Československé Akademie Věd 65, series SV 7. Prague: ČSAV, 1955.

_____. "Od bonifantů k mastičkářům" ["From Bonifantes to Apothecaries"], *Sborník historický* 9 (1962): 95–135.

Gebauer, Jan. "Staročeský Mastičkář a páně A. Šemberovy námitky proti jeho přesnosti" ["The Old Czech *Mastičkář* and Mr. A. Šembera's Objections Concerning Its Correctness"], *Listy filologické* 7 (1880): 90–121.

Havránek, Bohuslav, and Josef Hrabák, eds. *Výbor z české literatury odpočátků po Husovu* [*A Selection from Czech Literature from the Beginning to the Age of Hus*]. Prague: ČSAV, 1957. [Drama: 247–96.]

Hrabák, Josef, ed. *Staročeské drama* [*The Old Czech Drama*]. Prague: Československý spisovatel, 1950.

Jacobson, Roman. "Medieval Mock Mystery: The Old Czech *Unguentarius*." In Roman Jacobson, *Selected Writings*, 8 vols. Berlin, New York, and Amsterdam: Mouton, 1985. 6:2:666–90.

Kolár, Jaroslav. "Česká Hra veselé Magdalény a středověké divadlo" ["The Czech Play of Gay Magdalene and the Medieval Theater"], *Divadelní revue* 3 (1992): 39–50.

Máchal, Jan. *Staročeské skladby dramatické původu liturgického* [*The Old Czech Dramatic Compositions of Liturgical Origin*], Rozpravy České Akademie class III, 23. Prague: Česká Akademie, 1908.

Nejedlý, Zdeněk. *Dějiny husitského zpěvu* [*The History of the Hussite Song*], 2nd ed. Prague: ČSAV, 1954. Vol. 1.

Oberfalcer, František, ed. *Nejstarší české hry divadelní* [*The Oldest Czech Plays*]. Prague: Konservatoř hudby v Praze/Literárné historická společnost v Praze/ Lidové diadlo v Praze, 1941.

Plocek, Václav. *Melodie velikonočních slavností a her ze středověkých pramenů v Čechách* [*The Melodies of Easter Ceremonies and Plays from Medieval Sources in Bohemia*]. Prague: Státní knihovna, 1989.

Pujman, Ferdinand. *Zhudebněná mateřština* [*The Mother Tongue Set to Music*]. Prague: Melantrich, 1939.

Schamschula, Walter. "The Place of the Old Czech Mastičkář-Fragments within the Central European Easter Plays." *American Contributions to the Eighth International Congress of Slavists, Zagreb and Ljubljana, September 3–9, 1978, 2: Literature,* ed. Victor Terras. Columbus, Ohio: Slavica, 1978. 678–90.

Schmidt, W. "Der alttschechische Mastičkář und sein Verhältnis zu den deutschen Osterspielen," *Zeitschrift für Slawistik* 3 (1957): 223–42.

Škarka, Antonín. "Roudnický Plankt" ["The Roudnice Planctus"], *Listy filologické* 79 (n.s. 4), no. 2 (1956): 187–95.

Souček, Stanislav. "Ke Komedii vánoční o narození Syna božího, pocházející z Vlachova Březí" ("Concerning the Christmas Comedy about the Birth of the Son of God, Originating from Vlachovo Březí"], ed. Jan Lehár, *Strahovská Knihovna* 12–13 (1977–78): 122–58.

Svejkovský, František. "Dvě verze Mastičkáře—dva typy středověké frašky" ["Two Versions of Mastičkář—Two Types of Medieval Farce"], *Česká literatura* 11 (1963): 473–87.

_____. *Z dějin českého dramatu: Latinské a latinsko-české hry tří Marií* [*From the History of Czech Drama: The Latin and Latin-Czech Plays of the Three Marys*]. Prague: Universita Karlova, 1966.

_____. "Divadlo raného a vrcholného feudalismu a krize divadla za husitství" ["The Theater of the Early and High Feudalism and the Crisis of the Theater in the Hussite Era"]. In *Dějiny českèho divadla,* ed. Adolf Scherl. 4 vols. Prague: Academia, 1968. 1:24–98.

Trost, Pavel. "K staročeskému Mastičkáři" ["Concerning the Old Czech Mastičkář"], *Sborník Vysoké školy pedagogické v Olomouci: Jazyk a literatura* 3 (1956): 103–05.

Truhlář, Josef. "O starých dramatech velikonočních" ["About the Old Czech Easter Plays"], *Časopis Českého Musea* 65 (1891): 3–43, 165–97.

_____. "Paběrky z rukopisů Klementinských XVII: Latinsko-česká slavnost vánoční z doby okolo r. 1400" ["Gleanings from the Clementine Manuscripts XVII: A Latin-Czech Christmas Ceremony from around the Year 1400"], *Věstník České Akademie* 7 (1898): 660–62.

Veltrusky, Jarmila F. *A Sacred Farce from Medieval Bohemia: Mastičkář.* Ann Arbor: Horace H. Rackham School of Graduate Studies, University of Michigan, 1985.

_____. "Jeux de Pâques bilingues d'Europe Centrale: leur dualité et leur unité," *Revue de littérature comparée* 61, no. 4 (1987): 471–86.

_____. "Dialogues chantés et dialogues parlés dans le théâtre médiéval en Bohème." In *Le rôle des formes primitives et composites dans la dramaturgie Européenne,* ed. Irène Mamczarz. Paris: Klincksieck, 1992. 51–62.

_____. "The Old Czech Apothecary as Clown and Symbol." In *Festive Drama,* ed. Meg Twycross. Cambridge: D. S. Brewer, 1996.

Vilikovský, Jan. "K dějinám staročeského dramatu" ["A Contribution to the History of Old Czech Drama"]. In *Hrst studií a vzpomínek: A Beerovi*

[Festschrift for A. Beer]. Brno: Odbočka Jednoty českých filologů v Brně, 1941. 110–20.

_____. "Dva plankty svatojirské" ("Two *planctus* from St. Georges Convent"). In Jan Vilikovský, *Písemnictví českého středověku*. Prague: Universum, 1948. 41–47.

_____. "Latinské kořeny staročeského dramatu" ["The Latin Roots of Old Czech Drama"]. In Jan Vilikovský, *Písemnictví českého středověku*. 98–108.

Polish Saint Plays
of the Sixteenth and Seventeenth
Centuries

Andrzej Dąbrówka

With the revival of interest in the saint play in Western Europe, attention to plays associated with this genre in Central Europe, specifically in Poland, seems appropriate. By way of introducing the present list of Polish saint plays which is my objective here, some notice needs to be taken of the non-theatrical or non-literary (liturgical and festive) forms of the cult of saints in Poland; these are not to be seen as underdeveloped forms of theater or as its substitute, but rather as its "neighbor." And in an attempt to recover for our study those traditional developments that were discarded by modernist aesthetics as unimportant because non-innovative, the question of genre needs to be considered: do these sixteenth- and seventeenth-century plays belong to the same genre as the medieval saint plays?

For our purpose, three liturgical forms of the cult of saints can be distinguished: regular processions on the saint's feast day, special celebrations on extraordinary occasions such as beatification or canonization; and translations of the saint's relics. We have detailed programs of rich and spectacular processions celebrating the first feast of a new saint and the translation of relics (e.g., in Vilna, 1631).[1] These examples show the continuity and intensity of the cult of the saints—*the* crucial factor if we are to explain the shape of saint plays in terms of actual social circumstances rather than on the basis of some retarded "sacramental psychology" or the authors' unwillingness if not inability to purge "medieval elements" from literature.[2]

Certain rituals and customs developed around specific devotional traditions such as church benedictions that were ordained on saints' days. The connection with the saints' biographies here is mostly conventional (reflecting the church's patron) or nonexistent (the coincidence of an ancient tradition or a new custom with a specific day in the calendar).

It should be remembered that the annual feast of the patron saint of the parish was (and still is) connected with a church fair in Poland. Church fairs were a well-known meeting point for wandering merchants, beggars (singing beggars included), and entertainers, and they also provided an opportunity for local productions. We see this explicitly announced in the printed text of the Polish John the Baptist play (to be discussed below), which was "performed in Kamionka during the fair on the day of the named St. John the Baptist Anno Domini 1619."[3] Much could also be said about the different patron saints of other nations (such as St. Lucia or St. Patrick) who became emblems of popular celebrations. Another type is represented by St. Valentine, an example of the commercial afterlife of an old tradition, and St. Barbara, who is remembered in the official miners' feast that is still an occasion for parades, concerts, and dances in mining regions of Poland.

"Christian names" are a similar case. What today has become just the name-day—celebrated in Catholic countries rather than (or along with) one's birthday—was strictly associated with the patron saint a couple of centuries ago. A son writing (before 1700) congratulatory poems to his mother Anne and father Michael gave them the titles *Gratulatio pro festo Sanctae Annae* and *Gratulatio in festo S. Michaelis*[4] and addressed in them the qualities of these saints.

Popular traditions grew around saints and their feasts. Figures of particular importance for the study of Polish theater are Catherine, George, Gregory, and Nicholas. Others deserving of special attention are John the Baptist, who is of course internationally popular, while Boris and Gleb along with Stanislaus are important local saints. The available data on performances and texts are mainly drawn from the Polish, Lithuanian, and the German-speaking provinces of the Society of Jesus.

My list of Polish saint plays follows, and thereafter I will make some remarks by way of conclusion to place my concerns regarding them in perspective. The following abbreviations are used in my list and in the notes:

ARSJ: Archivum Romanum Societatis Jesu.
BJ: Biblioteka Jagiellońska, Cracow.
Korotaj: *Dramat staropolski od początków do powstania sceny narodowej.*
   Bibliografia, vol. 2, pt. 1: *Programy teatru jezuickiego*, ed. W.

Korotaj, J. Szwedkowska, and M. Szymańska (Wrocław: Ossolineum, 1976).
Lewański: Julian Lewański, *Studia nad dramatem polskiego Odrodzenia* (Wrocław: Ossolineum, 1956).
Okoń: Jan Okoń, *Dramat i teatr szkolny: Sceny jezuickie XVII w.* (Wrocław: Ossolineum, 1970).
Poplatek: Jan Poplatek, *Studia z dziejów jezuickiego teatru szkolnego w Polsce* (Wrocław: Ossolineum 1957).
Valentin: Jean-Marie Valentin, *Le Théâtre des Jésuites dans les Pays de la langue Allemande: Répertoire chronologique des pièces réprésentées et des documents conservés 1555–1773*, 2 vols. (Stuttgart: Hiersemann, 1983–84).

Alexis
Latin play in five acts with Polish arguments and choruses, performed 6 Nov. 1600, in Pułtusk, now lost.
Sanctus Alexius, performed 1600, in Pułtusk (Okoń, 358).
Sanctus Alexius, performed 22 July 1602 and 26 July 1605, in Poznań (Okoń, 369).
Three texts of Latin plays from the German-speaking provinces of the Society of Jesus, with 40 records of performances, 1589–1771 (15 programs preserved):
Drama de Sancto Alexio, Nationalbibliothek Wien, Cod.Vind. 13222 (93 pp.), performed in Vienna, 1589.
Alexius Moriens, Staatsbibliothek München, Cod. lat. mon. 2150 (48 pp.), performed in Munich, 1707.
Alexius Moriens, Staatsbibliothek München, Cod. lat. mon. 17797 (28 pp.).

Ambrose
De Sancto Ambrosio et Theodosio Imperatore, Calissia, 1592.
Written and performed by the English Jesuit Edmund Campion [otherwise Campian or Campianus], who was teaching at the Prague College in 1578. Full Latin text from this performance in Cologne, Staatsarchiv Univ. IX 659, fols. 304–340ᵛ (Poplatek, 177; see also Julian Lewański, *Dramat i teatr średniowiecza i renesansu w Polsce* [Warsaw: PWN, 1981], 515, 524).

Andrew
St. Andrew is a marriage divination feast for girls; see *St. Catherine*.

Still popular in Poland as an occasion for small feasts (*andrzejki*).
A dialogue about Andrew, performed 30 Nov. 1627, at Poznań
(Okoń, 370).

Anne and Joachim
Joachym y Anna, extant drama text in Polish (before 1600) (MS.
Ossolineum 6710, pp. 77–114; ed. J. I. Kraszewski, "Komedia o
niepłodności Anny," *Ateneum* 2 [1841], 95–126). The epilogue of
the play points to performance on her feast day of 26 July:
"Remember well this exemplary story / Which the day of today is
celebrating all over the world."[5]

Anonymous Martyrs
De martyrum constantia, performed Feb. 1585, in Połock. Recorded
in ARSJ Pol. 50 (Lewański, *Dramat i teatr*, 521).
*Tragoedia de duobus pueris martyribus sine nomine in Barono, hic
sub Caelestini et Feliciani nomine*, performed in Wilna, 1646. MS.
Zaluscianum Q.XIV.10, fols. 77–86 (lost).

Barlaam
Drama de duobus regibus ex parabola Barlaami, performed 26 Jan.
1616, at Poznań (Okoń, 369). See also approximately 50 performances and books on Josaphat (Okoń, 390).
Dialogue of Barlaam and Josaphat, Poznań, 1624 (Okoń, 370).

Boris and Gleb
The Spiritual Communion of SS. Boris and Gleb is a long historical
play on the Orthodox saints-princes of Rus' that was played in the
Polish Jesuit colleges before 1693.[6]
The play's heroes were two of the twelve sons of Prince Volodimir
(Vladimir) who baptized Rus' in 988. After Volodimir's death in
1015, twenty years of fraternal struggle followed which ended with
the rule of the only survivor, Jaroslav the Wise.[7] Boris and Gleb,
born around 990, were the first victims of this struggle's instigator,
Svyatopolk, who had them killed in 1015. The Greek Orthodox
Church recognized their cult, and they are regarded as the first
Russian saints.[8] Their feast day was established on 24 July. Before
1072 and in c.1080 their Old Church Slavonic *vitae* were written
down in the Basilian monastery of Kiev. The first was the
Skazaniye: Narrative and Passion and Encomium of the Holy

Martyrs Boris and Gleb,[9] the second *Čteniye: Lection on the Life and Assassination of the Blessed Passion Sufferers Boris and Gleb*.

Apart from the killing itself, only two motifs were used by the dramatist: the figure of Boris's retainer George, who "was loved by Boris beyond measure,"[10] and Boris' request to his killers to give him time for a prayer. There is no textual connection with the prayers in the *Narrative* except the last sentence—"Lord, lay not this sin to their charge, but receive my spirit in peace"—which derives from Acts 7:58–59; the drama has the following at this point: "I forgive, with all my heart I forgive you, and absolve you from your wrongdoings. Lord, receive, with this blood, my spirit" (1269–71).

The dramatization is developed by structuring the rather simple story in terms of tragic conflicts of loyalty vs. treachery, good lordship vs. egoism, brotherly love vs. hatred, pride vs. humility. The action abounds with intrigues, deceptions, disguises, forgeries, false rumors, and misunderstandings, and it contains a most famous *anagnorisis* (quite effective, admittedly)—all of this absent from the source. The anonymous author's contribution is decisive in the play. With considerable creative power, he created a drama from a source containing only an uneventful story of murder. We have here a drama created with very considerable technical skill—a drama which also comes very close to the baroque design that we would expect for a play of this period. Interestingly, as in the case of the John the Baptist tragedy, this drama also makes use of Ukrainian, here being used in the *accessus* (consisting of two parts, Antiprologus and Prologus) and the interlude.[11] The old story thus brings us closer to the early history of the region which became the Ukraine and in which the lives of these saints were embedded.

Cantius, St. John Cantius (of Kanti [Kęty])
De S. Cantio Doctore Almae Acad[emiae] Crac[oviensis] in vigilia Nativitatis Domini 1677; in Polish: incipit Żywot Jana Kantego Błogosławionego/Opowiedzieć myślemy wam dnia dzisiejszego—the text speaks about the blessed John (1390–1473). He was beatified only in 1680, and canonized in 1767. Ossolineum MS. 1125, fols.165ʳ–169ʳ; described Lewański, 44; performed by 15 students as a series of declamations.

Casimir Jagellon (1458–84, canonized in 1602; he was the son of

king Casimir IV).
We have a detailed description of the canonization feast of St.
Casimir, on 10 May 1604 in Vilna, contained in the most extensive
vita of the saint: Augustyn Lipnicki, *Życie, cuda i cześć św. Kazi-
mierza królewica polskiego, Wielkiego Księcia Litewskiego* (Vilna:
J. Zawadzki, 1858), 129–222.
Sanctus Casimirus, performed 2 March 1628, in Poznań (Okoń,
370).
[Title unknown], performed in the second half of the 17th century
in the Lithuanian province. Text lost from MS. Zaluscianum
Q.XIV.10, fols. 131–43.
Sanctus Casimirus, performed 1647, in Połock (Okoń, 370, 376).
10 performances in the German-speaking area (1628–1751), two
Latin programs extant (Amberg Lat. rec. 369 I 19; Staatsbibliothek
München, 8° Bavar. 4025), and one Latin text extant: *Mariana
vindicta in Casimiro*, performed in Dillingen, 1751; compare with
Nuremberg (Valentin, no. 6210).

Catherine of Alexandria
The eve of St. Catherine as well as of St. Andrew was dedicated to
marriage divination for young men and women curious about their
future partners. St. Catherine was the patron saint of students and
universities[12] which explains why she was so frequently the subject
of plays and why so many texts have survived. Eight Latin plays
from the German and Austrian provinces of the Society of Jesus are
preserved[13] as well as twenty-seven records of performances from
1563 to 1720 and three afterward. The three earliest dialogues (in
Latin) from Poland which are preserved in the Jesuit codex from
Calisia—performed on the feast of St. Catherine in 1584, 1586, and
1587—are not plays but rather theological disputes with some reference to her.
Dialogus in festo S. Catharinae exhibitus anno Domini 1584, performed at Kalisz on 25 Nov. 1584 (two-act play with choruses).
*Dialogus de vera Christianorum philosophia in festo S. Catharinae
exhibitus Anno Domini 1586* (same MS., fols. 37–56). This is a two-
act "theological" play with choruses and a strong anti-heretical message (Poplatek, *Studia*, 136), but a remarkable Echo figure appears
in a serious monologue.
Dialogus in festo S. Catharinae anno Domini 1587 (same MS., fols.
83–95ᵛ).

The last of these dialogues closes with a *Chorus in laudem D. Catharinae* (after the Epilogue), addressed as "Martyr et Virgo Catharina cuius / Laudibus summis resonare totus / Debeat orbis." No text is extant of the other performances.

Poznań on 26 Nov. 1574 (*de S. Catharina*; ARSJ Polonia 50, fol. 23, and 66, fol. 366.[15]

Vilna on 22 Oct. 1578 (*Tragoedia Divae Virginis et Martyris Catherinae*, Poplatek, *Studia*, 175).

Vilna on 26 Nov. 1584 (*Dialogus in die Sanctae Catharinae*, ARSJ Pol. 50, fol. 65; Lewański, *Dramat i teatr*, 520).

Calisia 1588 (*Eadem renovatione in festo S. Catharinae et Nativitate exhibiti sunt dialogi*, mentioned on fol. 106 of the same codex). Beyond these, there are no texts or titles extant from the performances in:

Vilna on 25 Nov. 1584.

Poznań in Nov. 1591.

Orsza on 25 Nov. 1636 (procession and dialogue performed in the church; Okoń, 375).

Ostróg on 25 Nov. 1688 (Okoń, 368).

Though *Dialogus pro festo Sanctae Catharinae virginis et martyris* by Jan Paweł Cichoński (1694) has a Latin title, it was written in Polish.[16] Very traditional and amateurish in its structure and dialogues, it is divided into six acts, two of them (3 and 6) containing only a single scene of one or two pages. The interludes are suggested by a title, without the full text. The action closely follows the Daily Office for St. Catherine's feast day on 25 November:[17] Emperor Maxentius is confronted by a group of Christians who refuse to make offerings to his gods. Their leader seems to be the virgin Katarzyna (Catherine). The drama involves a series of failed attempts to get her to abandon Christ. The famous dispute with the doctors—in this case five rather than the fifty specified in the saint's *vita*—is not missing, of course, and it has some charming naiveté. The first questions and statements about God and Christ having been exchanged, the First Doctor is ready to construct a syllogism proving that Christ cannot be God; at this point he switches to prose: "probo sic minorem propositionem: he has a beginning because of his birth, he has an end because of his death, ergo he cannot be god, ut ostendi." Katarzyna answers promptly: "Distinguo minorem propositionem, he has a beginning by his humanity, concedo, he has no beginning by his divinity, etc."[18]

When the question of the Trinity arises, things become serious, and the discussion switches to Latin prose exclusively, with the First Doctor asking: "Quo modo ergo tres personae possunt esse in uno?" Katarzyna answers with some twenty lines of a Latin lecture. This may be simple, compared, for instance, with the long discussion in the *Passio Sancte Katerine Virginis*. Our Katarzyna's achievement was "ruining the devil's building" by herself—that is, with her "perfidious cunning"! By avoiding the kind of denial of the saint's personal contribution that we find in the *Passio*—the angel's assurance in that text "that she could not be defeated"[19] meant reducing her to a mere passive vessel—our dramatist demonstrated a true instinct for the stage.

Cecilia
La Santa Cecilia (Italian opera, by Puccitelli, at court, Warsaw, 1637); see W. Tomkiewicz, "Widowiska dworskie w okresie Renesansu," *Pamiętnik Teatralny* 2, no. 3 (1953), 80–109, esp. 99, 103; Hannus Schüpli, *Kurtze Beschreibung, was sich verlofnen Jahr bey Abholung Caeciliae Renatae etc. zugetragen* (Vienna, 1638), fol. 3.

Celsus (young martyr of Antioch)
25 performances in Europe (three in Poland; Okoń, 383–84; for Polish programs, see Korotaj, nos. 118, 146, 422, 503).
Sublimitas virilis animi in puero nomine Celso, performed in 1712, at Calisia; program and text in MS. BJ 182 (Okoń, 51).
Akt o Celsie z innymi pacholęty od ojca zabitym, unknown date and place of performance; text in Zaluscianum Q.XIV.10, fol. 229 (lost) (Okoń, 308).
Celsus, sive Sapientia in schola fidei ad lauream martyri promota, performed in 1694, Warsaw; program in the University Library, Vilna, 3.XXIV.1/95 (full title in Okoń, 313).
De Celso, Martiani tyranni filio, performed on feast of St. Michael, 29 Sept. 1648, in Połock; no text (Okoń, 376).

Christopher (boy-martyr)
Idea Jesu Crucifixi in Christophoro octenni puero martyre, performed at Nieśwież, 19 April 1696; text in Zaluscianum Q.XIV.10, fols. 116–24 (MS. now lost).

Crispus (martyr)
Crispus, record of performance, Pułtusk, after 1603 (Lewański, *Dramat i teatr*, 531).

Edmund
Sanctus Edmundus, Poznań before 19 April 1615 (Okoń, 369).

Elisabeth
Comedy dated 1594: Bakałarzowi od Comedyej proxima festum s. Elisabethis ex mandato D. Proconsulis et Consulorum opłacono 30 gr (see Jan Dürr-Durski, "O mieszczańskim teatrze renesansowym w Polsce," *Pamiętnik Teatralny* 2, no. 3 [1953]: 69).

Elzear
De Eleazari constantia, Braniewo/Braunsberg, 1609 (ARSJ Lithuania, 38, fol. 36; Lewański, *Dramat i teatr*, 534).
Obrona przeciw gwałtowny imprezie grzechow od Swiętego Elzeariusza hrabie miana w ranach Jezusowych. Wynaleziona w kościele lubelskym Societatis Jezu przy wielkopiątkowym nabozenstwie do uwagi wszystkim, performed in Lublin, 1651 (*Kodeks konopczański*: MS. Ossolineum 6709/I, fols.131–57).
No text is preserved from the five performances in the German province of the Society of Jesus in 1621–1751; only two copies of a program remain from the 1624 performance at the Konstanz college:
Elzearius Comes Comoedien von dem H. Eltzeario Graven so zur Zeit Roberti Königs zu Neapel und Sicilien vor 300 Jahren mit Dalphina seiner Gemahlin Jungfräulich gelebt (Staatsbibliothek München 4° Bavar. 2193 I 19 and 21 [11 pp.]).

Eulogius (6th-century Greek-Byzantine stone mason, servant of St. Daniel the Hermit)
Around 20 performances in Europe, one in Vilna:
Antitheta morum in egestate et divitiis ab Eulogio latomo bizantino, 1681 (University Library of Vilna III, Cod. 10893; short content in Okoń, 199, 309; no full text).

Eustachius
Summarium tragoediae Eustachianae, ARSJ Lithuania, 38, fol. 112^v; performed at Vilna, 14 Sept. 1616 (Okoń, 115–16).

Summarium tragoediae Eustachianae in gratiam . . . Eustachii Wołowicz, performed and printed in Vilna, 1618 (Lewański, *Dramat i teatr*, 541).
70 performances in Jesuit colleges, 55 in the German-speaking area. Three texts of Latin plays preserved (Valentin):
Sanctus Eustachius Tragoedia Sacra, performed at Vienna, 1584 (Hessische Landesbibliothek Fulda C. 18, fols. 234–76).
Comedia de Eustacho martyre, performed at Graz, 1600 (Stifts- bibliothek Admont).
Comoedo-Tragoedia de Eustachio Martyre, performed at Mainz, 1603 (Landeshauptarchiv Koblenz, Sammlung Görresgymnasium Abt. 117, 593, I, 24).

Felicitas
Calisia, 1598: *Tragoedia S. Foelicitatis exhibita 6ª Octobris cum praemiorum solenni distributione* (no text).
Vilna, 1597: *Tragoedia Faelicitas*, by Gregorius Cnapius (Uppsala University Library, MS. R 380, fols. 38–90; ed. Lidia Winniczuk, *Gregorii Cnapii Tragoediae: Philopater, Faelicitas, Eutropius* [Wrocław: Ossolineum, 1965]).
Poznań, 1599, using same text as in 1597 at Vilna.

Francis Borgia (canonized 1671)
About 20 performances in Jesuit colleges all over Europe, 1625– 1760, excluding the year 1671; in this year a play about the saint was played "almost in every college" (Okoń, 385).

Francis Xavier
Krosno, 1631 (Lewański, 219).
Iudicium Dei horribile in Proregem Indiae, obstinatum ad poenitentiam ad libram pietatis Xaverianae, by A. Temberski, performed in 1699 at Lublin; MS. BJ 2384, fols. 70–79.

Genesius
Genesius histrio, performed in 1615, at Kalisz (Okoń, 363).
Tragoedia de sancto Genesio, performed 20 June 1619, at Poznań, with printed program in Polish:
Tragedia Genesius, to iest O Świętym Genezyusie męczenniku (Poznań: J. Wolrab, 1619), 4 pages in quarto (full description in Korotaj, 2, pt. 1, no. 296).

George
The powers of *St. George* and *St. Adalbert* (23 April), patrons of the
spring in Polish folk tradition, are addressed in agricultural apotro-
paism. St. George the knight was inspiration for young Kashubian
men to organize contests of strength: The winner was called
"George."[20] The later counterpart to SS. George and Adalbert was
St. Roch (16 August), patron of animals. On his feast day benedictions were ordained for flocks and domestic animals; living
animals could participate, or they could be represented by votive
figures of wax. Processions visited pastures.
Sanctus Georgius, performed at Poznań, 30 June 1603 and 1 May
1616 (Okoń, 369).
S. Georgius martyr, Magni Ducatus Lituaniae patronus, by Łukasz
Paprocki, performed by the class of rhetoric of the Vilna college in
1650; for program, see Korotaj, no. 510.
More than 15 performances of different St. George plays in Europe,
1586–1718 (Valentin).

Gregory
St. Gregory (12 March), as the patron saint of young people, gave
his name to a school tradition called *Actus Gregoriani*. In a record
from the seventeenth century, students split into different parties
and elected their "class king." The candidate of the Parnassus-group
was the winner. Coronation festivities followed. After being
crowned, the new king proclaimed war against the enemies of the
Latin language—the barbarisms, solecisms, and Polonisms—and
declared that all "rebels" should be eliminated.[21]

Hermenegild (canonized 1585)
Around 55 performances in Europe, four in the Lithuanian province
(Okoń, 387–88). Two programs, from Przemyśl in ?1761 and Vilna
in 1754, described in Korotaj, nos. 321, 660.

Ignatius Loyola
*Terminus anni literati principiis S. Ignatii coronatus, seu Heroica
ab Ignatio saeculi conculcatio* in scenam data ad decursum anni
literarii 1699 a rhetoribus Karnkoviani Collegii, performed in
Calisia, MS. Ossolineum, Biblioteka Pawlikowskich 204, fols.
135ᵛ–141; Latin dialogue in prose, historical and allegorical figures
(Grandis, Lojola, Rex Hispanus—Mars, Pietas, Furia), probably by
Franciscus Kwolek.

Japan, Martyrs of

The Martyrs of Japan were beatified in 1627. Three of the twenty-six martyrs—Paul Miki, John de Gota, and James Quigai—were Japanese Jesuits.[22] It was a great town feast in Kalisz/Calisia (5–6 February 1628) in which the Jesuit college participated, and a description of the triumph is preserved in the order's archives (Arch. Romanum Soc. Jesu, Polonia 66, fol. 25; quoted in Lewański, *Studia*, 220).

Tragoedia de Japonicis principibus martyrio affectis fratribus duobus de domo Finatorum et simul patruo (qui eos adoptaverat) in exilium misso anno 1629 ad Urbanum VIII–um Pontificem Maximum tota artis vi delata, performed in the second half of the 17th century in the Lithuanian province. Text lost from MS. Zaluscianum Q.XIV.10, fols. 38–65 (Okoń, 359).

John the Baptist

The vigil and feast of *St. John the Baptist* (23–24 June) comprise the oldest and still most popular festivity, called *Sobótki* (originally meaning St. John's Eve). Its traditional celebration with dances, singing, and bonfires is recorded, for example, by the greatest Polish Renaissance poet Jan Kochanowski.

Although the church festival of St. John the Baptist is an exception in that it commemorates the birth rather than death of the saint,[23] on this day an intriguing Kashubian ritual drama of "Beheading the Kite" ("ścięcie kani") was celebrated.[24] Its main actors were Dog-Catcher (who was the bird-catcher), Judge, Priest, Village Chief (*sołtys*), and Headsman. The actors were sometimes chosen from among herdsmen by drawing lots. Judging by its content, the drama should be called "Beheading the Scapegoat": the bird, caught earlier and kept in a cage until the day of the performance, was presented in a procession to the village's population as the seat of evil and bad luck, and declared responsible for all their misfortunes. It was brought to the place of judgment, bound to a pylon, sentenced to death, and executed. I would reject claims that the spoken texts preserve some old beliefs, and in the speeches of accusation I see mainly expressions of concern for local difficulties (e.g., workers not being paid for overtime) and problems of modern life (even, in 1964 at Strzelno, referring to women not using birth control pills![25]). The only traditional elements are eternally topical moralistic issues: men "and even women" spending too much time in

inns, couples betraying each other, boys refusing to marry girls, etc.
All this is the kite's guilt, and its beheading is intended as the
remedy.

Among dramatizations derived from the life of this very first
saint of the Christian Church is one written in Polish by Jacob
Gawatowic, whose *Tragedy or Picture of Death of the most holy
John the Baptist, God's Messenger* was performed and published on
24 June 1619.[26]
Calisia, *De S. Joannis Baptistae in eremum discessu* had been
played (22 July 1587).
Poznań, a Latin dialogue *De S. Joanne Baptista* is dated 26 June
1588.[27]
A drama on the decapitation of John was also staged in the second
half of the 17th century in the province of Lithuania.[28]
A program from a Cracow performance in 1700 is likewise pre-
served.[29]

Previously, the Beheading of John the Baptist seems to have
been the best-known saint play in Poland in the sixteenth century;
see Windakiewicz, *Teatr ludowy*, 127, whose source is a collection
of sermons on the Sacraments by the influential writer Piotr Skarga
(fl. 1600). Skarga took notice of the way in which the beheading
was represented: "they construct a dish around the neck, he looks as
if he is dead, but he is alive." A different method was used by performers of the Jesuit college of Połock at the beginning of the
nineteenth century: the beheaded body was played by one masked
actor, the head by another; it happened once that the "body" had
fallen asleep and began to snore; hearing that from its hole in the
stage, the "head" of the martyr began to laugh loudly (*Teatr ludowy*,
129).
One Latin text, entitled *Joannes Baptista*, from the German Jesuit
province is preserved; this was performed at the Dillingen college
in 1631.[30]
A summary of seven pages likewise survives: *Summarischer Inhalt
der comicotragoedi von Dem H. Tauffer Johann Christi Vorlauffer
und Martyrer.*[31]
In the German-speaking area there are twenty-three records of
performances between 1566 and 1741.
The saint additionally was a well-known figure in processions,
described in variants of the designation "In Kamels har, Johann
baptist."[32]

The Polish play by Gwatowic is a well-designed enactment of the main events of John's life: a hermit defends himself against devils and is called by an angel to start teaching ("the voice of one crying in the wilderness"); as a prophet, he chastises Herod's incest, the latter then promising "anything" to Salome and, inevitably, giving her John's head on a dish. The play closes with Herod's (fictional) punishment. He is not banished (as in the *Legenda Aurea*) but sentenced to death by Justice who hears the Subterranean Voice of innocent blood crying for vengeance. She summons Death, who beheads Herod with a scythe. The play shares this motif with (or maybe owes it to) the folk drama about Herod, very popular and played in some locations even today ("herody"). I remember seeing this scene as a child once or twice when it was performed by village mummers, who were visiting farmhouses.

The drama is more a *picture* and less a *tragedy*, but it has some merits: its simplicity, avoiding the burden of classical learning, and short choruses with a clear message, sometimes ironic. The verse is mostly hendecasyllabic and switches without a structural reason with octosyllabic passages. Unfortunately, the latter come too close to folkloristic diction, and it would be only by great effort on the part of a modern actor that they could be performed in a serious way. This is not a problem in the devils' roles, which are at times very authentic in their joy about successful intrigues and sorrow about failed attempts to conquer the saintly hermit.[33] Most remarkable from a linguistic point of view, however, are the two interludes that appear in Ukrainian. This is worth mentioning because these are the oldest specimens of drama extant in the Ukrainian language.[34]

John the Evangelist
Corvinus adolescens et b. Joannes Evangelista, performed at Poznań before 4 March 1615 (Okoń, 369).
A drama of John the Apostle and Evangelist, by Marcin Głębicz, performed in the school yard of the college at Wałcz, in 1676.

John of Damascus
Latin play, performed on 6 August 1600, at Pułtusk (not preserved).
Drama de Sancto Damascene per Deiparam olim sanato, performed April 1608, at Poznań (Okoń, 369).

Ars lucis et umbrae, performed 1733, at Vilna; copy of program in Cracow, Muzeum Narodowe 466; description in Korotaj, no. 631.

Lawrence
S. Laurentii tragoedia, performed at Jarosław, 1582 (Poplatek, 176).

Mark
The printed *Ordo processionis in die sancti Marci in Ecclesia Cathedrali Plocensis ita observatur*[35] is approximately 2,000 words in length. The route of this springtime procession connected three churches, none of them dedicated to St. Mark, and the directions for the participants differentiated between younger and older school-children: "Rectores incipiant Responsorium *Virtute magna.* Scholares minores remanent ante Ecclesiam: soli maiores intrant ut finiant responsorium: et vadunt ad partem Ecclesiae: soli presbyteri flectant ante pulpitum et cantent quae rectores intonabunt" (ibid., fol. 160ᵛ). The liturgical *ordines* for parish processions on particular saints' days could be very elaborate.

Martin
St. Martin is, among other things, the patron saint of poor people, and in Northern Europe he was regarded as the guardian of winter provisions.[36] In earlier times his feast day on 11 November was a consumption feast connected with the slaughter of animals to pro-vide provisions for the winter.
Kalisz, performed 10 Nov. 1586 (Poplatek, 136).

Nicholas
St. Nicholas, possibly today the most domesticated and exploited of all the saints, has been located by Polish ethnographers in two local traditions, different but very likely related to each other. One is a mummers' play called *Mikołaje* (*Nicholases*), connected with the church fair of 6 December organized at St. Nicholas church at the village of Łąka near Pszczyna in eastern Silesia.[37] The players, around ten young men in costume, are divided into three groups: (1) St. Nicholas, Bishop, Priest (they are collectively called "mikołaje" or "świynci"—i.e., saints); (2) Goat, Devil, Death, Jew, Female; (3) a band, consisting of one to four musicians (if only one, the instrumentalist is an accordionist), accompanying both or only the

second group. The troupe visits croft after croft, with first the Nicholas-group entering the house, greeting the family, singing two songs for them, and collecting offerings in the alms-box (no alcohol). During the presentation, the second group is waiting or producing some preparatory or background action outside the house. Their performance inside consists in wild dancing that includes the women of the family.[38]

The connection with our saint is stressed by the content of the two songs produced by the first group.[39] Both refer to the saint, the first by describing his helping powers: "he restores sight to the blind, he lets the lame walk again, he saves women in labor if asked with faith." The second song is a request for the saint's intercession: "open the way for us to the land above"; "those who take the way to God through him [Nicholas] will reach eternal peace and happiness." Among the actual meanings of these texts, non-liturgical imitation of church benedictions seems to be the most apparent. The functions, multiple as always in social phenomena, can include very divergent aspects from the trivial (a religious alibi for earning some money, drinking, and wild horseplay incognito[40]) to the philosophical (experiencing the sacred-profane duality, represented clearly by the two groups).

A more distinct ethical (or cognitive) duality is apparent in another Mikołaje tradition, which divides the players into two groups called the "whites" and the "blacks."[41] The first consists of Bishop, Priest, Acolytes, Soldier (master of ceremonies), Best Man, Young Peasant Woman, Bridegroom, Doctor, and Forester, while the second is made up of Lucifer, Devils, Bears, Mother-Bear, Jew, Gipsy and Gipsy Woman, Horseman (hobbyhorse), Death, Stork, Chimneysweep, and Potter. This organization is not always the same since the figures are not uniformly "white" or "black" (implying no racial characteristics) in everybody's opinion, but whatever the arrangement there are consequences for performance. Families with small children invite only the "whites." The connection with St. Nicholas is present only in the date of the performance and perhaps in the figure of the Bishop, but not in any other motif. This may be caused by the gradual loss of dialogue which has been observed in this and cognate traditions.[42] The good-bad ethical duality was also stressed by the angel and the devil who accompanied St. Nicholas when visiting children at their homes and bringing them

presents or punishment. What they actually received depended on how they answered his questions about their behavior.
A play: Vilna, performed in 1606 (Okoń, 118).

Paul
De S. Paulo, performed at Poznań on 26 June1588 (Poplatek, 136).

Pergentinus and Laurentius (brother-martyrs from Arezzo)
12 performances, one in Warsaw in 1690: *Promotio ad martyrii Lauream* (Okoń, 396).

Roch
A play about St. Roch (Annuae Literae Prov. Pol. Collegium Gedanense, ARSJ Polonia 52, fol. 119; Okoń, 116).

Stanislaus, bishop
We have a record of a sort of name-day drama, played on 8 May 1633 in the New Town in Warsaw, and for which one copy of the printed program is preserved. The full text on its title page is revealing: "*A Summary of the Tragicomedy of the History of the Life of St. Stanislaus, Martyr of Christ, Bishop of Cracow, and Patron of the Polish Crown*, dedicated by Mateusz Jagodowicz, vicar of the New Town . . . to Mr Stanisław Baryczka, mayor of the Town of Old Warsaw. Performed on his Feast Day in the New Town in Warsaw, to the veneration and glory of Our Lord, of St. Stanislaus, and to the renown and solace of the Polish Nation, on 8 May 1633 A.D."[43] Stanislaus is the hero of the oldest-preserved drama about a Polish saint.[44]

Stanislaus (died 11 April 1079, canonized 1253)[45] is the earliest notable saint-martyr of Polish origin whose death resembles that of Thomas Becket in many details. Both struggled with their respective kings and may be regarded as martyrs of the investiture controversy. Stanislaus became symbolic in Poland of the independence of the Church and its believers from the oppressive political power of the state—a symbolism that was invoked as recently as the imposition of martial law in 1981.[46] From the beginning authors and artists focused on the bishop and the king and arranged them between the poles of hero and anti-hero locked in an irreducible conflict,[47] which was thus presented in the saint's iconography and songs dedicated to him.[48] An important episode concerned a miracle story about the resuscitation of a dead witness to speak in favor of Stanislaus, who was accused at King Boleslaus' instigation.

The narrative must originally have been the principal attraction of this story, especially in stage dramatizations, though as the twentieth century approached priority shifted to interest in a second important motif, the struggle against tyrannical power. Stanislaus plays were performed about twenty-five times on Jesuit stages in the German-speaking area in 1574–1737[49] and at least ten times in Polish territories.

5 Dec. 1574: Poznań, *De vita et martyrio S. Stanislai* (Poplatek, 175).

26 Dec. 1616: Kalisz (Okoń, 363).

1624: Łuck: *Sanctus Stanislaus Cracoviensis antistes* (Okoń, 367).

8 May 1633: Warsaw (see n.19, below).

31 May 1638: Lublin (Stykowa, "Święty Stanisław Biskup," 152).

1679: Lwów (Okoń, 367); 1680: Bydgoszcz (Okoń, 361).

1693: Kroże (Stykowa, "Święty Stanisław Biskup," 152).

1723: Łowicz, (Stykowa, "Święty Stanisław Biskup," 152).

1737: Gdańsk: (Stykowa. "Święty Stanisław Biskup," 152).

17th century: ?Chełmno; see also Korotaj, nos. 170, 176, 376.

Some Old Polish plays introduce a figure of the saint as a secondary figure—e.g., in the *Dialogus*[50] where St. Stanislaus is pacifying the Ultio Divina with his experience as conqueror and helper of repenting sinners. The only extant dramatic text from early Poland dealing primarily with Stanislaus is the Latin *Tragoedia Boleslaus Secundus Furens* of Johannes Joncre, written before 1588 and only rediscovered shortly after World War II. This play, most likely not a Jesuit drama, was perhaps never performed.[51] Its main source was Długosz's *Vita S. Stanislai*, but thirteenth-century *vitae*—a shorter one from before and a longer one from after the canonization—and also printed legends were also available to the writer.[52] The author was probably a foreign humanist, perhaps a teacher of the Ostrogski family, as suggested by the fact that only the three most important figures of the story—Boleslaus, Stanislaus, and Peter—have their original names while all other proper names are changed, fictional, or non-Polish.[53] The drama is structured around the ethical conflict between the immoral king and the bishop trying to correct a sinner. The whole action, closely following the legend of the saint, has two strands, partially intertwined; alongside living people, a number of allegories present the most important points and turns of the conflict: Castitas and Cupido try to convert Boleslaus to their way; Avaritia and Conscientia discuss the false accusation; Fury tries to subject Boleslaus to her rule and brings him finally to Tartarus.

German performances with preserved texts (from Valentin); for Polish performances, see Korotaj, nos. 170, 176, 376.

Comico-Tragoedia: Das ist Ein Schawspill von dem H. Martyrer Stanislao Bischoffen zu Crackaw, performed in Eichstätt, 1652; copy of a German-Latin program in Staats- und Stadtbibliothek Augsburg 4° Bild II, 63 (8 pp.).

Schawspiel von dem H. Martyrer Stanislao Bischoffen zu Crackaw, performed in Soleure/Salzburg, 1659; copy of German-Latin program in Staatliche Bibliothek Dillingen XVII, 64, I, 16.

Petrus Polonus redivivus, performed in Lucerne, 1663, copy of German program, Freiburg i. Breisgau D. 8153.22.

Veritas Tragoedia, performed at Eichstätt, 1687; copy of German-Latin program in Bischöfliches Ordinariatsarchiv, MS. Eichstätt MV 85, 8.

S. Stanislaus Cracoviensis, performed at Amberg, 1700; copy of German-Latin program, Staatliche Provinzialbibliothek Amberg Lat. rec. 369, III, 61.

Boleslaus Furens Tragoedia, performed at Straubing, 1706; copy of German-Latin program, Bischöflisches Ordinariatsarchiv Eichstätt H.13, 14.

Rarum pro Justitia Testimonium Seltzamer Schutz und Zeug Der Gerechtigkeit, performed at Ellwangen, 1709; copy of German-Latin program, Württembergische Landesbibliothek Stuttgart R 17 I 73; Staats- und Stadtbibliothek Augsburg 4° Bild VI, 76).

Stanislaus Kostka (beatified 1604, canonized 1714)
More than 60 performances in Jesuit colleges all over Europe 1615–1763. For locations, see Okoń, 396–98; German data from Valentin. For Polish programs, see Korotaj, nos. 35, 72, 174, 188, 340, 386–87, 405, 664, 760.

In capite totus Stanislaus Kostka divinus, by A. Tamberski, performed at Lublin, Nov. 1698. MS. BJ 2384, fols. 161–64.

Flores rhetorici ad imaginem d. Stanislai Kostka a quodam Haeretico vulneratam, orations by A. Temberski, performed in 1699 at Lublin. MS. BJ 2384, fols. 43–50.

Latin drama on St. Stanislaus Kostka, with Polish songs, performed in Rawa in ?1699; text lost in the *Liber orationum, drammatum,*

salutationum in Collegio Ravensi S.J. (Biblioteka Uniwersytetu Warszawskiego, lat. F.XVII, 66).
Drama breve de fuga b. Stanislai Kostka Vienna Romam, performed at Pińsk in 1662 and Płock in 1664 (lost text in Q.XIV.10, fols. 209–16).
More than 30 performances with seven extant programs, and five preserved texts of Latin plays from the German-speaking area (Valentin, nos. 733, 3048, 4283, 4599, 6756).
B. Stanislaus Kostka, MS. Rein 175 (107 pp.), Bibliothek des Zisterzienser-Stiftes Rein, performed at Graz in 1615.
Ritterliche Gottseligkeit in Stanislao Kostka, Latin text in Stadtarchiv, Köln 1059, no. 19 (30 pp.); also in the same archive there is a German program from the performance at Cologne in 1692.
Litigium Amicum pro D. Stanislao Kostka honorando, by A. Maurisperg; ed. in *Dramata IV variis in theatris exhibitae* (Styrae, 1730).
Cor unum et anima una: SS Aloysius et Stanislaus, Dombibliothek Freising Hs. 72, fols. 2–39; performed at Munich in 1727.
Dominus Adjutor in Opportunitatibus (Stanislaus Kostka), Universitätsbibliothek Würzburg Rp XV, 72m; performance at Würzburg in 1757.

Stephan (King of Hungary, 997–1038)
De S. Stephano Primo, Koloszvar, Nov. 1587 (Transylvania; Poplatek, 177).

Vitus and Modest
De SS Vito et Modesto, Braniewo/Braunsberg college, performed in Autumn 1582 for the bishop of Warmia/Ermland (Poplatek, 176, with an Italian parallel text and more literature).

Conclusion. A general look at the matter of genre classification of the plays for which I have been able to provide a more extended discussion in the above list is now possible. Dimitrij Tschizewskij, without using the term 'medievalism,' quite explicitly defined "the literary baroque as an effort of an organic unification of elements of the renaissance and the late middle ages, in respect of form as well as of content."[54] Kevin Croxen, commenting on seven neo-Latin dramas (including *Boleslaus Furens*, which may be regarded as typical of the eleven extant Polish plays as well as of the twenty-

eight others for which records are extant), has argued that these
plays belong in the category of "medievalism." Polish neo-Latin
drama must be declared to be simply . . . *medieval*.[55] I recently have
come to a similar conclusion in my analysis of specimens of Polish
vernacular mystery plays and Eucharistic dramas of the seventeenth-century in a medieval context.[56]

Through Croxen's study the opportunity emerges to see the
similarities between the Latin and the vernacular streams of play-
writing. Two points are questionable: the concept of sacramental
psychology, and the falsely presumed uniformity of the genre
tragedy. Locating the hero's psychology as central to tragedy is
opposed to Aristotle's stress on reception, the impact on the
audience; for him it is only the action that really matters. A tragedy
in his view thus can reach its aim without fully developed characters.[57] In the case of Christian drama, however, other types of
characters are required. In this drama the means remain "unhappy
fate for the righteous, and the ruin of somebody like us."[58] Fear and
pity remain possible for the Christian audience, and, in spite of the
hard-line Jesuit exclusion of martyrs, such heroes of faith remain.
While for the hard-liner Sarbiewski, we cannot speak of pity in the
case of a martyr because many respectable people wish his fate for
themselves—and they see him rejoice in his sufferings[59]—not all
practitioners of Jesuit poetics accepted the exclusion of martyrs as
possible heroes of tragedies. There is, finally, not one sort of
tragedy: alongside the most sublime peripeteia-and-recognition
tragedy, we have the pathos-tragedy, the ethos-tragedy, and the
spectacle-tragedy.[60] Sarbiewski simply neglected the hero's suffering, the *pathos* as a source of tragic effect.

Influential as it was, Sarbiewski's prescriptive poetics must be
seen in contrast to an important Polish critical work, the anonymous
Poetica practica anno 1648.[61] In a chapter entitled "Monita com-
ponentibus comaedias, tragaedias, comicotragaedias etc.," the statement is made: "primum, sunt qui negant posse induci personas
ideales in comaediis et tragaediis; alii concedunt et de facto pro-
ducunt. . . . Discipulus sequatur quam voluerit opinionem."[62] This
author explicitly granted heroic status to Christian martyrs and, in
general, to "ideal persons." The student, a future writer of drama, is
not to be constrained in choosing his own way of composition.
Poetica practica thus defended the mixing of genres and gave a
great deal of attention to some of them, including tragicomedy.

[C]omicotragedia est actio poetica comicis et traicis rebus constans. Continet hoc genus utrumque actionis personas illustres et humiliores, laeta et tristia, finis tamen traicocomaediae est laetus, comicotragaediae vero tristis. Refertur traicocomaedia ad comaediam, comicotragaedia ab [ad?] tragaediam. . . . Materia traicomaediae sunt eventus laeti et tristibus nati; materia vero comicotragaediae sunt eventus ex latis tristes"[63]

The author was fully aware that while mixed genres were unknown to classic writers, the mixed sad-joyous *spectacula* were more frequent in his time than pure tragedies and comedies.[63] This means not only assimilation of the classical bipolar notions of "tragedy" and "comedy": it meant that theoreticians and also writers would not feel that these categories were binding. In the title of the Warsaw Stanislaus play of 1633 which appears in the list above, we see the use of the term *"comico-tragedy"* (that is, tragicomedy) correctly applied to a martyr drama prior to the writing and publication of the *Poetica practica*—proof that genre practices preceded their codification, and that this open-minded Jesuit author was indeed more interested in a descriptive than a normative study.[64]

In addition to the matter of genre, the plays that I have listed above also have many other medieval characteristics. The Catherine and John the Baptist plays in particular are more concerned with illustrating the *vita* than with affecting the audience with the tragic emotions of fear and pity. Nevertheless, martyrdom emerges as good subject matter for a tragedy, although it does not automatically produce a good play. Where classical influence is visible in such aspects as the use of choruses, genre division and labels, the number of actors allowed to speak in a scene, and certain stylistic devices and motifs, it produces a new contribution to tragedy only in the *Boleslaus Furens*. This play is programmatic in its allusion to Seneca's *Hercules Furens* and follows the Aristotelian-Senecan scheme for tragedy with its five-act structure, historical subject matter, complex action structure (*peplegmenoi*), *pathos* (of the purest sort: both the protagonist and his antagonist are Christians, with a king killing his bishop and cutting his body into pieces), decline of the noble hero ("dauntless but without integrity"[65]). But we also need to see such a play as the drama on the lives of Boris and Gleb as a tragedy if we consider the presence of the royal family, fratricide, functional *peripeteia*, effective recognition, and damnation of the wrongdoer.

The happiness of martyrdom, besides sharpening the contrast between good and evil, must be considered to be a common feature shared with the medieval saint legends and plays. This crucial characteristic thus affirms the continuity of the saint play genre in these later Polish plays.

To summarize: Legends of saints of the distant past were adopted by sixteenth and seventeenth-century writers as subject matter with a certain tragic potential. The stories derived from these legends were rewritten in a new "purged" tragic fashion. But new saints were also being canonized, and new stories about them were to be circulated. These stories were destined to be placed against a new humanist scholarly background, but the plays retained quite "medieval" ideas about the sacred and quite "medieval" expectations towards the saints themselves. The classical pattern of tragedy could not expunge medieval elements from the plays, assuming that the saint play genre retained its same functions from earlier times. What happened is that the apparatus of classical tragedy was adapted to maintain and heighten the impact of the old genre of the saint play on the post-medieval Catholic audience, not the other way round.

NOTES

[1] See *Summa procesjej na wnoszenie kości świętych*, in Korotaj, no. 50.

[2] See Kevin Croxen, "Thematic and Generic Medievalism in the Polish Neo-Latin Drama of the Renaissance and Baroque," *Slavic and East European Journal* 43 (1999): 265–98.

[3] "Odprawowany W Kamionce na jarmark przypadaiący na dzień tegosz Iana Świętego Chrzciciela Roku Pań, 1619" (title page reproduced in Lewański, *Studia*, 211).

[4] BJ MS. 3526, fols. 71–72.

[5] *Joachym y Anna: Comedia o niepłodności Anny S. z Joachimem mężem iey ktorych wdziewiędziesiąth lath vraczyłP. Bog Potomstwem Blogoslawioną Panną Marią między czorkami Syonskiemi nigdy nieporownaną*, ed. J. I. Kraszewski, "Komedia o niepłodności Anny," *Ateneum* 2 (1841):95–126; see Stanisław Windakiewicz, *Teatr ludowy w dawnej Polsce* (Cracow, 1902), 124–26.

[6] *Komunja duchowna SS Borysa i Gleba*, in Biblioteka Pawlikowskich, MS. Ossolineum 12778/I, fols. 401–72; Lewański, ed., *Dramaty staropolskie*, 6:303–406. Three other long miracle plays—e.g., *Sławna pomoc Ramirowego zwycięstwa przez anielskie pułki uczyniona*—appear in the same codex (fols. 1–102).

[7] Here we have a connection to St. Stanislaus: his killer Boleslaus was grandson of Jaroslav in the maternal line.

[8] Marvin Kantor, ed. and trans., *Medieval Slavic Lives of Saints and Princes* (Ann Arbor: University of Michigan, 1983), 13, with a parallel-text edition of the *Narrative and Passion and Encomium of the Holy Martyrs Boris and Gleb* (163–253) and complete facsimile of the Old Church Slavic copy from the *Uspenskij Sbornik*.

[9] *Skazanije i strast' i pochvała sviatuju mucenyku Borysa i Hleba*; Lewański, ed., *Dramaty staropolskie*, 6:691, points to this text as the main source of the drama.

[10] See Kantor, ed. and trans., *Medieval Slavic Lives*, 179.

[11] The latter is called *Scena quinta ludicra*, and is incorporated in the action of the first act; both texts edited by M. Markowski, "Južnorusskija intermedii," *Kievskaja Starina* 46, pt. 7 (1894): 32–45. To be sure, the area involved only later became known as the Ukraine.

[12] Lewański, *Dramaty staropolskie*, 6:676.

[13] Valentin, *Le Théâtre des Jésuites*, nos. 125, 126, 151, 160, 440, 2861, 3121.

[14] Biblioteka Pawlikowskich, MS. Ossolineum 204, fols. 30–36ᵛ.

[15] Julian Lewański, *Dramat i teatr średniowiecza i renesansu w Polsce* (Warsaw: PWN, 1981), 514.

[16] *Dialog na uroczystość świętej Katarzyny panny i męczenniczki*, BJ MS. 3526, fols. 130–42; ed. Lewański, *Dramaty staropolskie*, 6: 137–73.

[17] Ibid., 6:676.

[18] The text at "has a beginning" is corrupt, but the following proof clarifies the meaning: "he was always and he will be forever a King together with God and the Holy Ghost" (ibid., 6:151).

[19] *Passio Sancte Katerine Virginis, BHL 1663*, trans. Nancy Wilson van Baak, in *La festa et storia di Sancta Caterina: A Medieval Italian Religious Drama*, ed. and trans. Anne Wilson Tordi (New York: Peter Lang, 1997), 261; Jacobus de Voragine, *The Golden Legend*, trans. W. Granger Ryan, 2 vols, [Princeton: Princeton University Press, 1993], 2:334, 336. In Capgrave's version "Archaungell Mychael" himself grants her help after her long prayer, done "all in a traunce" (John Capgrave, *The Life of Saint Katherine*, ed. K. A. Winstead [Kalamazoo: Medieval Institute Publications 1999]; book 4, chap. 17).

[20] Barbara Ogrodowska, *Święta polskie: Tradycja i obyczaj* (Warsaw: Wyd. Alfa, 1996), 230. A useful comparison may be made with the English St. George plays and pageants, for which see Clifford Davidson, "Saint Plays and Pageants of Medieval Britain," *Early Drama, Art, and Music Review* 23 (1999): esp. 21–25, and Chambers, *The English Folk-Play*, 170–74.

[21] The content of two playlets of this sort (from the now lost Krasiński MS., fols. 33–37, 191–95) is preserved in a summary by Windakiewicz, *Teatr ludowy*, 130, n. 1; also in the same author's *Pierwsze kompanie aktorów w Polsce* (Cracow: Akademia Umiejętności,1893), 393; cited in Jan Dürr-Durski, "O mieszczańskim teatrze renesansowym w Polsce," *Pamiętnik Teatralny* 2, no. 3 (1953): 66.

[22] Sabine Baring-Gould, *The Lives of Saints*, 16 vols. (Edinburgh: John Grant, 1914), 2:141. For the Polish translation of the report on their martyrdom, see S.

Wysocki, *Opisanie chwalebnego męczeństwa dziewięci chrześcijan japońskich* (Cracow, 1612).

[23] The Beheading of John the Baptist is assigned a separate feast (29 August), which commemorates also the day when the saint's head was discovered (see Jacobus de Voragine, *The Golden Legend*, 2:137–38).

[24] See J. Rompski, *Ścinanie kani: Kaszubski zwyczaj ludowy* (Toruń: Muzeum Etnograficzne w Toruniu, 1974), and, for a literary Kushubian version, Jan Karnowski, "Scynanie kani: Widowisko kaszëbscie," *Gryf kaszubski*, nos. 8–9 (1932). The earliest record was published by Florian Ceynowa in 1851.

[25] J. Rompski, *Ścinanie kani*, 96.

[26] *Tragaedia albo Wizerunk śmierci przeświętego Iana Chrzciciela Przesłańca Bożego*, in *Dramaty staropolskie*, ed. J. Lewański, 6 vols. (Warsaw: PIW, 1959), 2:435–97; the only copy of the original 1618 edition, published in Jaworów, is in Muzeum Miejskie w Cieszynie, shelfmark 7827.

[27] Poplatek, *Studia*, 136, citing Annales collegii Posnaniensis 1588, Biblioteka Jagiellońska, MS. 5198/I, fol. 27, and Annuae provinciae Poloniae 1597, Collegium Calissiense, ASJ Pol. 50, fol. 158ᵛ; recorded also in Ossolineum Biblioteka Pawlikowskich MS. 204, fol. 107.

[28] Biblioteka Krasińskich, Zaluscianum MS. Q.XIV.10, fols. 131–43, now lost.

[29] *Depozyt łask i miłości Boskiej św. Jan Chrzciciel*, reproduced by K. W. Wójcicki, *Teatr starożytny w Polsce*, 2 vols. (Warsaw, 1841), 2:275–82. The play was also performed on the name-day of priest Jan Polnarowski by his students (Windakiewicz, *Teatr ludowy*, 127).

[30] Staatsbibliothek München Cod. lat. mon. 2124, as cited in J. M. Valentin, *Le Théâtre des Jésuites*, no. 1077.

[31] 4° Bavar. 2197 III, 25; reproduced in Szarota, "Boleslaus der Kühne und der hl. Stanislaus auf den Bühnen des 16. Jahrhunderts," 483–90; under 4° Bavar. 2197 III, 24 (same title), summary for a Innsbruck performance in 1623.

[32] Burkhard Waldis, *Das Päpstliche Reich* (1556), chap. 12; Oskar Sengpiel, *Die Bedeutung der Prozessionen für das geistliche Spiel des Mittelalters in Deutschland* (Breslau: Marcus, 1932), 27.

[33] The structural frame in which devil figures explicitly organize the dramatic action is known in medieval drama, for example in the Netherlandic *Spel vanden Heiligen Sacramente van der Nyeuwer Vaert* by Jan Smeken (c.1520); ed. W. J. M. A. Asselbergs and A. P. Huysmans (Culemborg: Tjeenk Willink, 1955); but see also, for a lesser example, the Paris *Passion* of Greban (Grace Frank, *The Medieval French Drama* [Oxford: Clarendon Press, 1954], 184).

[34] The two interludes were printed after the main text by M. Dragomanow in *Kievskaja starina* (Dec. 1883); they appear in Polish translation by M. Jurkowski and E. Łapski in Lewański, ed., *Dramaty staropolskie*, 1:480–97. For a study, see N. K. Gudzij, "Dwa najstarsze intermedia ukraińskie," *Pamiętnik Teatralny* 9 (1960): 519–24, who concludes that they were written by an unknown Ukrainian author whose work was then included into the Polish tragedy.

[35] *Agenda Ecclesiae cathedralis Plocensis* (Cracow: Mikołaj Szarfenberg, 1554), fols. 159ᵛ–162ʳ.

[36] Ogrodowska, *Święta polskie*, 317.

[37] For the following observations I am indebted to Jan Kurek, "Próba ustalenia genezy obrzędów dorocznych—'Mikołai', 'szlachciców' i dziadów', występujących współcześnie we wsiach Beskidu Śląskiego i Żywieckiego," *Polska Sztuka Ludowa*, 1973, fasc. 3:149–158, and, by the same author, "'Mikołaje'— obrzęd doroczny we wsiach Beskidu Śląskiego," *Polska Sztuka Ludowa*, 1973, fasc. 4:194–206.

[38] See the description of the production of 10 December 1972 in Aleksander Spyra, "'Mikołaje' z Łąki," *Polska Sztuka Ludowa*, 1973, fasc. 4:207–10; the show was sometimes shifted to the next Sunday. See also the articles by Kurek cited in n. 37 for a region near the Czech border.

[39] The texts of both are corrupt, as is the music, which originated in the repertoire of the Church.

[40] For the taboo regarding the identity of the players, their consequent anonymity, and their wildness in performance, see also Kurek, "'Mikołaje'—obrzęd doroczny we wsiach Beskidu Śląskiego," 200.

[41] Ibid., 200–04.

[42] Kurek, "Próba ustalenia genezy obrzędów dorocznych," 149.

[43] *Suma comico tragediey na historyą Żywota S. Stanisława Męczennika Chrystusowego, Biskupa Krakowskiego, y Patrona Korony Polskiey, przez Mateusza Jagodowicza, plebana nowomiejskiego . . . P. Stanisławowi Baryczce, woytowi Miasta K. I. M. Starej Warszawy, przypisaney, Dedykowaney, Na dzień Uroczysty Święta jego w Warszawie na Nowym Mieście na cześć y chwałę P. Bogu, y Stanisławowi S., Narodowi Polskiemu ku sławie y pociesze wystawioney. Dnia 8 Maia Roku Pańskiego 1633*, printed by the court printer J. Rossowski. The only extant copy is preserved in Biblioteka PAN Gdańsk, shelfmark Nl.83.24. On the term *comico-tragediey* ('tragicomedy'), see below. For another name-day performance of a saint play, see *Anne and Joachim*.

[44] For general introductions to the Polish saint plays, see Irena Sławińska, "Dramat religijny," in *Encyklopedia Katolicka*, 8 vols. [in progress] (Lublin: Towarzystwo Naukowe KUL, 1995–), 4:193–97, and Tadeusz Bańkowski, "Popularny dramat hagiograficzny. Uwagi o wybranych elementach twórczości autorów XX w.," in *Popularny dramat i teatr religijny w Polsce*, ed. Irena Sławińska and Maria Barbara Stykowa (Lublin: Towarzystwo Naukowe KUL, 1990), 65–94.

[45] *Acta Sanctorum*, 7 May, 2:215–21; Baring-Gould, *Lives of the Saints*, May, 110–13; Stanisław Bełch, *Saint Stanislaw, Patron of Poland* (London: Catholic Truth Society, 1979).

[46] In 1982 the publishing house Interpress, responsible for the propaganda covering the Communist rule, was the publisher of a 283-page book about this conflict of nine hundred years ago, with an English translation issued after the murder of Father Popiełuszko by the security police: Tadeusz Grudziński, *Boleslaus the Bold, Called Also the Bountiful, and Bishop Stanislaus: The Story of a Conflict* (Warsaw: Interpress 1985).

[36] See the bibliography of Stanislaus in M. B. Stykowa, "Święty Stanisław Biskup w dramacie i teatrze, Bibliografia," *Summarium. Sprawozdania*

Towarzystwa Naukowego KUL 7 (1978): 149–61; and, for all genres, see Z. Adamek, "Święty Stanisław ze Szczepanowa i Bolesław Śmiały w literaturze polskiej, Historia motywu," *Tarnowskie Studia Teologiczne* 7 (1979): 188–204.

[37] The oldest known specimen of iconography is a sculpture dated c.1350; among the most interesting illustrations is the twelve-episodes *vita* from an altar triptych at Szczepanów (now in the diocesan museum in Tarnów), dated c.1500; see W. Szczebak, "Motywy ikonograficzne postaci św. Stanisława Szczepanow-skiego na podstawie zabytków z terenu diecezji tarnowskiej," *Tarnowskie Studia Teologiczne* 7 (1979): 205–31, here 221–28. The oldest song dedicated to the saint is *Chwała tobie, gospodzinie* (*Praise be to you, Lord*), from 1452; see Mirosław Perz, "Staropolskie opracowania polifoniczne tekstów o św. Stanisławie," *Summarium: Sprawozdania Towarzystwa Naukowego KUL* 7 (1978): 103–18.

[49] E. M. Szarota, "Boleslaus der Kühne und der hl. Stanislaus auf den Bühnen des 16. Jahrhunderts," *Gegenreformation und Literatur*, ed. Jean-Marie Valentin (Amsterdam: Rodopi, 1979), 271–98; see also Szarota's commentary on the Ger-man program of the performance in Hall in 1733: *Veritas Tragoedia: Oder Die von denen Lebenden angefochtene/ Von denen Todten erfochtene Wahrheit*, Bavar. 2193, XII, 8, reprinted in her Periochen-edition, 1:5:22; for commentary, see Elida Maria Szarota, *Das Jesuitdrama im deutschen Sprachgebiet: Eine Periochen-Edition*, 4 vols. in 7 pts (Munich: Wilhelm Fink, 1979–87), 1:2:1783–86.

[50] BJ MS. 3526, fols. 1–10ʳ.

[51] Johannes Joncre, *Tragoedia Boleslaus Secundus Furens*, ed. Georgius Axer (Wrocław: Ossolineum, 1972); for the manuscript, see Biblioteka Kórnicka, MS. B IV 498,29, and, for the source, the *Vita Sanctissimi Stanislai*, in Joannis Długosz *Opera omnia*, ed. A. Przeździecki, 14 vols. (Cracow, 1863–87), 1:1–181. There was also a Polish dialogue of St. Stanislaus in the lost Chełmno codex, MS. Kras. 3495, pp. 45–59 (summary in Windakiewicz, *Teatr ludowy*, 134–35).

[52] Marian Plezia, introd., *Średniowieczne żywoty i cuda patronów Polski* (Warsaw: Pax, 1987), 105. With regard to early printed legends, see, for before 1600: Paulus of Krosno (Paweł z Krosna), Panegyricus ad divum Stanislaum praesulem Sanctissimum ac patronem Poloniae beneficientissimum in *Panegyrici et alia carmina* (Vienna, 1509; Cracow, 1513); *Legendae sanctorum Adalberti, Stanislai, Floriani, Regni Poloniae patronorum* (Cracow: Jan Haller 1517); Marszewski, *Vita et martyrium divi Stanislai* (Kraków, 1543); P. Roysius, *Carmen de sancto pontifice caeso dive Stanislao* (Cracow, 1547).

[53] As observed by Lesław Eustachiewicz ("Boleslaus Furens—nieznany dramat łaciński z XVI wieku," *Pamiętnik Literacki* 43 [1952]: 532), the river names are Nilus, Rhenus, and Rubicon with no mention of Vistula; also, Cracow is not mentioned. In the preface to his edition (10–11), Jerzy Axer proposed that the author could be Portugese or Spanish because three main rivers of Iberia are mentioned: Durius, Tagus, and Anas. The forms of both the first and the given name of the poet are, however, apparently not Spanish but rather Flemish or Dutch; the southern Netherlands were at that time under Spanish rule, and knowledge of the topography of Spain could have been based on experience.

⁵⁴ D. Tschižewskij, "Ausserhalb der Schönheit: Ausserästhetische Elemente in der slavischen Barockdichtung," in H. R. Jauss, ed., *Die nicht mehr schönen Künste: Grenzphänomene des Ästhetischen* (Munich: W. Fink, 1968), 209.

⁵⁵ Croxen, "Thematic and Generic Medievalism in the Polish Neo-Latin Drama," 265–98. "In summary, then, Polish neo-Latin drama to the end of the Baroque remained a profoundly medieval phenomenon with regard to length, content, characterization, and choral structure. The medievalism of Polish Latin drama places it up to two centuries behind Jozef IJsewijn's timetable for the purgation of medieval elements from Western European neo-Latin literature (*Companion to Neo-Latin Studies*, 2nd ed., 2 vols. [Leuven: Leuven University Press, 1990], 1:288). The classical bipolar notions of 'tragedy' and 'comedy' went unassimilated by most Polish playwrights, who could not reconcile these notions with the medieval sacramental psychology inherited more directly from the medieval Christian liturgy and liturgical drama" (ibid., 1:288, 290n).

⁵⁶ In my "Anything But a Game: Corpus Christi in Poland," read at the International Congress on Medieval Studies (Kalamazoo, 2000), and my book *Teatr i sacrum w średniowieczu* (Wrocław: FUNNA, 2001).

⁵⁷ See the concept of *ethos* (Aristotle, *Poetics* 1450a). Jacobus Pontanus, *Poeticarum Institutionum libri III* (Ingolstadt, 1597), 87–119, stressed the importance of character development in drama, but Sarbiewski followed Aristotle strictly; see M. K. Sarbiewski, *De perfecta poesi* (Wrocław: Ossolineum, 1954), for a bilingual Latin-Polish edition: *O tragedii i komedii czyli Seneka i Terencjusz*; cited in Teresa Banasiowa, "W kręgu tradycji Jakuba Pontanusa i Macieja K. Sarbiewskiego: autor 'Poetyki praktycznej' (1648) o dramatica poesis (Wybrane zagadnienia)," in *Jesuitica: Kolokwium naukowe z okazji 400. rocznicy urodzin Macieja Kazimierza Sarbiewskiego*, pod red. Jana Malickiego przy współudziale Piotra Wilczka (Katowice: Wyd. Uniwersytetu Śląskiego, 1997), 52.

⁵⁸ Aristotle, *Poetics* 1453a, 2–3.

⁵⁹ "Ex parte etiam ipsius martyris vix oriri potest commiseratio, cum et multi probi viri idem sibi optent et illum ipsum gaudere de cruciatu intellegant" (Sarbiewski, *De perfecta poesi*, 230; cf. Banasiowa, "W kręgu tradycji," 56).

⁶⁰ Aristotle, *Poetics*, 1452b, 35, and 1455b–1456a.

⁶¹ The *Poetica practica anno 1648* (MS. Zaluscianum Lat Q. XIV.229, now lost), as discussed and quoted extensively by V. I. Rezanov, *histori russkoj dramy: Ekskurs v oblast teatra jezuitov* (Nezhin: Izvestija Istoricesko-Filologiceskogo Instituta, 1910), 292–452.

⁶² *Poetica practica*, Tractatus IX [on tragedy], as quoted by Rezanov, *K istorii russkoj dramy*, 370.

⁶³ *Poetica practica*, Tractatus IX, as quoted by Rezanov, *K istorii russkoj dramy*, 368.

⁶⁴ "Apud antiquos traicocomaediae et comicotragaediae non fuit usu, apud nos vero frequens; imo frequentior est usus quam purae comaediae et tragaediae" (ibid., 368–69); this was opposed to the established tradition of Pontanus, Sarbiewski, and others (ibid., 369).

[65] This is a general conclusion from the analysis by Rezanov: "the author [of the *Poetica practica*] finds it quite normal to theorize about forms established by praxis and sanctioned by audience's approval" (ibid., 375).

[65] See the statement, referring to the John the Baptist play, by Lewański: "almost a regular tragedy of Herod" (*Dramat i teatr*, 237).

[66] Aristotle, *Poetics*, 1456a, 22.

The Descent from the Cross in Sixteenth-Century New Spain

Susan Verdi Webster

Public representations of the Passion of Christ were introduced to New Spain (Mexico) by Spanish friars during the early phases of the "spiritual conquest."[1] These and other forms of dramatic performances played a significant but often overlooked role in the evangelization of the indigenous people, especially during the sixteenth century. Texts of Passion plays from sixteenth-century New Spain are few in number, although many Nahuatl scripts likely await recovery and translation.[2] However, important visual and documentary evidence points to the early introduction and performance of Passion plays and indicates that the native people actively participated in the organization and production of these representations.

In a people already highly sensitive and attuned to the communicative power of visual spectacles and dramatic ritual enactments, the friars found a highly receptive audience. Indeed, religious drama and other forms of theatrical representation were particularly effective didactic and evangelical methods since they encouraged emulation and participation. Dramatic performances ranged from the ritual reenactment of battle scenes and episodes from the Nativity and Passion of Christ, using both sculpted and "live" actors, to simplified pantomime performances that dramatized Christian beliefs.

Dating from the second half of the sixteenth century, pantomime representations of scenes from the Passion, or dramatizations with minimal dialogue called *Neixcuitiles*, were performed on Fridays throughout the year in Mexico City.[3] Corpus Christi and Holy Week were often celebrated with numerous dramatic representations of biblical episodes, and these performances reportedly drew huge crowds of spectators.[4] Indigenous people performed as actors in many of these representations, and they were always present in great numbers as spectators.[5] Such spectacles encouraged native participation and presumably fostered a greater understanding of Christian religious practices and beliefs.

Following Spanish tradition, the native participants in these performances were typically members of religious confraternities founded by the Mendicant orders. In order to inspire devotion and loyalty among the newly-converted and actively to involve them in Christian devotional practices, the friars, instituting confraternities of natives, organized them into devotional groups dedicated to specific patron saints or biblical episodes. Among other activities, the confraternities celebrated their saint's day and other feast days with ritual public processions and performances in the open air of the monastery atrium.

The foundation of confraternities in New Spain began as early as 1526, and their numbers continued to grow, expanding dramatically in the last quarter of the sixteenth century and throughout the seventeenth century.[6] By all accounts, confraternities were especially appealing to the indigenous population, and in some towns virtually all the Indians belonged to a confraternity.[7] By 1585 there were said to be over three hundred native confraternities active in Mexico City alone.[8] The institution of confraternities provided the local populace with group identities similar to pre-Hispanic *calpulli*, or extended kin groups, and offered them a communal ritual role and dedication that accorded well with many earlier forms of indigenous ritual practices.

The most popular types of confraternities were the penitential groups dedicated to specific aspects or episodes of the Passion of Christ that celebrated Holy Week with elaborate rituals and flagellant processions. The earliest documented penitential confraternity was that of the Vera Cruz of Mexico City which in 1527 petitioned for two plots of land on which to construct a hospital and chapel.[9] In 1538, the Franciscan friar Toribio de Benavente Motolinía described the elaborate penitential processions held by the Confraternity of the Vera Cruz in Tlaxcala: "twenty thousand men, women, and children, cripples and disabled people . . . disciplined themselves with flagellant whips, and those that could not afford nor could have the small [metal] stars [attached to the whips], flogged themselves with whips of cord. . . ."[10] In 1541, Motolinía devoted several pages in his *Historia de los indios de la Nueva España* to a description of the impressive numbers of penitents that participated in the Holy Week processions in Mexico City and to the variety and vigor of the acts of self-mortification performed by the participants, especially the native groups.[11] Writing at the end of the sixteenth century, the Franciscan friar Gerónimo de Mendieta repeatedly marveled at the great devotion of the indigenous confraternities to penitence and to the Passion of Christ. Mendieta described Holy Week in Mexico City in 1595:[12]

> On Maundy Thursday the procession of the [confraternity of the] Vera Cruz went out with more than twenty thousand Indians, and more than three thousand flagellants, with two hundred and nineteen images of Christ and symbols of his passion. On [Good] Friday more than seven thousand and seven hundred flagellants, by count, went out in the procession of [the confraternity of] the Soledad, with images of the Soledad.[13]

The popularity of flagellant processions among the Indians prompted Mendieta to remark that "Among them [the Indians], he who does not carry a rosary and a flagellant whip is not considered a Christian."[14] The Augustinian friar Juan de Grijalva, writing in the early seventeenth century and lauding the intense devotion of the Indians to the penitential processions of Holy Week, declared that they far exceeded the Spaniards in their numbers and in the fervor of their self-mortification.[15] The native predilection for flagellation and other acts of self-mortification may on one level be seen as a continuation of the variety of pre-Hispanic traditions of ritual self-discipline.[16]

The penitential processions were not the only rituals of Holy Week in which the confraternities participated. They also witnessed and contributed to dramatic representations of the Passion, the most important of which was the Descent from the Cross.[17] Holy Week performances climaxed on Good Friday in the ritual reenactment of the Descent from the Cross and its related penitential procession. Although many sixteenth- and seventeenth-century chroniclers make note of the rituals and processions of Holy Week,[18] only one describes the ceremony of the Descent from the Cross in careful detail. The Dominican friar Agustín Dávila Padilla, writing in the late sixteenth century, recounts each step in a ceremony of the Descent from the Cross that was performed in the Monastery of Santo Domingo in Mexico City in 1582.[19] Although the Descent was performed by priests, the Monastery's newly established penitential confraternity of the Descent and Sepulcher of Christ likely provided

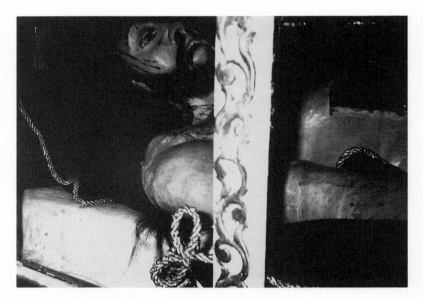

1. Sculpture of the dead Christ used in the Descent from the Cross. The figure has articulated shoulders that have been covered with leather and painted. Church of the Monastery of San Miguel, Huejotzingo, Puebla. Photo: Author.

many of the the images, properties, and elements of the stage set and also participated fully in the ritual and procession. Early membership in the confraternity consisted of Mexico City's elite but quickly burgeoned to include "the majority of the city's population."[20]

According to Dávila Padilla, the scene of the Crucifixion was erected on a large stage in front of the main altar of the Monastery of Santo Domingo. Three crosses bearing sculpted images of Christ and the two thieves were set atop a hill of jagged rocks and wild plants. Insignias of the Passion, the lance, the sponge, the crown of thorns, etc., were placed around Christ's cross. Sculptures of the sorrowing Virgin, St. John the Evangelist, and other images were arranged at the base. At two o'clock the sermon began, and as the discussion of the Descent from the Cross was reached, several priests accompanied by ladder-bearing acolytes emerged from the sacristy and knelt upon the stage. Another priest followed, swinging a censer. The first priest then asked permission of the Virgin to lower the body of her son. Two ladders were placed against the arms of the cross and were scaled by priests carrying long towels. One by one the insignias of the Passion were removed and placed in the hands of the image of the Virgin while the first priest described how each served as an instrument of salvation. Finally, the priests atop the ladders removed each of the nails from the image of Christ and, using the towels, gently lowered the body of Christ into the arms of those waiting below. The body of Christ was then placed in the arms of the image of the Virgin, which caused "great devotion" among the spectators. After permission to bury her Son was asked of the Virgin, the image of Christ was removed and stretched out on a bier, whereupon, to the sound of choral music, the penitential procession was organized.[21]

The Descent from the Cross was traditionally performed with sculpted images, and Dávila Padilla's account of the form and nature of the sculptures used at the Monastery of Santo Domingo coincides with this tradition. Life-size sculptures of Christ, the Virgin, St. John the Evangelist, and other variable images were specifically created for the representation of this drama.[22] Carved of wood or molded from a paste of macerated corn husks, as the images of New Spain often were, these sculptures were equipped with articulated limbs so that they could be posed or positioned to serve in a variety of scenes. Images of Christ were jointed at the shoulders and sometimes at the knees, allowing the arms to be lowered during the Descent from the Cross and moved to the sides of the body when the image was then carried in penitential procession as the dead Christ. Similarly, sculptures of the *dolorosa*, or sorrowing Virgin, were given articulated limbs so that the body of Christ, once lowered from the cross, could be placed in her arms to reenact the scene of the pietà. In some cases, sculptures of the *dolorosa* were outfitted with internal mechanisms of cogs and pulleys that, when activated, permitted the sculpture to incline its head, raise its arms, and bow from the waist. The *dolorosa* that Dávila Padilla describes was equipped with such a mechanism. The movements of the sculpture were manipulated by cords that extended below the platform on which the image stood. When each insignia of the Passion was placed in the hands of the image, the arms could be raised and the head lowered to make it appear that the Virgin was kissing or weeping over the object. Dávila Padilla notes that this act greatly moved the spectators to devotion.[23] Following the tradition of southern Spain, sculptures of the Virgin and other subsidiary images were made to be clothed in actual garments, and articulated limbs also facilitated the dressing of the sculptures and the affixing of any properties they might carry.

Articulated sculptures of the dead Christ are ubiquitous in Mexican churches and monasteries, where they serve as mute testimony to the dramatic performances of Holy Week during the colonial era (fig. 1). Many of them are undocumented, and frequent repainting has made them difficult to date with any certainty. However, there is another form of visual evidence that testifies not only to the visual appearance of such Holy Week performances but also to their extreme importance during the sixteenth century. During the past decades, a number of mural paintings depicting the Descent from the Cross and its related penitential procession have been uncovered in several sixteenth-century monasteries in central Mexico. The most elaborate of these murals was discovered in the 1980s under layers of whitewash along the north and south walls of the nave of the church at the Franciscan monastery of San Miguel, Huejotzingo, in the state of Puebla.[24] Close inspection reveals that these murals are not simply didactic illustrations of remote scriptural events; they literally document the form, appearance, and participants of the Good Friday performances enacted at the monastery during the sixteenth century.

The mural on the north wall, framing the *porciúncula* (north doorway), depicts a scene of the Descent from the Cross (fig. 2). Tonsured Franciscan friars on ladders, clad in the traditional brown sackcloth habits of the order, lower the body of Christ with long towels. Figures of the Virgin, St. John, and others are visible at the foot of the cross. Around the base of the hill are hooded confraternity members engaged in flagellation, and to either side (not visible in the illustration) are the crosses of the two thieves, surrounded by numerous confraternity members. The artist of this mural, probably a native painter working under the direction of the friars, clearly documents the local, contemporary elements of this pivotal Holy Week performance.

The south wall mural depicts the subsequent penitential procession with the body of the Dead Christ, known as the procession of the *Santo Entierro*, or Holy Burial. A reconstruction drawing (fig. 3) shows the members of the penitential confraternity opening the procession as they bear standards emblazoned with crosses,

2. Descent from the cross. North wall mural, Church of the Monastery of San Miguel, Huejotzingo, Puebla. Photo: Author.

3. Reconstruction drawing of the penitential procession. South wall mural, Church of the Monastery of San Miguel, Huejotzingo, Puebla. Photo: After José Alberto Vázquez Benítez, *Historia de un convento*, 26–27.

followed by rows of members dressed in white who engage in flagellation. The center row of black-garbed penitents carries the *Arma Christi*, or instruments of the Passion: the lance, the ladder, the dice, the veil of Veronica, etc. At the end of the procession, accompanied by a Franciscan friar, sculpted images are carried on platforms. The dead Christ, wrapped in a winding cloth, is carried under a baldachin, followed by figures of the Maries and St. John consoling the sorrowing Virgin. The artist of this mural has carefully documented the form and order of the procession, while the identity of the confraternity is clearly indicated by the escutcheons that each of the penitents wears on the chest of his tunic: a green cross on a red or ocher ground. This escutcheon is the traditional symbol of confraternities of the Vera Cruz, a type of penitential confraternity traditionally established and fostered by the Franciscans in Spain.[25]

A manuscript that belonged to a confraternity of the Vera Cruz founded by the Franciscans at the Monastery of San Miguel in the sixteenth century is preserved in the local parish archive at Huejotzingo. This manuscript, which indicates that the confraternity was almost exclusively composed of native members, contains several early seventeenth-century inventories of its belongings. The inventories demonstrate that this confraternity of the Vera Cruz is indeed that which is depicted in the monastery, for they include references to many of the images and objects pictured in the murals. An abbreviated inventory of 1649 lists the following items pertaining to the confraternity's processional activities: "two small banners one purple and the other black . . . three standards, one large and two small black ones . . . another purple standard . . . two boxes in which are kept the insignias [instruments of the Passion] and wax. . . ."[26] A more extensive inventory of 1663 lists the following:

Firstly the Holy Sepulcher of the Holy Christ of the Descent
. . .
two Wigs of the Holy Sepulcher one that he has on and the other that is among the said belongings
. . .
one large towel made of a decorated fabric with which the Holy Christ is lowered [from the cross] on Good Friday
. . .
One winding cloth of embroidered canvas with which the Holy Christ

is bound

. . .

two Embroidered Banners one white and the other black

. . .

five standards, four of them black with crosses and one purple and of
the black ones one is new with its fringe of silk

. . .

Two Small Painted Banners of Taffeta one black and one purple

. . .

All of the attributes and Instruments of the Passion of Our Lord that go
out in the procession on Good Friday

. . .

One St. John the Evangelist carved in the round made with articulations
placed on his processional platform with his alb and red silk cape and
[?] wig, with a black frontal.[27]

The absence of the more sacred images of the Virgin and Christ in
the confraternity's inventory suggests that these sculptures must
have been maintained in the monastery, where they served as devotional images throughout the year. Indeed, a 1663 inventory of articles in the Monastery of San Miguel lists a sculpture of "one holy
Christ with its baldachin or canopy which is in the cell of the
guardian friars."[28]

The Monastery of San Miguel, Huejotzingo, is only one of
many such establishments that staged Holy Week performances
with the assistance of penitential confraternities in the sixteenth
century. Mural paintings depicting the Descent from the Cross are
found in numerous sixteenth-century Mexican monasteries and may
serve as indicators that the rituals were performed in those places as
well. For example, at the sixteenth-century Dominican Monastery
of San Juan, Teitipac, in the state of Oaxaca, far more elaborate and
opulent mural paintings depicting Good Friday rituals cover a
significant part of the interior walls of the *portería* or exterior
cloister entrance (fig. 4). The *portería* was a public and highly
visible area of sixteenth-century monasteries and often served,
among other things, as a meeting place for friars and the native
community.

On the back wall of the *portería*, above the portal that leads to
the cloister, is a scene of the Descent from the Cross which is
performed by Dominican friars attired in traditional black and white
habits. One friar carefully lowers the body of Christ with a long

4. Descent from the Cross and penitential procession. Murals inside the *porteria*, Monastery of San Juan, Teitipac, Oaxaca. Photo: Juan and Eréndira de la Lama.

towel, while another prepares to remove the nail from the left hand. On the adjoining wall of the *portería*, the subsequent penitential procession is depicted. The procession is organized in two registers that are joined on the far right. In the upper left, the van of the procession, about to enter a portal, is led by two young boys and several black-garbed penitents carrying banners and standards. They are followed by rows of penitents, arranged in groups of three carrying the *Arma Christi* and guided by a friar.

The second half of the procession continues on the lower register, where it has just exited a portal (the form of which is strikingly similar to the actual portal that leads to the cloister). Groups of secular figures bring up the rear of the procession, and before them appear people dressed as the Virgin, Mary Magdalen, and, seemingly, St. John the Evangelist. These figures are preceded by eight rather opulently attired friars carrying a bier upon which is a sculpture of the dead Christ wrapped in winding cloths. Another group of friars leads the platform, one of whom swings a censer, sanctifying the space through which the image of Christ will pass.

Like the murals at Huejotzingo, these scenes appear to document with careful attention to detail the contemporary form and appearance of the performance and the procession. The archival evidence at Teitipac remains to be recovered; however, it is likely that a local confraternity organized and participated in these rituals as at Huejotzingo. The fact that in each case the scenes were recorded in important and highly visible public areas of the monastery attests to the importance of the rituals for their contemporary native audience. If the cases of Huejotzingo and Teitipac demonstrate that these murals served as markers of ritual activities that were performed at the monasteries during the sixteenth century, then other murals depicting scenes of the Descent from the Cross in Mexican monasteries may present similar evidence of the performance of Good Friday rituals. Any murals remaining to be discovered lie beneath centuries of whitewash.

Contemporary accounts, archival documents, and visual evidence demonstrate the importance and once-widespread popularity of this ritual in the sixteenth-century in New Spain. The ceremony of the Descent from the Cross continued to grow in popularity in the seventeenth century, but fell from favor in the eighteenth century when the Inquisition attempted to censor and eradicate such performances. Inquisitors filed charges leveled specifically against

Passion plays, and in so doing they cited a variety of indecencies, abuses, and scandals, including superstition and idolatry, associated with such performances.[29] Of particular irritation to the Inquisitors was the fact that most of these plays were performed in native languages, which purportedly gave rise to all manner of errors and unorthodox interpretations. Dictamens that were sent out to Inquisitors in central Mexico charged them with enforcing a ban on the performance of Passion plays and with advising their constituents of the fines, penalties, and a sentence of excommunication for their failure to comply. Inquisitors were also directed to "ascertain who the people are that have the written texts, what they [the texts] represent, and to collect them until they are completely extirpated."[30] A list of documents pertaining to the performance of Passion plays in specific *pueblos* included, among other municipalities, the town of Huejotzingo. Today, the Descent from the Cross is no longer performed at Huejotzingo, although some local confraternities still undertake penitential processions during Holy Week. The mural paintings inside the monastery church remain as the only visible testimony to the power and importance of the Descent from the Cross in the sixteenth century.

NOTES

[1] This article is based on research conducted in Mexico with the support of grants from the University of St. Thomas and the Program for Cultural Cooperation between Spain's Ministry of Culture and United States' Universities. I am grateful to Richard E. Phillips for encouraging my initial interest in the topic, and especially to Eréndira de la Lama for her invaluable knowledge, advice, and support during the on-site research. An expanded study on this topic, "Art, Ritual, and Confraternities in Sixteenth-Century New Spain: Penitential Imagery at the Monastery of San Miguel, Huejotzingo," *Anales del Instituto de Investigaciones Estéticas* 70 (1997):5–43.

[2] A notable exception is the Nahua Passion play recently translated and published by Louise M. Burkhart, *Holy Wednesday: A Nahua Drama from Early Colonial Mexico* (Philadelphia: University of Pennsylvania Press, 1996). Many such texts may have been destroyed by the Mexican Inquisition during the eighteenth century when such dramatic representations were banned. See "Las representaciones teatrales de la Pasión," *Boletín del Archivo General de la Nación* 5 (1934): 332–56.

[3] Othón Arroniz, *Teatro de evangelización en Nueva España* (México: Universidad Nacional Autónoma de México, 1979), 106.

[4] Fray Agustín de Vetancurt, among several other chroniclers, describes the popularity of representations of events from the Passion (*Neixcuitiles*) performed

during Holy Week in Mexico City and notes that "à las demas representaciones tan grande concurso, que no hay lugar vacio en el patio, y azoteas . . ." (*Teatro mexicano* [1698; facs. rpt. México: Porrúa, 1982], 42).

[5] See, for example, M. Ekdahl Ravicz, *Early Colonial Religious Drama in Mexico: From Tzompantli to Golgotha* (Washington, D.C.: Catholic University of America Press, 1970); Max Harris, *The Dialogical Theatre* (New York: St. Martin's Press, 1993); Arroníz, *Teatro de evangelización*.

[6] One of the earliest confraternities was that of Our Lady of the Immaculate Conception, which founded the hospital of Jesús Nazareno in Mexico City. Hernán Cortés wrote of the existence of this confraternity in 1529. See Adolfo Lamas, *Seguridad social en la Nueva España* (México: Universidad Autónoma de México, 1964), 140–41. According to Alicia Bazarte Martínez, *Las cofradías de españoles en la Ciudad de México (1526–1860)* (México: Universidad Nacional Autónoma de México, 1989), 34–35, the earliest documented confraternity is that of Los Caballeros de la Cruz, founded by Hernán Cortés in 1526. Although not all scholars believe that confraternities were established during the early phase of missionary activity, most agree that they began to proliferate in the late sixteenth and early seventeenth centuries. See, for example, Charles Gibson, *The Aztecs Under Spanish Rule* (Stanford: Stanford University Press, 1964), 127–33; James Lockhart, *The Nahuas After the Conquest* (Stanford: Stanford University Press, 1992), 218–19, 538n; John K. Chance and William B. Taylor, "Cofradías y cargos: una perspectiva histórica de la jerarquía cívico-religiosa mesoamericana," *Antropología* 14 (1987): 7; Ernesto de la Torre Villar, "Algunos aspectos acerca de las cofradías y la propiedad territorial en Michoacán," *Jahrbuch für Geschichte von Staat, Wirtschaft und Gesellschaft Lateinamerikas* 4 (1967): 418–19; Murdo J. MacLeod, "Papel social y económico de las cofradías indígenas de la colonia en Chiapas," *Mesoamérica* 4, no. 5 (1983): 67–68; Serge Gruzinski, "Indian Confraternities, Brotherhoods and *Mayordomías* in Central New Spain," in *The Indian Community of Colonial Mexico*, ed. Arij Ouweneel and Simon Miller (Amsterdam: CEDLA, 1990), 206–07; Bazarte Martínez, *Las cofradías de españoles*, 45–46. Missionary expansion on the northern frontier follows a similar trajectory. Confraternities, and especially penitential confraternities, were established almost immediately in the new cities and towns. See William Wroth, *Images of Penance, Images of Mercy: Southwestern Santos in the Late Nineteenth Century* (Norman: University of Oklahoma Press, 1991), 23–26.

[7] See Gruzinski, "Indian Confraternities," 206.

[8] Numbers cited by the Third Mexican Council of 1585; quoted in ibid., 207.

[9] Lucas Alamán, *Disertaciones*, 3 vols. (México: Editorial Jus, 1942), 2:259–60.

[10] Toribio de Benavente Motolinía, *Memoriales*, ed. Edmundo O'Gorman (México: Universidad Nacional Autónoma de México, 1971), 93: "veinte mil hombres, e mujeres, e mochachos, cojos y mancos . . . se disciplinaban con disciplinas de sangre, y los que no alcanzan ni pueden haber estrellitas, azótanse con disciplinas de cordel. . . ."

[11] Toribio de Benavente Motolinía, *Historia de los indios de la Nueva España*, ed. Edmundo O'Gorman, 5th ed. (México: Porrúa, 1990), 55–56.

[12] Gerónimo de Mendieta, *Historia eclesiástica indiana* (México: Porrúa, 1980), 286, 429, 433, 435–37; see also Motolinía, *Historia de los indios de la Nueva España*, 55–56, 64.

[13] Mendieta, *Historia eclesiástica*, 436: "El Juéves Santo salió la procesión de la Vera Cruz con mas de veinte mil indios, y mas de tres mil penitentes, con doscientas y diez y nueve insignias de Cristos y insignias de su pasion. El viérnes salieron en la procesion de la Soledad mas de siete mil y setecientos disciplinantes, por cuenta, con insignias de la Soledad."

[14] Ibid., 429: "Entre ellos, parece no es cristiano el que no trae rosario y disciplina."

[15] Juan de Grijalva, *Crónica de la Orden de N.P.S. Agustín* (1624; rpt. Porrúa, 1985), 161–62.

[16] Alongside the more well-known forms of auto-sacrifice performed by the pre-Hispanic cultures of Mesoamerica, public "penitential processions" are recorded in which the population of entire towns lashed each other with ropes. See, for example, Joseph de Acosta, *The Natural and Moral History of the Indies*, ed. Clements R. Markham, 2 vols. (1800; reprint New York: Burt Franklin, 1964), 2:399.

[17] This situation closely follows Spanish tradition. In Spain, Passion plays were traditionally fostered by the religious orders, who enlisted members of the local confraternities as actors, organizers, and sponsors of religious drama. In the sixteenth and seventeenth centuries, Spanish representations of the Passion were often performed outside the churches on the steps or on makeshift stages erected in the patios of monasteries. Passion plays were generally, although not exclusively, enacted during Holy Week, beginning with the Entry into Jerusalem on Palm Sunday and culminating with the Resurrection on Easter Sunday. Although confraternity members often performed as actors in these dramas, certain characters, notably Christ and the Virgin Mary, were portrayed using sculpted images. The pivotal scene of the Passion, the Descent from the Cross, was enacted almost entirely with sculpted images.

The relationship between confraternities and theatrical production has a long history in Spain. Madrid's first two permanent public theaters were established by the local penitential confraternities of the *La Pasión* and *La Soledad* in the sixteenth century. Confraternities often sponsored public theatrical productions in order to support their pious works, and either collected alms or charged admission. None of the formal, commercial aspects of theater were apparently present in the performances sponsored by confraternities in sixteenth-century New Spain, but the link between popular devotion, confraternities, and dramatic production was clearly continued in the New World. For example, see Hugo Rennert, *The Spanish Stage in the Time of Lope de Vega* (New York: Hispanic Society of America, 1909); Melveena McKendrick, *Theatre in Spain, 1490–1700* (Cambridge: Cambridge University Press, 1992), 47; Casiano Pellicer, *Tratado histórico sobre el origen y progreso de la comedia y del histrionismo en España*, ed. José María Díez Borque (1804; reprint Barcelona: Editorial Labor, 1975), 48.

[18] See, for example, Vetancurt, *Teatro mexicano*, 435–36; Mendieta, *Historia eclesiástica*, 435–36.

¹⁹ Agustín Dávila Padilla, *Historia de la fundación y discurso de la Provincia de Santiago de México de la orden de predicadores*, 3rd ed. (México: Editorial Academia Literaria, 1955), 561–68.

²⁰ Ibid., 563.

²¹ The preceding description is a synopsis of Dávila Padilla's lengthy and carefully detailed description of the performance (ibid., 563–65).

²² Sculpted, and often articulated, images were commonly used in European representations of the Descent from the Cross during the late Middle Ages and Early Modern periods. Spain appears to have maintained the tradition far longer than many other parts of Europe. See Richard B. Donovan, *The Liturgical Drama in Medieval Spain* (Toronto: Pontifical Institute of Mediaeval Studies, 1958), 51–63, 130–45; William Shoemaker, *The Multiple Stage in Spain during the Fifteenth and Sixteenth Centuries* (Princeton: Princeton University Press, 1935), 66–77; Neil C. Brooks, "The Sepulchre of Christ in Art and Liturgy," *University of Illinois Studies in Language and Literature* 7 (1921): 139–250; Ulla Haastrup, "Medieval Props in the Liturgical Drama," *Hafnia* 11 (1987) 133–70; Gesine and Johannes Taubert, "Mittelalterliche Kruzifixe mit schwenkbaren Armen," *Zeitschrift des Deutschen Vereins für Kunstwissenschaft* 23 (1969): 79–121; Alonso Sánchez Gordillo, *Religiosas estaciones que frecuenta la religiosidad sevillana*, ed. Jorge Bernales Ballesteros (Seville: Consejo General de Hermandades y Cofradías, 1983), 164–65; Rafael Martínez González, *La Semana Santa* (Palencia, 1984), 24–53; Antonio Cea Gutiérrez, "Del rito al teatro: Restos de representaciones litúrgicas en la provincia de Salamanca," in *Actas de las jornadas sobre teatro popular en España* (Madrid: CSIC, 1987), 33–37; Rafael Martínez, "La función y paso del descendimiento de Cristo de la Cofradía de San Francisco de Palencia," in *Actas del primer congreso nacional de Cofradías de Semana Santa* (Zamora: Diputación Provincial, 1987), 679–86; Susan Verdi Webster, *Art and Ritual in Golden-Age Spain: Sevillian Confraternities and the Processional Sculpture of Holy Week* (Princeton: Princeton University Press, 1998), chap. 4.

²³ Dávila Padilla, *Historia de la fundación*, 563. The mechanism that Dávila Padilla describes follows Spanish tradition. In Seville, a Gothic sculpture of the Virgin, the Virgen de los Reyes, still retains this system of cogs and pulleys designed to allow the head, arms, and waist to move. See Juan Carrero Rodríguez, *Nuestra Señora de los Reyes y su historia* (Seville: J. Rodríguez Castillejo, 1989), 31; Juan Martínez Alcalde, *La Virgen de los Reyes* (Seville: Editorial Miriam, 1989), 70; Benito Caetano Guerrero López and Antonio Zoido Naranjo, *La Virgen de los Reyes y el pueblo de Sevilla* (Seville: CajaSur, 1996), 85–87. However, the Virgen de los Reyes is not a *dolorosa*. The image is enthroned with the Christ Child in the pose of the maestá. The movements of the sculpture, described as *humillaciones*, were effected at certain points while it was carried in public procession. A sculpture of Santa Ana from a nearby church in Triana was similarly equipped with mechanical devices; see Bernardo Luis de Castro Palacio, "Tratado de algunas ceremonias que se guardan en la Santa Iglesia desta ciudad de Sevilla [1717]," Biblioteca Capitular y Colombina, Sevilla, MS. 83–4–9, fol. 97. References to sculptures outfitted with such mechanisms are relatively rare. From around 1621, archival records from the Cathedral of Mallorca document a

sculpture of the Virgin that was equipped with a device that allowed her head to nod in *reverencia*. The occasion of this action was a procession held on Easter Sunday, in which sculptures of the Virgin and Christ were carried in procession through the city and met in a ritual "encounter" (*encuentro*) in front of the Palacio de la Almudaina. In the *encuentro* ritual, as the sculpture of the Virgin was moved toward that of Christ, it stopped to "make reverences" every four steps. These *reverencias*, which Gabriel Llompart asserts involved the inclination of the head of the sculpture, are undoubtedly the same acts of *humillación* performed by the sculptures of the Virgen de los Reyes and that of Santa Ana in Seville and Triana. The Mallorcan sculpture of the Virgin is extant, and is maintained in the Cathedral Museum; see Gabriel Llompart, *Entre la historia del arte y el folklore* (Palma de Mallorca, 1984), 225–26.

[24] To date, the only scholar to study these murals in any detail is Elena Estrada de Gerlero, "El programa pasionario en el convento franciscano de Huejotzingo," *Jahrbuch für Geschichte von Staat, Wirtschaft und Gesellschaft Lateinamerikas* 20 (1983): 642–62. See also Webster, "Art, Ritual, and Confraternities."

[25] The identical escutcheon is employed by the Confraternity of the Vera Cruz of Seville; see "Regla de la Cofradia de la S[antí]s[i]ma Vera Cruz," Biblioteca Universitaria de Sevilla, MS. 331/224. On the Franciscans and the establishment of confraternities of the Vera Cruz, see J. Meseguer Fernández, "Las Cofradías de la Vera Cruz: Documentos y notas para su historia," *Archivo Ibero-Americano*, 109–10 (1968): 1–15; José Sánchez Herrero *et al.*, "Los cuatro tipos diferentes de Cofradías de Semana Santa, desde su fundación hasta la crisis de finales del siglo XVIII en Andalucía bética y Castilla," in *Actas del primer congreso nacional de Cofradías de Semana Santa* (Zamora: Diputación Provincial, 1987), 259–97.

[26] Archivo Parroquial de Huejotzingo, "Libro de la Cofradía de la Vera Cruz": "dos guiones chicos uno morado y otro negro . . . tres estandartes uno grande y dos chicos negros . . . otro estandarte morado . . . dos caxas donde se guardan las ynsinias y sera. . . ."

[27] "Libro de la Cofradía de la Vera Cruz": "Prim[er]a[men]te el S[an]to Sepulchro del S[an]to Christo del desendim[ien]to . . . dos Cauelleras del Santo Sepulchro una que lo tiene puesto y otra que esta entre los d[ic]hos bienes . . . Vna toalla grande con que se deçiende el S[an]to Xpo el Viernes S[an]to de ruan florete con sus trapaselos . . . una toalla de linesuelo desilada co[n] que se sine el S[an]to Xpo . . . dos Guiones Bordados uno blanco y otro negro . . . cinco estandartes los quatro negros con cruces y el uno morado y de los negros el uno es nuevo con su fleco de ceda . . . Dos Guiones Pequenos de Tafetan negro y morado Pintados . . . Todos los atributos e Ynstrumentos de la Pacion de n[uest]ro S[eño]r que salen en la proçeçion del Viernes S[an]to . . . un San Juan Ebanxelista de Bulto echo de gonses pendiente en sus andas con su abua y capa colorada de seda y su [?] cauellera con su frontal negro. . . ."

[29] For a catalogue of Inquisition documents denouncing Passion plays, see "Las representaciones teatrales de la Pasión," 332–56.

[30] Ibid., 335.

The Cloud: A Medieval Aerial Device, Its Origins, and Its Use in Spain Today

Francesc Massip

Let me begin by commenting on the phenomenology of flight as it relates to its scenic realization. Once, according to Ramon Llull, there was a king's daughter who was playing in the garden; suddenly a crow stole the golden jeweled diadem and "flew through the air for a long distance while many men followed it to see where it would deposit the crown."[1] To fly was until very recently a most fervent desire of men and at the same time a limitation posited by the laws of nature. Of course, while it is an aptitude not inherent in the human body, flight was nevertheless considered proper to *super*natural creatures, and hence to achieve such a skill would mean to make contact with higher orders of beings. From the human standpoint, "flight and divinity were intimately connected."[2] Yet until 1783, when the first flight of an aerostatic balloon was accomplished, every attempt at human flight had failed.

However, if suspension in mid-air formerly seemed in reality to be impossible for humans, scenic fictions could achieve this feat, as had already been the case in Greek tragedies, which included tricks for transporting the actors who played the roles of heroes and divinities. Machinery of this type on stage was, to be sure, disapproved in part by Aristotle since in his view it threatened the credibility of the tragic action.[3] On the other hand, if the spectator believes in the possibility of divine or suprarational intervention, then the use of gadgetry to achieve suspension in the air or flight can be accepted. This would be the case in early Christian drama from the medieval mysteries to Calderón.

Not surprisingly, therefore, the medieval theater began to use elevated places which were determined by the architectural structures in which the plays were produced—e.g., pulpits, galleries, etc.—for locating space to be associated with God. But the wish to achieve realism would lead over time to the search for material

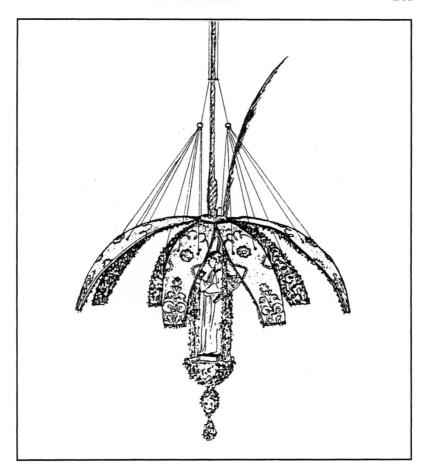

1. Cloud or pomegranate from *El Misteri de l'Assumpcio d'Elx* (País Valencià). Sketch by A. Serrano Peral (1940).

solutions to the visualizing of celestial interventions. Aerial machinery was thus invented so that the theatrical scene might more adequately achieve the desired effect. When we search for analogues in art, we need to realize that since the appearance of photography, including film and television, we are able to see more scenes in a single day than Giotto did in the seventy years of his life. It is thus difficult to look adequately through medieval men's eyes to perceive with similar surprise and hypnotic delight the appearances, disappearances, or angelic flights that were realized on the medieval stage by machines in the spectacles of those times.

One of the most vigorous reinterpretations of the legacy of antiquity occurred during the Gothic period, which has verticality, *anagogicus mos*, and the conquest of height and of light as crucial premises. For Llull, light is the symbol of wisdom—a symbol which established a new architectonic spirit for Abbot Suger at St. Denis.[4] In comparison with the penumbra and horizontality of the liturgical space of the romanesque, the new French style was striving for the maximum expression of ascendent luminosity. We need therefore to remember the treatises on methods of construction and mechanical techniques written by Banu Musa in the twelfth century and Al-Jazari in early thirteenth century—two men who probably met in Arab Hispania—and also the civilization's predisposition toward verticality at this time. It is within this context that we need to examine the reappearance of aerial machinery in scenic action.

The Cloud. Among the different kinds of mechanical devices in medieval spectacles, the spherical machine representing a cloud, normally opening during its descent to show in its interior its celestial nature, has been given various names during its development: *núvol* or *nuve* (cloud), *peanya* (pedestal stand), *caixa* (box), *grua* (hoisting device), *bola* (ball), *globo* (sphere or balloon), *magrana* (pomegranate), *carxofa* (artichoke), *taronja* (orange). It is in fact one of the most interesting gadgets of the medieval stage both for its symbolism and its complexity[5] (fig. 1).

This apparatus is documented for the first time at the coronation of Martin the Humane in Saragossa in 1399. In the Aljafería's palace

> there was an new work of a great spectacle in the manner of a heaven
> with stars which had diverse gradations, and in them there were various
> figures of saints with palms in their hands, and at the top God was
> painted in the middle of a multitude of seraphim. . . . From this heaven
> came down a large bulk that looked like a cloud. . . . From inside of this
> cloud appeared an angel singing wonderfully, and, going up and down
> several times, he let fall all around many small letters and couplets
> written on colored paper, some in yellow and others in blue, inscribed
> with different colors of ink, all for the purpose of solemnity and cere-
> mony that was done there.[6]

Fifteen years later, the new Trastámara king, Ferdinand de Ante-
quera, was furnished with the same ceremony with similar apparatus: "And [as they were] eating the first dish, God moved the
heavens and from them came a large cloud which came down in
front of the table . . . and out of the cloud came an angel singing."[7]
At his wife's coronation the same machinery was used to play an
elaborate joke on the famous royal jester, Borra:

> This jester was in the hall where the Queen was feasting, and when
> Death appeared in the cloud . . . the jester became agitated at the sight
> of him and screamed at him not to come near him. The Duke of Gandía
> sent word to the King . . . that when Death came down and the jester
> began to scream, he should lead him out and tell Death to throw a rope
> down and pull the jester up to him. And this was done. When Death
> came in his cloud in front of the table, Borra started to scream, and the
> Duke led him up; Death threw down a rope, they tied it round Borra,
> and Death hanged him. You wouldn't believe the racket Borra made,
> weeping, expressing his terror, and, as he was pulled up, he urinated
> into his underclothes, and the urine fell on the heads of those below. He
> was quite convinced he was being carried off to Hell. The King
> marvelled at this and was much amused. . . . And Borra the jester went
> up to Heaven as Death's prisoner.[8]

If the fear, the weeping, and passing of his urine of Antoni Tal-
lander, a court jester but also a respected grammarian and ambas-
sador, were real as the chronicle relates, we will have uncovered
evidence of the effectiveness of aerial tricks in the creation of
verisimilitude and of the enormous power of enchantment that
scenic fiction possessed in medieval society.

In the kingdom of Aragon the spherical machine was used early
in the fifteenth century in the Assumption drama staged in Valencia
Cathedral[9] for the descent of the angel who announced to the Virgin
Mary that she was to die—a dramatic form inherited at Elx (Elche),
where it survives to the present time, and at Lleida, where the
gadget was described in 1508 as a "cadira amb ales" ("chair with
wings").[10] But it was also used for royal entries at city gates where
monarchs would meet local dignitaries and be invited to enter the
city. An example of the latter was the *araceli* that opened during its
descent at the entry of Isabella I in Barcelona in 1481,[11] the *caxa*
that came down from a structure representing heaven built on top of
the Gate of St. Anthony in Barcelona at the entrance of Charles V
in 1519, the *grua* that came down at the entrance of Phillip II in

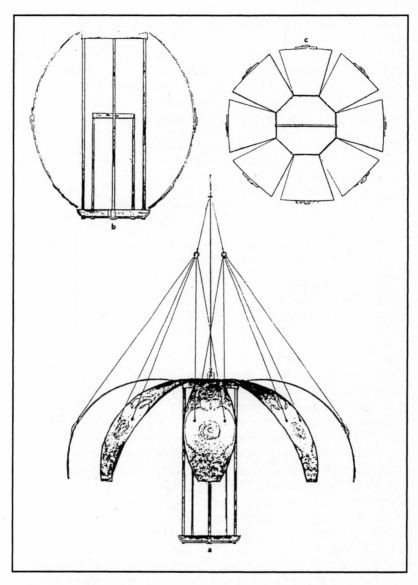

2. The interior structure of the pomegranate. Diagrams by A. Serrano: (a) frontal view; (b) section; (c) end view.

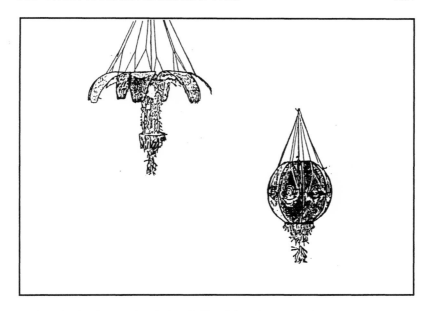

3. The Elx cloud opened and closed. Sketch by Pierre Paris (1897).

1564, and the *magrana* that descended at the entry of Phillip III in 1599 and Phillip IV in 1626.[12] This type of machine was also used in 1599 for the entrance of Phillip III and again in 1632 for Phillip IV when it was described as a *bola* and *mangrana* coming out of a tower in Valencia.[13] In other cases the spherical device was used for the descent of the Virgin, as in the artichoke of Tárrega in 1612[14] or the *globo* of Mallorca.[15]

In Italy the cloud was used to enwrap Christ during his elevation into heaven, as in 1425 in the representation of the Ascension in the Church of the Carmine in Florence,[16] but it was also utilized in dramas of the Assumption (as in the pageant of the *Assumptione* at the feast of St. John in 1514[17]) and in solemn entrances, e.g., at the entrance of Borso da Este at Reggio Emilia in 1453 when a spherical machine came down with St. Peter to crown the Duke of Ferrara.[18]

Cloud machines were introduced, probably by the carpenters or scene designers of Valencia, into Castille at the end of the fifteenth century. In the urban Corpus Christi spectacles of Toledo such

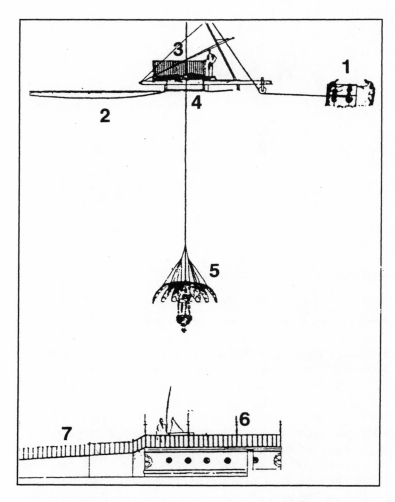

4. Diagram showing vertical cross section of the scene of the *Misteri d'Elx:* (1) elevation winch; machines on terrace of church; (2) heaven canvas covering dome of church; (3) heaven platform where descent originates; (4) door of heaven; (5) cloud or pomegranate; (6) platform (*cadafal*) for scene in transept; (7) ramp to platform (corridor: *andador*). Diagram by A. Serrano.

clouds were used; here the clouds were covered with wool and cotton, decorated with tinsel stars and painted seraphs in the interior, and appropriated for the representations of the *Auto del Juicio Final* (1496, 1510), *Auto de la Ascensión* (1500), *Auto del Sacrificio de Isaac* (1504), and *Auto del Bautismo* (1508).[19] Within the Cathedral, in the famous quasi-dramatic ceremonies of the Boy Bishop, "a cloud was coming down from the arches, and, stopping in the middle, it opened," revealing several angels who were placing a miter on the head of a young "prelate."[20] Also, in the Corpus Christi procession of Seville at the end of the fifteenth century a pageant wagon appeared with a blue and white cloud that opened sparklingly and showed the character of Christ,[21] while in some references in the *Códice de Autos Viejos* we find numerous references to a cloud.[22]

Such machines were even exported to America as part of the program of evangelization in which religious drama played a role. At the representation of the Assumption at Tlaxcala in 1538, "Our Lady" was raised "in a cloud from a platform to another height that they had prepared for heaven." González de Eslava used this machine, and there were others who likewise made use of this technology.[23] However, lest it be assumed that machines of this type were only developed and used in Southern Europe, with allowance made for export to the New World, it should be noted that clouds are documented for celebrations, spectacles, and plays in France,[24] Holland, and England.[25]

The Survival of the Cloud Machine. The mystery of *Festa d'Elx*, originating at the end of the Middle Ages and produced without interruption in the Valencian city of Elx (Elche) until the present, is unique in Europe in being a medieval spectacle preserved in traditional use, and it presents the most ambitious examples of machinery of the type under discussion here, for the play includes a splendid *núvol* or *mangrana*. This mechanism involves a framework of 174 cm. in height and 60 cm. in breadth and consisting of four metal bars joined at the top and bottom by two octagonal frames of wood. In the interior of this structure an angel (nowadays a boy, but in the eighteenth century sometimes a *castrato*) is suspended; he is standing and supported at the waist by four more iron rods that are attached at the lower socket and joined at the top with a strap.

5. The present Elx pomegranate in the "interior" of heaven.

Above the upper support frame is a ring that joins the machine to a rope, and in the socket's sides there are hinges to which the wings of the pomegranate are attached (fig. 2). From the lower base, reinforced with lead, is suspended a tassel covered with tinsel. The spectacular covering, which can reach a diameter of 145 cm. in width, is formed by eight leaves or wings made of canvas reinforced with iron (fig. 3). Externally painted blue to identify the mechanism as a cloud symbolically and with a cherub in each wing, its original meaning is now forgotten; since 1906 these wings have been painted to replicate a color associated with the pomegranate, reflecting its name in popular usage (*mangrana*), while the ornamental angels have been replaced by gold flowers. The interior of the wings, the rods and beams, are completely decorated with tinsel.

The cloud emerges completely closed from the door of heaven, which is situated in the canvas which encloses the cupula, and, in the open space (about five meters beneath the celestial canvas), it opens its wings majestically to reveal to the audience the sight of the boy angel, who begins to sing[26] (figs. 4–5).

Similar machines are preserved in other Valencian localities, but they are more rudimentary, all of them being set up in the street. For example, the *carxofa* of Silla is a wooden apparatus which has an interior shaft that stands out from the framework where the singer, a boy angel, is placed. Sixteen wooden wings which open and close extend from it externally. The whole apparatus is painted green to evoke the vegetable that gives its name to it; even the wings invoke a resemblance to the artichoke. Only the interior is painted with little clouds, stars, and cherubs' heads. In contrast, the *carxofa* of Aldaia is not suspended in the air but is attached to a cylindrical pole whose apex is covered with twenty wings arranged in two rows of ten leaves each; these wings are adjusted by means of a wooden hoop. This example is also painted in green externally, but internally it is blue, decorated with clouds, heavenly bodies, and seraphim. A third *carxofa*, in the Carmen district in Valencia, is formed by twelve wings that open mechanically and are painted in colors similar to those described above. The interior has a metal chair which is like a swing, and the illumination is by incandescent lighting at the edges. The angel, a boy or girl, sits in his or her chair and sings from a musical score held in the hand. The *Taronja* of Morella is a completely spherical machine, painted in orange and suspended with ropes which reach from one balcony to another across the street; in the interior there appears a small angel singer.[27]

In Castille there are still similar machines which are used in the Procession of the Virgin Mary and the appearance to her of her resurrected Son on Easter Day. In Aranda de Duero (Burgos) or in Peñafiel (Valladolid) in the *Fiesta del Angel*, "a boy dressed like an angel inside a sphere [*globo*] comes down until he arrives where the Virgin is covered with a black cloth; in that moment the sphere opens, and the boy uncovers the face of the Virgin, who appears also with the image of the resurrected Christ."[28] In Caudete (Albacete), a boy emerges from the *Alcachofa* and sings for the Virgin del Carmen as part of the festivities.[29]

Among the examples of the spherical cloud machines surviving from medieval scene technology in Spain, the cloud of Elx stands out for its complexity and its splendor. Though changes have occurred in the production of this drama over the centuries, the techniques and resulting magnificence in this aspect of the depiction of the Assumption of the Virgin are replicated by the singers of Elx each year in much the same manner as five hundred years ago.[30]

NOTES

[1] Ramon Llull, *Llibre de Meravelles* (1288), book 7: *Llibre de les Bèsties*, Els Nostres Clàssics 34 (Barcelona: Barcino, 1931), chap. 4.

[2] Isidre Vallés, *La màgia del vol. Primeres proves aerostàtiques a Barcelona, València i Castella al final del segle XVIII* (Barcelona: Altafulla, 1985), 18.

[3] Aristotle, *Poetics*, XV (1454b). See also Plato, *Cratylus* 425D.

[4] "'Dear friend,' said Felix, 'by light we understand knowledge, and knowledge means light; and by light we understand glory, and by darkness we understand pain and ignorance'" (Llull, *Llibre de Meravelles*, 3.1). "Claret enim claris quod clare concopulatur,/ et quod perfundit lux nova, claret opus," wrote Suger, patron of arts and organizer of liturgical spectacles (quoted by Erwin Panofsky, *Abbot Suger on the Abbey of St. Denis* [Princeton: Princeton University Press, 1979], 67).

[5] See Francesc Massip, "*Aeris mirabilia*: el meravellós aeri en l'escena medieval. Concomitàncies italo-catalanes," *XIV Congresso di Storia della Corona d'Aragona, Addenda* (Sassari-Alghero, 1990), 800–19.

[6] Gerónimo de Blancas y Tomás, *Coronaciones de los serenísimos Reyes de Aragón, con dos tratados del modo de tener cortes (1585)* (Zaragoza, 1641), 75 (1.8), who translates into Spanish the passage from Pere-Miquel Carbonell, *Chròniques de Catalunya* (1513), published in Barcelona in 1547 under the title *Cròniques d'Espanya*, fol. ccxx. Though the copy of the narrative of Martin the Humane's coronation prepared by P. M. Carbonell (1434–1517) is lost, there is a reference in *Rúbriques de Bruniquer: Ceremonial dels Magnífichs Consellers y Regiment de la Ciutat de Barcelona*, 5 vols. (Barcelona, 1912–16), 1:233: "There

is described the Entrance and Coronation of the monarchs Martin and Maria with details in the *Libre de Solempnitats* [1383–1409]." For the realization of this spectacle noteworthy artists were employed as painters—e.g., Lluís Borrassà and Berenguer Llopart (F. Massip, "Eiximenis, Borrassà i el teatre," *Revista de Girona* 144 [1991]: 42–45).

⁷ Alvar García de Santamaría, *Crónica de Juan II*; Paris, Bibliothèque Nationale, MS. Esp. 104, fol. 199ᵛ.

⁸ *The Staging of Religious Drama in Europe in the Later Middle Ages*, ed. Peter Meredith and John E. Tailby, Early Drama, Art, and Music Monograph Series 4 (Kalamazoo: Medieval Institute Publications, 1983), 94–95 (translation); for the original text, see García de Santamaría, *Crónica de Juan II*, fol. 204ᵛ.

⁹ In this play the angel comes down in an apparatus called *peanya*, a term which describes a design similar to that of the *carxofa* still in use in the Valencian community of Silla (see below). For the Valencian text, see Manuel Sanchis Guarner, "El misteri assumpcionista de la Catedral de València," *Butlletí de la Reial Acadèmia de Bones Lletres de Barcelona* 32 (1967–68): 97–112; the rubrics are translated in *The Staging of Religious Drama*, ed. Meredith and Tailby, 230–39.

¹⁰ See Josep Romeu i Figueras, "El teatre assumpcionista de tècnica medieval als Països Catalans," *Miscel·lània Aramon i Serra* 4 (Barcelona, 1984): 276.

¹¹ *Dietari o Llibre de Jornades (1411–1484) de Jaume Safont*, ed. Josep M. Sans Travé (Barcelona: Fundació Noguera, 1992), 283.

¹² *Llibre de les Solemnitats de Barcelona*, ed. A. Duran and J. Sanabre (Barcelona, 1930–47), 1:396–97 (for 1424–1546), and 2:8–10, 131–33, 162 (for 1546–1719). The description of the entry at Barcelona in 1519 is translated in *The Staging of Religious Drama*, ed. Meredith and Tailby, 94. A "celestial sphere, moveable with golden stars," in which "there was a boy who represented the armed emperor" at Messina in 1535, was used for the entry of Charles V. While Rodo Santoro considers this machine only to be one of the Italian family of scenic devices ("La 'Vara' dell' Assunta di Messina: cosmografia, teologia e scenotecnica," *Beni culturali e ambientali Sicilia* 5, nos. 3–4 [1984]: 112), it is instead very clearly of a Catalonia-Aragon origin. Such machines were already present in 1399 in Saragossa, as we have seen, where they were used in similar circumstances. Political linkage between the kingdoms of Aragon and Sicily was certainly a factor.

¹³ See Salvador Carreres Zacarés, *Ensayo de una bibliografía crítica de libros de fiestas celebradas en Valencia y su antiguo reino* (València, 1925), 175, and the same author's *Llibre de Memòries de diversos sucesos e fets memorables e de coses senyalades de la Ciutat e Regne de València (1308–1644)* (València, 1930), 2:1111.

¹⁴ Ramon Miró, *Activitat teatral a Cervera (XIVth–XIXth Century)*, Ph.D. thesis (Universitat Autònoma de Barcelona, 1993), 1442.

¹⁵ *Representation of santa Isabel*; see Mercè Gambús Saiz, "La ciutat de Palma com a escenografia festiva en el segle XVII," in *El Barroc Català* (Barcelona: Crema, 1989), 392.

¹⁶ Alessandro D'Ancona, *Origini del teatro italiano*, 2 vols. (Turin, 1891), 1:253, 408. See also Clyde Brockett, "Reconstructing an Ascension Drama from Aural and Visual Art: A Methodological Approach," *Fifteenth-Century Studies* 13

(1988): 195–205.

[17] See Nerida Newbigin, *Nuovo Corpus di Sacre Rappresentazioni fiorentini del Quattrocento* (Bologna, 1983), xlix. A similar representation of the Assumption occurred in 1881 at Canicatti's Church where Maria "goes up on big *nuvole* [clouds] that go up high, full of divine light" (G. Pitré, *Spettacoli e feste popolari siciliane* [1881; reprint Palermo, 1978], 360). See also Francesc Massip, "The Staging of the Assumption in Europe," *Comparative Drama* 25 (1991): 17–28.

[18] See Elvira Garbero and S. Cantore, *Le entrate trionfali*, in *Teatro a Reggio Emilia*, ed. S. Romagnoli and E. Garbero (Florence, 1980), 1:13. For further details, see Francesc Massip Bonet, *La Festa d'Elx i els misteris medievals europeus* (Alacant: Institut Juan Gil Albert, 1991), 189.

[19] Carmen Torroja Menéndez and Maria Rivas Palá, *Teatro en Toledo en el siglo XV: "Auto de la Pasión" de Alonso del Campo*, Boletín de la Real Academia Española 35 (Madrid, 1977), 49, 57, 62–63, 68.

[20] Sebastián de Covarrubias Orozco, *Tesoro de la lengua castellana o española* (Madrid, 1611), "Obispillo."

[21] See Jean Sentaurens, *Seville et le théâtre de la fin du Moyen Age à la fin du XVIIᵉ siècle*, 2 vols. (Talence and Bordeaux, 1984), 1:73–74.

[22] E.g., the *Aucto de los Triunfos de Petrarca* or the *Aucto de la Paciencia de Job*; see Mercedes de los Reyes Peña, *El 'Codice de Autos Viejos': Un estudio de historia literaria*, 3 vols. (Seville: Alfar, 1988), 3:1030ff. Other examples are the *Las Cortes de la Muerte* by Miguel de Carvajal and Luís Hurtado de Toledo, the *Comedia de san Segundo* by Lope de Vega, and the spectacles organized by Calderón at the courts of Phillip III and Phillip IV; see William Hutchinson Shoemaker, *The Multiple Stage in Spain during the Fifteenth and Sixteenth Centuries* (Princeton: Princeton University Press, 1935).

[23] Isabel Martínez Cerdà, "El Misterio de Elche y su posible influencia en la evangelización de América," *Archivo Ibero-Americano* 45 (1985): 162–63.

[24] Note especially the sphere that brought down the dove of the Holy Spirit in the Valenciennes *Passion* (1547) and the clouds used in the *Mystère des Actes des Apôtres* at Bourges (1536); see also *The Staging of Religious Drama*, ed. Meredith and Tailby, 95.

[25] For further details, see Massip, *La Festa d'Elx*, 190–91 and notes, and see also *The Staging of Religious Drama*, ed. Meredith and Tailby, 94–96.

[26] More details in Massip, *La Festa d'Elx*, 197–98.

[27] Ibid., 201–02.

[28] Mª Angeles Sánchez, *Guia de fiestas populares* (Madrid: Atenea, 1982), 41–42.

[29] *El Auto religioso en España* (Madrid, 1991), 102.

[30] I am grateful to Joana Helms for translating this article.

Medieval Ideas of the Ancient Actor and Roman Theater

Sandra Pietrini

While the Roman stage was not entirely unknown throughout the Middle Ages, the crumbling theaters that remained were the subject of speculation that on the whole did not do justice to the drama that had flourished in antiquity. Though John Capgrave could connect the Roman amphitheater with places for playing and wrestling in the fifteenth-century Britain ("a place all round swech as we haue her in this lond"), his knowledge of that theater was nevertheless severely limited.[1] Indeed, in spite of a manuscript tradition of illustrations of Terence's plays that involved close copies of originals dating from the Roman empire,[2] the memory of the ancient theater otherwise was handed on during the Middle Ages mainly through the writings of Tertullian and other Christian writers, who had been the most severe adversaries of Pagan culture. Their harsh condemnations of jesting, dancing, and other performances that survived during the period of the decline of theater as an institution had been repeated for centuries, from St. Augustine to St. Thomas Aquinas. Scattered comments referring to Roman theater, mingled with observations from contemporary spectacles, also were derived from early medieval glossaries and found their way into the antiquarian reconstructions of learned humanists. To assemble even a part of this puzzle, inevitably doomed to incompleteness, we must turn to heterogeneous sources such as Christian treatises, commentaries on ancient works, glossaries, and the miniatures illustrating these texts.

Throughout much of the Middle Ages, however, Isidore of Seville's seventh-century encyclopedia, the *Etymologiae*, would be the most widespread source of information about antiquity. Isidore was primarily responsible for the perpetuation of partial or untrue notions about the ancient theater: erroneous etymologies, commonplaces, and misunderstandings of previous definitions were passed on and nourished a series of flawed conclusions.[3] These were profoundly influential and taken up in the terms defined in dictionaries,

275

and used in the other literary sources surveyed by Mary H. Marshall, whose scholarship is a precious contribution to the reconstruction of medieval ideas about ancient theater.[4] The aim of this article is to add some pieces to this puzzle, especially in taking a fresh look at the medieval conception of the stage and acting. In this effort, I propose to take into consideration some literary and iconographical sources often neglected by theater historians such as the translations of St. Augustine's *De civitate Dei* and Titus Livius's *Ab Urbe condita*.

I

The well-known confusion of genres and other blurred notions concerning the antique stage, some of them drawn from the fourth-century grammarians such as Servius and Aelius Donatus, were reflected in the medieval glossaries. In the twelfth-century *Derivationes* by Osbern of Gloucester, for instance, tragedy is typically defined as "a mournful writing, since it begins with joy and ends in unhappiness, while comedy begins on the contrary with unhappiness and ends in joy" ("carmen luctuosum, quia incipit a letitia et finit in tristitiam, cui contrarium est comedia, quia incipit a tristitia, et finit in letitiam").[5] This distinction had become a commonplace, as had the understanding of character in these genres. Tragedy was held to concern people of high status and qualities, comedy common and modest persons. These generalizations concerning dramatic forms were endlessly repeated and were interpreted as absolute categories, while at the same time memory of the nature of the physical performance in antiquity had been essentially lost. Tragedy could even be defined within this scheme as a sorrowful poem.

The confusion already appears in Isidore's view of drama, for while he seems to recall that dramatic genres require dialogue, which would exclude the use of a narrator,[6] he nevertheless enumerates Horace, Persius, and Juvenal among the new comic dramatists, regardless of the structure of their works. Perhaps he was misled by Horace's writing concerning tragedy and comedy in his *Ars poetica*, a text that was very well known and frequently glossed, or, more likely, he was thinking of Horace's *Odes*, in which the leading voice often addresses an imaginary interlocutor.

The blurring of concepts was even more pronounced by the late Middle Ages. In the thirteenth century, Geoffrey of Vinsauf defined

comedy as a "iocosa materia,"[7] while according to John of Garland
it was a "quasi villanus cantus, quia materia vili et iocosa con-
textitur."[8] In his *Genealogia deorum* Giovanni Boccaccio still included Catullus and Ovid among dramatic writers,[9] though he knew
very well what tragedies and comedies were—an odd contradiction
which reveals the overwhelming power of traditional *topoi*.

The commonplaces which allegedly described the physical
staging of the drama are even more puzzling. The most striking
description of the manner in which comedies and tragedies were
performed appears in a frequently cited statement by the humanist
Nicholas Trevet, who says that in the middle of the semicircular
theater "there was a little house [*parva domuncula*], called 'scene,'
in which there was a pulpit, on which the poet recited [*pronun-
ciabit*] the verses [*carmina*]," while outside it were mimes who
performed the action with their gestures.[10] This understanding of
dramatic action is reflected in the frontispieces of two famous
Terence manuscripts (*Térence du Duc de Berry*, Paris, Bibliothèque
Nationale, MS. Lat. 7907a, and *Térence des Ducs*, Paris, Bibliothèque de l'Arsenal, MS. Lat. 664)[11] and in a fourteenth-century
codex of Seneca (*Tragoediae*, Vatican Library MS. Vat. Urb. 335,
fol. 1).

Trevet's description of the ancient theater was again derived
ultimately from Isidore, who had understood the *scaena frons* as a
house and the pulpit as a misinterpretation of the stage itself
("Scena autem erat locus infra theatrum in modum domus instructa
cum pulpito"[12]). The lexicographer Papias the Lombard influentially
passed on Isidore's description in his *Elementarium* and simplified
it by affirming that "Scaena domus in theatro erat."[13] If such descriptions nod at those manuscripts of Terence deriving from the
tradition of illustration reflected in the ninth-century Vatican
Library MS. Vat. lat. 3868—a manuscript that is presumed to be the
closest of this group to a third century original—they nevertheless
on the whole ignore the evidence.[14] There is nothing in this group
of manuscripts like the stage described by medieval scholars, who
instead took the word of Isidore in imagining pulpits, constructions
not surprisingly influenced in design by contemporary pulpits in
churches. Both houses and pulpits were imagined by them as a little
roofed construction used as an orator's pulpit, with a lectern for the
reader.

1. Terenzo, *Commediae*. Tours, Bibliothèque Municipale, MS. lat. 924, fol. 13ᵛ. By permission.

    Some echoes of this confused idea of ancient theater and scene might be seen in two miniatures in Terence manuscripts dating from the twelfth century. One (Rome, Vatican Library MS. lat. 3305, fol. 8ᵛ) offers a general view of the staging of ancient comedies: the reader (Calliopius) is sitting in a little pulpit (with Terence on one side and his detractors on the other), while the spectators are ranged in the medium level. The staging in fact shows a public reading, though some dramatic characters are gesticulating in the lower part of the depiction, which is inserted within a frame shaped like a house, perhaps a reminiscence of the literary description of the ancient scene. In the other miniature (Tours, Bibliothèque Municipale, MS. lat. 924, fol. 13ᵛ) the reader is sitting on a raised little roofed platform that in the aim of the illustrator would likely represent the *pulpitum* (fig. 1). The space under this two-level wooden construction is occupied by some men pointing out to another group of persons, probably the spectators, who are standing in front of the reader. The illustrator appears to have a very garbled notion of Roman staging but nevertheless aims to design a hypothetical scene that is clearly inspired by the description of the *pulpitum* as a structure for the reader—that is, an orator's pulpit.

A further complication arises since another tradition, derived from Servius, described the scene (*scaena*) as a sheltered place (*umbraculum*). This tradition draws its inspiration from a bucolic and mythical image of the origin of theater according to which the *skenè* was named after the shade (*skía*) where shepherds once sang their songs. This too was absorbed and combined with Isidore's image of the little house. The most organic integration is in Uguccione of Pisa's *Magnae Derivationes*, which defines the stage as a "shady place in the theater covered by tents, alike to seller's shops covered with planks or cloth, and therefore the stage may be named from *scenos*, that is, 'house,' since it is built up like a house."[15] Apart from the incorrect etymology (Uguccione did not know Greek), the whole image is an acceptable juxtaposition of the two original elements, the shade and the house. Further, Uguccione's comparison with medieval market shops reveals that his starting point was a visual image and not only a received text, and in this he differs from many medieval scholars who used lexical fantasies to build up an impossible stage. Uguccione's description also extends to a method of acting not very different from the one proposed by Trevet: "in that shade the masked actors hide, and at the reader's voice came out making gestures" ("In illo umbraculo latebant persone larvate, que ad vocem recitantis exibant ad gestus faciendos").[16] It is worth noting that in the two miniatures from the Paris manuscripts of Terence the little house is covered on each side by cloth, and the mimes hide inside it before performing their parts (one of them is just emerging from behind the curtain). The illustrators in these cases probably knew the widely disseminated description of the scene which had been proposed by Uguccione.

Aside from the design of the stage in the theater building, there may be much yet that we can learn also about the idea of acting that prevailed. I hence do not intend to discuss here Trevet's reconstruction of the ancient theater, which would later be re-elaborated by other humanists such as Pietro Alighieri in his commentary on his father's *Comoedia*,[17] but I do want to recall a detail often overlooked by scholars, who have quoted Trevet's description merely to exemplify the oddity of the medieval concept of ancient theater. The separation between declamation of the text and acting is not in fact a groundless fantasy since it derives (more or less directly) from a passage in Livy's *History of Rome* (7.2.9–10). The Roman historian reports an anecdote concerning the actor Livius Andronicus: Asked many times for encores, he became hoarse and called a young boy to sing while he acted and made the appropriate gestures.[18] In this way, it is said, began the division of functions which also character-ized ancient pantomime, and this practice seems generally to have prevailed in the medieval memory of acting. But in fact it was not the only idea of representation that was circulating among the learned, as we discover if we delve into the rich and still unexplored sea of literary imagery concerning the theater.

The identity of the actor in the medieval conception of ancient theater owes something, of course, to the conflicting descriptions of their performances in the early Christian sources where the theater is frequently evoked as a metaphor and a negative example. The in-consistencies extend to Isidore's *Etymologiae*. The most often quoted definition from this source refers to the *mimi*, who are said to be "imitators [*imitatores*] of human things; in fact, they had their author who, before the mimes played, told the story" ("nam habe-bant suum auctorem, qui antequam mimum agerent, fabulam pro-nuntiaret").[19] While this description foreshadows the separation of function between voice and gestures described by Trevet, the se-quence is different since in Isidore's reconstruction the narration of the "author" *precedes* the pantomimic action and might be under-stood to describe a reader reciting a prologue. It might be assumed that Isidore's description was simply transformed into simultaneous action—a reduction of acting to pantomime since the nobler task of declaiming the text was attributed to the poet. However, the idea of a separation between declamation and mimicry could have come to the late Middle Ages through another surviving tradition. Before the humanistic rediscovery of classical sources, occasional fragmentary notions about the Roman theater were in circulation.

Isidore's understanding of ancient actors, however, clearly ex-tends to more than mime since he connects them with impersonation and speeches or singing. *Histriones* thus are identified with cross-dressing: "those who, in women's attire, performed by their gestures the attitudes of indecent women; and dancing they told stories and heroic deeds."[20] They are called *histriones* either because they came from Istria or because they drew ambiguous stories from history such as *historiones*[21]—a fanciful etymology that nevertheless under-lines their peculiar function as story-tellers. The *tragoedi* are "those who sang with sorrowful verses the ancient deeds and misdeeds of villainous kings before the people," while the *comoedi* are "those who sang the acts of private men by words and gestures."[22] The definition very concisely shapes an image of the comic actor as an interpreter of the dramatic character *through voice and gestures* —an understanding consistent with the masked and gesturing actors shown in the group of Terence manuscripts of which Vatican Library MS. Vat. lat. 3368 is the earliest example.[23] Even in defining the *hypocrita* (etymologically connected to the art of acting) Isidore alludes to the masked actors playing different character roles.[24] The recycling of Isidore's definitions by late medieval writers would inevitably lead to a range of conflicting ideas about the actor.

This multiplicity of definitions in whatever combination is a sign of vagueness. In spite of the spread of professional performers such as the jesters (*joculatores*), the figure of the actor became less and less fixed. Medieval entertainers exhibited themselves in a wide range of spectacles, but the actor in the modern and strict sense of the term had disappeared. The variety of entertainers is clearly reflected in the multiplicity of Latin and vernacular terms employed to describe them. In some cases the terms allude to a specialization such as *saltator, grallator, tumbeor*, and in others they may be considered to be a sign of vagueness and inconsistency in the idea of the actor.[25] Mime had survived and bore similarity to actors in antiquity since its practitioners represented characters or types, but their use of expressive means of course differed from the interpretations of characters by the actors of the past. The difference between antique past and the present could not but affect the way in which the classical theater was imagined in the Middle Ages—a sign of even more confusion and conflicting descriptions. The medieval idea of acting thus ultimately embraces a considerable variety of performances from public readings to pantomime. Just as narrative and drama may be conflated in discussions of genre, acting in antiquity in some cases is assimilated with epic narration.

Such differing and conflicting ideas concerning acting are partly due to the misunderstanding of the ancient sources. An eleventh-century commentary on Horace's *Poetica* explains that a comedy could be either represented by actors on stage—that is, within the curtains from which these actors came out—or simply narrated: "aut agitur, idest per actus personarum tantum ostenditur in scaenis, idest in cortinis, de quibus exibant illae personae, aut refertur tantum acta sine personis."[26] But when Horace had affirmed in his *Poetica* (179) that "either an event is acted on the stage, or the action is narrated" ("Aut agitur res in scaenis aut acta refertur"),[27] he certainly was alluding to the *rhesis*, the violent deeds that in the Greek theater were not shown but reported by messengers. Through a misinterpretation of this sentence, medieval commentators would claim that the *whole performance* could be either acted or narrated. Joseph R. Jones has suggested that the error might have been due to a medieval misunderstanding of an ambiguous sentence from the fourth-century work, the *Ars gramatica* by Diomede, in which the line from the *Poetica* was quoted.[28]

By the thirteenth century the image of the ancient *hystrio* as a player had become a faded reminiscence but nevertheless re-emerged from time to time. In these cases the idea of the actor was frequently confused with diverging notions inherited from diction-aries and glossaries or from contemporary experience. Indeed, the term *histriones* changed in meaning so much that it was not any longer associated with the notion of playing a character, and it was often used to refer to the jesters who exhibited themselves in tests of skill or performed tricks. Late medieval culture seems almost completely to have lost the concept of stage character. In the four-teenth-century *Variloquus* of Johannes Melber of Gerolczhofen, a description of the ancient stage as a shade (*umbraculum*) is fol-lowed by an explanation concerning the way of acting: "a peasant plays a king or a soldier, and when the performance is over he again returns to be the peasant he was" ("rusticus efficitur rex vel miles, et ludo peracto quodlibet est sicut prius rusticus fuit").[29] This is a peculiar description, but it shows how the entertainer's role had fallen in esteem.

II

The misunderstanding of the role of the actor is particularly evident in relation to Roman *ludi scenici*. Around the 1370, in order to spread the work of Christian authors among the unlearned, the French king Charles V commissioned an aged scholar, Raoul de Presles, to translate St. Augustine's *De civitate Dei* into the ver-nacular. Though the *ludi scenici* to which Augustine refers actually derive from Titus Livius's *Ad Urbe condita*, the presentation in Raoul's *Cité de Dieu* emphasizes the Christian reinterpretation of the episode. Since the Romans resorted to plays (*ludi*) in order to appease the gods and avert the plague ravaging the city, the theater is reinterpreted as dependent on superstition, and its origin is attributed to the devil's influence on the earthly city. In his commentary on St. Augustine's text, Raoul emphasizes the connection between the pagan cult and the *ludi scenici*, and, insisting on the demonic details concerning the theater which the Church Fathers had drawn out, he traces analogies with contemporary forms of spectacle.

In most cases, Raoul, who quotes Isidore of Seville, Papias, and other scholars, simply reformulates the concepts stated by his predecessors. Many observations derive without acknowledgment of their source from the Latin commentary on the *City of God* by Thomas Waleys, a Welsh Dominican who had been imprisoned in 1333–38 on a charge of heresy.[30] In contact with the Parisian academic milieu and in service as a chaplain of Matteo Orsini in Avignon, Waleys probably drew most of his descriptions of ancient theater from the elder Nicholas Trevet, who around 1332 had previously annotated all twenty-two books of the *De civitate Dei*. In this virtual set of learned humanists, there was a free circulation of ideas, and it is sometimes difficult to ascertain the authorship of a concept.[31]

Raoul's starting point is moral disapproval. Describing ancient comedies, he underlines their licentious character: "comedy is made of the facts of private people and the whorish tricks [*puteries*] of women and men and the filthy things [*conchiemens*] made during such debaucheries [*ribaudies*]."[32] Following this definition, he describes the staging in more detail: during the representations of comedies "they [*ilz*] so much lost their composure that they removed their clothes before all the people and without shame they came to embraces and kisses and completed to excess their impudence [*puterie*] and filthiness [*laidure*]."[33] The disorder and discomposure attributed to comedies in consideration of their subjects give rise, in Raoul's imagination, to stripping and lascivious behavior. But who is the referent of the pronoun *ils*? Since he does not allude to the characters of the *fabula*, he certainly seems to be referring to the performers. The figure of the actor is a sort of immoral, unnamed *monstrum* in Raoul's blurred and shadowy view of the ancient theater.

With the commentaries of Trevet, Waleys, and Raoul de Presles, a rich imagery is grafted onto the *topoi* of learned tradition,

which had associated the theater with excess and debauchery. Yet
Raoul adds some observations that seem to reflect a glimpse of the
performances of his own time. Mentioning Isidore and closely following Trevet's definition of the ancient stage, he describes it as a
little house in the middle of the theater with a lectern for the reader
and masked people representing the story by gestures "such as you
can see now in the plays of characters and charivari" ("aussi comme
tu vois que l'en fait aujourdui les gieux de personnaiges et chari-
valis").[34] The plays (*jeux de personnages*) to which he refers were
short farces based on a comic dialogue, performed either by professional entertainers or by simple citizens or peasants. The account
book of the duke of Orléans records, for example, some expenses
for three "joueurs de personnages" in 1392–93.[35] The *charivari*, on
the other hand, was not performed by professionals and belonged
more to folklore than to theater in any strict sense of the term.[36]

   Professionalism thus was not considered to be a distinguishing
element of the theater, and indeed the only common feature of the
two theatrical forms—*jeux de personnages* and *charivari*—
mentioned by Raoul is the assumption of different identities than
the actor's own. This is in fact the primary requisite of the actor in
the modern conception of theater, but in the thought of Raoul and
those who influenced him this characteristic was not emphasized
above other factors. The comparison traced by Raoul reveals a weak
re-emergence of this notion, taken in its most general meaning.
What do the *jeux de personnages* and the *charivari* have in common? Not interpreting of character, but the wearing of masks, conceived as the fundamental feature of personification.

   Yet further echoes from his contemporaries and earlier writers
creep into Raoul's understanding of the professional literary men of
antiquity: *Lirici, Comedi, Tragedi*, and *Theologi*. The first are tale
singers, who derive their name from their musical instrument (*lyra*);
the *Comedi* and *Tragedi* are dramatic writers, and the *Theologi* are
inventors of songs and ditties about the gods. In fact this last
typology derives from the *Etymologiae*, which defines *theologici* as
poets "since they write verses about the gods" ("quoniam de diis
carmina faciebant").[37] In elaborating Isidore's definition, however,
Raoul was very likely thinking about medieval entertainers who
sang saints' lives, which were very popular in France at that time.
The *ditz* were in fact the typical work of the troubadours and
trouvères. Raoul thus employs a contemporary term to define an

ancient, fabulous form whereby he traces an implicit parallel between such saints' lives and the histories of pagan gods. A similar superimposition of typologies appears in the description of ancient theater contained in the fifteenth-century *Troy Book* in which John Lydgate repeats various commonplaces drawn from previous writings: "in Troye/ Were songe and rad lusty fressh comedyes/ And othir ditees that callid been tragedies."[38]

A more direct allusion to the theatrical practice of the fourteenth century emerges from Raoul's definition of the *comedi*, so called "pour les lieux ou ilz avoient accoustume a chanter c'est assavoir aux places et aux carrefours qui en grec sont appellez comas ou pour comestion c'est assavoir mengier pource que apres mengiez l'en va veoir volentiers telz gieux aussi comme l'en fait aux festes le chanteur en gieuc ou aux halles et autres places."[39] The two possible etymologies derive from Isidore's encyclopedia,[40] but Raoul's explanation introduces a new perspective since it combines unusual Greek reminiscences—the peasants' villages (*komas*) mentioned also by John of Garland[41]—and allusions to the common practice of interludes, played during banquets and feasts organized inside the halls of aristocratic palaces. Trying to reconstruct the spectacles of the past, Raoul also evoked something of the contemporary "theater," especially court performances, when he wrote that "they are properly called interludes because they are acted between two meals" ("Et son proprement appellez interludia pource que ilz se font entre deux mengiers").[42] At this time we know that court banquets had become grand occasions for spectacle. For example, in 1378 Charles V organized a magnificent banquet at the Palais Royal in Paris that included a performance, depicted in a well-known miniature from Jean Froissart's *Les grandes Chroniques de France*, featuring the sailing away of the Crusaders and their capture of Jerusalem.[43] At a banquet in honor of Charles VI in 1389, the siege of Troy was performed—a subject revealing the new interest in ancient history—and many jesters performed in various entertainments.[44]

As we have seen, Raoul de Presles absorbs into his idea of ancient theater different forms of entertainment, including performances of folklore, entertainments at court feasts, and professional jesters. The emergence of the image of the jester in connection with the ancient theater is of particular interest, as a few examples will demonstrate. An eleventh-century manuscript which

also contains the *Etymologiae* equates *istriones* and *ioculatores*
("Istriones sunt ioculatores"), while the *pantomimi* are defined as
imitators who rely entirely on gestures.[45] Osbern of Gloucester in
his *Derivationes* defines the term *ludius* as *ioculator* and *ludia* as
ioculatrix.[46] While in the fourteenth century Trevet still uses the
term *mimus* in his description of the ancient staging, Pietro
Alighieri identifies the actors as *mimi ioculatores*. The same super-
position of jesters and Roman actors, in fact reduced to panto-
mimes, clearly appears in the two fifteenth-century miniatures in the
Paris manuscripts of Terence. But in late medieval reconstructions
of ancient theater, jesters are generally considered to be a decadent
form of the actors. In Pierre Bersuire's French translation of Titus
Livius's *Ad Urbe condita*, dating from the middle of the fourteenth
century, *ludi scenici* are described (as in the original text) as performances by Etruscan dancers, accompanied by some musicians.[47]
Bersuire, however, adds some details, in particular identifying these
performers as *baleur ou iugleur*—that is, resorting to the image of
jester to clarify the nature of *ludi*. In his discussion of the ancient
histriones he also claims that "in the Tuscan language the jesters
were called *ystres*" ("istrions pour ce que a la langue tuscaine l'en
appelloit le iouglars ystres")[48]—a direct comparison between ancient and contemporary professional performers. But jesters seem
to him to be degenerate and thus inferior to the sober tradition of the
theater's alleged origins, and Bersuire summarizes his moral disapproval in a significant sentence: "Et ainsi doncques vindrent les
iougleurs,"[49] corrupted inheritors of the ancient theater.

III

Raoul de Presles' assimilation of the Roman *ludi* into contemporary performances—the *jeux de personnages*, the *charivari*, the
dits of the troubadours, and the interludes—demonstrates that the
theater was no longer a surviving memory of the past but a real
presence in everyday life. The imaginary theater of antiquity is thus
seen as directly related to the vast range of performances taking
place in medieval society. The medieval conception of theater was
much broader than our own and could include even capital exe-
cutions (often performed on a platform surrounded by spectators,
like the staging of the farces). The difference from our own idea of
the stage is particularly striking in the iconography to be observed

2. Le cité de Dieu. The Hague, Meermanno-Westreenianum Museum, MS. 10 A11, fol. 36ᵛ. By permission of the Meermanno-Westreenianum Museum.

3. *La cité de Dieu*. The Hague, Meermanno-Westreenianum Museum, MS. 10 A11, fol. 311ᵛ. By permission of the Meermanno-Westreenianum Museum.

in a fifteenth-century miniature in the *Cité de Dieu* (The Hague, Meermanno-Westrenianum Museum MS. 10 A11, fol. 36ᵛ).[50] This illustration (fig. 2) represents the origin of the *ludi scenici* in a narrative sequence: the dead corpses lying in the Roman streets, the inhabitants prostrated in front of the altars and asking for guidance to avert the plague ("Quid facturi sumus ut cesset plaga"), the gods' response ("Facite ludos scenicos, et plaga cessabit"), and the opposite opinion of St. Augustine ("Placate Deum celi et non fiant hii ludi"). But clearly Augustine's virtuous and virtual admonition remains unheeded. In the lower frame of the miniature we see the *ludi scenici*, represented as a circular dance by two women, a devil, and jesters who are accompanied by a pipe and tabor player. In the iconography of the *Cité de Dieu* the presence of jesters suggests weighty moral implications. Because they incite to worldly pleasures and sensual joys, jesters are accomplices of the forces of evil and are defined by no less a person than Peter Abelard as priests of the demonic[51]—and it is not by chance that one of the dancers is wearing a devil's mask. The dance is a clear allusion to lust, symbolized by the women's nakedness and long hair. While the performance is a typical court dance (*carole en rond*) and the presence of the jester can partly be referred to a court context, the dancers' nakedness imparts a strong moral significance to the scene. The image seems to reinstate the harshest condemnations of dancing, which the preacher Jacques de Vitry had defined as "a circle in the middle of which there is the devil," clearly referring to the *carole en rond*: "Chorea enim circulus est, cujus centrum est diabolus: et omnes vergunt in sinistram, quia omnes tendunt ad mortem eternam."[52]

In another miniature in the same manuscript (fol. 311ᵛ), the round dance alluding to the theater is taking place in a sumptuous palace hall and is associated with the pleasures of the table, represented by a banquet, and with idol-worship, symbolized by two statues of pagan gods (fig. 3). The men and women who participate are accompanied by a pipe and tabor player, just as in the *caroles* actually performed in the late medieval courts. Three naked flagellants in the foreground are flogging themselves as penance, while a gloss is provided by the figure of St. Augustine, dressed in bishop's vestments and commenting: "Immolaverunt demoniis et non Deo." The Pagan and sinful origin of the *ludi* is recalled and underlined by the counterpointing of the two actions: the deprecable entertainments (the banquets and the dance) representing the theater are opposed to another form of spectacle which is self-flagellation. To stress their mutual relationship and direct opposition, both these performances are presented in the round. We must recall that self-flagellation, having originated from the *flagellanti* movement founded in Perugia by Raniero Fasani around 1260, had spread even outside Italy in spite of numerous interdictions designed to suppress it.[53] The illustrator of the *Cité de Dieu* miniature, however, appears to suggest that the processions of *flagellanti* are a positive model of theater, inspired by religious devotion and set against immoral entertainments.

In a Flemish manuscript of the *Cité de Dieu* illustrated c.1470 for King Edward IV of England (British Library, Royal MS. 17.F.III, fol. 54), the *ludi scenici* are represented as a circular dance of four men around a column (fig. 4), which recalls the altar mentioned in literary sources and sometimes depicted in the middle of the stage. The dance is again a representation of theater by metonymy, while the altar alludes to the origin of the *ludi scenici* in pagan cult and superstition. But on the column, instead of the usual statue of a pagan idol, there is a golden calf, a clear biblical reminiscence and apparent anachronism since the dancers wear expensive medieval clothes with just a touch of the exotic in their headdresses. By representing the adoration of the golden calf, the dance acquires a double negative significance. It not only is a sinful entertainment leading to excess but also connects with idol worship and hence with behavior that rightfully should be proscribed.

Particularly bizarre is the representation of the *ludi* as a duel between two knights in Turin, Biblioteca Nazionale MS. L.I.6, fol. 44[v], and British Library Royal MS. 14.D.I, fol. 41[v]—a sort of minimalist version of the late medieval tournament. This iconography probably derives from the comparison between ancient theater and medieval jousts traced by Raoul de Presles to explain the *ludi circenses* "qui estoient une maniere de ioustes."[54] In the late Middle Ages the performances most akin to the spectacles of fighting in the imaginary antique theater were jousts and tournaments. The illustrators of the *Cité de Dieu* hence might choose the image of the duel as an emblem referring to the origins of the theater, while at the same time they might enrich the scene with allusions to both historical context and dramatic tradition. Thus Cassio and Messala, the two censors mentioned by St. Augustine, are shown, and two men hold a flag on which we read the words "tragédie" and "comédie." The historical and the "mythical" levels overlapped and helped to create a hybrid view of the theater which understood ancient customs in a contemporary guise.

4. London, British Library, MS. Royal 17.F.III, fol. 54. By permission of the British Library.

In the miniatures representing the *ludi* as a court dance or a duel, their modernization implies disapproval of the medieval performances but also a full awareness of their theatrical nature. In spite of the moral condemnation of secular entertainment, the theater in the later Middle Ages was extending its scope and its importance, as the illustrations accompanying the *Cité de Dieu* suggest. To be sure, when the theater is represented through metonymy in illustrations of dancing, the dissolution of the image of the actor is evident since there is no necessary borderline between performers and spectators. And since the theater itself tends to be identified with various forms of spectacle, the figure of the actor shatters in a multiplicity of partial functions, or, looking at the matter from another point of view, it disappears and is replaced by the emergence of non-professional performers, ostensibly caught in the trap of wicked entertainments. If a professional figure does appear on the European scene, this is the jester, supposedly a receptacle of vices and inevitably compromised with the devil. On the one hand, the idea of theater, losing its boundaries, becomes indefinite, while on the other it acquires an astonishing pervasiveness: if the theater is a nebulous and dangerous ghost of the past, any kind of contemporary performance can evoke it and even revive it.

NOTES

[1] *Ye Solace of Pilgrimes: A Description of Rome, circa A.D. 1450*, ed. C. A. Mills (London: Oxford University Press, 1911), 17–18, as cited in Clifford Davidson, *Illustrations of the Stage and Acting in England to 1580*, Early Drama, Art, and Music Monograph Series 16 (Kalamazoo: Medieval Institute Publications, 1991), 148.

[2] See C. R. Dodwell, *Anglo-Saxon Gestures and the Roman Stage* (Cambridge: Cambridge University Press, 2000), 4–6, for a summary of current opinions concerning the Terence manuscripts, and especially Leslie Webber W. Jones and C. R. Morey, *The Miniatures of the Manuscripts of Terence Prior to the Thirteenth Century*, 2 vols. (Princeton: Princeton University Press, 1931).

[3] See Joseph R. Jones, "Isidore and the Theater," in *Drama in the Middle Ages, Second Series*, ed. Clifford Davidson and John H. Stroupe (New York: AMS Press, 1991), 1–23, esp. 5.

[4] Mary H. Marshall, "*Theatre* in the Middle Ages: Evidence from Dictionaries and Glosses," *Symposium* 4 (1950): 1–39, 366–89.

[5] Osbern, *Derivazioni*, ed. Ferruccio Bertini and Vincenzo Ussani, Jr., 2 vols. (Spoleto: Centro italiano di studi sul Medioevo, 1996), 2:715.

[6] Isidore of Seville, *Etymologiarum libri*, ed. W. M. Lindsay, 2 vols. (Oxford: Clarendon Press, 1962), VIII.7.

[7] Geoffrey of Vinsauf, *De modo et arte dictandi et versificandi*, in *Les arts poétiques du XIIᵉ et du XIIIᵉ siècle: Recherches et documents sur la technique*

littéraire du Moyen Age, ed. Edmond Faral (Paris: Champion, 1923), 317.

[8] John of Garland, *Poetria magistri Iohannis Anglici de arte prosayce metrica et rithmica*, ed. G. Mari, in *Romanische Forschungen* 13 (1902), 918: "Comedia dicitur a cosmos quod est 'villa' et odos quod est cantus, quasi villanus cantus, quia materia vili et iocosa contexitur."

[9] Giovanni Boccaccio, *Genealogia Deorum*, ed. Vincenzo Romano, 2 vols. (Bari: Laterza, 1951), 2:743 (XIV.19.9–14).

[10] Nicolas Trevet, *Expositio Herculis furentis*, ed. Vincentius Ussani, Jr. (Rome: Edizioni dell'Ateneo, 1959), 5: "Et nota quod tragedie et comedie solebant in theatro hoc modo recitari: theatrum erat area semicircularis, in cuius medio erat parva domuncula, que scena dicebatur, in qua erat pulpitum, super quod poeta carminapronunciabat; extra vero erant mimi, qui carminum pronunciationem gestu corporis effigiabant per adaptationem ad quemlibet ex cuius persona loquebatur."

[11] The miniature in the *Térence des Ducs* is reproduced in William Tydeman, *The Theatre in the Middle Ages* (Cambridge: Cambridge University Press, 1978), 50.

[12] Isidore, *Etymologiarum*, XVIII.43.

[13] Papias, *Elementarium Doctrinae Rudimentum*; quoted from an edition entitled *Vocabulista* (Venice, 1496) by Marshall, "*Theatre* in the Middle Ages," 21: "Scaena domus in theatro erat, structa cum pulpito quae orchestra vocabantur, ubi cantabant comici, tragici atque saltabant histriones et mimi, dicta graece quod in specie domus erat illustrata."

[14] Dodwell, *Anglo-Saxon Gestures and the Roman Stage*, 4, cites Kurt Weitzmann's opinion in his *Late Antique and Early Christian Book Illumination* (London, 1977), 13, that the Vatican Terence is "a most faithful copy" of an original from the late classical period.

[15] Uguccione da Pisa, *Magnae Derivationes*, in Bodleian MS. Laud 88, fols. 164[v]–165, as quoted in Marshall, "*Theatre* in the Middle Ages," 25: "scena, id est umbraculum, scilicet locus adumbratus in theatro et cortinis coopertus similis tabernis mercennariorum que sunt asseribus vel cortinis operte, et secundum hoc posset dici a scenos quod est domus, quia in modum domus erat constructa. In illo umbraculo latebant persone larvate, que ad vocem recitantis exibant ad gestus faciendos."

[16] Uguccione, *Magnae Derivationes*, in Bodleian MS. Laud 88, fol. 165, as quoted by Marshall, "*Theatre* in the Middle Ages," 25.

[17] *Il 'Commentarium' di Pietro Alighieri nelle redazioni ashburnhamiana e ottoboniana*, ed. R. Della Vedova and M. T. Silvotti (Florence: Olschki, 1978), 8–9: "Antiquitus in theatro, quod erat area semicircularis, et in ejus medio erat domuncula, quae scena dicebatur, in qua erat pulpitum, et super id ascendebat poeta ut cantor, et sua carmina ut cantiones recitabat, extra vero erant mimi joculatores, carminum pronuntiationem gestu corporis effigiantes per adaptationem ad quemlibet, ex cujus persona ipse poeta loquebatur."

[18] Livy, [*History of Rome*], ed. and trans. B. O. Foster *et al.*, 14 vols. (London: Heinemann, 1919–58), 3:362–63.

[19] Isidore, *Etymologiarum*, XVIII.49.

[20] Ibid., XVIII.48: "Histriones sunt qui muliebri indumento gestus in-

pudicarum feminarum exprimebant; hi autem saltando etiam historias et res gestas demonstrabant."

[21] Ibid., XVIII.48.

[22] Ibid., XVII.45–46. "Tragoedi sunt qui antiqua gesta atque facinora sceleratorum regum luctuosa carmine spectante populo concinebant." "Comoedi sunt qui privatorum hominum acta dictis aut gestu cantabant, atque stupra virginum et amores meretricum in suis fabulis exprimebant."

[23] See Jones and Morey, *The Miniatures of the Manuscripts of Terence,* *passim.*

[24] Isidore, *Etymologiarum,* X, 119: "Nomen autem hypocritae tractum est ab specie eorum qui in spectaculis contecta facie incedunt, distinguentes vultum caeruleo minioque colore et ceteris pigmentis, habentes simulacra oris lintea gipsata, et vario colore distincta, nonnunquam et colla et manus creta perungentes, ut ad personae colorem pervenirent et populum, dum in ludis agerent, fallerent; modo in specie viri, modo in feminae, modo tonsi, modo criniti, anili et virginali ceteraque specie, aetate, sexuque diverso, ut fallant populum, dum in ludis agunt."

[25] See J. D. A. Ogilvy, "'Mimi, scurrae, histriones': Entertainers of the Early Middle Ages," *Speculum* 38 (1963): 603–19; R. Morgan, "Old French 'Jogleor' and Kindred Terms: Studies in Medieval Romance Lexicology," *Romance Philology* 7, no. 4 (May 1954): 279–325; and Sandra Pietrini, "Il disordine del lessico e la varietà delle cose: le denominazioni latine e romanze degli intrattenitori," *Quaderni Medievali* 47 (1999): 77–113.

[26] *Scholia in Horatium,* ed. H. J. Botschuyver (Amsterdam: Van Bottenburg, 1942), 468.

[27] *Diomedis Ars grammatica,* ed. H. Keilii (Leipzig: Teubner, 1857), 490: "Ideoque Horatius utraque significatione interpretatur, cum ita de fabula dicit, *aut agitur res in scenis aut acta refertur,* sicut in choro."

[28] Horace, *Satires, Epistles, and Ars Poetica,* ed. and trans. H. Rushton Fairclough (London: William Heinemann, 1961), 464–65.

[29] Johannes Melber, *Vocabularius Praedicantium sive Variloquus,* as quoted in Marshall, "*Theatre* in the Middle Ages," 380: "Scena, -e, id est umbra, vel umbraculum, vel locus obumbratus in theatro, ein stat des schattenss, a scenos, id est umbra, sic romani fecerunt hutten cum frondibus et asseribus propter umbram. Etiam pro ludo capitur in huiusmodi loco facto ubi rusticus efficitur rex vel miles, et ludo peracto quolibet est sicut prius rusticus fuit."

[30] Beryl Smalley, "Thomas Waleys O.P.," *Archivum Fratrum Praedicatorum* 24 (1954): 50–107.

[31] T. Kaeppeli, "Une critique du commentaire de Nicholas Trevet sur le *De Civitate Dei,*" *Archivum Fratrum Praedicatorum* 29 (1959): 200–05, and Beryl Smalley, *English Friars and Antiquity in the Early Fourteenth Century* (Oxford: Basil Blackwell, 1960), 88.

[32] *La Cité de Dieu,* trans. with commentary by Raoul de Presles, in Paris, Bibliothèque Nationale MS. fr. 6272, fol. 30. This manuscript was executed, probably in Burgundy, at the beginning of the fifteenth century and contains eleven miniatures, but it only includes the first ten books of the *City of God.*

[33] Ibid., fol. 30: "ilz se desordonnoient tellement que ilz se despouilloient

devant tout le peuple et sans vergoigne venoient iusques aux accolemens et baisiers et au surplus achevoient leur puterie et laidure."

[34] Ibid., fol. 29ᵛ.

[35] Edmond Faral, *Les Jongleurs en France au Moyen Âge* (Paris: Champion, 1910), 247.

[36] See F. Lebrun, "Le charivari à travers les condamnations des autorités ecclésiastiques en France du XIVᵉ au XVIIIᵉ siècle," in *Le Charivari: Actes de la table ronde organisée à Paris (25–27 avril 1977) par l'École des Hautes Études en Sciences Sociales et le Centre National de la Recherche Scientifique*, ed. Jacques Le Goff and Jean-Claude Schmitt (Paris: La Haye, 1981), 221–28.

[37] *Etymologiarum*, VIII.7.

[38] John Lydgate, *Troy Book*, ll. 842–926, as quoted by Clifford Davidson, ed., *A Tretise of Miraclis Pleyinge*, Early Drama, Art, and Music Monograph Series 19 (Kalamazoo: Medieval Institute Publications, 1993), 161.

[39] Paris, Bibliothèque Nationale MS. fr. 6272, fol. 39.

[40] Isidore, *Etymologiarum*, VIII.7: "Comoedi appellati sive a loco, quia circum pagos agebant, quos Graeci κώμας vocant, sive a comisatione. Solebant enim post cibum homines ad eos audiendos venire."

[41] John of Garland, *Poetria*, 918.

[42] Paris, Bibliothèque Nationale MS. fr. 6272, fol. 39.

[43] Paris, Bibliothèque Nationale MS. fr. 2813, fol. 473ᵛ.

[44] Ibid., as quoted in E. Manselli, "La festa nel Medioevo," in *Spettacoli conviviali dall'antichità classica alle corti italiane del '400*, Atti del VII Convegno di Studio, Viterbo, 27–30 Maggio 1982 (Viterbo: Agnesotti, 1983), 219–41.

[45] Paris, Bibliothèque Nationale MS. lat. 4883A, fol. 67.

[46] Osbern, *Derivazioni*, 1:360.

[47] Titus Livius, *Histoire Romaine*, Paris, Bibliothèque Nationale MS. fr. 30, fol. 136: "Sans nul chant et sans nul ditties et sans faire nul mouvement au son d'aucune chanson li baleur ou iugleur les quelz il avoient fait venir d'Estruerie sailloient et trepoient au son des cornemuses et des monidies et si faisoient gracieux mouvemens ala maniere tusque."

[48] Ibid.

[49] Ibid.

[50] For further study of the illustrations of Raoul's de Presles's *Cité de Dieu*, see Sandra Pietrini, *Spettacoli e immaginario teatrale nel Medioevo* (Rome: Bulzoni, 2001).

[51] Peter Abelard, *Theologia Christiana*, 2.129, in *Opera Theologica*, ed. Eligius M. Buytaert, 2 vols., Corpus Christianorum, Continuatio Mediaevalis 12 (Turnhout: Brepols, 1969), 2:192–93: "Quid enim sunt tales histriones nisi praecones, et, ut ita dicam, apostoli daemonum per quorum ora vel gestus praedari miseras non cessant animas?"

[52] Jacques de Vitry, MS. 17509, fol. 146, as quoted in Étienne de Bourbon, *Anecdotes historiques: Légends et apologues tirés du recuél inédit d'Étienne de Bourbon, dominicain du XIIIᵉ siècle*, ed. A. Lecoy de la Marche (Paris: Librairie Renouard, 1877), 162.

[53] See *Il Movimento dei Disciplinati nel settimo centenario del suo inizio*

(Perugia 1260), Convegno internazionale, Perugia 25–28 September, 1960 (Perugia, 1962), and *Le laudi drammatiche umbre delle origini, Atti del V Convegno di studio, Viterbo, 22–25 May 1980* (Viterbo: Centro di studi sul teatro Medioevale e rinascimentale, n.d.). The *flagellanti* are also discussed in Cyrilla Barr, *The Monophonic Lauda and the Lay Confraternities of Tuscany and Umbra in the Late Middle Ages*, Early Drama, Art, and Music Monograph Series 10 (Kalamazoo: Medieval Institute Publications, 1988), esp. 31–60.

[54] Paris, Bibliothèque Nationale MS. fr. 6272, fol. 30ᵛ.

The Flyting of Yule and Lent: A Medieval Swedish Shrovetide Interlude

Leif Søndergaard and Thomas Pettitt

This article introduces to English-speaking scholarship a remote but potentially significant document of medieval theater (or, more properly, dramatic custom), the Swedish *Flyting of Yule and Lent* from the fifteenth century.[1] The text is preserved in Stockholm, Royal Library MS. D 4a (Codex Verelianus) from 1457, a substantial miscellany of popular vernacular material, and comprises forty-six lines of verse divided by rubrics into ten speeches evenly distributed between two speakers named *Fastan* (i.e., Fast, Lent) and *Julen* (i.e., Yule, Christmas).[2] The dialogue is introduced with the words "Next follows how Yule and Lent they dispute" (the English title is ours, based on the *Julens och Fastans Träta* conferred by Swedish editors), and breaks off in what is clearly the middle of a speech. The loss with regard to action if not words may be considerable, for as the fragment ends the two figures are clearly squaring up for a fight, possibly with the intervention of a third party, since both seem to anticipate the entry of "Mortification."

Given this incomplete state of the text, we have opted for a doggedly accurate line-by-line translation rather than something more lively and suited for performance; nor have we attempted to reproduce its metrical system (*knittelvers*: irregular four-stress lines rhyming in couplets).[3]

Next follows how Yule and Lent they dispute.

Lent
It is my duty first to wish
Health and happiness to King and Bishop!
I am the one who is called Lent,
I am accustomed to keep watch over sin and vice;
Anyone who knows he has been sinful,   5

297

He is afraid to come to me.

Yule
My lords King and Bishop both,
I crave of you help and mercy.
I am she who is called Yule,
I do not hide myself from Lent.   10
Lent will be against me,
My lord King, be my servant,
I hope that I shall live well.
My lord King, you must give me my rights,
For both poor and rich know   15
That Lent will never be like that.

Lent
I shall teach you a better attitude:
Drink and eat a good deal less,
Do not sit long at your table,
But also go and listen to God's Word sometimes.   20

Yule
I'll tell you, Lent, what you must do:
Go to the sermon now as always;
Let me sit here with my food,
And fill my horn, we'll not be parted.

Lent
That won't do you much good,   25
Scoffing so many sweet things:
You fill your habituated belly with rubbish,
So the soul is diseased with your sin.

Yule
I think you are too haggard, Lent,
You're too pale and thin, weedy and brownish;   30
God will fully know how to judge
Which of us will first come to heaven.

Lent
I'm trying to give you a lesson:

Let us all scourge our backs,
Ready to meet our father confessor, 35
And humbly do penance for all our sins.

Yule
It's your occupation to hear confessions,
To sit in church and do nothing else;
If I come to you Good Friday night
I reckon that should be good enough. 40

Lent
So comes he who is called Mortification,
He will scourge your back
So you won't be able to get away,
And you'll be punished for old and new sins.

Yule
I shall surely see to it 45
That he doesn't scourge my bare back

.   .   .

First published in Gustaf Ljunggren's *Svenska Dramat* in 1864 and appearing in what is still the standard critical edition in G. E. Klemming's *Svenska Medeltids Dikter og Rim* (1881–82), the piece has been strangely neglected in recent Scandinavian accounts of medieval literature despite receiving some notice in international scholarship (though not in English).[3] The fragmentary state of the text (not due to loss in the manuscript) and several obvious instances of scribal copying errors indicate that it is a copy and that the play itself may be somewhat older than the mid-fifteenth-century manuscript, but it has not been subjected to sufficient philological analysis for this matter to be settled with confidence. Nor can we be perfectly confident about the regional affiliation of the play.

Of the various suggestions which have appeared from time to time concerning the genre of the text, its function, and its context, we are persuaded that it was designed to be performed rather than merely read as a poetic dialogue, and that it was intended for presentation during Shrovetide revels, most probably by the revelers themselves or just possibly in the context of a customary house visit by a small group of men or boys in quest of refreshment and largess—analogous, if at a different season, to the more recent English mummers' plays—in a tradition closely affiliated to the roughly contemporary *Fastnachtspiele* of Nuremberg. As such it joins the Danish *The Unfaithful Wife* (*Den Utro Hustru*) and *The Judgment of Paris* (*Paris Dom*),[4] the only other known Scandinavian Shrovetide interludes from the late medieval and Renaissance periods. There is no appropriate term available in English, probably because this tradition was not strong—or died out early —in England. We have adopted 'Shrovetide interlude' as an English equivalent of the German *Fastnachtspiel* and the Danish *Fastelavnsspil*, both of which carry the meaning literally of "eve-of-Lent plays." The graphic and precise early English 'Fastyngong' having been lost from the language, the slightly somber 'Shrovetide' (i.e., period for confessing, "shriving") is preferred to the more festive 'carnival' since the latter, a post-medieval term in any case, in common modern usage has connotations of outdoor processions, and in scholarly discourse it has been emptied of its calendrical significance by sub-Bakhtinian historicism to mean almost any kind of popular (and preferably subversive) merrymaking. 'Shroving' in the early modern period meant precisely a disguised and convivial house-visit with an entertainment. And we take 'interlude' (with some justification in late medieval usage) to mean a short dramatic entertainment performed in the context of seasonal revelry—i.e., a play "between the games" rather than, as usually explicated, "a game between" something else. In the absence of any external evidence concerning the Swedish texts provenance and function, we shall briefly support our thesis by literary and dramaturgical analysis, combined with reference to the analogous Danish plays, the German *Fastnachtspiele*, and the English mummers' plays.[5]

That the text is designed for performance and not merely recital is suggested negatively by the absence of narrative transitions ("and then Yule said," and the like) and positively by the rubrics specifying speakers of all except the first speech, reinforced by two parallel lines in the margin beside each. Before interacting with each other, both speakers address the audience, and in so doing identify themselves in clearly formulaic phrases ("I am the one who is called Lent"; "I am she who is called Yule"), all of which is paralleled in the German *Fastnachtspiele* ("Ich pins di Fasnacht") and the mummers' plays ("In comes I, St. George"). Equally indicative of performance and festive auspices, and likewise matched in the analogous traditions, are Lent's opening greeting and good wishes ("Health and happiness") to the audience, although here Lent usurps a task more often undertaken by a Presenter (e.g., Preco in *The Unfaithful Wife*: "Wassail! Good day, dear friends, / All you who are in here"; the *Praecursor* or *Vorläufer* of the *Fastnachtspiele*: "Got gruss euch, ir herren uberal"). The *Fastnachtspiele* also use the technique of the Swedish play in having the introductory business performed by one of the characters (a peasant, say, or a fool) in the action to follow.

In each tradition this opening business is symptomatic of the circumstance that the performers are visitors to the venue at which they perform and that they have first to attract the attention and gain the good will of an assembly of people who are already engaged in seasonal revelry at a tavern or private house or guild hall. In the case of the later mummers' plays, the classic auspices are provided by the Christmas revels of the squire in the hall of the "great house" or by the Christmas feast accorded by a farmer to his workmen in the kitchen of his farmhouse. In late medieval Germany and Scandinavia the equivalent was the Shrovetide revelry of the urban trade and craft guilds and of educational institutions such as universities and church schools. Our Swedish text seems to fit best this third context if we consider the likely identity of the "King and Bishop" ("konunga och biscopa") singled out for greetings and appeal by both speakers. They could just feasibly be real historical worthies of this rank, but it is much more likely that they are the mock-leaders selected by lot or by vote to preside over the feast—or, indeed, over the entire festival season from Christmas to Shrovetide —as the "King of Christmas" or "Lord of Misrule" of the winter revels in domestic or institutional households, or as the "boy bishop" of the schoolboys and the choristers of ecclesiastical institutions.[6] It need not confuse matters that such festive leaders are just as often encountered as *visitors* offering festive entertainment at other households, and it is presumably this context that provides the only reference from medieval Scandinavia to the boy bishop, a record in the household accounts of Queen Christine of Denmark of a payment to "the Christmas bishop in Odense on the day after Circumcision" (i.e., on 2 January) in the Christmas season of 1508–09.[7] The Christmas leader also presided over revels "at home" (the feast financed by the largesse received in the preceding per-

ambulations) at which he in return received visiting performers
from outside. This is evidently the context for the Christmas
"Mumming of the Seven Philosophers," a series of seven (increasingly unphilosophical) speeches followed by a song, whose
Presenter brings ironic greetings from Seneca "Vnto yow hys
brother, kyng of Crystmas."[8] In 1415 Winchester College paid
twenty pence "to various men from Ropley coming to the College
on Holy Inncents Day dancing and singing in the hall in the
presence of the bishop of the scholars."[9] The reference in the
Swedish text to *two* such festive leaders may suggest that the
auspices were provided by the joint revels of a complex household,
the King (of Christmas or Shrovetide) from, say, the domestic sub-
household (of abbot, bishop, or nobleman), the (Boy) Bishop from
the institutional sub-household (of abbey school, cathedral choir, or
private chapel, respectively). An alternative (and calendrically
closer) contextual model is provided by the late medieval French
confréries of young people who elected a King of Carnival to
preside over the festivities, sometimes accompanied by a Carnival
Prince and (more relevant here) an Abbot.[10] The Carnival King is
attested in medieval Scandinavia by the observation in a Swedish
moral work from the early sixteenth century (Peder Månsson's
Barnabok) that the rich clothing of the king in itself does not
distinguish him from "the king who is dressed up at Shrovetide."[11]

The specific *seasonal* context is indicated by the Swedish interlude's characters and themes, for it is a "Shrovetide interlude" in
a double sense. Like many *Fastnachtspiele* and *fastelavnsspil*, it
was designed for performance at Shrovetide revels, and its content
with regard to both words and action is generally appropriate: the
dispute between antagonistic figures is familiar from both Shrovetide and Christmas (e.g., mummers') interludes (knights vs. peasants, Christians vs. Turks, husband vs. wife), as is the combat which
seems to be in the offing. The references to scourging the back are
appropriate to the penitential aspect of Shrovetide but may, given
that the "bak" of the Swedish text might also mean "backside," hint
at horseplay consistent with festive dramatic custom elsewhere; the
connotations also could include the beatings traditionally inflicted
by Shrovetide gangs on passers-by. The additional qualification is
of course that this play's content and characters are not merely
appropriate to Shrovetide, they are *about* Shrovetide and dramatize
the conflict inherent in the season—a confrontation between the

season of revels drawing to an end on Shrove Tuesday, and the period of Lenten fasting beginning on Ash Wednesday. As such it is matched by only two *Fastnachtspiele*, both of the 1440s, *Das spyl von der Vasnacht und Vassten recht* and *Der Vasnacht und Vasten recht*.[12] The theme of the conflict between carnival (in this strictest calendrical sense) and Lent is familiar of course in non-dramatic literature from the beginning of the thirteenth century onwards, and there is other evidence of its popularity in drama—e.g., the French *Jeu de carneval, La dure et cruelle bataille et la paix de Sainct Pensard à lencontre de Carême* (1485) and *Le Testament de Carmentrant* (1540).[13] In contrast to the Swedish play where the conflict (at least what we have of it) is restricted to a verbal stand-off, French tradition involves a real battle involving bakers, butchers, and others connected with the victualing trades, figures with parodic food names (*Lechebroche*, "Fork-licker"; *Tirelardon*, "Pork-snatcher"; etc.) or food terms (for example, on Lent's side, Onion and Herring).[14]

This thematic factor is in many ways less significant than the dramaturgical considerations already noted above. A sense of calendrical propriety (although it was lost by the time of Shakespeare's *Twelfth Night* and *A Midsummer Nights Dream*) would presumably mean that plays on this theme were performed at Shrovetide, but not necessarily in the context of visitors at household revels. Pieter Bruegel the Elder's celebrated painting of the *Combat between Carnival and Lent* of c.1559 may well, despite its evident symbolism, reflect actual tradition, but the scale and nature of the show suggests performance in the context of a street parade rather than a house visit.[15] The same is true of the one English—and highly significant—account of Shrovetide revelry, concerning the parade through the streets of Norwich in 1443 by the appropriately named John Gladman, dressed in tinfoil and crowned as "kyng of cristmesse," accompanied by figures representing the twelve months of the year (each dressed accordingly) and another as Lent in white and red herrings skins: they performed "myrth and disportes and plays," according to the record, "in diuerse stretis of the cite."[16] This last record, incidentally, explains an odd feature of the Swedish play in a Continental context, the appearance of Yule rather than Carnival as Lent's antagonist. The Norwich procession was "in tokyn that all mirthis that seson sculd end . . . [and] that sadnese shuld folowe and an holy tyme." Both traditions are clearly working with a festive calendar in which the winter revels, having started at Christmas (perhaps with a preliminary bout at All Hallows), are deemed to persist through to Shrovetide rather than (as in some local traditions) ending at Twelfth Night (6 January) or Candlemas (2 February).[17]

Occurring in a manuscript explicitly dated 1457, this Swedish Shrovetide interlude, as we shall now assume the right to call it, is a significantly early document in the history of eve-of-Lent plays in the German-Scandinavian cultural landscape. The earliest German *Fastnachtspiele* manuscript, dated in the manuscript itself, is some four years later, in 1461. The plays themselves may go back earlier, perhaps even to the mid-fourteenth century, yet it is difficult to find anything convincing much earlier than the reference, in the already mentioned *Der Vasnacht und Vasten recht*, to a papal decree of 1445. But the Swedish play, of which the Stockholm manuscript is unlikely to be the original, may well go back this far. The two Danish *fastelavnsspil* are from the beginning of the sixteenth century, while the earliest Danish record of Shrovetide interludes (*ludos carnispriviales*) is from 1447 and from Odense, probably the home of the plays concerned.[18]

On the manner of performance the text offers only the slightest hints, which must then be correlated with the proposed context. Both figures are doubtless dressed appropriately, Lent (to judge from the Norwich record and the Bruegel painting) a lean figure with costume symbolic of Lenten fare (e.g., fish scales). When Yule taunts Lent with being "brownish" (Swedish: *jarp*), the reference is probably to the penitential color of the dress, perhaps like the russet of medieval hermits and nuns. Yule is something of a puzzle, however; while everything in the seasonal symbolism and in both dramatic and pictorial tradition would lead us to expect a fat, sausage-eating Falstaffian figure, the text unequivocally designates the character as female: "I am she [*hon*] who is called Yule." We know of no precise analogue for this in the texts or records of medieval seasonal symbolism, perhaps the closest being the personification of *Lent* as a female (*donna Quaresima*) in Juan Ruiz's *Libro de buen amor*, a Spanish verse epic of c.1330,[19] but self-indulgent female figures (played by men) do figure in dramatic and semi-dramatic seasonal revelry, from the *Mère Folle* of medieval France to the Old Dame Jane of the English mummers' plays. The Swedish play requires no properties or scenery beyond what can be carried (a stick for the beating threatened at the end) or found *in situ*. In the manner of the tradition of the German *Fastnachtspiel*, food and drink loom large in the play's mental world and action, and we are doubtless to imagine Yule sitting at a table (see ll. 23–24) eating and drinking with gusto. In the earlier English *Dame Siriz* from the end of the thirteenth century which anticipates the Shrovetide interludes in many ways, Siriz herself is similarly served with bread, meat, and wine.[20] The play may end with a combat, or more likely a tussle since one of the figures is a woman. In purely literary treatments of the conflict between Carnival and Lent, the outcome can be determined on the basis of the author's view of the two attitudes to life which they represent, and indeed in the first few centuries of the tradition the victory can go either way. But the calendrical logic of performance at Shrovetide (reinforced after c.1500 by the onset of a more moral and didactic ethos) would suggest that Lent be victorious, as in the analogous combat between "fasting days" and Christmas "gambolls" in the second antimasque of Thomas Salusbury's *Knowsley Masque* of 1641.[21] The defeated Yule (and the revelers at the feast) might well be consoled, however, with the reassurance that her reign would resume next year, or, alternatively, as in one of the German *Fastnachtspiele* on the theme (*Das spyl von der Vasnacht und Vassten recht*), a compromise might be reached on the superiority of a joyful feasting not marred by overindulgence (as represented by the approaching Easter festival).

NOTES

[1] What follows is a translation of the Swedish text, undertaken jointly by the authors, accompanied by a note formulated by Thomas Pettitt, who has contributed some additional matter and discussion from an Anglo-Saxon perspective to commentary derived from Leif Søndergaard's two published articles on the play: "La lutte de Carnaval contre Carême: un jeu de carnaval suédois dans la tradition européene," *Théâtre et Spectacles, hier et aujourdhui: Moyen âge et Renaissance*, Comité des travaux historiques et scientifiques (Paris: Editions du CTHS, 1991), 227–43; "Julens og Fastans träta—en svensk fastelavnsspil fra midten af 1400-talet," *Rig* 74 (1991): 33–56. The translation is based on Søndergaard's transcript of the manuscript, published in the Danish article cited above.

[2] In the Scandinavian languages, *jul* encompasses both the Christian and the secular-pagan aspects of the season.

[3] See, for example, Wilhelm Creizenach, *Geschichte des neueren Dramas*, I: *Mittelalter und Frührenaissance*, 2nd ed. (1911; reprint New York: Benjamin

Blom, 1965), 462; Martine Grinberg and Sam Kinser, "Les Combats de Carnaval de Carême: Trajets dune métaphore," *Annales E.S.C.* 38 (1983): 90.

⁴ The verse form of the Swedish text is also shared with the Danish plays and many *Fastnachtspiele*, but since it is a fairly common form in the Germanic languages this is not suggested as providing evidence of relationships.

⁵ On the analogy between the *Fastnachtspiele* of the fifteenth and sixteenth centuries and the English mummers' plays of the nineteenth and twentieth, see Thomas Pettitt, "English Folk Drama and the Early German *Fastnachtspiele*," *Renaissance Drama*, n.s. 13 (1982): 1–34. This article also provides illustration of the common dramaturgical features of the two traditions mentioned, without specific documentation, in the present article.

⁶ For one or both of these figures in various contexts, see Karl Young, *The Drama of the Medieval Church*, 2 vols. (Oxford: Clarendon Press, 1933), 1: 104–10; R. L. DeMolen, "*Pueri Christi Imitatio*: The Festival of the Boy-Bishop in Tudor England," *Moreana* 45 (1975): 17–28; Jacques Heers, *Fêtes des Fous et Carnavals* (Paris: Fayard, 1983), 105–89; and Sandra Billington, *Mock Kings in Medieval Society and Renaissance Drama* (Oxford: Clarendon Press, 1991), chap. 2.

⁷ *Dronning Christines Hofholdningsregnskaber*, ed. W. Christensen (Copenhagen: Gyldendal, 1904), 309. On a fascinating and significantly early Boy Bishop's play, probably from Constance, see Eckehard Simon, "Das Schwäbische Weihnachtsspiel: Ein neu entdecktes Weinachtsspiel auf der Zeit 1417–1431," *Zeitschrift für deutsche Philologie* 94 (1975), *Sonderheft*, 30–50, and "The Home Town of the 'Schwäbische Weihnachtsspiel' (ca. 1420) and Its Original Setting," *Euphorion* 73 (1979): 304–20.

⁸ *Secular Lyrics of the XIVth and XVth Centuries*, ed. Rossell Hope Robbins, 2nd ed. (1955; reprint Oxford: Clarendon Press, 1968), no. 120 (ll. 8, 11).

⁹ E. K. Chambers, *The Mediaeval Stage*, 2 vols. (London: Oxford University Press, 1903), 2:246.

¹⁰ Martine Grinberg, "Carnaval et Société urbaine XIVᵉ–XVIᵉ siècles: le royaume dans la ville," *Ethnologie française* 4 (1974): 218–20.

¹¹ Peder Månsson, *Skrifter*, ed. R. Geete (Stockholm: Svenska Forsskrift Sællskapet, 1913–25), *Barnabok*, 666.

¹² *Fastnachtspiele aus dem fünfzehnten Jahrhundert*, ed. A. von Keller (1853–58; reprint Darmstadt: Wissenschaftliche Buchgesellschaft, 1965), nos. 72–73.

¹³ *Deux jeux de carnaval de la fin du Moyen âge*, ed. Jean-Claude Aubailly (Paris: Droz, 1978). French scholarship seems to use the term *jeu de carnaval* in this special sense of a play *about* carnival (and probably performed at carnival time); it is very likely that French late-medieval tradition, like the German and Danish, also had Shrovetide interludes (i.e., plays performed at Shrovetide) on other themes.

¹⁴ Kinser and Grinberg, "Les combats," 65–98, provide a list of known texts, dramatic and otherwise, in the tradition featuring the combat between Shrovetide and Lent.

¹⁵ For this painting in the context of Bruegel's life and career, see Walter S.

Gibson, *Bruegel* (London: Thames and Hudson, 1977), 79–80, and for perceptive discussion of its detailed depiction of a variety of seasonal (including Shrovetide) custom, see Claude Gaignebet, "Le combat de Carnaval et de Carême de P. Bruegel (1559)," *Annales E.S.C.* 27 (1972): 313–45, and Elke M. Shutt-Kehm, *Pieter Bruegels d. Ä "Kampf des Karnevals gegen die Fasten" als Quelle volkskundlicher Forschung* (Frankfurt, 1983).

16 *Records of the City of Norwich*, ed. W. Hudson and J. C. Tingey, 2 vols. (Norwich and London: Jarrold and Sons, 1906), 1:340. This record seems to reflect a genuine Shrovetide custom in Norwich, even though in this particular instance the procession actually occurred at a different date and with insurrectionary purposes, the document having been written to provide an innocuous explanation to the authorities.

17 On varying conceptions of Christmas and Carnival and the link between them, see Claude Gaignebet, *Le Carnaval* (Paris: Payot, 1974), 17–39, and Siegfried Wagner, *Der Kampf des Fastens gegen die Fastnacht* (Munich: Tudur, 1986), 23.

18 Gerd Simon, *Die erste deutsche Fastnachtspieltradition* (Hamburg: Matthiesen, 1970), 66–69; Leif Søndergaard, *Fastelavnsspillet i Danmarks senmiddelalder* (Odense: Odense Universitetsforlag, 1989), 53–54.

19 Juan Ruiz, *Libro de buen amor*, ed. Raymond J. Willis (Princeton: Princeton University Press, 1972), 294–333.

20 *Dame Sirith*, ll. 312–26, in *Early Middle English Verse and Prose*, ed. J. A. W. Bennett and G. V. Smithers (Oxford: Clarendon Press, 1968). On the likelihood that *Dame Siriʒ* was designed for performance, and most likely "in a banquet situation," see Martin W. Walsh, "Performing Dame Sirith: Farce and Fabliaux at the End of the Thirteenth Century," in *England in the Thirteenth Century*, ed. W. N. Ormrod (Woodbridge: Boydell Press, 1986), 155.

21 James Turner, *The Politics of Landscape* (Oxford: Blackwell, 1979), 146. On the increasing tendency for Lent to be victorious (breached by only one exception after 1500), see Siegfried Wagner, *Der Kampf des Fastens gegen die Fastnacht: Zur Geschichte der Mässigung* (Munich: Tudur, 1986), 79–80.

Index